HENRY ADAMS

Books by R. P. Blackmur

Criticism

The Double Agent
1935

The Expense of Greatness
1940

Form and Value in Modern Poetry
1952

Language as Gesture
1952

The Lion and the Honeycomb
1955

Eleven Essays in the European Novel
1964

A Primer of Ignorance
1967

Henry Adams
1980

Poetry

From Jordan's Delight
1937

The Second World
1942

The Good European and Other Poems
1947

Poems of R. P. Blackmur
1977

HENRY ADAMS

Drawing by John Briggs Potter, 1914

R. P. BLACKMUR

HENRY ADAMS

Edited and with an Introduction by Veronica A. Makowsky

Foreword by Denis Donoghue

New York and London

HARCOURT BRACE JOVANOVICH

Printed in the United States of America

Library of Congress Cataloging in Publication Data

Blackmur, Richard P   1904–1965.
Henry Adams.

Bibliography: p.
Includes index.
1.   Adams, Henry, 1838–1918.   2.   Historians—United States—Biography.
I.   Makowsky, Veronica A.
E175.5.A2B55   1980   973'.07'2024 [B]   79-1812
ISBN 0-15-139997-2

Set in Linotype Waverly

First edition
B C D E

Foreword

by Denis Donoghue

Richard Blackmur's first major essay on Henry Adams was published in 1936. At that time Adams' presence in American
literature and history had to be assumed in the virtual absence
of evidence. His reputation was hardly more than a shadow. In
1933 James Truslow Adams, publishing the first biography of
Adams, complained that the occasion for which he had written
the book had found no use for it: originally planned to accompany a collected edition of Adams' *Works* "in many volumes,"
it had come into existence only to discover that it had nothing
to accompany. "Adams himself," his biographer maintained,
"would have enjoyed the irony of the fact that the very breakdown of our economic system—whether temporary or not—
which he predicted a generation before it occurred has pre-
cluded the possibility of publishing his own *Works* for the time
being on the scale contemplated." It was in those circumstances
that Blackmur took on a project which, in the event, he never
completed. The essays on Adams which he published over the
following seven or eight years were read for their immediate
interest but also as chapters of his work-in-progress. It was clear
that the relation between Adams' mind and Blackmur's was
extraordinarily intimate, and that the big book on Adams would
count as Blackmur's autobiography, or at least as the most sa-
lient parts of it. In the end the book was only partially written,
the relation only partially defined. But we now have most of it,
and the most finished parts.

I cannot offer any particularly cogent explanation of Blackmur's failure to complete the work, except to note that his mind worked best in the essay of twenty or twenty-five pages. Every writer has a congenial space. Some take pleasure in latitude, the exercise of control over a wide range of material, the work gathering momentum. Blackmur's mind reached instead for "the emphasized example." Even when he dealt with a writer's entire work, he chose to come upon it obliquely, gaining entry by an acute angle of vision. If the example were well enough chosen and the emphasis sustained, he would come to the center of the work in the end, with every advantage gained from quirkiness and risk. But the trouble with the procedure is that when you compose a book by bringing your forays together you never know when the book is finished: another experimental insight is always feasible. So with Blackmur on Adams. Some of the most remarkable chapters in this book are written as if by stealth; they come upon their theme in the way you least expect, a way opened by hunches rather than by method. That he had a plan, or plans, is clear, but he did not allow himself to be intimidated by such things. Far out in the book, Blackmur writes of Adams and James that to both men "the judgment of education called for a specialized form of autobiography in which the individual was suppressed in the act only to be caught in the style." That is where Blackmur, too, is best caught. If he were caught in the act, the proof would be a method: caught in the style, the evidence is a steady tone, a distinctive way of responding to Adams' themes, chasing his shadow and coming to love its darkness.

Not quite so far out in the book, Blackmur writes of Adams' relation to Pascal, that Pascal was part of Adams' spiritual biography. And he goes on to make a general observation from the relation between one writer and another, referring to "the great creative labor in which men have to make use of others in order to see demonstrated the truth of that which in themselves alone they cannot believe, though they suffer it." So, too, Blackmur made use of Adams. By another formulation, he rehearsed himself in Adams, as again in James, though the scores are different and only the intensity of concentration is the same. I have sometimes thought of Blackmur's criticism as a supplication of texts. When the text is secular, he woos it. When it is spiritual or religious, he brings to it his devotion, not as faith but as the felt need of it—to use a phrase you will find in this book. If chronology would bend a little, we could fancy that Blackmur came to understand criticism as supplication when he saw what Adams' relation to the Virgin made possible and necessary in the devoted chapters of *Mont-Saint-Michel and Chartres.* In supplication you create the thing you see, and your sense of it is the strongest testimony to its value; you respond to one form of energy, enhancing it with your own.

Blackmur knew from the start what form his supplication of Adams' text should take. Adams' theme was early identified as "thought or imagination conceived as the form of human energy"; in another version, the theme was a predicament: "man had been put in possession of vast stores of new energy which as he learned to use them carried him away, and which his intelligence could neither keep up nor cope with." By the end of the nineteenth century, "the ordinary man's knowledge amounted to a kind of detailed helplessness before enormous aggregates of supersensual energy." Sometimes Blackmur's account of the theme emphasized the disproportion between energy and mind: mind, itself a form of energy, seemed puny by comparison with energy at large and mainly beyond control. Sometimes he thought the loss of control was not yet complete. Both emphases, with variations running between them, were ascribed to Adams.

In the first chapter of *The Lion and the Honeycomb* Blackmur said that Henry Adams "used to argue that the great question was whether the American mind could catch up with American energy: he doubted it, but thought a good jump might do it." In his study of Adams he does not specify what direction the jump should take, but only the urgency of trying it. Thus his supplication. And the rituals of supplication were adopted from Adams. In *The Education of Henry Adams* each person described is treated as an expressive part of society and significant for that reason. Adams wonders aloud about the nature of a society of which the particular person could be a part. A person was interesting, dismal, or edifying, chiefly as an example. Blackmur took up the procedure, with this difference—that he did not identify the whole with society in general or any society in particular but with life itself, so far as it could be felt and known: each person considered then became a fragment of what might be felt and known, a point at which some force, not elsewhere available, became articulate. Supplication, in that context, became the energy released by comparison and contrast.

When Blackmur, commenting on *Mont-Saint-Michel and Chartres*, reflects upon St. Francis and then upon St. Thomas, he measures each as the cost of the other, each as the defect of the other's merit. Criticism is mind conceived as one of the forms of human energy, and it is lavished upon Adams' text mainly in supplication. Blackmur's procedure, for the moment, is to feel each form of energy in the light or the field of another. So with his account of Adams and James, between whom, in Blackmur's mind, there is "a wooing both ways." By seeing each according to this light or in this field, Blackmur's vision becomes more intense than ever: the light reflected from one is bestowed upon the other, with whatever consequence.

The main distinction is that James's sense of form, pattern, and type always waits upon his sensibility: his intelligence is the kind that comes after the intuitions that provoke it. Adams' feeling for form, pattern, and type always insists on anticipating the experience and imposing the terms in which it is received. "Adams' set of intellectual instruments more or less *predicted* what he would discover; James resorted to instruments only to ascertain what his sensibility had *already* discovered." Each paid a price not for his intelligence but for the form it insisted on taking. "The thinness in James comes from excess of feeling; in Adams thinness comes, not from want of feeling, but from excess of consideration." It is clear that Blackmur's own talent was on James's side in this distinction, and for that reason he is more severe with James than he has to be. Thinness is rarely attributed to James's fiction nowadays: to us it appears, in the central novels, substantial, opulent. The light reflected from James upon Adams is more judicious: excess of consideration is what we still feel Adams' work to labor under if not to suffer from. What we feel in him, and what we have reason to think Blackmur felt in him, is the amount of experience from which his consideration has exempted him, the things that mock prediction.

If Blackmur was, as I think, of James's party in this difference of temper, we can substitute him for James and consider him and Adams now, each in the other's light. We see then that Adams' demand for order was premature. It often appears that he goaded experience to disappoint him, and waited to see how far and deep the disappointment would go. Since every form of knowledge is fragmentary, he set impossible conditions for its success, conditions that could be fulfilled only if he allowed that in practice the part would be equal to the whole—a concession he was not willing to make. We catch him best in the act of looking behind him, seeing the objects of vision emerge only to recede nearly at once. Mostly, he is explaining why some interest or excitement or passion failed to survive, and the form his disappointment has taken. And yet in each going there is a remaining, the rueful but sturdy force that keeps him open to the next possibility, for interest and truth. In this, as Blackmur says, Adams is a type of the imagination which is always "a little posthumous to its actual inspiration: it celebrates, as in epic and tragedy, exactly what survives out of what has been lost: what is still real, however desperately held."

If the pattern of Adams' intelligence were set as rigidly as we have implied, the verdict of disappointment and loss would be complete, there would be no remainder. "So full of aspiration and dismay," as Blackmur describes his mind, Adams would clear the ground of every trace of the old interest, dispose of it, before starting afresh. But he is not like that, or not entirely. What makes us care about him is his detailed helplessness, the unofficial feelings he could not wave away so as to begin again. We are touched by his residue. What touches us in Blackmur is a different force. He always thought that order was best when it was not sought too earnestly; best if it came with luck and only enough judgment to know luck when you felt it. To Blackmur's kind of criticism, as to Adams' Virgin, prudence was necessary, but as an afterthought.

Blackmur is tender toward Adams in this book as elsewhere. Indeed he avoids saying what might be said, that Adams combined appreciation with enough malice to sharpen it though not enough to sour it: he could patronize people like Hay and George Cabot Lodge if he thought them merely minor versions of himself and his own predicament. Blackmur is not troubled enough by Adams' malice to mention it. The only moment in this book which contains an expression of impatience on Blackmur's part is when he refers to Adams' refusal of risk; how he ran in thought to principle, "to summarized intelligence." Blackmur was all for principle, but not for summary, and espe-

cially not for a summarized intelligence that would prevent
you from responding to what the summary excluded. The proof
is his language, which is often so daring that it seems nothing
but risk. It is truer of Blackmur than of most other critics that,
as he says in this book, "one does not know a thing until one has
put it down to see what will happen to it in a new medium and
what it will attract to itself; what one knows is what one did not
put, but what comes otherwise to be there—what was dragged
into being by the agency of the language used and by the symbol made." A critic who writes that sentence does not live on
"the subsistence level of imagination" or on the level of what
corresponds to it in language. He supplicates the language, giving words not only respect but devotion and allegiance, knowing that they have further possibilities beyond their local
meaning. So he treats words as though they were proper objects
of affection, which in his case they are: such words as unity,
symbol, energy, force, failure, loss, inertia, thought, faith,
form, eccentricity.

I have been speaking of Adams and Blackmur as different
forms of intelligence. The differences are substantial. Adams
felt a need—which many people do not feel—to find life not only
actual but intelligible. His interest in people was mainly in
the hope that each might be an instance of the intelligible already achieved. Each might embody not only experience but its
syntax, or a version of its syntax. Blackmur was content to discover the syntax later rather than sooner, and he suspected syntax that came before the need of it. But it is possible to exag-
gerate, by this emphasis, the differences between the two men.
The sense of ignorance brings them together again.

Early in the book, Blackmur is discussing the tendency of
mind in the nineteenth century to create its symbols merely as
slogans: *laissez faire*, survival of the fittest, and so forth. Each
of these, he says, "superseded and confounded the energy of the
values which should have illumined them." As symbols these
slogans failed because they thought themselves equal to their
field and authoritative all the way, while none of them "held in
reserve the power of the occult, the mysterious, the unknowable; none, in short, was itself, as well as what it stood for." We
are close, in this quotation, to the poetics of ignorance, a theme
that Blackmur supplicates two hundred pages later when he
cites Adams' observation that "true ignorance approaches the

infinite more nearly than any amount of knowledge can do." Blackmur takes care to say what Adams means by true ignorance as distinct from the common sort: it is "a present sense of the 'unknown' other than in the consciousness that uses words and ideas." Trying again: it is limited to cover "the absence of articulable knowledge in the presence of another and positive skill of knowing." And then, in a glowing sentence, Blackmur says: "One has to possess one's ignorance like knowledge." The nineteenth century, according to Adams, was indifferent to what it could not understand: it did not possess true ignorance. The thirteenth century "cared little to comprehend anything but the incomprehensible": that is, it valued true ignorance more than any legal form of knowledge. Adams and Blackmur meet in these perceptions; in the felt relation between knowledge and ignorance, where each is true; or between education and failure. In "The Expense of Greatness," referring to Adams as a representative example of education, Blackmur says that it is "education pushed to the point of failure as contrasted with ordinary education which stops at the formula of success."

I shall end with a hateful thing, a formula, a summary. In *The Lion and the Honeycomb, Language as Gesture,* and *A Primer of Ignorance,* Blackmur's concerns are mostly those he first saw in Adams' books, with only the further exacerbation of seeing them in even more desperate straits in the world at large. The subtitle of *The Lion and the Honeycomb* reads: "Essays in Solicitude and Critique." The solicitude, like the rituals of supplication, comes mainly from Adams, in the sense that Blackmur has taken up Adams' themes to see what has become of them twenty, thirty, or forty years after his death. The critique comes not only or directly from Blackmur's intelligence but from the diverse and complementary forms of intelligence he found in Adams and James. The public themes are prompted mainly by Adams, and they amount to one crucial problem: how to convert energy and momentum into intellect. The possibilities implicit or latent in literature, especially in the novel, are prompted mainly by James. What Blackmur made of James, we have long known and admired. What he made of Adams, and what Adams made of him, we are now in a better position to see.

Editor's Introduction

"The more he thought of it the less difference it seemed to make whether the Presidential Election that confronted him was that of 1868 or 1928. Neither in the perspective of history nor in the unseen focus of the present, so far as he had them in mind, was his heart ever at stake. The young man was saddened; his own experience palled him, and he tried every facility of sophistry to make his negative seem a choice and his abstention from the Polls the only possible exertion, for him, of political power."

This paragraph's concern with the insignificant individual amid uncontrollable forces, the tone of ironic indifference, the confessional use of the third person—all would seem to declare it the work of Henry Adams. It is, however, part of an essay written by Richard Palmer Blackmur (1904–1965) in an attempt to decide between Herbert Hoover and Alfred E. Smith in the 1928 Presidential election ("Politikon," *Hound & Horn*, 1928). Throughout his life Blackmur used Adams as a standard by which he could measure his own age. As he wrote in "The Expense of Greatness" (1936), "In Adams the attractive force is in the immediate relevance his life and works have for our own. The problems he posed of human energy and human society are felt at once to be special and emphatic articulations of our own problems." Throughout his life as a critic Blackmur used the figure of Adams as a point of reference in his intense study of the problem of the artist in modern society, a process that he hoped would culminate in a definitive, book-length study of Henry Adams.

When Blackmur died in 1965 he left approximately seven hundred pages of manuscript and several boxes of notes on Adams. Among these papers are eighteen pages written in October 1936, shortly after "The Expense of Greatness," and entitled "Plans for Work." Even at this early stage Blackmur did not visualize a chronological biography or a standard work of literary criticism. He savored the complexity of human character and wished to do full justice to the reticent and paradoxical Henry Adams. He therefore planned a book that would exhibit four aspects of Adams, in the hope that by revolving these facets he could compose a full "portrait" of the man. He wished to consider Adams in the following contexts: (1) his familial, social, and historical background; (2) his written works evolving from the "personal" critic to the "impersonal" artist; (3) his contemporaries' opinion of him; and (4) his significant "notions" about friendship, eccentricity, ignorance, failure, and education. Blackmur believed that these perspectives on Adams would demonstrate his unity and value as an "American archetype," proving the theses of "The Expense of Greatness."

Like many great American works, Blackmur's book grew by accretion over a long period of time. The order in which he wrote the sections was dictated by his current interests and the availability of sources, not by his "Plans for Work." In the late 1930s and through most of the next decade, he concentrated on Adams the historical figure, as opposed to Adams the archetypal artist. He was greatly helped in his research by Mr. and Mrs. Ward Thoron. Mrs. Thoron, the former Louisa Hooper and niece of Adams' wife, Marian ("Clover") Hooper Adams, granted Blackmur access to manuscripts in the family's possession. He, in turn, sent her his manuscripts about Adams and she replied with praise, criticism, and suggestions. The frankness and warmth of their correspondence help to explain the immediacy and vividness of Blackmur's "personal" portraits of Adams written during those years.

Blackmur first concentrated on the third category of his 1936 "Plans for Work"—the criticism of Henry Adams by his contemporaries. In a series of essays written in the late 1930s

he evaluates Adams by comparing him with three of his inti-
mates: his wife, his brother Brooks, and Henry James. A review of *The Letters of Mrs. Henry Adams* appearing in a 1937
issue of the *Virginia Quarterly Review* documents her importance in Blackmur's view of Henry Adams. "Henry and Brooks
Adams: Parallels to Two Generations" was published in the
Southern Review in 1939. In the late 1930s Blackmur wrote
"King Richard's Prison Song," a study of Adams during the
last six years of his life in which he is compared with Henry
James. Three parts of "King Richard's Prison Song," including
the section on James, were published in the *Kenyon Review*
(1940) as "Henry Adams: Three Late Moments."

During the 1940s Blackmur turned to Adams' place in history, the first category of his 1936 "Plans for Work." In 1942
he completed four essays under the heading "National Politics
1868–1885." In these unpublished essays he considers Adams'
journalistic writings, his *History of the United States*, and his
biographies of Albert Gallatin and John Randolph. As World
War II came to an end, Blackmur wrote three additional essays
on "Foreign Affairs 1895–1908," in which he examines Adams'
role as "stable-companion to statesmen" from the Spanish-
American War to the transatlantic alliances preceding World
War I. The third of these historical essays, "The Atlantic
Unites," appeared in the *Hudson Review* in 1952. Blackmur
never revised these studies in the light of the wealth of materials which became available to scholars in later years. Although all seven essays are interesting as examples of a kind
of historical criticism atypical of Blackmur, they have not
worn so well as his more characteristic work and are omitted
from this volume.

In the mid-1940s Blackmur evaluated Adams as a novelist
and a pedagogue, two roles that he believed were united in
Adams' late masterpieces, *The Education of Henry Adams*
and *Mont-Saint-Michel and Chartres*. In "The Novels of
Henry Adams" (*Sewanee Review*, 1943) Blackmur examines
Adams' somewhat awkward attempt to resolve fictionally what
he considered the twin problems of his age, the fragile nature
of democracy and the impossibility of religious belief. "The
Pedagogue of Sensibility," published in *Chimera* in 1944,
treats some of Adams' letters to his niece, Louisa Hooper, as
exemplary of the artist as teacher. "The Pedagogue of Sensi-

bility" compares Henry Adams and Henry James as rather unusual pedagogues.

In the late 1940s Blackmur re-evaluated his work on Henry Adams and wrote another outline for his projected book. In this new plan he focused on the second category of his 1936 "Plans for Work": Adams' written works as evidence of a development from "personal" journalist and historian to "impersonal" artist. He reordered what he had already written and estimated the length of what remained to be done. The new study of Adams was to be divided into two books. Book I would take Henry Adams from his undergraduate years at Harvard to the threshold of his last great works in the late 1900s. Book II would include "The Virgin and the Dynamo" and "King Richard's Prison Song" (the heart of the present volume).

Blackmur did not proceed chronologically and never wrote the projected sections for Book I on Adams' career before 1868, his marriage, his trips to Japan and Tahiti, and his social life after his wife's death. His essays on Adams in national politics and foreign affairs were completed but, except for "The Atlantic Unites" (*Hudson Review*, 1951), they were never published. Book I, then, was fragmentary and less than half-complete at the time of Blackmur's death. All his published essays on Adams would have been included in the final study, with the exception of an early article, "The Failure of Henry Adams" (*Hound & Horn*, 1931).

Although Blackmur did not finish the book he had planned, his enduring interest in Adams elicited some of his best criticism. His most luminous and sustained work on Adams came, as one would expect, during the late 1940s and early 1950s, when Blackmur—at the height of his powers—turned his attention to the final and most fruitful decades of Adams' life. These studies, which he titled "The Virgin and the Dynamo" and "King Richard's Prison Song," appear here in their entirety for the first time. I have prefaced them with "The Expense of Greatness" (*Virginia Quarterly Review*, 1936), which announced the essential themes of Blackmur's later works on Adams. I have also included one fragment, "At Rock Creek," Blackmur's meditation upon Adams' frequent visits to his wife's tomb at Rock Creek Cemetery in Washington, D.C., since it demonstrates Blackmur's remarkable identification with Adams in what amounts to an intensely lyrical prose poem.

The text of *Henry Adams* is based on Blackmur's typescripts with the exception of "The Expense of Greatness," which is taken from his collection of essays of the same title. I have altered obvious typographical errors, but have not tampered with Blackmur's syntax or style. Wherever possible, I have verified his quotations and corrected misquotations.

Blackmur's work on Adams is interesting not only for its unique insights into Adams' mind and character but also because its development paralleled Blackmur's growth as a critic. In "The Expense of Greatness" (1936) Blackmur sought to demonstrate that his own artistic ideal, the "rational imagination," was the goal toward which Adams was striving. The rational imagination is the perfect balance between objective, formal reason and subjective, creative imagination: "For the great poet, craft is the whole act of the rational imagination. It must combine the relish and hysteria of words so as to reveal or illuminate the underlying actuality—I do not say the logic— of experience."

At the beginning of "The Expense of Greatness" Blackmur projects his current interest in the rational imagination on to Adams as though he were setting the stage for a tragedy: "For great failure we want the utmost unrelenting imagination and the impersonal agony of knowledge searching the haven of objective form. . . . A genuine failure comes hard and slow, and, as in a tragedy, is only fully realized in the end." The climax of Blackmur's drama is the inability of the artist to realize his ideal. This impotence stems from the paradox that language and thought, the objective forms which are the only means to convey experience, change that experience as they express it. This is essentially the problem described by T. S. Eliot in the fifth section of "East Coker": ". . . one has only learnt to get the better of words / For the thing one no longer has to say, or the way in which / One is no longer disposed to say it." In almost all of his essays on contemporary artists written during the 1930s, Blackmur grapples with this paradox, but it is most movingly presented in "The Expense of Greatness":

Adams, by attempting to justify experience and so to pass beyond it, had like Milton and Dante to push his mind to the limit of reason and his feeling to the limit of faith. Failure, far from being incidental, is integral to that attempt, and becomes abstract, or faith fails and pretends to be absolute.

Like Oedipus, who can only see when he realizes that he is blind, Adams can achieve partial success only when he realizes that he has failed: "His scrupulous sophistication made him emphatically aware of his own failure; and this awareness is the great drive of his work." "Scrupulous sophistication" is another phrase for Blackmur's concept of the provisional imagination, which resembles Keats's "negative capability" or the suspension of belief in the reader of poetry that Eliot advocates in his 1929 essay on Dante. Not surprisingly, therefore, the "provisional imagination" is best expressed in Blackmur's early essays on Yeats and Eliot, where he states that the critic must imaginatively adopt a writer's belief, such as Yeats's magic or Eliot's Anglicanism, in order truly to appreciate his work. As he says in "From 'Ash Wednesday' to 'Murder in the Cathedral' " (his 1935 essay on Eliot), "The literal believer takes his myths, which he does not call myths, as supernatural archetypes of reality; the imaginative believer, who is not a 'believer' at all, takes his myths for the meaning there is in their changing application." Adams' greatness, then, lies in his ability to be both critic and artist, imaginative and literal believer:

Again and again he [Adams] describes unifying conceptions as working principles; without them, no work could be done; with them, even at the expense of final failure, every value could be provisionally ascertained. That is the value of Adams for us: the double value of his scrupulous attitude toward his unifying notions and the human aspirations he was able to express under them.

"King Richard's Prison Song," completed in 1938, adumbrates Blackmur's later interests. In it he explores Adams' attempts to express his life through a pre-existing symbol, as opposed to one that he might create for himself. Throughout Adams' letters and published works a certain pair of lines from Grétry's opera *Richard Coeur de Lion* haunted him, as it had his grandfather, John Quincy Adams: "O, Richard! O, mon Roi! / L'univers t'abandonne." According to Blackmur, when Adams found the medieval original of Richard's Prison Song, it seemed to serve "as an objective and actualizing symbol of his [Adams'] own suffering."

As he describes Adams' relation to the Prison Song, Blackmur transforms his theory of the rational imagination into what he would call in 1946 the "symbolic imagination." According to this criterion, reason and imagination find expression in an objective form or symbol. The symbol provides a focus for belief in an age without faith. Music succeeds best as a symbol because it eludes the snares of thought, language, and personality: it is a "translation from verbal sound with all its accidents and barriers of sense and commitments to place and person to pure, and uncommitted, statement." Blackmur's conclusion is worth quoting as the most explicit example of the transition in his thought from the rational imagination to the symbolic imagination:

> The representative imagination is driven constantly to force its experience to the crisis of expression. By expression we mean the achievement of external or objective form, where as a rule the experience becomes impersonal in just the degree that it is expressed, however personal its origin. The first paradox is, as any age of faith will show, that in objectivity is our only sight of unanimity; and the worse paradox is that even in the best—the most objective—expression of private emotion there is an arbitrary or willful element which makes the moment of crisis the verge of collapse or emptiness. Hence we turn as Adams turned in his Prison Song to the support of some existing form or convention of the general imagination, as if merely by existing and because we share it, its own profoundly arbitrary character might virtually lose itself in the exacting actuality of form. All that we are truly capable of believing is what we put into our gesture, our buildings, our images, or our song.

Buried here also, in the complexities of his prose style, is the seed of his famous essay of 1946, "Language as Gesture," in which he examines the symbolic potential of language.

In "The Novels of Henry Adams" (*Sewanee Review*, 1943), largely a plot summary of two little-read novels, Blackmur evaluates *Democracy* and *Esther* in terms of the symbolic imagination and finds them false starts in Adams' search for artistic unity. For Blackmur, art with a polemical purpose, such as that of Adams' novels, is not genuine art, which should be a pure expression of the artist's vision of reality without the distortion of ideology:

The artist must always reserve the right to exhibit what he sees or feels of the human predicament, and the only thing that we may require of him is that he does not exhibit what he neither sees nor feels, but only thinks, for political or other reasons, that he ought.

The "fables and symbols" created by reason alone are inadequate for the expression of experience. He concludes "The Novels of Henry Adams" by identifying the choice of the imaginative life with intellectual maturity:

[The novels] represented the gropings of a mature mind after its final theme. Taken together they make the turning-point of a mind which had constructed itself primarily for a life of political action into a new life, which should be predominantly imaginative and prophetic.

With this essay on Adams' novels Blackmur, too, had reached a "turning-point." In the first chapter of "The Virgin and the Dynamo" he takes on Adams' concern for the "imaginative and prophetic nature" of created symbols.

With what was merely "said" in the *Education* we have already dealt: the biography, the anecdote as illustrative, the history as narrative: here the job is deliberately to attach and rehearse the symbolic elements in the effort to catch the echo. At the right point, an analogous exploration of Chartres must be made; and finally, if possible, the symbolic values must be compared and joined and encouraged to work upon each other so that we may feel them, however complex and disparate in structure, as a single element fading and fulling in our own minds.

Blackmur believed that he could approach an understanding of Adams as an artist by a "rehearsal" or creative imitation of the structural "values" of Adams' great works, *The Education of Henry Adams* and *Mont-Saint-Michel and Chartres.* In creating his own masterpiece, "The Virgin and the Dynamo," he provided a consummate demonstration of his theory of the symbolic imagination.

In the first chapter of "The Virgin and the Dynamo," entitled "The Problem Laid Out," Blackmur outlines what he believes to be the position of modern man. After discussing the inability of Church and State to provide unity, he characteristically shifts the level of discussion to artistic failure as symptomatic of a diseased world: "What seemed to have disappeared was the means to express human reaction and aspiration in terms of great symbols." The "symbols" of the nineteenth century, such as *laissez faire*, suffered from the same overreliance upon reason that is demonstrated in Adams' novels. For Blackmur a true symbol expresses what thought cannot reach: "As symbols such phrases failed because each claimed to describe accurately, literally, authoritatively some vast field of human or natural energy; each asserted itself equal to its field; none held in reserve the power of the occult, the mysterious, the unknowable." This theory of symbols resembles his earlier ruminations about the nature of thought and language, but with the difference that Blackmur now seems to believe that language itself can be a source of symbols.

In Chapter 2, "A Boy's Will," Blackmur considers Adams' personal symbols, such as Quincy (multiplicity) in contrast to Boston (unity). Idiosyncratic symbols can fulfill a unifying function for the individual if they arise organically from circumstances, instead of being created by the intellect:

Associations are intended for what thought cannot express; systems of ideas are reared to take care of ignorance or uncertainty in the field of association. . . . Life was lived in instances and their associations and was understood by seeing what happened when they were put together in some form of discourse.

In the remaining chapters of "The Virgin and the Dynamo" Blackmur follows Adams' development from the idiosyncratic to the universal symbol.

In Chapter 9 Blackmur explores the nature of the universal symbol by concentrating on Adams' belief that the Virgin of Chartres was such a symbol for the twelfth century. In a lengthy discussion of the divergent philosophical schools of the twelfth century, Blackmur maintains, as Adams did, that there was little actual unity in the Church. For Adams, religious faith, as expressed in the Virgin of Chartres, provided unity despite theological controversies. Blackmur builds on the argument by transforming the Virgin into a symbol of imaginative or artistic unity. For Blackmur, art, not faith, produces unity, even in the twelfth century:

One of the curiosities in studying such extreme theological schools is that the relation often becomes clearest in the art that lies between;

for it is art that shows what happens to the extremes when actually experienced by minds otherwise. Art, in any fixed relation, is always the extreme of the ordinary.

In the last chapters of "The Virgin and the Dynamo" one can see Blackmur drawing an intellectual and psychological distinction between Adams and himself. Adams believed that he never attained the unity for which he was striving, and this sense of failure informs his last, embittered, works, such as the "Letter to American Teachers of History." According to Blackmur, however, Adams achieved unity but never realized it because he was looking in the wrong place and in the wrong way. Adams was seeking a physically demonstrable, rationally verifiable unity, and never perceived that he had achieved what Blackmur considers man's only form of unity, the imaginative and artistic unity of the twelfth century's Virgin or of Adams' masterpiece, *Mont-Saint-Michel and Chartres:*

Truth was not a relation in the twelfth century, as it tends to seem in the twentieth century, but the source of the relatedness of things; and the difference between two kinds of universe, that in which unity is grasped precariously by faith, and that in which centralization is imposed by incessant and always inadequate measurement of relations. Adams seemed to feel that it was not man who had changed the universe, but that it was the universe, by showing a different aspect as it moved, that changed man's mind. But he also seemed to feel that the consequent weakening of intensity in man's mind was relative rather than absolute, and that therefore the work was all to do over again under new and more difficult conditions [an allusion to Eliot's "East Coker," v]. Some kind of organic unity was his own ideal and he had come on it by having grasped it imaginatively, in its last apparition, at the height of the Middle Ages. *Mont-Saint-Michel and Chartres* is the record of imagination.

At the end of his study Blackmur no longer accepts Adams' pessimistic definition of his life as a tragedy, but finds in Adams' ability to perceive imaginative unity sufficient cause for optimism about the fate of the unaided imagination.

I wish to thank Professor A. Walton Litz, Chairman of the Department of English at Princeton University, for many helpful suggestions. I wish also to thank the staff of the Department of Rare Books at Princeton University Library, the repository of Blackmur's papers, for unfailing courtesy and helpfulness in the years I worked with the Blackmur collection.

Princeton University V.A.M.
September 1979

Contents

THE EXPENSE OF GREATNESS

Three Emphases on Henry Adams

Where your small man is a knoll to be smoothed away, Henry Adams is a mountain to be mined on all flanks for pure samples of human imagination without loss of size or value. That is the double test of greatness, that it show an attractive force, massive and inexhaustible, and a disseminative force which is the inexhaustible spring or constant declaration of value. As we elucidate our reaction to the two forces we measure the greatness.

In Adams the attractive force is in the immediate relevance that his life and works have for our own. The problems he posed of human energy and human society are felt at once to be special and emphatic articulations of our own problems. The disseminative, central force, which we find objectified in his works, may be felt and seen as the incandescence of the open, enquiring, sensitive, and skeptical intelligence, restless but attentive, saltatory but serial, provisional in every position yet fixed upon a theme: the theme of thought or imagination conceived as the form of human energy. We feel the incandescence in the human values and aspirations that were fused by it, from time to time, in persuasive form; and the cumulus of his life and works makes a focus, different as differently felt, whereby the particular values actually rendered shine concentrated as it were in their own best light. We make the man focus upon himself, make him achieve—as he never could for himself in the flux and flexion of life—his own most persuasive form. To make such a focus is the labor and the use of critical appreciation.

The approaches to such a labor are varied and must be constantly renewed and often revised. No single approach is omniscient or even sufficient. Here, in this essay, I want to take Henry Adams in a single perspective and submit it to three related emphases. I want to regard him as he often chose to regard himself, as a representative example of education: but education pushed to the point of failure as contrasted with ordinary education which stops at the formula of success.

The perspective is worth a preliminary emphasis of its own. It was as failure both in perspective and lesson by lesson that Adams himself saw his education. Success is not the propitious term for education unless the lesson wanted is futile. Education has no term and if arrested at all is only arrested by impassable failure. Surely the dominant emotion of an education, when its inherent possibilities are compared with those it achieved, must strike the honest heart as the emotion of failure. The failure is not of knowledge or of feeling. It is the failure of the ability to react correctly or even intelligently to more than an abbreviated version of knowledge and feeling: failure in the radical sense that we cannot consciously react to more than a minor fraction of the life we yet deeply know and endure and die. It is the failure the mind comes to ultimately and all along when it is compelled to measure its knowledge in terms of its ignorance.

Most failures we have the tact to ignore or give a kinder name. That is because we know by instinct at what a heavy discount to put most proffered examples of failure. There was no effort of imagination in them and only private agony, where for great failure we want the utmost unrelenting imagination and the impersonal agony of knowledge searching the haven of objective form. Most failures come too easily, take too little stock of the life and forces around them: like the ordinary failure in marriage, or business, or dying; and so too much resemble the ordinary success—too solemn and scant and zestless for realization. A genuine failure comes hard and slow, and, as in a tragedy, is only fully realized at the end. A man's success is in society, precarious and fatal; his failure is both in spite and because of society—as he witnesses its radical imperfection and is himself produced by it, its ultimate expression. Thus in a great man we often find inextricably combined the success which was his alone, though posthumously recognized, with the failure which as we feel it is also our own in prospect.

Let us take for our first emphasis Adams as a failure in society. If we assume that an education means the acquisition of
skills and the mastery of tools designed for intelligent reaction
in a given context, it will appear that Adams' failure in American political society after the Civil War was a failure in education. Society was bound for quick success and cared only for
enough intelligence to go on with. It cared nothing for political
mastery, and commonly refused to admit it had a purpose beyond the aggregation of force in the form of wealth. The effect
on Adams as a young man was immediate but took time to recognize. If *vis inertiae* was enough for society, any education was
too much; and an Adams—with the finest education of his times
—was clearly useless. The question was perhaps not initially of
Adams' failure but of society's inability to make use of him: its
inability to furnish a free field for intelligent political action.
Washington was full of wasted talent—of able young men
desperately anxious to be of use—as it is now; but no one knows
what talent might accomplish, then or now, because talent has
never been given a chance without being at the same moment
brutally hamstrung.

The discovery—that he was to be wasted whether he was any
good or not—was all the bitterer to Henry Adams because he
had three generations of conspicuous ability and conspicuous
failure behind him. Every Adams had ended as a failure after
a lifetime of effort—marked by occasional and transitory success—to handle political power intelligently. Their intelligence
they had kept; none had ever succumbed to the criminal satisfaction of power on its lowest terms—whether power for interest, or, worst of all, power for its own sake: the absolute corruption, as it seems to a scrupulous mind, of giving in; but all
equally had failed at the height of their abilities. If times had
changed for Henry it was for the worse. Where his ancestors
found in a combination of scruple and temper an effective termination of useful public careers, Henry found his scruple
alone enough to preclude a public career altogether. Scruple is
sometimes only a name for snobbery, stiffness, or even an inner
coldness—all, forms of disability; but in an Adams scruple was
the mark of ability itself, and its limit, as it made intelligence
acute, responsible, and infinitely resourceful, but a little pur-
blind to the advantage of indirection. An Adams could meet an
issue, accept facts, and demonstrate a policy, but he could never

gamble with a public matter. Jefferson's epitaph for John applied to them all: as disinterested as his maker. If the odds grew
heavy against an Adams he resorted to an access of will—or, if
you choose to call it, a wall of stubbornness, which is merely
will grown hysterical. But acts of will or stubbornness are
merely the last resorts of minds compelled to act scrupulously
against the unintelligent or the unintelligible.

Thus it is that many great men, if seen as examples of intellectual biography, seem either sports or parasites upon the society that produced them. They were compelled to act against
or outside it; and our sense of radical connection and expressive
identity is only re-established in the examples of their works
aside from their lives. Certainly something of the sort is true,
with different emphases, of Whitman, Mark Twain, Henry
James, Melville, and in our own day of Hart Crane and George
Santayana. They stand out too much from their native society:
all outsiders from the life they expressed and upon which they
fed. If all knew the ignominy of applause, applause from the
wrong people, for the wrong thing, or for something not performed at all, it only accented their own sense of eccentricity
and loneliness. That is how Adams stood out, but without much
applause ignominious or otherwise, eccentric and lonely; but
within him, as within the others in their degrees, was an intelligence whose actions were direct, naked, and at their best terrifyingly sane.

If, as I think, it was the scruple of his mind that made Adams
an outsider and that at the same time gave precise value to his
eccentricity, then the scruple should be defined both for itself
and in terms of Adams. It is what I have been deviously leading
up to: as it represents the single heroic and admirable quality
of the modern and skeptical mind as such; and a quality not
called for by the occasion but crowning it, even when dis-
astrously.

Scruple, generally speaking, is the agent of integrity, what
keeps action honest on the level of affairs, or on the level of
imagination when actuality or truth is the object. The etymol-
ogy of the word refreshes the meaning I emphasize, where we
have the Latin *scrupulus*, a small sharp stone, a stone in one's
shoe, an uneasiness, difficulty, small trouble, or doubt. Scruples
differ with the type of mind and education. Most men either get
rid of them or show pride in their calluses. In either case the

process of thought is made easy and reaction insensitive; you give in, you are practically carried along, but you get nowhere except where you are taken, and you know nothing at all of what you have been through, or of its meaning.

Specifically, with Henry Adams, scruple of thinking and thence of action was the whole point of his education for public life. Men without scruples either victimized power or succumbed to it; and if you had the wrong scruples you succumbed, like Grant, without knowing it. Political education was meant to supply the right scruples at the start, to teach sensitiveness to new ones as they came up, and to ingrain a habit of feeling for them if not apparent. It is scruples that compel attention to detail and subordinate the detail to an end. When excess atrophies the mind, whether of scruples or the lack of them, it is because either an impossible end or no end was in view. In science the adjudication of scruples is called method and taken for granted; but the whole test of the democratic process is whether or not the seat of power attracts the scrupulous intelligence and gives it rein. Here we may conceive Henry Adams as a provisional focus for that test.

In a sense no test is possible. Adams never held office. He only made himself embarrassingly available in the near background of Grant's Washington. Power was what he wanted, but on his own terms: the terms of his training. Perhaps he offered too much; perhaps his offers seemed too much like demands; at any rate he got nothing. But if we take him as a type—whether of 1868 or 1932—we can see that he was in the predicament of all young men whose abilities seem to lie in public life but who refuse waste motion. Society has no use for them as they are, and the concessions it requires are fatal to self-respect and taste, and lead either to futility, the treason of submission, or an aching combination of the two.

Both Adams and society saw politics was a game, but the difference in their angles of vision made their views irreconcilable. Adams saw the game as played impersonally with, as ultimate stake, the responsible control of social energy. Since ultimate value was never sure, every move ought to be made with the maximum intelligence and subject to every criticism your experience provided. If you stuck scrupulously to your intelligence you had the chance to come out right in the end under any scruples, democratic or not. You had a chance to put your society in control of itself at the center of its being. That was Adams' idea of the game, the idea of any honest young man.

Society played differently. The stake was immediate power, the values were those of personal interest. Thus the actual stake —control of social energy—was left for the ventures of interests irresponsible to the government meant to control them. Society in its political aspect cared more for chaos than unity; and the democratic process was an unconfessed failure, obliviously committing itself to social anarchy. Yet the failure remained unconfessed; the society lived and gathered energy; it was omnivorous, rash, and stupid; it threatened to become uncontrollably leviathan; it seemed occasionally on the point of committing suicide in the full flush of life. Always it had been saved, so far, by its vitality, its prodigious capacity for successive ruination, or by the discovery of a new and available source of power.

There was the young man's predicament. Should he assume that society was no field for intelligence and that its own momentum was sufficient to its needs? Should he rather enter the field, outwardly playing society's version of the game, while inwardly playing his own as best he could? Or should he work on society from the outside, accepting his final defeat at the start, and express the society rather than attempt to control it?

The first choice is the hardest; taken mostly by weak minds, it resembles more the dullness of indifference than disconsolate impartiality. Most men of ability, fortunately, make the second choice; it is they that make the administration of society possible and intermittently tolerable. Individually, most of them disappear, either lose office or succumb to it; but the class is constantly replenished from the bottom. A few survive the struggle in their own identity, and these are the ideals the young men hope to cap. J. Q. Adams was one of these, Gallatin and Schurz are clearly two more, as Senators Walsh and Norris make two examples for our own day. Men like Cleveland and Theodore Roosevelt are partial survivals. Adams thought his friend John Hay not only survived but succeeded in establishing a sound foreign policy; history is a harsher judge than friendship. As a general thing promise in politics not only dies early but is resurrected in the corruption of party or unwitting interest, which is what happened to Adams' friend Lodge. For the most part Adams' reiterated sentiment remains apt: "A friend in power is a friend lost." Small men might pass unnoticed to honorable graves but the great were lost.

Henry Adams lacked the dimensions suitable to a small man in public life and lacked the coarseness of will and ability to dissimulate to seize the larger opportunity, had it offered. Hence he made gradually the third choice, and brought the pressure of all the education he could muster upon society from the outside. It took him seven to ten years to make the choice complete. The first form of pressure he exerted was that of practical political journalism, of which the principal remaining results are the essays on "The New York Gold Conspiracy," "The Session, 1869–1870," and the essay on American financial policy called "The Legal-Tender Act." The second form of pressure was also practical, and combined the teaching of history at Harvard with the editorship of *The North American Review*. Already, however, the emphasis of his mind was becoming imaginative and speculative. Seven years in Cambridge taught him the impossibility of affecting society to any practical extent through the quarterly press, or through any press at all. Two of his essays were made campaign documents by the Democrats—their import reduced to the level of vituperative rhetoric—and then forgotten; so that by the test of the widest publication possible their practical effect was nil. There remained a third form of pressure not so much indirect as remote, and that was pressure by the imaginative expression, through history and fiction and philosophy, of social character and direction; and the aim was to seize the meaning of human energy by defining its forms and to achieve, thus, if it was possible, a sense of unity both for oneself and one's society.

Expression is a form of education, and the form that was to occupy the rest of Adams' life, the subject of our second emphasis. Put another way, society had failed to attract Adams to its center, and Adams undertook to see whether or not he could express a center for it. Unity or chaos became the alternative lesson of every effort. Here we have gone over or climbed up to a second level of failure, which is the failure of the human mind, pushed to one of its limits, to solve the problem of the meaning, the use, or the value of its own energy: in short the failure to find God or unity. What differentiates Adams' mind from other minds engaged in the same effort is his own intense and progressive recognition of his failure; and that recognition springs from the same overload of scruples that made him eccentric to the society that produced him. What he did not recognize was the ironical consolation that the form his work took as a whole was itself as near the actual representative of unity as the individual mind can come; which is what we have now to show.

Henry Adams' mind acquired, as his work stretched out, a singular unity of conception and a striking definiteness of form. It was the idiosyncrasy of his genius to posit unity in multiplicity, and by exploring different aspects of the multiplicity to give the effect, known to be false or specious but felt as true, of apprehending the unity. In reading *The Life of Albert Gallatin*, so successfully is the effect of Gallatin's career composed, we have to think twice before realizing that it is meant to show one aspect in the story of the failure of the democratic process to unite American society. Published in 1879, when Adams was forty-one, it so well struck the theme of Adams' whole career that it can be bracketed with Adams' own autobiography and be called "The Education of Albert Gallatin."

As important here, striking his theme gave Adams his first mature prose. The previous essays had been comparatively metallic, brittle, and rhetorical, and carried a tone of intermittent assertiveness rather than of cumulative authority. It was the subject perhaps that matured the style: Gallatin was the best in character, ability, and attainment that American history had to offer. At any rate, the biography of John Randolph, which came in 1882 and portrayed the worst waste in ability and personal disintegration in American history, showed a reversion to the earlier immature style. If Adams was, as Hay said, half angel and half porcupine, then it was altogether the porcupine that got into this book. The tragedy of Randolph was personal eccentricity, his constant resorts hysteria and violence, and Adams brought those elements over into his own style. Later, in his *History*, Adams repaired his injustice and treated him with charity of understanding, as an energetic sample of his times.

Meanwhile and just afterward, in 1880 and 1884, Adams published his two novels, *Democracy* and *Esther*. These suffer about equally from Adams' incompetence as a novelist, and the reader can take them best as brilliant documentary evidence of

Adams' insights and preoccupations. To intrude the standards of the art of fiction would be to obviate the burden the books actually carry. *Democracy* exhibits a political society full of corruption, irresponsible ambition, and stupidity, against the foil of a woman's taste and intelligence. So brilliant and light is Adams' execution, it is hard to decide which vice is worst of the three.

Madeleine Lee, Adams' foil, is struck a heavy blow in the face by her first and only Presidential reception. She stands fascinated and aghast at the endless wooden procession. "What a horrid warning to ambition! And in all that crowd there was no one beside herself who felt the mockery of this exhibition. To all the others this task was a regular part of the President's duty, and there was nothing ridiculous about it." It was Adams, not Mrs. Lee, who felt the full force of the blow. He remembered what he had seen at Devonshire House a few years back when Mme de Castiglione, the famous beauty of the Second Empire, entered.

How beautiful she may have been, or indeed what sort of beauty she was, Adams never knew, because the company, consisting of the most refined and aristocratic society in the world, instantly formed a lane, and stood in ranks to stare at her, while those behind mounted on chairs to look over their neighbors' heads; so that the lady walked through the polite mob, stared completely out of countenance, and fled the house.

In *Democracy* Mrs. Lee received a second blow, which we may obscurely feel as a consequence of the first, when, after his corruption is discovered to her and she taxes him with it, her suitor, Secretary of the Treasury Ratcliffe, defends himself by minimizing his offense, passing it off as commonplace, and asks her to purify American politics through marriage to him and with his aid.

The audacity of the man would have seemed sublime if she had felt sure that he knew the difference between good and evil, between a lie and the truth; but the more she saw of him, the surer she was that his courage was mere moral paralysis, and that he talked about virtue and vice as a man who is color-blind talks about red and green; he did not see them as she saw them; if left to choose for himself he would have nothing to guide him.

Which blow was the harder to bear? Was corruption, like stupidity, only an atrophied form of intelligence? Given the system and the society, did not the practice of politics necessarily produce one form or the other?

Adams himself did not feel the full force of the second blow until twenty years later when Theodore Roosevelt inherited office from McKinley. Secretary Ratcliffe in *Democracy* was the archetype of all he hated and Roosevelt represented an approximation of a good deal he admired. Ratcliffe was about the worst you got and Roosevelt was the best you could expect. But the lesson the two men taught about the disease of power was much the same, however they taught it on different levels. At heart Roosevelt, as a type, was more source of despair than Ratcliffe.

Power is poison. Its effects on Presidents had always been tragic, chiefly as an almost insane excitement at first, and a worse reaction afterwards; but also because no mind is so well balanced as to bear the strain of seizing unlimited force without habit or knowledge of it; and finding it disputed with him by hungry packs of wolves and hounds whose lives depend on snatching the carrion. Roosevelt enjoyed a singularly direct nature and honest intent, but he lived naturally in restless agitation that would have worn out most tempers in a month, and his first year of Presidency showed chronic excitement and that made a friend tremble. The effect of unlimited power on limited mind is worth noting in Presidents because it must represent the same process in society, and the power of self-control must have limit somewhere in face of the control of the infinite.

"Here," Adams goes on, "education seemed to see its first and last lesson." Certainly it is part of the lesson of the second Roosevelt as well as of the first; and certainly it is a lesson that in one form or another can be drawn not only from Presidents, but from every concentration of power in single hands. Power is greater than the hands that hold it and compels action beyond any tolerable volition. No wonder men make a game of it, as they make mathematics of time and space, since it is only as converted into a game that the experience of fatal struggles is commonly found tolerable.

But the lesson had other forms, as the energy it attempted to express took other forms than the political. There is the well of character, the abyss of science, and the aspiring form of religion, all expressions of human energy, and a wakened and scrupulous mind was compelled to respond to them all. Experience is only separated into its elements in the *tour de force* of expression, and as in *Democracy* Adams separated the bottom level of political experience, in *Esther* he separated the highest level of religious experience he could find in America and measured it against the response of a woman's intelligence. The question asked and the lesson to be learned were simple and fundamental and desperate. Assuming the Christian insight in its highest contemporary form, could the Church supply a sense of unity, of ultimate relation with God or the sum of energy, to which intelligence could respond? If the Church couldn't—and the Church had no other motive for being—nothing else could, and the soul was left on its own and homeless. Or so it seemed to Adams; hence the desperateness of the question; and hence the disproportionate importance relative to its achievement that Adams himself assigned to the book. Writing to John Hay from Japan in 1886, he suggests that it was written in his heart's blood, and again to Elizabeth Cameron from Papeete five years later, he says: "I care more for one chapter, or any dozen pages of 'Esther' than for the whole history, including maps and indexes." The nine-volume history represented the predicament of the society he had abandoned, and *Esther* represented his own predicament in relation to that God or unity the hope of which he could never in his heart altogether abandon. Like Spinoza, Adams was god-intoxicated, like Pascal god-ridden. His heart's hope was his soul's despair.

That the responding intelligence in *Esther* as in *Democracy* should have been a woman's, only reflects a major bias of Adams' imagination. Women, for Adams, had instinct and emotion and could move from the promptings of the one to the actualities of the other without becoming lost or distraught in the midway bog of logic and fact. Impulse proceeded immediately to form without loss of character or movement. More than that, women had taste; taste was what held things together, showing each at its best, and making each contribute to a single effect. Thus the argument of a woman's taste dissipated every objection of logic, and at its highest moments made illogicality itself part of its natural charm. Taste was the only form of energy sure enough of itself—as all non-human energies may be—to afford beauty; elsewhere the rashest extravagance.

Thus Adams tried everywhere to answer great questions in terms of a woman's taste and intelligence. Who else but Esther Dudley could form the center of the book she named? Only the strength of her instinct could accept the Church if it showed itself alive, and only the courage of her taste could reject it if it proved dead or a shell. That she might be confused in instinct and unconscious of her taste, only made the drama more vivid and its outcome more desperate. The problem was hers, but an artist could help her solve it, and perhaps a scientist, too, if he felt the struggle as an artist feels it. So Wharton, the artist, puts the question to her and answers it. "It all comes to this: is religion a struggle or a joy? To me it is a terrible battle, to be won or lost." The object of the battle is Nirvana or paradise. "It is eternal life, which, my poet says, consists in seeing God." The poet is Petrarch, and his words: *Siccome eterna vita è veder dio.* Strong, the scientist, for his part tells her: "There is no science that does not begin by requiring you to believe the incredible. I tell you the solemn truth that the doctrine of the Trinity is not so difficult to accept for a working proposition as any one of the axioms of physics." Between them—between art as it aspires to religion and science that springs from the same occult source —Esther might have been able to accept religion as that great form of poetry which is the aspiration of instinct and informs the whole of taste; but the Church itself, in the person of the Reverend Mr. Hazard, her lover, failed her both in persuasiveness and light. Power in politics and pride in the Church were much alike.

The strain of standing in a pulpit is great. No human being ever yet constructed was strong enough to offer himself long as a light to humanity without showing the effect on his constitution. Buddhist saints stand for years silent, on one leg, or with arms raised above their heads, but the limbs shrivel, and the mind shrivels with the limbs.

There is a kind of corruption in the best as well as the worst exemplars of each—which I suppose the Church would admit sooner than the State; a corruption in each case that makes for the self-falsifying effort of fanaticism. Hazard in his last argument appeals neither to instinct, intelligence, nor taste; he appeals to Esther's personal desperation and fear and so shows the ruination of emptiness within him. Esther can only answer him from the depth of revolted taste. "Why must the church always appeal to my weakness and never to my strength! I ask for spiritual life and you send me back to my flesh and blood as

though I were a tigress you were sending back to her cubs."
Although she loves him, the inadequacy of his church to its own
purpose compels her to dismiss him, but neither for science nor
for art, but for despair. That is the blood in which the book was
written.

As *Democracy* foreshadowed the major theme of the *Education*, the theme of *Esther* is given deeper expression throughout
Mont-Saint-Michel and, as well, in at least one place in the
Education. *Esther* is a representation of the failure in fact of
American society to find God in religion. As he grew older,
especially after the tragic death of his wife, and felt more and
more that society had abandoned him, Adams grew more pre-
occupied with the ultimate failure of imagination itself, as illustrated in every faculty of the mind, than with the mere
indicative failure of fact. Not facts which could be met but
their meanings which could not be escaped were his meat. The
meaning of *Esther* is intensified and made an object of inexhaustible meditation in the meanings Adams found in the monument Saint-Gaudens made for his wife in Rock Creek Cemetery. Part of the meaning lay in its meaninglessness to most of
those who saw it, and part in the horror of the clergy who saw
in it their defeat instead of their salvation. In a letter, Adams
gave the monument the same motto he had embedded in *Esther:
Siccome eterna vita è veder dio;* you could, in a gravestone, if
you had the will, see what life needed but never provided. In the
Education Adams suggests that the monument mirrors to the
beholder whatever faith he has.

In *Mont-Saint-Michel and Chartres* the problem of *Esther* is
made at once more universal and more personal. There Adams
made an imaginative mirror of his own effort toward faith in
terms of the highest point of faith—that is, of effective unity—
the world had ever seen: the Christianity of the great cathedrals
and the great intellectual architecture of the Schools. The Virgin dominated the cathedrals as a matter of course; and St.
Thomas dominated the Schools by an effort of will; but without
the Virgin the Schools would merely have paltered, as the
cathedrals would never have been built. The Virgin was pure
energy and pure taste, as her spires and roses were pure aspiration. Adams' book is the story of her tragedy; not that she was
destroyed or even denied, but that men no longer knew and

loved her, so lost their aspiration with the benefit of her taste, and no longer felt any unity whatsoever. The Virgin herself is still there, "but looking down from a deserted heaven, into an empty church, on a dead faith." She no longer gave orders or answered questions, and without her the orders and answers of St. Thomas were useless; and similarly, for Adams, the orders and answers of all later authorities.

Thus the education that led Adams to the Virgin was the greatest failure of all; the highest form of unity was, in effect, for the modern man, only the most impossible to recapture. Where Esther had very simply repulsed the Church because it appealed only to her weakness, Adams was in the worse ail of having no strength with which to seize it when it called for all the strength there was: he had no faith, but only the need of it. The Virgin's orders were the best ever given; obeyed, they made life contribute to great art and shine in it; but he had nothing with which to accept her administration. Her answers to his problems were final; she was herself the cumulus and unity of energy, and she removed, by absorbing, all the contradictions of experience; but seven centuries of time had made life too complicated for the old answers to fit. The same energy would need a new form to give the same meaning.

The failure of education was the failure of the unity which it grasped; the pupil was left with a terrible and weary apprehension of ignorance. Thinking of the Virgin and of the Dynamo as equally inexplicable concentrations of energy, Adams was led into the last phase of his education in the application of the mechanical theory of the inevitable change of all energy from higher to lower forms. What he wrote may be found in the later chapters of the *Education*, and in his two essays "A Letter to Teachers" and "The Rule of Phase Applied to History." It was, I think, the theory of a desperate, weary mind, still scrupulous in desperation and passionately eager in weariness, in its last effort to feel—this time in nature herself—the mystery in energy that keeps things going. It was the religious mind applying to physics on exactly the same terms and with exactly the same honest piety that it applied to the Virgin.

The nexus between the two was shown in the need for either in that fundamental condition of the mind known as *ennui;* and Adams quotes Pascal, the great scrupulous mind of the seventeenth century.

"I have often said that all the troubles of man come from his not knowing how to sit still." Mere restlessness forces action. "So passes the whole of life. We combat obstacles in order to get repose, and, when got, the repose is insupportable; for we think either of the troubles we have, or of those that threaten us; and even if we felt safe on every side, *ennui* would of its own accord spring up from the depths of the heart where it is rooted by nature, and would fill the mind with its venom."

Nature was full of *ennui* too, from star to atom. What drove it? What made energy change form in *this* direction and not that? Adams tried to find the answer in the second Law of Thermodynamics—the law that assumes the degradation of energy; the law which sees infinite energy becoming infinitely unavailable; and he tried hard to *feel* that law as accounting for change in human society. The attempt only puts his ignorance on a new basis. As analogues, the laws of physics only made the human predicament less soluble because less tangible. You might learn a direction, but physics prevented you from feeling what moved.

Reason, in science, as Adams had discovered earlier in *Esther*, deserted you rather sooner than in religion; and the need of faith was more critical. Had Adams had the advantage of the development of the quantum theory from the thermal field to the whole field of physics, had he known that all change was to come to seem discontinuous and that nature was to reveal a new and profoundly irrational face, he would have given up his last effort before he began it. A *discontinuous* multiplicity cannot be transformed into unity except by emotional vision. Adams had earlier said it himself. "Unity is vision; it must have been part of the process of learning to see. The older the mind, the older its complexities, and the further it looks, the more it sees; until even the stars resolve themselves into multiples; yet the child will always see but one." In 1915 Adams wrote to Henry Osborn Taylor that "Faith, not Reason, goes beyond" the failure of knowledge, and added that he felt himself "in near peril of turning Christian, and rolling in the mud in an agony of human mortification." But he had not the faith; only the apprehension of its need which made him struggle toward it all his life.

Failure is the appropriate end to the type of mind of which Adams is a pre-eminent example: the type which attempts through imagination to find the meaning or source of unity aside from the experience which it unites. Some artists can be content with experience as it comes, content to express it in the best form at hand. Adams gives La Farge as an instance: "His thought ran as a stream runs through grass, hidden perhaps but always there; and one felt often uncertain in what direction it flowed, for even a contradiction was to him only a shade of difference, a complementary color, about which no intelligent artist would dispute." Shakespeare is another instance. In such artists failure is incidental, a part of the experience expressed. But Adams, by attempting to justify experience and so to pass beyond it, had like Milton and Dante to push his mind to the limit of reason and his feeling to the limit of faith. Failure, far from incidental, is integral to that attempt, and becomes apparent just so soon as reason falters and becomes abstract, or faith fails and pretends to be absolute. Aside from the question of magnitude, one difference between Adams and his prototypes is, to repeat once more, just this: that his scrupulous sophistication made him emphatically aware of his own failure; and this awareness is the great drive of his work.

Here is our third emphasis. The failure of Adams in society—or society's failure to use Adams—was perhaps self-evident when stated. The singular unity of Adams' subsequent efforts to express the unity he felt has, I hope, been indicated. There remains the question of Adams' special value in the light of his avowed failure. The value is double.

The greatness of the mind of Adams himself is in the imaginative reach of the effort to solve the problem of the meaning, the use, or the value of its own energy. The greatness is in the effort itself, in variety of response deliberately made to every possible level of experience. It is in the acceptance, with all piety, of ignorance as the humbled form of knowledge; in the pursuit of divers shapes of knowledge—the scientific, the religious, the political, the social and trivial—to the point where they add to ignorance, when the best response is silence itself. That is the greatness of Adams as a type of mind. As it is a condition of life to die, it is a condition of thought, in the end, to fail. Death is the expense of life, and failure is the expense of greatness.

If there is a paradox here, or an irony hard to digest, it is not in the life experienced or the failure won, but in the forms through which they are conceived, in the very duplicity of language itself, in the necessarily equivocal character, earned by long use, of every significant word. Thought asks too much and words tell too much; because to ask anything is to ask everything, and to say anything is to ask more. It is the radical defect of thought that it leaves us discontented with what we actually feel—with what we know and do not know—as we know sunlight and surfeit and terror, all at once perhaps, and yet know nothing of them. Thought requires of us that we make a form for our knowledge which is personal, declarative, and abstract at the same time that we construe it as impersonal, expressive, and concrete. It is this knowledge that leads to the conviction of ignorance—to the positive ignorance which is the final form of contradictory knowledge; but it is the triumph of failure that in the process it snares all that can be snared of what we know.

The true paradox is that in securing its own ends thought cannot help defeating itself at every crisis. To think straight you must overshoot your mark. Orthodoxy of the human mind—the energy of society in its highest stable form—is only maintained through the absorption into it of a series of heresies; and the great heresy, surely, is the gospel of unity, whether it is asserted as a prime mover, as God, or, as in art, as the mere imposed unity of specious form. In adopting it for his own, Adams knew it for a heresy. Again and again he describes unifying conceptions as working principles; without them no work could be done; with them, even at the expense of final failure, every value could be provisionally ascertained. That is the value of Adams for us: the double value of his scrupulous attitude toward his unifying notions and of the human aspirations he was able to express under them. To feel that value as education is a profound deliverance: the same deliverance Adams felt in the Gothic cathedral. "The delight of its aspiration is flung up to the sky. The pathos of its self-distrust and anguish of doubt is buried in the earth as its last secret." The principles asserted are nothing, though desperate and necessary; the values expressed because of the principles are everything. For Adams, as for everyone, the principle of unity carried to failure showed the most value by the way, and the value was worth the expense.

THE VIRGIN
AND THE DYNAMO

CHAPTER ONE

The Problem Laid Out

Dans certains états d'âme presque surnaturels,
la profondeur de la vie se révèle tout entière
dans le spectacle, si ordinaire qu'il soit,
qu'on a sous les yeux. Il en devient le symbole.

—*Baudelaire*

In the year 1858 Henry Adams graduated from Harvard College. In 1859 appeared Darwin's *Origin of Species*. Thermodynamics, Accounting, Electromagnetism were new and explosive studies. Nationalism, Imperialism, Political Realism, and the Corporation were new institutions—or new forms of old institutions—drawing energy and materialistic bias from the new studies. Political Europe—and European culture—expanded in scope and speed and fragmented both internally and externally because it was not able to maintain unity in the interests of its new intensities. Industry was stronger than the family; interest was stronger than doctrine; the inevitable that could not be controlled was stronger than the necessary that must be controlled.

The Crimean War of 1855 showed Europe at its least military potential in modern history; the War of 1870, coming on top of the American Civil War, showed military power as the agent and creator of independent, aggressive, and fatal political power in a new, unprincipled form, the more portentous because plainly uncontrollable in any common interest. By 1870 the common or confederative polity of Europe—with its limited sovereign ties and limited competitions, its concert of nations and balance of powers, its predominant civil and human rights and its rising notion of parliamentary responsibility—had been destroyed except in Great Britain and her colonies, and in the

United States, where they survived, but only in their internal political aspects. In its place came the system of armed peace, territorial nations each claiming absolute sovereignty, unrestricted competition, and the increasingly irresponsible centralization of political and economic power. The Russian, German, French, British, and later the Japanese and American empires competed in terms of increasing and increasingly naked power—what was called *Realpolitik*—to control the rest of the world and eventually each other. The ideal of concert had been replaced by the obsession—and the fear—of dominion.

Something similar seemed true of the State's old doublet, the Church. It would seem part of the same process—an act responsive to the same stimuli—but moving if anything a little faster and a little ahead of its time—that the Roman Church in its Council of 1870 should issue a claim to greater and more nearly absolute sovereignty than it had ever before had the need to assert: the Bull of Papal Infallibility in matters of faith and morals. The process was technically complete when, in 1880, Leo XIII founded the Academy of St. Thomas at Rome and made medieval Scholasticism the official philosophy of the Church. In one sense the Church was reacting to a materialistic age by excluding the age; but in another and more consequential sense it was following the political states of the age by creating for itself an inclusive authoritarian basis. Where the State gave liberty within its limits and took authority where it could find it, the Church already took the next step and asserted authority without granting liberty, and thus found itself in the common competition for the naked power which it had been its historic and religious mission to redeem by the occult powers of imagination and charity and love.

What had happened—to continue this highly simplified account with an even more simplified explanation—was that man had been put in possession of vast stores of new energy which as he learned to use them carried him away, and which his intelligence could neither keep up nor cope with. In 1858 the sciences were still popular—extensions of common sense in terms of common interests—and were largely concerned with the development, economy, and synthesis of knowledge and skills of energy that had long been in human possession: the ordinary intelligent mind needed to push itself very little to catch up with what was then known. By the end of the century the ordinary man's knowledge amounted to a kind of detailed helplessness before enormous aggregates of supersensual energy. It was a new form of the oldest helplessness in the world—helplessness in the dark, helplessness in the felt, overawing presence of unseen forces, helplessness of the mind to understand the force that moved it, the helplessness, finally, of the spirit to maintain, or even to discover, its own aspiration in the face of the infinite.

The science, the technics, and the cities which revealed, deployed, and absorbed the new energies expressed themselves only as incomprehensible dogmas, novel routines and pressures, and incalculable wastes of inertia. There was violence, randomness, flatness: a kind of new ignorance willfully acceded to, a raw determinism, a mechanics of fate, which taken literally obliterated or at least mutilated the individual in the mass of his society. There were none by office or ability to see the dignity of the mass as it moved; so it was thought there was no dignity in the motion. Dignity is when man reacts to himself in his motion: never of the mass alone but of the individuals in the mass. Dignity is in human authority. In the part of this materialistic age which reaches from 1858 to 1900, human authority was in most dominant positions replaced by the authority of extra-human law, whether in Church or State or art or science. What seemed to have disappeared was the means to express human reaction and aspiration in terms of great symbols.

The disappearance was of course illusory, and even the illusion showed only in high places. Men and women still lived lives for the most part shaped between the third century B.C. and the Reformation; history was still transmitted, only its rate had changed; tradition was still manifest and available, only some of the modes of its expression needed renewal to meet the actual situation. What had crumbled was not the will and the imagination, but belief in the will and in the daringness or passion of the imagination. The optimism of materialism dumped great rampages of energy noisily into the sink of inertia; only the pessimist had the will and the passion to struggle for images—for symbols—in which to create the human significance, the significance to humans, out of the energies which moved him and which, as he aspired to affirm himself, he must move.

Henry Adams was such a pessimist, and of a special streak which he may have come by through his Puritan inheritance,

though it cannot be insisted upon since there have always been
minds which like his needed darkness against which to force
the passion of intelligence to luminosity. At any rate the inherited streak is worth emphasizing as a parallel in its own
right. Perry Miller, toward the end of *The New England Mind*,
expresses the character of that streak and its attractive force:

The Puritans were gifted—or cursed—with an overwhelming realization of an inexorable power at work not only in nature but in themselves, which they called God; whatever may have been the factors
in their society and their experience that so sharpened the edge of
their awareness, the acuteness and poignancy of the awareness are
phenomena which psychology will recognize though it cannot explain, and which history must take into account. And by a necessity
which both students of the soul and students of the past must en-
deavor to comprehend, whenever men conceive, in whatever guise,
that they confront this gigantic power, either in the visible world or
in their souls, they invariably must find means of coming to terms
with it, of bringing it into friendship, for the furtherance of their
common interests and for their respective sanctifications, not merely
for that of humanity but for that of the lawless, brutal force itself.

Adams' experience and insight were much like those of the
Puritans, his impulse of reaction was similar, but his means of
coming to terms—his operative incentives—were very different,
were in part indeed a reaction against the Puritan means. As he
had to deal with brutal forces that the Puritans did not know
because man had not yet released them, he had also to deal in
terms of previous efforts at reaction—in sex and art and aspiration—which the Puritans had tried to exclude from their ideali-
zations. The very passion of the Puritan rejection of sex was
perhaps the basis of Adams' obsession of assent to sex; perhaps,
too, the old Puritan arrogance against innovation and new revelation made Adams the more greedy to seize and tenacious to
understand the newly created energies. Having to assent to his
own age—having to discover where it shaped him and how, if
at all, he might shape it—he had also to assent to, to recreate
symbolically, the perspective experiment of history as it focused
at some point.

The Puritan point would not do because its configuration and
mutilation of Renaissance and Reformation—its special case of
the Christian experiment—still roiled his blood. The Puritan

configuration was what he could not focus with. When he looked back, it was how he saw what he did not have; it was for him the configuration of exhaustion—the weariness of denial from which he was never free—and he could feel neither its energy nor its assertion of unity. He found his focus therefore in those symbols which the Puritans seemed especially to deny, that made a cluster, or a crystal, in the cathedrals, the color, the mysticism, the Scholasticism, and the Virgin of thirteenth-century Normandy. Then, it seemed to him, the Christian experiment had reached its most intense and most absorptive stage of human significance. Then the revelation of God seemed continuous because impartially unified in all the aspirations, and given deeply related expression in all the dominant arts, of the whole society. Then the unity seemed deep as well as broad because it was asserted in the same congruity of emotion with which, transformed, it was crowned. Whatever logic of syllogism or architecture or manners came between, the revelation of God's energy ended as it began in emotion, kept human and made divine in the symbols of Christian imagination.

No doubt the thirteenth-century Christian lived much of his life apart from and even in conflict with his Christian emotion just as the creatures of nineteenth-century determinism lived apart from and even in ignorance of scientific law; the peasants' revolts in the fourteenth century seem to have been against the Church or at any rate against the clergy. No doubt, too, the institution of the Church acted more to its own aggrandizement than to the salvation of the people or to the nurture of saints, just as the finance capitalists and politicians of our own time developed the corporation and the state in the interests of immediate power rather than of the common good. Adams was aware of the corrupting conditions. The difference—and the value—lay in his conviction that for about a century—from 1215 to 1315—the emotional symbolism of Christian culture penetrated and enriched the recesses of the whole being, in terms of actual values felt, whereas the meaning of scientific and economic law did not penetrate but flattened out the beings who suffered from their operation, and did so precisely because the powers they dealt with had not been translated or expressed in adequate symbolic form. It was therefore natural that, feeling within him both the old and the new energies, and rediscovering for himself the vitality of the old symbols, he should attempt to discover symbols which should express his vital relation with the new energies, and that, further, he should attempt to feel both sets of symbols together and in their relations. Feeling their concert would give him unity; feeling their relation or sequence would give him history. And this was exactly the program of the *Education* and the *Chartres*, a deliberately undertaken program of what Kenneth Burke would call symbolic action by one man against the infinite forces that drive upon and within him.

That the *Chartres* pretended to be conversation with nieces and that the *Education* took the form of memoir suggests how fully Adams felt that one man, trying for great symbols, was not likely to create more than tokens of his intent: the palmer's withered leaves, which yet, to him who had crusaded, represented the maximum human adventure. In the Middle Ages, said Adams, all men were pilgrims, and he called himself, now a pilgrim of the Virgin and, again, a pilgrim of power. It was only the form of his books that suggested doubt of their validity; the experience within them was unquestionably serious, and the intent clearly major. The waywardness of form and lightness of tone reflected doubt of his audience—doubt of the possibility of any bridge between the audience and himself—but of the validity of the symbols toward which he worked he had no doubt at all.

The chasm between the self which creates and the symbol created has always been great, and was bound to be especially so in an age which tried for legal description and literal authority and which created its symbols either as convenient slogans, or inadvertently, or under the illusion that they were descriptions: *Laissez faire*, survival of the fittest, or the laws of thermodynamics, none of which was the source of the values each engaged, but each of which superseded and confounded the energy of the values which should have illumined them. As symbols, such phrases failed because each claimed in little to describe accurately, literally, authoritatively some vast field of human or natural energy; each asserted itself equal to its field; none held in reserve the power of the occult, the mysterious, the unknowable; none, in short, was itself, as well as what it stood for. They were asserted formulae rather than discovered creations: much as though the Trinity were conceived as a means of theological manipulation rather than as the mode of a mystery in which the many were also one and the one was also many.

True symbols, in the sense that the term is here used, are the means by which we express our understanding, or our helplessness in understanding, of what we cannot articulate verbally or by any other intellectual means. Symbols actually accrete and store the power with which we credit them, and become the more inexhaustible of that power the more they are used, providing the user still feels within himself what that power is. But true symbols cannot do the work of the intellect, and whenever either the intellect is actually able to do the work of the symbol, or deludes itself that it can do so, the power in the symbol disappears. Thus the validity and necessity of symbols depend on the human situation in which the mind realizes that it is dealing with energies beyond its descriptive knowledge or that it is helpless under the pressure of energies of which it has no direct knowledge at all. This was the human situation of Henry Adams. Neither the descriptive laws of energy made by his own age nor the symbols which happened to survive from the last age seemed to him adequate to cope with the energies he actually felt at work. Nor did the private symbols he had discovered in his own life satisfy his needs once he put them in a full context. He had therefore to repeat, to attempt to re-create, old symbols for old energies and to discover new symbols for new energies, and he had to do this on the most objective possible level, which would alone be adequate. He had to do this not as an imposed or a sought duty; the sole *corvée* was in the type of his mind, which could work in no other way, and which indeed reached for the symbolic mode of the mind as for a second nature.

Both in his historical work and in his private life he turned men into types, and phrases into fetishes, as for example in the portraits of Burr and Randolph and Calhoun and Gallatin— where the men are themselves felt as the alternating modes of politics, or again in such phrases as *Impavidum ferient ruinae*, *Sac* and *Soc*, the *C.C.A.*, and the Salmon Family—where each phrase both stood for a critical focus and created in Adams' mind something superior in reality to what it stood for. It was by such means that Adams composed his work and clung to himself; and it is by such means that the chapters of the *Education* are composed and cling to themselves; it is the function of these memoirs as a work of art to make types and symbols in permanent form of Adams' effort to respond and assent to his own time. So, too, in the *Chartres*, Adams attempted to restore to symbolic being the unity, in art, of sex and thought and occult force without the felt need of which his own times seemed meaningless.

Adams thought that if he could imaginatively recapture the aspiration of the Christian experiment at its highest symbolic value, he might better understand the aspiration—or, if his mind failed, the lack of it—in his own time. In each case he made symbols for the forces to which he had reacted or needed to react, in order to understand—to express—the mystery of himself in the forces and of the forces in himself. It is as if he had to dream the same theme twice, in two worlds, before he could find what the theme was or that the worlds were the same, and that both, imaginatively, were reversible, raising the same questions, tempting the same hopes, exacting the same despairs, depending on whether the sensibility that suffered and enjoyed them felt itself more driven or more attracted, old or young.

He had tried the same thing before, in *Democracy* and *Esther*, on simpler motives and in relatively fleshless symbols, in his forties, when the whole question had to do with ascertaining drives; now, in his sixties he resumed his theme, absorbed, as it were, both alternately and simultaneously, in forces which drove *and* attracted him. The difference is illustrated in the scope of emotion expressed and in the intensity of imaginative intelligence called out in symbolic form. No reader could doubt the intent of the novels either as to emotion or criticism; the intent was plain, and stopped with the words. But the later books, with the same or similar intent, must raise in the reader a kind of vital, continuing, uncertifiable, not quite formulable response—as to an actual situation unfolding—precisely because the emotion and the meaning go on, in symbols, after the words have stopped. There is the plummet echo of the unsayable in the said.

With what was merely "said" in the *Education* we have already dealt:* the biography, the anecdote as illustrative, the history as narrative; here the job is deliberately to detach and rehearse the symbolic elements in the effort to catch the echo. At the right point an analogous exploration of the *Chartres*

* A reference to his published articles and planned chapters on Henry Adams.—*Ed.*

must be made; and finally, if possible, the symbolic values of the two books must be compared and joined and encouraged to work upon each other, so that we may feel them, however complex and disparate in structure, as a single echo fading and fulling in our own minds.

CHAPTER TWO

A Boy's Will

For a job of such delicate issues, the critic's tools of analysis, specification, and comparison are rough and awkward, or would be if Adams had not himself made the first approaches simple and inevitable: by showing the accidents of childhood as creative forces. The forces existed and he had felt them; what had happened to him as a result of the forces was what he was—his identity. If, then, he could attach the forces to objects and situations and places, he would have gone a long way toward being able to handle, in a way to use, the forces which otherwise only handled and used him. It is part of the effort to achieve actual understanding of themselves that leads men to cultivate intense and inaccurate memories of the places where they have lived, just as it is another part of the same effort that leads to the erection of more or less rigid and always biased abstractions of behavior into systems of thought. Associations are tended for what thought cannot express; systems of ideas are reared to take care of ignorance or uncertainty in the field of association. Adams veered constantly between the two efforts, but wherever there was a question of necessary choice he chose to stick on the associations rather than on the formulas. He took strength in the fact that no one could deny the validity of the associations which he felt, and he saw weakness in the fact that any one, including himself, could question, in the instance, any formula. Life was lived in instances and their associations and was understood by seeing what happened when they were put together in some form of discourse. More might be necessary later—more from art and philosophy and science and religion—but in the beginning were instances. That was the simplicity of approach in the first chapters of the *Education*.

Thus Quincy and Boston, where his family lived alternately with the halves of the year, were joined in Washington at the level of primitive sensual and emotional experience, not merely as congeries of memory but because "winter and summer, cold and heat, town and country, force and freedom, marked two modes of life and thought, balanced like lobes of the brain." Boston was education and roused resistance and rebellion; Quincy was the value behind the resistance and was somehow included in the smell and taste and color of seaside country. Yet Quincy, too, involved education inescapably, if the value was to be maintained. The charming anecdote of the old President dragging his grandson to the country school becomes an image to bridge the two halves of the problem—or the lobes of the brain; and the President represented the ideal Washington: order or discipline achieved with intelligence and without cant. "From cradle to grave this problem of running order through chaos, direction through space, discipline through freedom, unity through multiplicity, has always been, and must always be, the task of education, as it is the moral of religion, philosophy, science, art, politics, and economy; but a boy's will is his life, and he dies when it is broken, as the colt dies in harness, taking a new nature in becoming tame."

A boy's will is his life; and the question of education is whether its dying is a termination or another birth, whether the boy is driven into either slavery or rebellion against his society, or whether he becomes a "consenting, contracting party and partner" to his life as a whole. To Adams summer, country, Quincy, and the old President represented freedom, duty, truth, and moral resistance to the material values of Boston. The trouble was that these Quincy values were warped by being expressed in terms of his ancestral revolutionary eighteenth century.

At the age of ten he had been deeply impressed by "the last services at Quincy over the body of one President and the ashes of another," but the later oration by Edward Everett at Faneuil Hall had in it nothing of his grandfather and nothing of himself. In Boston, Quincy values disappeared because the problems they raised were denied existence except as shadows. Clerical Boston had watered religion till it was a harmless solution, like its appendage Concord philosophy and its literary twin in the combined work of Ticknor, Prescott, Motley, and Holmes. Politics had become a choice between interest—in Webster, and temper—in the Abolitionists; though the boy's father and young Charles Sumner stood between, the one a model, the other a hero of the old statesmanship. Suffrage, the Common Schools, and the Press made Education; Education made Perfection; and Unitarianism was Perfection. "Boston had solved the universe; or had offered and realized the best solution yet tried." But it had done so by ignoring the old convulsive problems which hitched on man's anxiety about past and future, his dread of the energies which inhabited him, and his insight into the ends to which he must conform. Boston had lost its original impulse and had kept its old forms only for literature and party politics. Thus: "The children reached manhood without knowing religion, and with the certainty that dogma, metaphysics and abstract philosophy were not worth knowing. So one-sided an education could have been possible in no other country or time." The practical consequence was that "Boston girls and boys were not nearly so unformed as English boys and girls, but had less means of acquiring form as they grew older." They were safe from the problems of maturity, which Boston thought solved.

Of course, in opposing Quincy to Boston, Adams was looking back sixty years, and what he saw was more typical than it had ever been actual. The boy whose will had been broken under a double strain was not the man who had been tamed, but the man had need of some measure of what had been tamed—or changed—or grown; for whatever it was still lingered as a primal force in the man. Quincy, or summer, or freedom, or instinct, or truth—Quincy in its relations to Boston—made the best summary form to measure by: Quincy was life, Boston was what happened to life when Quincy was ignored: a mere manipulation of degraded—or ungraded—values. Quincy as ideal might be impossible in the actual world: Boston was limited to the possible, that is to say, the respectable, which hides rather than copes with the queer and the dark and the virtuous in man's nature, so that the respectable itself unconsciously became a little warped, inconsequential, and eccentric. Boston, then, represented what reason and habit can do when emotion and direct knowledge are gone; Quincy represented the underlying powers which must be acknowledged through imagination and reason, if reason is to be valid. Quincy was the will in imagination, soaked in sense, the moving faith in nature; Boston dispensed with imagination by atrophying, with its manner, the need for it. Both were clustered with associations, Quincy of nature, Boston of blackguardism and slavery mobs on Court Street. Quincy was the movement of nature, Boston the violence of man. Which broke the boy's will was a true question, unanswerable by logic of formula, but deeply answerable in the echo of the names themselves, in the strike or ring of their metal.

But Quincy and Boston made only a pair and showed only a shuttling relation, as simple as two fixed ideas, irreconcilable but apparently inclusive, which might wear each other out. The idea of Washington destroyed the inclusiveness, and did so first by striking the boy in the face with slavery, rousing not only response and rebellion but positive reaction. "Slavery drove the whole Puritan community back on its Puritanism," and in the community of anti-slavery emotion, Adams felt that he was, not a shuttled atom, "but a sort of herring-fry in a shoal of moving fish." But Washington the city meant also Washington the man, and the man stood above slavery and Southern Senators and the bad Virginia roads; he stood alone, "an ultimate relation, like the Pole Star," a product and judge of the corruption he stood on, and also the image of the ideal that lay beyond. Washington the man was the ideal force, as Washington the seat of government was the actual force, that could unite Boston and Quincy, not only through slavery but through whatever convulsive problem might come up. Washington, man or city, could cope with and survive whatever corruption of principle or institution might intervene between the American people and their aspiration; Washington was the fixed relation that made other relations intelligible and tolerable.

Adams at seventy saw clearly what at thirteen he could only have felt as one of the worst relations. "The first vague sense of feeling an unknown living obstacle in the dark," he says, "came in 1851." Much as Boston degraded the values of Quincy, so the party organizations degraded the values of statesmanship. In order to get Sumner a seat in the Senate, the Free Soil managers had to bargain with the Massachusetts Democratic managers, with the state government equivalent to the Senate seat. Sumner, C. F. Adams, and Dana—the Free Soil statesmen—would have nothing to do with the bargain in process but they took the benefit of it. Adams says the boy learned "the nature of a flagrantly corrupt bargain in which he was too good to take part, but not too good to take profit"; but it was learning by experience, by stumbling on foulness in the dark, not learning in terms of the maxims either of Boston or Quincy: it was learning to cope with the forces that actually confronted him. Washington represented the lesson by marking the gap between Mount Vernon and political practice, which was crossed only by bad roads; and Sumner represented the lesson, so far, by maintaining a unity of principle and value with a strength and purity all the greater for the forces they conciliated in order to concentrate and guide. Sumner like Washington came from political corruption to incorruptible power, and Sumner and Washington were right; but the rightness was hard for Boston or Quincy to bear. "As a politician," said Adams, the boy bringing Sumner the news of his election from the State House to Mount Vernon Street, "was already corrupt, and he never could see how any practical politician could be less corrupt than himself." Washington, then, represented the predicament of principle when action is necessarily impure and yet must be taken if the values behind the principle are to endure. "Apology, as he understood himself, was cant or cowardice."

The judgment is severe, even if taken as a form for the assertion of original sin in politics. Its practical result was the obliteration of Boston as a satisfying symbol; that is, in old age, Adams expressed his lifelong dissatisfaction with Boston by making of it a symbol of what he rejected: the inability either to assert principle or to take competent action in a contingent situation. That is what he means when he says he never regarded himself as a Bostonian, but always felt himself somewhere else. Quincy was real in morals and nature; Washington was real in principles and action; Boston—the force, the order, the education of his boyhood against which he rebelled—was an unreal compromise; of the three, Boston had to go. That is why he closes his third chapter, after rejecting Boston, with the promise that his story "will show his reasons for thinking that, in essentials like religion, ethics, philosophy; in history, literature, art; in the concepts of all science, except perhaps mathematics, the American boy of 1854 stood nearer the year 1 than to the year 1900." Quincy was alive as multiplicity, Washington as the struggle for unity, and both were positive; Boston, whatever the life underneath or in the power to come, was in its type neither one nor the other but a balance of both which if not dead was negative. The judgment is severe, but it is a judgment by interpretation and the association of feeling rather than by fact.

CHAPTER THREE

Education Reversed

The next triad of chapters—on Harvard College, Berlin, and Rome—takes rise from that judgment and begins by developing it; for Harvard College represented a kind of solvent for Boston and Quincy alike. It was a matter of course for the sons of both to submit to the *mesure*—the notion of balance by restraint, of judgment by moderation—which under the Unitarian clergy the college provided. There the mind was led to move, not by intellect, emotion, and will, but by gravitation; for the aim was to produce a type, but not a will, "a mind on which only a water-mark had been stamped," and the "water-mark" was social like that in letter paper. The students seemed to stand alone, respectable citizens, not leaders. "It seemed a sign of force; yet to stand alone is quite natural when one has no passions; still easier when one has no pains."

The position seemed even clearer in memory when Adams put beside himself and other Bostonians his three Southern classmates, who had temperament rather than mind, the habit of command rather than the means of control. Neither type was fitted to run the railways, which would be the major overt expression of the energy of their generation. Only the literary world seemed to recognize the coming change to industrial capitalism, and instead of trying to understand and develop and modify the significance of the change, instead of responding to it, the literary world reacted against it in satire. The middle class had the power; the satirists and idealists, says Adams, seized the press and attached the power by social means alone. The power that made railways was not to be deflected by social disdain or contempt or even fury, for the social power was a dispossessed power like the professional classes that expressed it. Neither the *beau monde* nor the *ancien régime*, in their American forms, governed; and aside from their actual professional functions, existed only as an inherited class that was rapidly becoming inferior, a social luxury rather than a social intensity. Harvard, which helped produce the class, had struck bottom somewhere in the 'fifties, and Harvard men afterward competed for the distinction of having graduated in the lowest year. Adams put it that at Harvard, "he was slipping away from fixed principles"—away from both Boston and Quincy toward Concord, that is to say, even farther from the proper, educational object of creating men of the world. For Harvard did not make men of the world: "it helped only to make the college standard permanent through life. The Bostonian educated at Harvard College remained a collegian, if he stuck to what the college gave him. If parents went on, generation after generation, sending their children to Harvard College for the sake of its social advantages, they perpetuated an inferior social type, quite as ill-fitted as the Oxford type for success in the next generation."

If the judgment seems harsh of Harvard in 1858, it is because its justice remains implacable, or has again become implacable, not of Harvard alone but of the whole college system, a century later. It is not now, nor was it then, the only just judgment upon the higher education; but it is the judgment with the least smugness and the least cant, and it condemns what ought to be condemned, the failure of the college to keep even with its time. In a nation and a culture which assert their dependence on popular education in the effort to maintain a democratic polity, the college, as a quasi-public institution, has a double function: to transmit the living past, and to train men in the ability to respond to, and perhaps lead, actual society. Harvard College in Henry Adams' time fulfilled the first function poorly and the second not at all. By transmitting largely what was dead in the past it cut itself off, as an institution, from living society, and tended to make its students indifferent to the problems they would have either to meet or succumb to. It is not an accident, and it is certainly in part a responsibility of the colleges, that so many of the writers and artists and teachers between 1870 and 1900 should have created themselves so far outside their time as to have earned the description of "The Genteel Tradition." Today the emphasis is different, but what is emphasized is the same: too many of our best minds have been cultural isolationists, doctrinaire radicals, escapists, feeling no part or only the wrong part—the failing, faltering part—of our actual society; and again the colleges cannot be held without direct fault.

It was because Henry Adams was himself a victim, and in a way a member, on the political side, of the genteel tradition that he rejected as nearly useless and nine-tenths wasted time his four years at Harvard College. What he seems to have rejected can be expressed most simply as the tacit, perhaps the unconscious, denial that human intelligence can develop in terms of newly couched human problems. The college as institution housed no symbols—whether saved from the past or seized from the future—with the compulsive power to overcome that denial. Without them it could not keep its purpose valid, except, as Adams felt, at a progressively inferior level. Adams' case is one more in the common experience with institutions, that as they profess to guide us through life, they are willing to do so only if they can cheat us on the way of half of life itself.

It is worth noting that the chapter on Harvard College has no represented associational clusters, unless it be the trio of wild Southerners; there are no landscape images and no images with a dramatic tenor. That is to say, there was no sense of the nether world, the unknown world, and no obstacle in the dark, that had to attach themselves to the college. The next chapter—Berlin—though it has in its center a death deader and colder than Boston's and a smugness of rote smugger than Harvard's, has at its beginning and end a multiplicity of images impinging as richly as Quincy on the boy's consciousness.

Adams went to study at the University of Berlin as the next natural step after graduation at Harvard, but before he got there he made several strides in education along novel lines. The first was seasickness, to which he was ever afterward prone, and which struck him hard: seasickness was the daily cost of pilgrimage. The second was the Black District—the first great industrial blight: an unknown society in the pit, a new and perhaps fatal obstacle in the dark. The Black District was the cost, in its new form, of society itself. The third stride was London, his first great city, which was insolent and large and had style, but had also the Bank and the Royal Exchange, which were not only insolent but hateful, and which were hated. London was the profit of the Black District, and as it grew larger the profit grew smaller: "The great city grew smaller as it doubled in size; cheaper as it quadrupled in wealth; less imperial as its empire widened; less dignified as it tried to be civil." In short, London became less the result of effort and more the result of unintelligible momentum, and so showed as a kind of blackening district itself.

The fourth stride was of another order—indeed of another age —and made the first three intelligible. On the route to Berlin he stopped at the sixteenth-century city of Antwerp, and felt it "thick, rich, ripe, like a sweet wine," as sensually alive as Quincy in summer or Washington in spring, but alive—though handed down, like Boston—from another age. Antwerp was his first taste of the Middle Ages, though he failed in response to the cathedral and the Cross, and was a high point in education. It was the renewal of an old ascent: "thick, rich, ripe, like a sweet wine."

His second taste of the Middle Ages, in Berlin, was a descent: the University operated on thirteenth-century methods—the lecture and the notebook—without the thirteenth-century excuse of the absence of books. "He had thought Harvard College a torpid school, but it was instinct with life compared with all he could see of the University of Berlin." After one lecture he quit the University and entered a Gymnasium in order to learn German through the study of Latin. His experiences and contemporary conclusions are related in an earlier chapter.* Here the interest is in the symbolic value of the German system of state education as a mode of institutional preparation for life. Reason, which very near unaided had solved or ironed out the problems of Boston, was excluded in the new Prussian education, and rote of both memory and thought, of skill and substance, was made omnipotent.

The German state was becoming military, a little ahead of and precipitating the militarization of Europe. Where the American polity relied upon an independent popular education

* Not found among Blackmur's papers.—*Ed.*

and suffered from relaxation, the new European polity identified education with standardization, and standardization with
discipline; and discipline in turn was to be the sole mode by
which the individual participated in the state. The new system
had the advantage of energy so great as to be free of doubt;
characteristically, the energy was the state, and was, therefore,
its own authority. Adams summed the intention and the method
with a figure out of his late life. "All State education is a sort
of dynamo machine for polarizing the popular mind; for turning and holding its lines of force in the direction supposed to
be most effective for State purposes."

It is this vocabulary—neutral in tone, neuter in sex, determined only in its authoritativeness—that was the creation of
the generation between 1870 and 1900; and the Prussian Gymnasium of 1858–1859, along with the Academy of St. Thomas
and Darwin's *Origin of Species*, helped make the creation possible and desirable. It was, in the Prussian form, a long descent
from Washington and Quincy, let alone Antwerp: it was man's
thought sunk to the level of the Black District, the well of energy
and sink of spirit. Whether from the same energy and, at least
in part, through the same vocabulary, another and different
effort might be made which should use rather than mutilate all
man's faculties was the looming, deceptive, haunting, impossible question, that asked itself first, as always, at Rome.

But before Rome, and on a par with Antwerp but deeper and
more personal—rather as if Antwerp were crossed with Quincy,
as if a cathedral grew in a hayfield—Adams had experience of
another order of man's thought, which had nothing to do with
St. Thomas or Darwin or Bismarck, except that it had in itself
the authority they claimed. Adams thought that this "his only
clear gain—his single step to a higher life—came from time
wasted; studies neglected; vices indulged; education reversed;—
it came from the despised beer-garden and music-hall; and it
was accidental, unintended, unforeseen." After years of listen-
ing to music in boredom, he one day found that he was following
the movement of a "Sinfonie."

He could not have been more astonished had he suddenly read a new
language. Among the marvels of education, this was the most marvellous. A prison-wall that barred his senses on one great side of life,
suddenly fell, of its own accord, without so much as his knowing
when it happened. Amid the fumes of coarse tobacco and poor beer,

surrounded by the commonest of German Haus-frauen, a new sense burst out like a flower in his life, so superior to the old senses, so bewildering, so astonished at its own existence, that he could not credit it, and watched it as something apart, accidental, and not to be trusted.

The experience itself must be taken for granted; it either happens or does not happen to those whose sensibilities are plastic to the *experience* rather than molded to the *idea* of new forces, or of old forces in new occasions. No doubt the possibility of this experience was liberated in Adams by the change in the conditions in which he heard music. At Cambridge and Boston, music was a social function; heard in drawing rooms or in concert halls, or produced by undergraduates, it was in any case either official or vicarious and had to do with the organization of social relations. In the Berlin beer garden, music was superficially casual and required no official attention; hence it was able to do its own work and reveal its own meaning almost exclusively by its own means: like landscape and architecture.

Most official education, short of the expert, got in the way of and devitalized direct perception. The question, of course, is how much direct perception in matters of importance even the most plastic sensibility can stand without being overwhelmed and disorganized. The sensibility instinctively grasps for the maximum, and official education as surely insists on the minimum as optimum. Adams clearly felt that an accident had shown the estimate of official education inadequate, and the interest in the sentences quoted above lies in what he says about the accident of the experience rather than its substance. It was education reversed; it was not education organizing and preparing for perception—essentially abstracting and accounting for perception; it was, rather, direct perception, achieved by indirect and customary exposure, organizing and adding to education, and in a dark, recessive sense contradicting the precepts, along with the prison walls, of education. So interpreted, it is again, as in its counterweight—the sentence about the dynamo of state education—the vocabulary of these sentences about the apparition of music in Adams' life, it is the vocabulary and the phrasing, that is important: it is sensual, nervous, poetic, sexual, as of a force running through chaos, a singleness created in multiplicity, not authoritative by law but known as authentic by experience. Here was a realm of experience in which it was

education to participate, like the yellow sunlight and the taste
of apples at Quincy. It remained, wrote Adams, for line and
color and metaphysics to make possible their upward strides.
But before that should happen, there had to be a vast amount
more education reversed.

Rome was an instance, partly of itself and partly by its contemporary and personal associations in the winter of 1859–1860.
Napoleon III had just declared war on Austria, with Italy as
pawn and loot and scene of battle; and to Adams both France
and Austria were wicked, which left him in a dilemma. "As long
as he could argue that his opponents were wicked, he could join
in robbing and killing them without a qualm; but it might happen that the good were robbed. Education insisted on finding a
moral foundation for robbery." That is—by both Quincy and
Boston standards—self-interest had to be justified. This was one
accident of personal and historical association; and his dilemma
was solved by the will of his sister, Mrs. Kuhn; and through her
influence Italy, like Beethoven, was one of the ends attained in
life.

Mrs. Kuhn was Italian, like most Americans, but she was
also a young woman in whose charm and intelligence the force
of life asserted itself as personal will; she combined in human
form the imperiousness and the sympathy and the quality of
justice-in-action which had been idealized in the twelfth-
century Virgin. Adams thought that of the forces that drove
him, those represented by men drove him wrong and those
embodied in women drove him right: which was a symbolic
apposition he was to develop. Here he expressed it simply as the
superiority of will over self-interest. "Women have, commonly,
a very positive moral sense; that which they will, is right; that
which they reject, is wrong; and their will, in most cases, ends
by settling the moral." The moral was Italian, and was made
somehow shining if not clear, when, with his sister, he saw
the double line of sentries of the opposing armies at armistice
in the Alps: "The flash of the gun barrels was lost in the flash
of the snow." The moral was doubtful, but actual.

Here Adams supplied two notions, or two attitudes, which
must alternate in the mind of any man widely traveled and
widely exposed to the accidents of experience. One is the notion
that "all experience is an arch, to build upon," which is the
notion of experience as liberation, leading to affirmation and

aspiration. The other is the notion—consequent upon the experience but resulting from the conflict with official education —that one can be no more than a tourist, which is the notion of distrust and uncertainty protecting itself, with reason, against participation in experience lest it encroach too much and abscond with the mind that suffered the experience. It is the conflict between these notions which Adams joined in the following terms. "In theory one might say, with some show of proof, that a pure, scientific education was alone correct; yet many of his friends who took it, found reason to complain that it was anything but a pure, scientific world in which they lived." Thinking back on the Rome of May 1860, and thinking what he could recapitulate that he failed even to see then, he could hardly have written otherwise, unless he had joined the issue by saying that, like a pilgrim, he was a tourist where his understanding was easy and a builder upon the arch of experience where it was troubling or difficult. His recapitulation was all on the troubling side: it had to do with the cultivation of knowledge by ritual through common symbols.

The symbols with which Rome bristled were by general agreement—even in Protestant Boston—thought the chief symbols both of Christendom and of the classical world. Boston might think England the Old Home and snobbish, Paris wicked, and Berlin highbrow, but she sent her sons and daughters to Rome without qualm of risk or doubt, for she did not see that Rome represented the failure of Christendom and the classical world—the very momentum of failure which is in survival—as well as their striving. This Adams did see, not so much at the time as when he was old enough to know what he had seen: that the nature of the failure was in the qualm of the striving. In the striving was the arch of experience; in feeling the qualm without the striving arose the temptation of secular withdrawal —the temptation to reduce oneself to a mere tourist. For Rome was the immorality of history: there was neither relation nor sequence between St. Peter's and the Forum, or the Forum and the Vatican; there was nothing but flat contradiction. Rome was where Gibbon dedicated himself to the mystery of the fall of Rome; was where Browning was shocked by a guillotine; and where, in retrospect, Adams was himself both shocked and dedicated. "Rome was a bewildering complex of ideas, experiments, ambitions, energies; without her, the Western world was pointless and fragmentary; she gave heart and unity to it all." Adams, like everybody else, asked the eternal question, Why, then, had Rome failed? which is the equivalent of asking what is failure.

No one ever had answered the question to the satisfaction of any one else; yet every one who had either head or heart, felt that sooner or later he must make up his mind what answer to accept. Substitute the word America for the word Rome, and the question became personal.

Adams nowhere says either what answer he accepted or on what terms he felt the American experiment continued the Roman. Those who distrust Adams will think it was the tourist in him that would not speak; but it would seem as true to say that the answer was rather the unsayable in what he said, that Rome was another example of education reversed, like Beethoven in Berlin, where his words do not present his experience but set up the conditions in which it will echo. At any rate he thought his Rome "the happiest month of May that life had yet offered, fading behind the present, and probably beyond the past, somewhere into abstract time, grotesquely out of place with the Berlin scheme or a Boston future. Adams explained to himself that he was absorbing knowledge. He would have put it better had he said that knowledge was absorbing him." Which is the flat definition of education reversed, and one definition of education through ritual, where the values rehearsed are only gradually and intermittently grasped.

May in Washington was the month of dogwood and judas tree, the month in which the forces of nature burst upon the sensibilities of men, flaunting her force as flowers, more bewildering and inexplicable in her appeal to the senses than she was ever in her pressure upon the mind. Washington was a kind of Rome, but with a future rather than a past. Rome in May 1860 had a future in the offing too, which as Adams looked back upon it had something in common with the future of Washington. The young Adams was drawn to the spectacle of Garibaldi's piratical, operatic revolution at Palermo and managed to see Garibaldi—to "look this sphinx in the eyes"—for about five minutes.

Here, as usual, memory did a bigger job with the experience than the contemporary record. It is the difference between looking at Garibaldi as an adventure and using him as a symbol. As a symbol he gathered and articulated the forces which as a man

he blindly represented. The habit of projecting perspective without diminishing the direct impact no doubt has something to do
with Adams' rediscovery of Garibaldi; and the weight of Rome
was sure to force perspective. "At that moment, in the summer
of 1860, Garibaldi was certainly the most serious of the doubtful
energies in the world; the most essential to gauge rightly. Even
then society was dividing between banker and anarchist. One
or the other, Garibaldi must serve. Himself a typical anarchist,
sure to overshadow Europe and alarm empires bigger than
Naples, his success depended on his mind; his energy was beyond doubt." But his intelligence was precisely what Adams
could not estimate, nor whether he was of the type of Napoleon,
Spartacus, or Condottiere: "in the eyes of history he might, like
the rest of the world, be only the vigorous player in the game
he did not understand." A double nature—pirate and patriot—
he did not understand his own acts, and was an instrument of
the classes he least wanted to help.

One sees here nineteenth-century materialism as moral fatal-
ism, but making a poem of itself: anarchy and finance, patriotism and finance, no matter how they were paired, seemed to set
up a relation in which the unconstrued forces were greater than
intelligent reaction to them. Garibaldi, because he was himself
a major energy, seemed to embody the forces, though he was
only their victim. He stood for the greater thing, and the thing
was inhuman. But he was also an individual, and tilted power
in ways that, like Rome, did not seem to fit any relation; the
puzzle was that in tilting power he uttered political common-
places. It was not necessarily that he lacked intelligence, but
there was no way to tell if it was there. "Precisely this class of
mind was to be the toughest problem of Adams' practical life,
but he could never make anything of it. The lesson of Garibaldi,
as education, seemed to teach the extreme complexity of extreme
simplicity; but one could have learned this from a glow-worm."

Adams meant that he was to find the same puzzle in different
degrees through a whole series of men who wielded great power
in great causes without conscious, or continuous, or developed
use of the intelligence. President Grant, Senator Cameron, and
perhaps Lord Russell and Theodore Roosevelt were examples.
There was a streak of Garibaldi in all of them; Garibaldi was
only the extreme Italian example, with the old violent immorality of Rome backing and as it were justifying his explosive

energy. This again was education reversed: it suggested how little in the actual conduct of men can be predicated on intelligent lines, and it demonstrated, more important, how little official education can do in understanding human conduct: education and conduct do not operate in harmony, though they may strike on the same fields. Accident might lead to Beethoven, education might lead to Berlin. As in Rome, there seemed neither sequence nor relation. The question was whether in this situation conscious intelligence had a lesser or a greater role to play; and Adams' next five chapters lay out the materials for the answer.

CHAPTER FOUR

Quantula Sapientia
Mundus Regitur

The question asked itself all the more sharply at Washington in the winter of 1860–1861 because of Rome and Garibaldi in the previous spring. We have seen how Adams, having looked on during a middle stage of the Italian struggle for liberty and unity, suddenly found himself participating with his father and W. H. Seward in another struggle for liberty and against disunion. Washington was not yet Rome but it gave promise of becoming so; it would either succeed in reasserting American unity or it would be the scene of one more failure in the effort to assert it. The policy of Seward and Charles Francis Adams was the intelligent balancing of conflicting forces subject to the principle of unity. Adams outlined the policy in the paper he sent to his brother Charles, and ascribed its failure to the inability of human nature to choose the means of intelligence when the same ends could be gained by brute force; but he insisted, at twenty-three, that it was "right to make the effort even if overruled." At sixty-nine he held the same conviction but tended, in the chapter called "Treason," to ascribe the failure of an intelligent policy to a radical weakness in one type of human intelligence itself. The treason was in the mind of Charles Sumner: that treason to principle which consists in making it fanatic. The Forum and the Vatican—the source of reason in debate and its end in dogma—were never farther apart than in the councils of the Republican Party during the Secession Winter. It was Sumner himself who quoted Oxenstiern to Adams: *Quantula sapientia mundus regitur.*

Thus Adams builds up images of precariousness and risk, of instability and conspiracy. The government buildings were Greek temples in the wilderness: there were Southern conspirators in Cabinet and Senate, and Northern conspirators in both houses of Congress. "The Government had an air of social instability and incompleteness that went far to support the right of secession in theory as in fact; but right or wrong, secession was likely to be easy where there was so little to secede from. The Union was a sentiment, but not much more, and in December, 1860, the sentiment about the Capitol was chiefly hostile, so far as it made itself felt." The Southern Senators in their violence of opinion showed Adams "his first object-lesson of the way in which excess of power worked when held by inadequate hands." Sumner, by his own violence of opinion, made the second lesson.

Comparing Sumner to Seward only pointed the moral. Seward gave the effect of unselfish large-mindedness devoted to the national interest. Together with C. F. Adams, Andrew Johnson, and Winter Davis, he tried to maintain a government for Lincoln to take over. Sumner, on the same anti-slavery principles, at first followed Seward in the policy of conciliation and Constitutional amendment; suddenly he began denouncing him and his policy and broke relations with the Adams family. He could not brook a superior. His principles had become his ego, and his ego had outraged his principles with a violence as excessive as the physical beating he had received in the Senate. It seems he never recovered balance from either violence.

Adams drew a desperate lesson. "Many a shock was Henry Adams to meet in the course of a long life passed chiefly near politics and politicians, but the profoundest lessons are not the lessons of reason; they are sudden strains that permanently warp the mind." The defection of Sumner from policy to faction was one of these strains: "[The] shock opened a chasm in life that never closed, and as long as life lasted, he found himself invariably taking for granted, as a political instinct, without waiting for further experiment—as he took for granted that arsenic poisoned—the rule that a friend in power is a friend lost." Sumner was the symbol of human treachery in rigid egoism: the treachery which, to repeat, by losing contact with the conditioning values involved, turns principle in application to mere fanaticism. Then the light acts like the dark. That is why Adams could say the Rebels' defections mattered nothing, but "Sumner's struck home."

If Sumner's case presented one type of the failure of intelligence—what might be called a Boston failure in a Roman situation—Charles Francis Adams' adventures as Minister to England suggested that whole nations might behave like Sumner at one moment and at another behave as a result of motives which only reached intelligence through the disfigurement of confusion. This meant that intelligence operated only on a fraction of its claimed field, and did that only by gross self-deception. As a result, the temptation to secular withdrawal almost overcame the temptation to build on the arch of experience. Conscience, if it put together the avowals and the acts of the British Government to find an intelligible policy that would explain both, might well gnaw itself with the suspicion that intelligence was good only for tourist purposes. Yet if the suspicion were taken as proved, conscience would be worse hit by the fact that it was by the operation of one's own and one's friends' efforts at intelligence that the failure of intelligence in one's opponents was discovered and, gradually, dealt with. The sensible conclusion would be that inadequate intelligence was common enough but adequate intelligence was rare and even at its best required constant support outside itself. The elements of the story of American relations with England, as Adams reflected upon them, did not come out so simply, and the four chapters which he took to lay them out reached only a double—a Yes-and-No—conclusion which was not sensible at all and which led to impractical as the only practicable action.

The stages by which Adams reached this way station are complex, but enough of them can be exhibited to make them acceptable. At first reaching his post Minister Adams found that the British Government had already recognized Southern belligerency. The Minister's job was therefore either to prevent that recognition from becoming intervention or to force intervention to take the form of war, as American policy should require. At home the Minister enjoyed the enmity of Sumner, who was chairman of the Senate Committee on Foreign Relations, and the support of Secretary Seward. Unfortunately, Seward's support was at first tainted by his recurring temptation to believe that the rebellion might be put down by resort to an English war. He thought both sides would unite against the common enemy.

In England the Government asserted strict neutrality, and so long as that assertion was maintained, it gave the Minister a point for reasoned argument from which he could not be dislodged: strict neutrality, in American opinion, would support the Union. But British policy as it actually unfolded seemed to look toward the diminution of a dangerous, because competing, power; the last object of policy was the promotion of American unity. England as a whole insisted on neutrality, but the dominant voices in government directed her neutrality as far as was feasible against the North and for the South. It was a case of competition between interest and morals, and produced the characteristically ambiguous pattern which is the result of such competitions. She recognized belligerency, but she did not make war out of the *Trent* Affair, where, from the point of view of interest, honor might have justified war. She held out as long as evasion of Minister Adams' arguments was possible with regard to releasing armored cruisers to the South, but she gave in when evasion was no longer possible. Furthermore, she believed Lincoln's Government to be on the verge of collapse, and naturally sought her advantage in the collapse. In taking this advantage, the French were clearly willing to help; and perhaps French willingness had something to do with developing shifting policy in England. At any rate, when her mistake in judgment became evident—when Lincoln's Government survived and strengthened, and the North began to win—England changed her policy. Something like this makes up a natural view of the bases of an intelligent American policy for England, if the moral consideration and long-term English-American interests were left out.

Minister Adams had therefore the task of persuading the English Government that his own Government had strength which it would develop, that English interests, English law, and the Law of Nations lay with the North, and that the moral consideration was integral to Anglo-American relations intelligently understood. The Minister had the further advantage that for the first time he represented the principle, in America's name, of legitimacy and order, which since 1815 represented a chief avowed cause in the international actions of European govern-

ments. The advantage was only in argument so far as the English Government went, but it helped indirectly to solidify the
liberal anti-slavery elements and the Lancashire millworkers
on the American side, and this in turn pressed the Government
back upon a line of actual neutrality. In essence, then, Minister
Adams' object was to bring England into intelligent cooperation
with American interests, and the great obstacle was a series of
apparently coherent and purposive acts, contradicting all professions of neutrality, which seemed to lead to intervention. The
question was whether the professions or the acts represented
policy.

The situation seemed the more ambiguous the more it was
explored. On the face of it Lord Russell lied, Lord Palmerston
laid traps as well as lied. Policy was a compound of lies and
truth on the basis of interest, so that the problem was to discover the motive behind the lie. If the statesmen lied one way,
in declarations of neutrality, English society lied another way,
by transforming Lincoln and Seward into brutes and by identifying the interests of Lancashire millworkers with the support
of a feudal slave-labor in the Southern states. Lord Palmerston,
the Prime Minister, sometimes joined society, and tried to pick
a quarrel with Minister Adams over Butler's Woman Order at
New Orleans, but the Minister prevented the quarrel by refusing to communicate with Palmerston except through Lord Russell, the Foreign Minister. The lies, said Adams, were necessary,
since otherwise English society would have had to acknowledge
itself morally wrong in promoting the Southern cause. Though
it lied, society was civil; Lady Palmerston was "sympathique";
but what in a way most emphasizes the ambiguity of the situation is Adams' account of the visit to Fryston, where he met
Swinburne. Swinburne was *moyenâgeux*, "medieval with grotesque turn," and gave education by prodigy or genius, an experience no more comprehensible, though more enjoyable, than
English foreign policy. Perhaps neither poetry nor policy was
conscious of its motive; perhaps intelligence was possible only
in response to either, not in creation.

Adams certainly entertained the first suspicion; whether or
not he entertained the second, he seems to have laid out the
chapters on "Political Morality" and "The Battle of the Rams"
as if he did. He writes about the men who made British policy
as if he were examining the motives in a play in which the au-

thor is credited with pure, and inconsistent, creation, but no
intelligence, as if he had been predetermined in every line,
without possibility of choice. The ambiguity in Hamlet or the
ambivalence in Iago is less than in Russell and Gladstone, and
each has to be dealt with by the process of detaching symbolic
values and adding speculative context to replace the simple
drama lost by analysis. The form of the process is interrogative;
questions cut deeper than statements, and are good for any
situation that has the capacity to be unfolded. The situation
stated is merely an instance. The main question Adams asked
can be put serially. Is it possible to trust a competition of forces
to produce a single interest? Can national policy have a conscious motive? Do political decisions depend more on intelligence in terms of motive and interest, or more on that inertia
of accumulated interest that intelligence does not touch? In
short, is it possible to react to a situation from a clear motive?

Somewhere among these is the question Adams was in reality
asking; just as—and this is what contradicts his self-accusation
of being a tourist—there is somewhere also in the very asking
the reality of his conviction that one must always make the
attempt to act on intelligent grounds, and that, further, one
must always impute the effort at intelligence in one's opponent.
The effort is one thing, and the actuality, which may be
another, cannot be judged without it. Great suspicion can only
be built on the basis of profound trust. "Never distrust the sincerity of your opponent," said T. E. Lawrence, thinking of war.
It should follow that one ought not to count on much more immediate policy in one's opponent than one finds in oneself.

The problem is central and unsolvable, whether the struggle
for choice is not the struggle to be chosen, and takes different
emphases from differently coordinated stresses. Perhaps one
ends by finding a long-term policy which gradually absorbs the
immediate im-policy as the inertia of instinct absorbs the accidents of will, and as the pressure of interest consolidates, while
it aggravates, choice. Then Adams' question can be sought in
another series: Can one trust a politician? Is policy possible?
One does what it is possible to do; also, one tries a thing, out of
tykishness, to see if it is possible, to see what would happen
if—! That is, one experiments in order to find out what one must
do. The Puritan, the positivist, the nineteenth-century materi-
alist—and Henry Adams was rebelliously all three—in trying

the experiment, usually invents some new form of inexorable will, and contrives to make of the experiment a *corvée*—an inescapable imposed task. The *corvée*, then, *is* the experiment. To Adams the *corvée* in politics was, to repeat once more, the effort to create policy—a clear, persistent intent, involving risk—out of principle and intelligence, with each modifying the other.

This was the lesson of aspiration, of the ideal reduced almost to the possible level; and it had to come to terms with the lesson of what actually went on. His teachers were the three Americans, Thurlow Weed, William M. Evarts, and Minister Adams, and the three British, Lord Russell, Lord Palmerston, and Gladstone, as they had to do with the struggle over Britain's American policy. The more he reflected on what they taught, the clearer it seemed that they taught the limitations and relative intensities of their different types of character as they pressed, or were pressed by, the mass of government in motion. Though government is set up of laws not men, men still sit at the center and filter laws through their personality. So it is also true that men must filter their words through the acts to which they are impelled by laws and interests. The filters alter the force and value of the laws without altering either the intent of the laws or the interests. Thus there is conflict and contradiction which require treatment, either by self-deception or readjustment, by the men who experience them, in order to make action possible. Action emphasizes the values actually at work, with expense to the consistency of the principles which are supposed to guide the action. Action is a constant revelation of the inadequacy of principle to a given situation without necessarily affecting the adequacy of principle to all situations. The lesson is simple in the abstract but aggravating in the concrete instance.

As it happened, Adams' three British teachers resorted to self-deception and his three American teachers were able to readjust the relation of their laws and their interests in the face of the given situation. In the end the story showed that each trio was honest within the limits of character and ability; and if the difference in limits had a measure it was in degrees of intelligence and stupidity. Adams' natural prejudice sharpened the contrast in favor of the Americans, and the ordinary caution needed in assessing prejudice should be applied in following his account, especially where he seems to credit the Americans with greater freedom of action than the British. The real issue, historically, is between relative intelligence and relative stupidity; to us it is a symbolic rendering of the possibilities of political action.

Each of the three Americans is presented as expressing an attitude appropriate to the highest feasible practice of politics, yet each touches somehow on an obstacle in the dark. Thurlow Weed, he said, inspired confidence partly by his skill and address in the management of men, but even more by his apparent unselfishness. He was "a rare immune" from the violent egotism of power. "He had the instinct of empire: he gave, but he did not receive." When Adams asked him if no politician could be trusted, Weed answered: "I never advise a young man to begin by thinking so." Adams decided that Weed's point was that in a world of relative values young men could not trust a general rule, and he elaborated the opinion in a kind of general rule for himself. "Principles had better be left aside; values were enough." The whole passage is one of the most seminal passages in the *Education*; here the single sentence just quoted may be re-emphasized along narrow lines. Applied to the diplomatic conduct of Russell and Palmerston, it meant that their fidelity to or deviation from principles did not matter so much as the values—things of felt worth—their actions affected, with or without the aid of principles. Addiction to principle should be in oneself, subject only to the security of one's values. Too much worry about the principles of the British Cabinet might distract attention from the values which were its object. When all the values were known, principle might illuminate further value; so might the absence of principle. If the name of Weed brought such an attitude to Adams' mind, it was of great symbolic significance.

The character of Evarts only enforced the lesson from a slightly different angle. To Adams he seemed to play for the stakes and not for the game; which was to say that he played for primary values, which ought to be represented in primary principles. He was also "an economist of morals, but with him the question was how much morality one could afford." Put the other way around, in practice too much morality ruined both primary principles and values by becoming cant. A just morality depended on more values than were usually available, and mere moral principles could never substitute for the missing values.

Thus when Russell and Palmerston pointed in act toward intervention and yet swore to impartial neutrality, young Adams asked himself, and his father, whether he was wrong in taking their bad faith for granted. Young Adams thought he was right and that Russell lied; the Minister thought not, but had to act as if he did. In short, for practical purposes, in action not judgment, the Minister had to behave with indifference to the moral question; truth or lie was one more value to be determined. Thus, when young Adams repeated the question in another form—Could he risk trusting anyone in politics?—his father's example seemed to assume that one had to trust and not to trust at the same time, and the real question was how far one could trust oneself.

As a young man Adams rebelled against this position as a fatal breach of principle. "Life changed front, according as one thought one's self dealing with honest men or with rogues." And to some extent the rebellion persisted when, as an old man, he found Russell admitting in his Memoirs that he had been at fault in letting the Rebel cruisers escape. "The true issue lay not in the question of his fault, but of his intent. To a young man, getting an education in politics, there could be no sense in history unless a constant course of faults implied a constant motive." This was a concession of principle, and he was to make more as various memoirs became available. The facts seemed to run as follows. When on one occasion the Federals took a beating, Palmerston suggested to Russell that intervention would be desirable should Washington fall. Russell replied that intervention might be desirable in any case: to which Palmerston answered that they had better wait and see. The records show the two men alternating in position, one cautious and the other positive. Gladstone alone remained a firm interventionist; and when he delivered his famous "and what is more, they have made a nation" speech, he was promptly disavowed by the Cabinet as a whole.

Gladstone, the one moralist of the three, had blown up in rhetoric a possibility, and in the explosion the possibility itself collapsed; it was political "realism" in a moral nature, leaving the nature and destroying the morality. Adams calls it unex-

ampled political turpitude; yet by bringing the project of intervention into the open Gladstone showed both its inacceptability
to the country and its weakness in the Cabinet itself. On the
American question Minister Adams' supporters, Cobden and
Bright, were stronger both in the Cabinet and in the country
than the three principal members of the Cabinet itself.

But the three persisted. Shortly after disavowing Gladstone's
speech, Russell called a Cabinet to see whether it was not the
duty of Europe to intervene; if words meant anything they
meant that the disavowed Gladstone had expressed his dis-
avower's intent. Gladstone and Russell had been pursuing the
matter with Napoleon. Napoleon wanted Mexico, the three
Englishmen wanted to submit a divided America to a European system; but only Gladstone the moralist held firm. Yet
on the day of the Cabinet Russell assured Minister Adams that
no change in neutrality was contemplated. Whether the Cabinet voted intervention down, or whether he lied, Russell was
right. The trouble was, says Adams, that Russell habitually said
one thing and did another, unconscious of contradiction. Palmerston, in his Memoirs, turned out to have been cautious, con-
ciliatory, and consistently honest. Gladstone charged himself
with stupidity and the inability to view "subjects all round."
Meditating on these, Adams found his answer, that he might as
well have trusted as distrusted; there was nothing there to distrust worth the distraction and the temper. "His whole theory
of conspiracy—of policy—of logic and connection in the affairs
of men, resolved itself into 'incredible grossness,' "—which was
Gladstone's phrase for himself.

The other conclusion, which neither Adams nor any of the
three British statesmen drew, was that, whether connected and
logical or not, the three had made tentative and reversible but
consistent moves in a game of wait and see. If the South had
won the war, the moral question would have been lost in the
fact that both North and South would have been drawn into the
European system at the military as well as the economic level;
and whether England needed to promote that contingency, no
English Ministry should have failed to anticipate it. Yet it does
not seem to have been anticipated. English opportunism under
Russell and Palmerston was unintelligent. So far as England
was concerned, Adams had now the answer to that version of
his question which asked, Is political action the result of intelli-

gent decision? English action was the result of indecision. "The old-fashioned logical drama required unity and sense; the actual drama is a pointless puzzle, without even an intrigue."

If the chapter called "Political Morality" shows the demoralization of intelligence in politics over the issue of intervention, the next chapter, "The Battle of the Rams," shows the triumph of morals and intelligence in the deepest possible contrast to the last. Charles Francis Adams, as symbol of the whole Adams creed, is presented in the act of making a small triumph of righteous, consistent, reasoned policy otherwise, till the end, without weapons. But the triumph needs detail to be understood.

The material points at issue between Adams and Russell had to do with the ironclads then being built at Birkenhead by the firm of Lairds on the apparent order of a M. Branay of Paris but actually and notoriously for the Rebels. The *Alabama* had already been built, and had "escaped" into Rebel hands. The question was of technical collusion between the British Government and the Rebel agents—whether virtual, tantamount, actual. Adams argued there was criminal negligence in the *Alabama* and that it was about to be repeated. It was at heart a question of policy, not of law. The British were no doubt within *some* construction of the law, at least until Adams could prove that the ships were Rebel property, but they were very certainly outside the spirit of the law if their policy was in fact neutrality. What happened to the two new ironclads would determine the policy. But Adams had to argue in terms of law, he had to argue collusion in order to reach considerations of policy. If he could prove collusion, he could demonstrate that in fact Russell exercised a policy which, if held, could only mean war. And that is what he did. As each step of his argument showed Russell nearer to intervention, Adams raised his tone; and he no doubt felt the better able to do so because at about that time Vicksburg fell, and it was clear that Lincoln, Seward, and Stanton had begun to effect a mature policy at home.

To young Adams the experience was giddy and exalting. "One began to dream the sensation of wielding unmeasured power. The sense came, like vertigo, for an instant, and passed, leaving the brain a little dazed, doubtful, shy. . . . Little by little, at first only as a shadowy chance of what might be, if things could be rightly done, one began to feel that, somewhere

behind the chaos in Washington power was taking shape; that
it was massed and guided as it had not been before." Young
Adams felt that his father was swinging some of that power in
London. The father kept on raising his tone until he reached his
famous sentence: "It would be superfluous in me to point out to
your Lordship that this is war!" It was superfluous because
Russell knew it and meant it; war was the logical outcome of his
policy. Minister Adams was pointing out to the world, not to
Russell, that he was accepting Russell's war.

The curiosity is that Adams' policy succeeded in reaching
strength only because he assumed that Russell's policy was
equally consistent and tenacious in opposition. It is important
that Russell had actually given in to Adams' argument before
he received the note containing the statement of war. It was not
to the threat of war that Russell succumbed, but to the absence
within himself of a tenacious, risky, convicted undertaking: the
absence of a conscious policy. It may be argued that Russell had
an unconscious policy; if so, the point is that when it became
conscious—when it had to react to conscious opposition—it became American policy. The power of tenacious mind—the mind
conscious of the power behind it and of the values at stake—was
great enough to focus, intense enough to concentrate, that part
of English policy which bore upon it. The contribution to the
diplomatic success of the growing military power at home was
of course greater than the moral considerations, at least in the
sense that if military power had failed moral considerations
would not have counted. But there was a point of balance, and
it was at that point that Adams won his case, and he did so
partly by the impeccable moral form in which he presented his
argument for international obligation through law.

The whole "Battle of the Rams" argues that it is right, and
proper, and possible to conceive a policy on principle when the
values at issue fit the principle, and that it is sometimes possible
to effect that policy. Taken with the argument in the previous
chapter [of the *Education*], that English policy was a pointless
puzzle, there is the suggestion of these rules, that policy exists
but has to be discovered, and that the conscious policy which intelligently asserts its values may sometimes triumph over conflicting values which have not been formulated in conscious
policy. This is one form of the relative triumph of intelligence
over inertia. Perhaps, better, it suggests that intelligence is the

intensification, amounting to a transformation to a new phase, of relevant inertia. Reduced to its smallest, the suggestion is that Charles Francis Adams had, by reason of his knowledge of his own policy, a sense of the English policy which the English did not have. Thus he was able to make the necessary assumption of trust. On the intelligence of the assumption hung superiority in power.

But this is a dramatic simplification, made more on behalf of human need than on the facts. If it happened, it is rare enough to be accidental, as all the great forms of understanding seem to be. Thus at the very end of the chapter Henry Adams quotes Gladstone to the effect that politicians are the hardest type to understand, and that he, Gladstone, had never felt he had understood more than one or two. To Henry Adams it seemed at the time that Seward and Charles Francis Adams, Russell and Palmerston, had all showed strength, ability, and tenacity; history seemed rather to follow Gladstone and showed that the British had not known what they were doing—that they had erred rather than lied. By some accident the American Minister had successfully used intelligence in an unintelligible field. Similarly, John Adams had beaten Lord North, and John Quincy Adams had beaten Canning. It was an accident that had happened three times. No matter what its meaning, such an accident, digested into a living will, becomes aspiration. Made objective, that aspiration seems to imply that the foundation of the modern state which means to continue beyond adventure must be in the principle of the combining validity of the human intelligence and the human will. The accident might yet be law. *Quantula sapientia mundus regitur!*

CHAPTER FIVE

Terebratula and *Pteraspis*

If the difficulty in using intelligence and principle in politics was the difficulty of understanding the type of man who rose to political power, and if the greatest possible success was both accidental and questionable, it might help to ask if types other than the political were also to be understood only by accident and in questionable terms. One might discover, at the end of such a pursuit, that intelligence and principle were restricted means to their own larger end, and that something had been left out of the consideration that was actually being used all along. Adams was an American dealing with English statesmen, and although he—or his father—learned to deal with them, they remained incomprehensible on his chosen grounds. What other grounds were there? What forces were there that bore only an accidental and occasional relation to the force of intelligence? The next batch of four chapters—called "Eccentricity," "The Perfection of Human Society," "Dilettantism," and "Darwinism"—carry the skill in handling the puzzle a little further. But as in mastering a difficult knot, the skill was developed by habit in the mind's fingers; and if the skill had passed through the brain it had left no conscious mark.

The experience explored was English. Had it been French, one would have found Napoleon incomprehensible in a different way from Palmerston or Russell. Napoleon had begun in 1854 to set the tone of Europe in a series of random and grandiose military gestures which seemed to serve no rational purpose of his empire and which had as their only discernible purpose the strengthening of his personal dynasty by extravagant and, as it turned out, futile means. He meant to compel the monarchs of Europe to address him as Brother. To an American such a motive might seem ridiculous and intolerable, but it was intelligible; it was what the American experiment was meant to destroy, and thinking of it filled the American intelligence with the strength of emotion. Nothing in England led to the same reaction. To Adams the English mind of the 'sixties, and all its motives, seemed an eccentric version of the American mind. It either worked off center or its center was not located where the American center was and had other attractive forces unknown to Americans—especially to Americans from Quincy.

Adams inclined to the view of straight eccentricity. His absolute right to his view does not lie in its justness in measuring his English experience, but in a combination of his inner need for a satisfactory symbol, on the political level, of human eccentricity, and in the fact that his family had been in political combat for three generations with what they regarded as inexplicable British stupidity. For this need and because of this fact the view that the English mind was eccentric did very well.

But nowhere does Adams exactly define English eccentricity; rather he works around and through examples of it in generalization and character and makes contrasts to it both American and English. One knows what it does and what it is not, but not what it is; one knows its associations and its frictions but not its purpose or plot. But the question in greatest doubt was whether as a force it was strong or weak. Would a mind gain or lose, respond better or worse, by cultivating eccentricity? Could a mind vitally engaged in anything but play afford to take experience as a glancing blow which one flung off, with energy, but randomly? If so, was not the method wasteful? When Adams looked around and summed up, it seemed to him that though the English mind could not be plotted from a whole view, by system or by logic, it yet had an unsystematic system and an illogical logic. By experience one could learn to predict its eccentricities. The English, said Adams, thought Americans had not a mind but a "cutting instrument, practical, economical, sharp, and direct." That it was no more was due to the absence of a felt tradition, the narrowness and superficiality of the conventions upon which it rested. The point was that Americans needed all their energy for vital purposes; the English, at this time, evidently did not. The characters in Thackeray and Dickens were not satire: they were what England could afford in the way of eccentricity. "Often this eccentricity bore all the marks of strength; perhaps it was actual exuberance of force, a birthmark of genius." Yet Charles Francis Adams, Thurlow Weed, and William M. Evarts showed themselves as strong or stronger. In politics, then, eccentricity was weak; but in society it made amusement and softened bad manners with tolerance.

The trouble was that "by natural affinity the social eccentrics commonly sympathised with political eccentricity. The English mind took naturally to rebellion—when foreign—and it felt particular confidence in the Southern Confederacy because of its combined attributes—foreign rebellion of English blood—which came nearer ideal eccentricity than could be reached by Poles, Hungarians, Italians or Frenchmen." On the other hand, to Adams' mind the Federal sympathizers all had relatively balanced minds, and all were concerned directly with the problem of creating policy by means of the intelligence. W. E. Forster's "chief ideals in politics took shape as working arrangements on an economical base." Cobden used rational persuasion; Bright was self-assertive, but hammered his point. Monckton Milnes, whose eccentricity was merely that he had "ideas a little in advance of the time," remarked that Gladstone, boxing the compass of thought, was "furiously earnest on both sides of every question." On the whole, "society" was eccentric and rebel: the Church, the universities, and the philanthropists were all rebel. The dissenters—religious and political—were union; and they represented the country better than "society" did. But the worst example was from the class of trimmers and doctrinaires: Henry Reeve, editor of the *Edinburgh Review*. Ponderous and pompous, he "avoided taking sides except where sides were already fixed." To an American this attitude of "oscillating reserve seemed more eccentric than the reckless hostility of Brougham or Carlyle, and more mischievous, for he never could be sure what preposterous commonplace it might encourage."

Two matters were of extreme importance in Adams' catalogue of English eccentricity, and a third was of subordinate importance. The third stands out least, and has to do with the need of any lively mind, given to extravagance and rashness of imaginative adventure, to see eccentricity and waste in the other fellow's action in order to feel confident in one's own. The eccentricity one sees elsewhere is the satire upon one's own vital conviction: it marks the element of pretense that must go with any serious commitment to action. There is a little pretense in Adams on English eccentricity, but it was necessary if he was to express what was important in his experience of it. Adams seems to have felt the element of pretense in his thought in the last paragraph of his chapter on "Eccentricity," for he there first excludes it and then transforms it into a metaphor. Let us take the exclusion first.

The sum of these experiences in 1863 left the conviction that eccentricity was weakness. The young American who should adopt English thought was lost. From the facts, the conclusion was correct, yet, as usual, the conclusion was wrong.

Here is the transformation.

A young American in 1863 could see little or nothing of the future. He might dream, but he could not foretell, the suddenness with which the old Europe, with England in its wake, was to vanish in 1870. He was in dead-water, and the parti-colored, fantastic cranks swam about his boat, as though he were the ancient mariner, and they saurians of the prime.

Saurians are lizards, but ordinary people in using the term as a rule name lizards of another age: Adams was cruising in a sea of swimming fossils.

Being interpreted, these six sentences have a meaning that is overwhelming because recurring; thinking of it, one has the fear that it is recurring this day—whatever this day may be—and not by accident but as the inevitable end product of any society. It was not that eccentricity was weak, but that the weakness in the structure of society made its official leaders eccentric. It was Boston and Harvard College all over again in English parts. In France, Napoleon had suppressed the intellectual élite; in England, the élite was made official, devitalized, eccentric; in America, the élite was unofficial, but when it tried to be otherwise aped the English model. Eccentricity is the fanaticism that happens when classes of men remain structurally dominant in a society after the power they represent is no longer the power that actually moves society, but before the new power has become sufficiently recognized to envisage a clear conflict between what is dead and what is living. Since new power is absorbed into and thrown off by society at different rates—none of which, except by accident, is ever the rate of the mind—the conflict is never wholly clear; so that there is always a good deal of eccentricity in both official and lonely minds.

There is a question, too, as to whether there is likely to be greater eccentricity in minds behind the times or in those ahead. The only certainty was that those behind were fossils and the more they were mistaken for live, the more they weakened their society. That was one of the important matters Adams' experience symbolized. The other important matter was in the contrast of temper that permitted him to see the first matter; the cross of Quincy and Washington in him that left him rebellious against Boston and Harvard College and Berlin, also left him rebellious against English eccentricity, and the stronger for rebellion. But the whole experience did nothing but make more ambiguous, and more doubtful, the underlying question whether, supposing intelligent men in office, intelligence could be used in politics at all and, if so, how far—for the stakes, or merely for the game?

Even the best intelligence was likely to mistake the one for the other. Boston generally had a snobbish regard for English society. Sumner and Lowell and Motley in their different ways took the opposite view from Adams. Motley, rather less warped than Sumner and less "social" than Lowell, was the best that Boston could produce, and Motley told young Adams that England in the 'sixties was "the Perfection of Human Society." Adams never, then or later, could see what Motley meant, and rather thought he had idealized experience he had not rather than that which he had.

To Adams the eccentricity in politics swept over into the social relation where it showed as bad manners, bad clothes, bad cooking, and company without companionship. Eccentricity was as weak in one relation as the other, without sequence and without coherence. Once one was "in" society, one was alone, solitary in crowds. "Society had no unity; one wandered about in it like a maggot in cheese; it was not a hansom cab, to be gotten into, or out of, at dinner-time." What happened in the cheese, Adams illustrates with two images. One was of the noblest lords and ladies in England, forming two lines, those behind on chairs, but all craning to disgrace themselves at the sight of Mme de Castiglione; that great beauty fled from her reception. The other image was of three duchesses worshiping Garibaldi with his gray capote over his red shirt. The "Perfection of Human Society" did not know what to do with either great beauty or great energy in human form. Against this society Adams put as foil his Yorkshire friends, Milnes and Gaskell, and found them solid of the center. Yorkshire was either outside England or was all England. Yorkshire took one into the family, and the family was real. Yorkshire might be perfect human society—for friendship and indolence and wit; but it was the past: it was not what Motley meant, and it was not what Adams could use, except as a vantage point for being a tourist.

About the only profession which the perfections of London and Yorkshire could fit a young foreigner for was dilettantism. Combat with London might fit him for the State Department, but the American System could not insist on using his training. Only the press was open to him as an alternative to dilettantism when his father's term in London should be over. It was very near the choice between becoming flotsam or jetsam: to float back and forth on the surface of action or to be cast up a smooth-worn relic of ancient action, to change uselessly or to represent that which had stopped changing. Like an Englishman, Adams began to cultivate his tastes in both directions. He collected watercolors and drawings and bric-à-brac, and he drifted toward the antiquarian side of history. As he could not guess the future of history, neither could he guess the future meaning to him of the adventure of the Raphael drawing, and so recorded it with no hint of its meaning except the length and detail of the record. Both history—in the shape of a paper on John Smith and Pocahontas—and Raphael were at the moment what they seemed to be, the occupations of a restless mind in "deadwater." What saved him and changed them, was that he was conscious of his restlessness. "In spite of personal wishes, intentions, and prejudices; in spite of civil wars and diplomatic education; in spite of determination to be actual, daily, and practical, Henry Adams found himself, at twenty-eight, still in English society, dragged on one side into English dilettantism, which of all dilettantism he held the most futile; and, on the other, into American antiquarianism, which of all antiquarianism, he held the most foolish."

Foolish and futile though he might know they were, it must have been the eccentricity or restlessness of his own race that kept him from succumbing to them, as Americans without number had done and were to do at Rome and Paris and London. Poverty forces most men from indolence; the convention of work as blessing forces others; but Adams suffered neither from poverty nor convention. The temptation to power and three generations of the habit of it in his own family were not enough alone to conquer the deeper temptation to disguise indolence with puttering and small affairs. The world being what it is, the temptation to secular withdrawal, when there are means to take advantage of the chance, is almost irresistible. It was the strain of abnormal energy in the Adams blood, no longer concentrated but split and intermittent, no longer bound to action and prisoned in contest but liberated as reflective and imaginative power—it was this strain in Henry Adams which gave him the energy to try for full response to the actual world, and gave him also the standard by which he was to call his struggle failure. Filial piety has done worse; and the human vanity involved, much worse.

Even piety and vanity required the additional support of the accident by which Adams was thrown into the stream of modern science, and which took shape through his father's friendship with Sir Charles Lyell, the great geologist. In the 'sixties the sciences still expressed themselves in ordinary intellectual terms, but had made such strides in reach and scope that they seemed on the verge of a great generalization that would be the end of education. Eccentric or "fragmentary" the British mind might be, "but in those days it was doing a great deal of work in a very un-English way, building up so many and such vast theories on such narrow foundations as to shock the conservative, and delight the frivolous." Under the excitement of envisaging a universe apparently at once expanding and united, Adams became a Comtist: positive knowledge of the world seemed at hand. He should have become a Marxist, too, he wrote, "but some narrow trait of the New England nature seemed to blight socialism."

Precisely the narrow trait that kept him from socialism prevented him from remaining either a Comtist or a Darwinian. Nothing he meant as progress and little that he valued as human was expressed in either gospel. Nor did he need liberation from the excesses of ancestral Puritanism; between the Unitarian teaching of his youth and the Roman lesson at the edge of manhood, he was not only sufficiently liberated, he was deprived. He knew something was missing that had to do with the sense of unity and the sense of purpose. Both geology and biology tried for unity and invented purpose; but in the rigor of their science they had forgotten the rigor of intellect, and had ignored the existence of emotion. As representative adventures of the whole human mind they were as one-sided, as eccentric, and as reckless of principle as Russell and Palmerston. Their unity was unbroken evolution under uniform conditions, and their purpose was measured in survival. Geology and biology were like Boston and Harvard College: they had solved human problems by dismissing them and had solved the universe by sanctioning it. The narrow trait that led Adams to reject socialism led him to reject Boston and Comtism and Darwinism and English eccentricity and dilettantism; it was the trait which had its source in Quincy—the multiplicity of nature—and which was developed by contact with Washington—the human attempt to balance all the forces of nature under a unifying aspiration. The trait was narrow only if it was not renewed, through new experience and new reactions, in each generation. If Rome could have taught Adams a lesson, it would have taught him the means of renewal.

It was considerations of this sort that brought Adams to frame his rejection of Darwinism with both irony and a declaration of ambition. Irony and ambition were what he felt when he looked back. The idea that life evolved without break under uniform conditions was very suitable to a young man who had in the Civil War helped "to enforce unity and uniformity on people who objected to it." The idea was "only too seductive in its perfection; it had the charm of art." That was the irony; the ambition was a full retreat to the wall, where he would insist "on maintaining his absolute standards; on aiming at ultimate unity." The irony represented what happened to principles in the violence of experience; the ambition represented what might happen if intelligence were substituted for violence. To some who believe only positively and must needs make their facts into dogmas, there will seem more irony in the ambition than in the remarks about achieving uniformity by force and unity by assertion. To Adams, Darwinism meant the substitution for religion—in which principles become both human and divine through emotion—of a common-law deity, which is the average of actions as they are, or the cheapest form of pantheism: what survives.

But Darwinism was a serious force, and Adams handled it by means of two ambiguous symbols which he first came upon in the course of reviewing Sir Charles Lyell's *Principles of Geology* for the *North American Review*. He asked Sir Charles for the simplest case of uniformity on record, and Sir Charles gave him a kind of shellfish called *Terebratula* which had been uniform from the beginning to the end of geological time. He then asked for the first vertebrate and was given *Pteraspis*, a kind of sturgeon, not very different from contemporary sturgeons whose fossils Adams might find under Wenlock Abbey, the Gaskells' country place, along with other fossil ancestors, and coeval with all of them. From time to time, looking back on his life, Adams found both these creatures standards or symbols to set against fresh bewilderments. *Pteraspis* was himself stopped short, man at his limits, and a warning of fresh limits to come. *Terebratula* was the energy in man that never changed, as other energies changed from diffusion to intensity when charged with intelligence, but changed only from torpor to violence and back again. *Terebratula* was protected by his carapace from all but the fatal blows of experience; *Terebratula* was the incalculable element of pure energy in other human beings: the natural man. *Pteraspis* was more sympathetic; he fossilized one's past successes and failures, putting them in a perspective that was outside time all together, was both past and present, both admonitory and unavailing. It was right he should sleep at Wenlock.

At Wenlock everything existed at once, whether in the Abbey ruins, the Roman marks, or looking away over the Welsh Marches—everything, Roman, medieval, primitive and geological, and as everything, became an emotion of landscape. As Quincy and the Georgetown woods represented the emotion of Nature at her work, purposive, maternal and engulfing, the scenery at Wenlock, with *Pteraspis* as clue, seemed work done, done but troubling. "The peculiar flavor of the scenery," Adams thought, "has something to do with absence of evolution: it was better marked in Egypt: it was felt wherever time-sequences became interchangeable. One's instinct abhors time." *Pteraspis* at Wenlock represented the instinct for withdrawal.

But the full meaning of these symbols is elusive. They belong

to the class of private and obsessive names used to indicate special possessiveness or special sentiments which never reach the
dictionary since their value cannot be defined. Such symbols
stand for the part of one's meaning that mocks itself, the part
of one's thought one cannot quite think, or the part of judgment
that in the act of decision turns on itself. Adams' symbols of this
order are intended to carry both parts of his meaning, thought,
or judgment in a single vehicle, so that they make one stroke
upon the sensibility; but there is a little plain nonsense in them,
too, a little of *hoc est corpus* turned hocus pocus.

Yet nonsense has a right in one's symbols; for there is nonsense at the center of the major as well as the minor contradictions in man's mind. *Pteraspis* and the Wenlock landscape was
what Adams pitted against the nonsense of Darwinism. "He
could detect no more evolution in life since the *Pteraspis* than
he could detect it in architecture since the Abbey. All he could
prove was change. Coal-power alone asserted evolution—of
power—and only by violence could be forced to assert selection
of type. . . . In geology as in theology, he could prove only
Evolution that did not evolve; Uniformity that was not uniform;
and Selection that did not select." To Darwinians, evolution was
a religious hope of perfection; but Adams saw in it the failure
of determinism: "what he valued most was motion, and . . .
what attracted his mind was Change." His sturgeon and his
crab seemed to suggest that there was neither motion to value
nor change to attract, but an unchanging, unmoving truth in
the midst of moving value and overwhelming change. *Pteraspis*
and *Terebratula* were the symbols by which he referred to the
annoyance of that universal contradiction.

These symbols also made tolerable a blasphemy against the
human by putting it in an alien idiom; for the position in which
Darwin and Lyell left him was one in which "he did not really
care whether truth was, or was not, true": which was the intolerable extreme of secular withdrawal, or tourism. Whether
Adams is exact in the biographical sense is immaterial; he is
imaginatively just in showing his young actor finding his stimulus to the recovery of energy, not from the fossils, political and
social, of a society in dead-water, but from much older fossils
newly seen. The older geological fossils stood for the social fossils and put them in perspective, even those fragments of eccentricity and dilettantism which had become part of Adams' habit

of expression. Besides that, he seldom afterward forgot the skepticism which was the source of his reaction: "Whether truth was, or was not, true" was a recurrent question and a renewable stimulus, which led him to insist "on maintaining his absolute standards; on aiming at ultimate Unity," since they alone could put down the question and exhaust the stimulus. The old fossils proved that the great generalizations that the science of the 'sixties was making were inadequate; they touched neither what was changing nor what had never changed, but in a sense only what had stopped changing, what had run down in motion, or offside in direction; they generalized, so to speak, only that part of life which had neither value nor motion, neither quality nor aspiration—and these, which were untouched, Adams was bound to bring in by every power of mind he could manage. *Pteraspis* and *Terebratula* might mock the effort, but they proved that it might be made: it was the same effort which they recorded.

As an American, Adams' effort had to be made in America and, until he found his profession for sure, it had better be made in terms of some immediate and open questions. He therefore attacked the question of specie payments in two long articles for the *North American Review*. The lesson of his whole English experience sank in, in a new place, when he discovered, to the horror of his principles, that "the best treatment of a debased currency was to let it alone." *Pteraspis* and *Terebratula* should have warned him that his principles were more urgent, if not more right, for being horrified. But he went again to Rome and sat again on the steps of Ara Coeli, and found only that in ten years of accidental education, "he had learned nothing whatever that made Rome more intelligible to him, or made life easier to handle." Yet the materials were gathering themselves together, reaction and response upon reaction and response, contradiction upon contradiction, felt limit upon limit, until they were nearly ready for true composition. The questions already asked had only to ask themselves in new and living terms, at home, to the grown man, in order to precipitate either silence or an answer, or silence followed by an answer. The next five chapters may seem to some literally the preparation for failure that Adams, for dramatic reasons, so insists on; to others, the literal failure will seem a great preparation: a withdrawal in order to return.

CHAPTER SIX

The Withdrawal

The difference between the ordinary secular withdrawal or normal half-use of the mind and a genuine withdrawal is like the difference between a vacation and a vastation, between a daydream and a vision. The one comes by accident and by succumbing to facility, the other comes by deep shock, like that of conversion, and by a maximum cultivation and intensification of perception. The one is a surrender, the other is the accomplishment of central experience. Yet the two kinds of withdrawal may sometimes be made by the same person, either alternately or at the same time, and the road to the one may from the outside look like the road to the other; for either withdrawal is the experience of loss, of which all persons are capable, and it is only the return, which is possible seldom and to few on an expressive level, which shows the experience of gain.

Perhaps it is only the religious, in the strict sense, who experience complete withdrawal and return; to an outsider it looks like more withdrawal than return: there are too many limp souls. But there are others—and Henry Adams was perhaps one of them—among all kinds of men, who make partial withdrawals and returns or who at any rate only partially express what may have been a more complete experience. It is these men who quicken the actual, who by seeing in it what they bring back, wring from it the double cry of aspiration and

73

the defeat of aspiration. Their works—their gestures, images, symbols—are the tokens of the impossible, whatever it is, to which in some part of us we fatally shape ourselves; but the values of these tokens are all actual values, dubious, virtual, contingent, even reversible; the impossible is only present, like the Muse, as a haunting echo.

When we come on the lives or works of such men, they have the peculiar warrant of something we have experienced before, less perfectly but more deeply; they have the persuasiveness, the inevitable mistakenness, and the uncontrollableness of sharp memory. The tokens have values in the actual world which we had not known we felt, but the tokens have other values, too, which may belie the actual and the reasonable and the desirable—values which are precise without being recognizable —and these are the values created between the withdrawal and the return: we feel their pressure quickening the actual without knowing what they are. And then—whether we are these men themselves or are merely those who rehearse ourselves in the works of others—then we cannot help mutilating, trapping, prisoning this direct central experience in the conventions of the mind, for the sake of our ordinary safety. Men are not so much marked by experience as by the precautions they take against it, and by the devices to which they resort to reduce to tolerable form the experience they could not help having. Like Dostoevsky's Idiot, we are not worthy of our suffering and transform it into religion or philosophy or history or art; when it is not ourselves but our suffering that becomes worthy, how-ever, it fails to reach our experience. Thus our deepest knowl-edge is that which we reject in order to live.

It may not be argued what sort of withdrawal Henry Adams made from life; no doubt it was of several orders at once, and imperfect in all of them. We know that he thought he with-drew, after his wife's death in 1885, and that he thought that he returned—that part of him returned—in 1891. His wife's death was the shock of conversion that deepened the mere loss into central experience. We do not know that experience but we do know something of how he reduced that experience to tolerable form by submerging it in the conventions of the mind. We know because we can see how the conventions were trans-formed, how they quickened with the actual, under the pressure that seems to have been built up in his imagination between his withdrawal and his return.

The reason for introducing these considerations here, rather than either earlier or later in this study, is that Adams seems to have become able to apply that pressure first in writing the chapters of his own life which began with his return to America in 1868. Perhaps his years abroad constituted in perspective an earlier withdrawal, in which he had accumulated energy enough to convert innocence into experience and experience into revolt, which is halfway the course the mind can run. His book is parallel to his life; through the symbols which he dragged from life into the book, the pattern which had been blurred in action and restlessness began to transpire. That which happened later began to seem to have been conditioned earlier; the book began to be a discovery that this which is just now happening was foretold long since; memory became prophecy, and prophecy became law.

The sequence of innocence, experience, revolt required as a next step failure of the revolt or despair: that is to say, withdrawal—either into the self or into the vision of that other world which furnished the standard of failure and the value of despair. Retirement into self is suicide; retirement into vision is to the ordinary religious the limit the human mind can reach —just beyond the standards which could determine whether it is the transcendence or the obliteration of experience. Those in whom the transit to self or vision is less complete have a pattern which comes full circle in one more stage, no less inevitable, no less the substance of prophecy, to those who endure it, than the earlier stages. This is the stage of creative return; the stage in which vision suffers rebirth into the imperfection of the actual world, yet presses beyond it. Henry Adams is a singularly imperfect, singularly actual instance of this experience; at least, the peculiar intractable quality in his life and work makes itself clear as a tragic drive, if we adopt this view. He could not, in his return, act completely upon the substance of vision, nor completely build it into the conventions of the mind; yet he was driven to try both at once, because neither vision nor conventions were adequate.

But it is not what happened after the return with which we are here concerned, except insofar as the conditions that led to revolt and withdrawal also attracted his return. We are concerned rather with the symbolic picture Adams made of a mind none of whose principles and few of whose values could be represented in action, because, as he felt, American society in the 'sixties and 'seventies had a dominant minority that responded neither to the values nor to the principles, and because the society as a whole moved faster than the conventional mind of its legitimate government, and along different lines. Whether the mind of Adams or of the Government was more at fault was a serious question: certainly society as a whole could not be at fault. Adams sometimes blamed himself, and sometimes the men who composed the Government, but he never blamed the American people, as John Hay sometimes did, for the shortcomings of either.

What he saw, in 1868, was that Washington was a tidal "slack-water." At slack water, especially low water slack, in muddy marsh creeks such as he had seen as a boy at Quincy, the water is foul with wide scums and dirty bubbles, debris of last year's growth eddies a little, and the general limited sense of motion is of drainage rather than of current, like a well emptying. Adams did not himself develop his slack or "deadwater" images; they were part of his equipment from birth; but they must have carried with them associations such as these, when used both for Washington and for London. He rather tended, by such an image, to develop his portrait of Charles Sumner in his further metamorphosis from the evangel as hero to the fanatic as gentleman. Sumner was cordial when he met Adams instead of resentful as might have been expected after the quarrel of 1861. Adams explained that Sumner could not resent because he had become impervious to feeling. "Sumner's mind had reached the calm of water which receives and reflects images without absorbing them; it contained nothing but itself. The images from without, the objects mechanically perceived by the senses, existed by courtesy until the mental surface was ruffled, but never became part of the thought."

Sumner was a kind of intellectual slack water; yet he was presumed, by office and reputation, to be a man with great power. The power had outrun the man; he was a barrier to handling power, not a handle: he was a theory of power, grown senile. The other men in power—Seward, Evarts, Johnson, McCulloch, and Chase—as Adams describes them, had no theory of power and so had no means of controlling the power actually abroad. They were slack water in another sense: the tide did not run through them or despite them but indifferently to them. They were, so to speak, marooned in the current without knowing it. These men, the best in Washington, were in a critical sense unavailable to the offices that they held. At the political level the trouble was easy to express.

The whole government, from top to bottom, was rotten with the senility of what was antiquated and the instability of what was improvised. The currency was only one example; the tariff was another; but the whole fabric required reconstruction as much as in 1789, for the Constitution had become as antiquated as the Confederation. Sooner or later a shock must come, the more dangerous the longer postponed. The Civil War had made a new system in fact: the country would have to reorganize the machinery in practice and theory.

The old Constitution had balanced the old forces of agriculture, handwork, and learning; the reformed Constitution would have to balance the new, and superior, forces of coal, iron, and steam. Until it did so, theory could never catch up with practice, and practice could never catch up with the forces themselves or the collateral forces they threw off and concentrated in single men or groups of men who were amenable neither to the old theory nor the old practice but who behaved as if they were themselves forces released directly by nature. Until politics could again govern the relations between the forces men actually employed in the work of society, power would be usurped by ungovernable men, and, in effect, society would be under the blind control of the forces themselves. The surrender to blind force is the surrender to inertia, and that surrender can never be made more fully than through reliance upon a system of intelligence whose techniques were designed to control quite different forces. The intelligence disappears and the system is taken over by the forces. The problem is perennial.

The problem is perennial, but its new form never turns up all at once, nor can all its elements be seen as related; the attack must be piecemeal and sometimes as chaotic as the problem itself. One has to feel along familiar paths with new corners and uncertain shifts of direction; the old guides have altered meanings at the new rate of motion. Henry's brother, Charles Francis Adams, Jr., pitched on the railroads, which, spanning the continent, were clearly concentrating a great deal of the energy of their generation. Henry stuck to Washington and attempted to work through the press with articles on finance, Civil Service Reform, and the imbalance of political powers under the stress of the new forces. Part of what survived in him of the old system was the belief that young men like himself could vitally affect public opinion and through public opinion bring the forces of society into intelligent control. Later, he felt that the new forces had ejected him from his heritage and that he had become bric-à-brac; but at the time, hardly knowing what the new forces were, he struck out at the plain evils he saw.

Adams' scheme seemed to him to have broken down in President Grant and the Senate. "One may be more or less certain of organized forces; one can never be certain of men." The Senate in 1869 was clearly, by the Constitutional standard, a disorganized force, it was not national either in constituency or in spirit; individually egotistic, it was in combinations factious, and worked in the milieu of bargain rather than of compromise; it achieved concert only in its struggle to advance its prerogative at the expense of the Executive and the Judiciary. President Grant as a force was intermittently organized, hence as a man permanently uncertain. To Adams the Senate and Grant, as types of men to whom the American people habitually delegated political power, became symbols he could never quite let alone, since he could never either quite accept them or understand them, or even be quite sure that he wanted to reject them. Of the two the Senate was more human—a defective organization of human foibles and forces—and Grant was more a plain force of nature. The Senate could be tinkered with and individual Senators criticized according to the rules of experience. Grant could be studied as a phenomenon and handled only by sympathetic means and repeated contact. The Senate was an endless irritation; Grant had to be swallowed whole.

But he stuck in the throat; thought could not digest him, because he was not a creature of thought. His staff officers said the only way to influence Grant was to talk a plan out within earshot until finally Grant presented the plan as his own and carried it out. Grant was "an intermittent energy, immensely powerful when awake, but passive and plastic in repose." Seeing him, Adams was reminded of Garibaldi: "in both, the intellect counted for nothing; only the energy counted." Yet the type was common and normal, and certain attributes could be listed to make up an uncertain whole. He was one of those "men whose energies were the greater, the less they wasted on thought; men who sprang from the soil to power; apt to be distrustful of themselves and of others; shy; jealous; sometimes vindictive; more or less dull in outward appearance; always needing stimulants, but for whom action was the highest stimulant—the instinct of fight. Such men were forces of nature, energies of the prime, like the *Pteraspis*, but they made short work of scholars."

Worse than *Pteraspis*, "Grant fretted and irritated him, like the *Terebratula*, as a defiance of first principles. He had no right to exist. He should have been extinct for ages. . . . The progress of evolution from President Washington to President Grant was alone evidence enough to upset Darwin." Washington had avowed a policy of conscious intelligence in balancing forces under principle. "Grant avowed from the start a policy of drift; and a policy of drift attaches only barnacles." Yet because of his position as President, and perhaps more because of his prestige as a great general, he exercised vast powers in a negative sense precisely to the degree that he did not exercise his proper powers positively. The spectacular corruption of his administration was itself witness of the mere waste of the powers actually at work.

Harding's administration fifty-six years later showed that similar corruption came about from similar causes. Harding's "Back to normalcy" and Grant's "Let us have peace" measured similar minds; only Grant was purer than Harding in every sense of the word, purer in energy, in torpor, in superficial political honesty, and therefore purer as a victim. No wonder Adams looked at Grant all around, and no wonder he thought of Garibaldi. It was not only in their energy and absence of intellect that they were alike. Both men turned out to have been managed by interests which they hated; their great energies had advanced causes which were fatal to their own. Would taking thought have saved either? Let alone Garibaldi, who had Rome at his back, where was the thought for Grant to take?

It was not in Washington. Outside Washington were the dogwood and the judas tree, the azalea and the laurel. Adams loved "the soft, full outlines of the landscape," which "carried no hidden horror of glaciers in its bosom." "He loved it too much, as though it were Greek and half human." The charm of

Washington was greater than the force of Boston. King told him
that the two mistakes of nature were the inclination of the
ecliptic and the differentiation of the sexes. "Adams, in his
splenetic temper, held that both these unnecessary evils had
wreaked their worst on Boston. The climate made eternal war
on society, and sex was a species of crime." To Adams these
evils showed at their least because they showed as charm at
Washington. Charm was not thought.

But in Adams, charm affected thought and sometimes seems
its self-contrasting underlying substance; it was the other force
in nature that fed thought. These images of a landscape "Greek
and half human" are used to introduce the consideration of,
first, what absence of thought did to the Executive, and, second,
the worse effect of thought turned faction in Senate and Executive. The first was the scandal of the Erie Railroad and the New
York Gold Conspiracy, which was in essence a single, not altogether conscious, effort on the part of a small group of men to
absorb old social forces into the orbit of the new forces of which
they were the managers: the effort of the power symbolized by
the railroads to absorb morals as morals was symbolized in
the social relations made coherent by money. Had they sought
only to absorb money, society might have tolerated their acts;
but they sought to absorb the control of the value of money in
the direct sense. "The worst scandals of the eighteenth century
were relatively harmless by the side of this, which smirched
executive, judiciary, banks, corporate systems, professions, and
people, all the great active forces of society, in one dirty cess-
pool of vulgar corruption." Adams "foresaw a life of wasted
energy, sweeping the stables of American society clean of the
endless corruption which his second Washington was quite
certain to breed." He "noticed with horror that the grossest
satires on the American Senator and politician never failed to
excite the laughter and applause of every audience. Rich and
poor joined in throwing contempt on their own representatives.
Society laughed a vacant and meaningless derision over its own
failure." Intelligent people left Washington. "The people would
have liked to go too, for they stood helpless before the chaos;
some laughed and some raved; all were disgusted; but they had
to content themselves by turning their backs and going to work
harder than ever on their railroads and their foundries. They
were strong enough to carry even their politics."

The effect, then, of the absence of intellect in Grant was the virtual surrender to corrupt manipulation of that major fraction of the power of government that was imputed to the Treasury Department. Most of the remaining significant power of government was supposed to be lodged in the State Department. Besides the two great Departments, there was the balancing or parallel power of the Supreme Court. In the focus of the State Department, Secretary Fish tried for one foreign policy, Senator Sumner set up another in his Foreign Relations Committee, and President Grant worked intermittently at one of his own in the War Department. In the focus of the Supreme Court, Attorney General Hoar fought Chief Justice Chase for personal victory over the public issue of legal tender. Thus national policy became the private interest of men otherwise honest.

Adams puts it that under the lax rule of Grant, "his four most powerful friends had matched themselves, two and two, and were fighting in pairs to a finish; Sumner-Fish; Chase-Hoar; with foreign affairs and the judiciary as prizes!" It was a free fight and Adams expressed his sense of it in a deeper, more sober horror than the money corruption of the Gold Conspiracy had aroused. "The statesmen of the old type, whether Sumners or Conklings or Hoars or Lamars, were personally as honest as human nature could produce. They trod with lofty contempt on other people's jobs, especially when there was good in them. Yet the public thought that Sumner and Conkling cost the country a hundred times more than all the jobs they ever trod on; just as Lamar and the old Southern statesmen, who were also honest in money-matters, cost the country a civil war." In short, where the Erie gang corrupted the morals of money, the Senator and the Secretary, the Attorney General and the Chief Justice, safe in their "money-morals," corrupted in fact the chief principle of the political system they were sworn to defend: the principle that government should rest upon laws, not man.

The three chapters—"The Press," "President Grant," and "Free Fight"—in which Adams, looking back at the ordinary affairs of the nation, saw in the spectacle itself one of the profound contradictions of life revealed, are worth generalization. Generalized, the spectacle becomes its own symbol: of man's might useless.

Grant, having been established as a personal symbol of blind or drifting or inert political power, is then shown, as such a symbol must be, gathering in energy which he was powerless to control. The power of government is powerless not to be used, and may be all the more powerful in fact when direct political power and intelligent principles for its control are absent or negligible, for it is in such circumstances that power is most easily grasped by men and organizations nominally outside government. Unaccountable men—or torpid men—at the seat of power attract the play of unaccountable forces by men accountable only to themselves or to their immediate interests. Further, men otherwise accountable become reckless of every consideration not personal and every agreement not arbitrary. In sum: when in government men are weak, laws and the sense of laws become weak also, and the random or whimsical power of men becomes strong—becomes catastrophic. Institutions let alone and unreformed by constant character and insight lose their institutional strength and corrupt themselves along with the men. Weakness in men is the corruption of institutions, because their strength is then unredeemed. The process then continues: the weakness of institutions is the corruption of men. Grace for either must come from the strength of the other. Without grace, laws become men and men become weak laws.

But there is a point—of resentment—when strength is resumed. Resentment is the primitive form of responsibility, and requires institutions for development. Out of resentment wells destruction. But the power to destroy is also the power to create. It is the business of the statesman to anticipate resentment and move across destruction to creation. This requires a system capable of attracting such men into its orbit. It is in practice equivalent to seeing that creative men who are also balanced men, mature men, are enabled to respond to the pressures of power. To respond, the statesman must distinguish and cling to what is vital in the institutions with which he is entrusted by office, but he must also cut away what he can of what is dead. What is alive is what is capable of supporting clear human intent, and what is dead is what lends dominance to interests otherwise secondary and censurable.

Adams' picture shows the processes of political decay issuing from Grant's torpor (and, of course, partly from his energy, too); but the picture shows that the system was unable to use the men—when by accident it attracted them—who could reform it. There is, rather, the invasion and usurpation of political power by random, private hands of which the New York Gold Conspiracy and the Whisky Ring were only extreme cases; and there is the friction and faction and fraction of personalized offices in the seat of power itself, of which the Legal Tender suits and the "private" foreign policies of Sumner and Fish and Grant were only casual cases.

Both usurpation and faction along these lines were conspicuous and characteristic in the political history of the United States from 1870 to 1900; they made American politics negative by removing the moral consideration from any effective part in their operation. It is no less significant because a similar course was run elsewhere. This negative politics—this will-less surrender of the use of forces that one must as a statesman represent if one represented anything—was the American version of the European conversion, during the same period, from the ideal of rational cooperation and the balancing of forces to realism and military nationalism along fatal lines. The same process that militarized Europe, and produced dogfights in Latin America, led in the United States to a demoralized, depoliticalized, economized sovereignty by social forces hitherto unknown either in vastness or intensity. The pain of the resumption of political and moral sovereignty may be seen in both the First and the Second World War. The powers abroad were too vast and precariously pitched to permit universal piracy—whether in large or small universes. Adams lived in the generation of interim, before it was seen that piracy, like usury, is self-interest carried to the point of maximum—not optimum but maximum—intensity: when morals become *merely* private.

Yet resentment began soon enough, as Adams himself witnesses; but the resentment was factious and tended to become more so the nearer it got to power. The Gold Conspiracy made a beautiful paradigm of the corruption of private individuals who might or might not retain their private morality. The Legal Tender cases illustrated the seed form of corporate corruption which was outside private and public morality, except that the individuals so corrupted must be *otherwise* respectable. The two together made a single moral which, so far as it was accepted, made the translation of resentment into political thought unnecessarily difficult.

Men thought the attempt to corner gold evil because they be-

lieved gold in its social uses was as much a natural and inevitable force as coal or iron. Thus money was a fetish power,
which might be misused; government had the task of putting
down misuse of that power, because it was the one power to
which, of the several equal or superior to it, it was sensitive.
In the absence of political sovereignty, money necessarily became sovereign: money was to common feeling the only co-
hesive force among forces otherwise anarchic. No wonder men
tended to think the force of money almost supernatural; and no
wonder that many men, striving to direct that force to their own
interests, should take to piratical methods. It is always more
tempting to plunder and destroy than to secularize and make
responsible. The paradigm, though it never applied exactly even
to Gould and Fisk, yet applied more nearly as time went on and
to more and more of the forces of society.

The symbolism of every day was so clear to Adams that he
could only repeat himself, as if his words might show deeper
meaning with repetition, and the deeper meaning somehow
enlarge the mind that saw it.

The political dilemma was as clear in 1870 as it was likely to be in
1970. The system of 1789 had broken down, and with it the eighteenth-century fabric of *a priori*, or moral, principles. Politicians had
tacitly given it up. Grant's administration marked the avowal. Nine-
tenths of men's political energies must henceforth be wasted on
expedients to piece out—to patch—or, in vulgar language, to tinker
—the political machine as often as it broke down. . . . Yet the sum
of political life was, or should have been, the attainment of a working
political system. Society needed to reach it. If moral standards broke
down, and machinery stopped working, new morals and machinery
of some sort had to be invented.

Between the two halves of the passage just quoted, after remarking that Garfield and Blaine laughed at Senators, Adams,
who had no such laughter, inserted a question: "What kind of
political ambition was to result from this destructive political
education?" The question was rhetorical in the good sense, and
in two respects. The answer depended on where you looked: at
those who held office or at those who either never held it or could
not keep it if they did; the cost to the country is great in either
case. If you looked at Adams, the answer needed the help of
emotion—of nature rising to emotion and of thought dissolving
in emotion—a condition to which the very process of composing

his *Education* committed Adams more and more deeply. No one wanted reform in the spring of 1870, but Adams went on fighting, through the press, with all the more excitement and enjoyment. "When spring came he took to the woods, which were best of all, for after the first of April, what Maurice de Guérin called 'the vast maternity' of nature showed charms more voluptuous than the vast paternity of the United States Senate. Senators were less ornamental than the dogwood or even the judas-tree. They were, as a rule, less good company. Adams astonished himself by remarking what a purified charm was lent to the Capitol by the greatest possible distance, as one caught glimpses of the dome over miles of forest foliage. At such moments he pondered on the distant beauty of St. Peter's and the steps of Ara Coeli."

It is often complained of Henry Adams that he failed to adjust himself to the life of his times, and Adams himself almost as often asserts that he was a full and consenting partner to that life. Perhaps both views are correct. If Washington represented life in America, then it is correct to believe that Adams failed in adjustment to the actual Washington symbolized by President Grant and the Free Fight of Senators, Judges, and Secretaries of the Executive; he could not adjust to the horripilation of principles. But if the Washington is meant which is better symbolized when joined by dogwood and judas tree to St. Peter's and Ara Coeli, then Adams was in a deep—and a deeper because constantly struggling—adjustment to it.

It is sometimes forgotten that full assent is an exhausting and shocking labor of nerve and emotion and vision; that habit is never enough; and that radical rejection in act is part of assent in imagination. As a young man Adams may be said to have accepted his actual society by fighting it till the fight drove him out of it. Then shock supervened and converted the terms of the struggle. As an old man Adams assented to all of his society he was able to create objectively in the new terms, but the creation was as much of a fight as the earlier adventure. Fighting his way back—like the fighting in the heart—was never finished, any more than the fighting that drove him out. Only the terms had changed, and they changed, as Adams gives it, in a revelation of Chaos and Failure.

It is in these chapters that the preparation for withdrawal is completed. In the first of the pair, "Chaos," is the image of man's revolt against those depriving conditions of nature and society which he must accept if he is to live at all; in the second, "Failure," is the image of a particular man's revolt, Henry Adams' revolt, against human conditions which he must reject if he is to live by his aspiration. Chaos is the condition which makes aspiration necessary; failure is when man, not nature, brooks aspiration; but the two conditions are often found interchangeable and interfused, and will alter in emphasis—perhaps in substance—depending on the vantage from which the relation is seen. A man may think his Failure Chaos, or Chaos his Failure, depending on his age or on the degree to which his habits have become instincts.

How shall we say, thinking of the chapter called "Chaos," from what vantage Adams regarded the symbols which he there offers? The date for the chapter is 1870; the date of composition is a full generation later; almost exactly halfway between, the violence of his wife's death, by its necessity and by its absolute lack of necessity, by its personal intensity and by its human purposelessness, struck him empty; it was the shock of death which gave a vantage looking both forward to the date of composition and backward to his sister's death in 1870. In his wife's death died a part of him, and by her death a new part lived in him, living backward and forward like memory, with that double force of the richness of the possible and the devastation of the actual which memory alone gives. This is the force of vantage. And it is because it is so that Adams did not need, for the purposes of his *Education*, to deal directly with it: it was there; and it ought to be possible to point out how it is there by the sequence and kind of images.

Adams begins his scene in a low key, pointing to himself on a pleasure trip to England and finding himself an oldtimer in new times. As a tourist he was "the great conservative who hated novelty and adored dirt." When Frank Palgrave told him war was coming, Adams denied it, as the chances were always against catastrophes. He felt not war, not any kind of collapse, but rather "the velvet smile of trained and easy hostess." His first shock—his first warrant in the present context that times had changed the relationships of society—was when Henry Reeve refused to print Adams' Gold Conspiracy article for fear of libel, showing that the new corruption had some control of the institution of the English quarterlies. "Respectability, everywhere and always, turned its back the moment one asked to do it a favor." The radical *Westminster*, which did not need favors, accepted and later printed the article. His second shock—his first warrant that it was nature not man who was immortal—came in his sister's death after "ten days of fiendish torture." Yet it was less his sister's death that shocked him than the contrast between her death and its circumstances, and the warping of his own sensibilities as they were compelled to digest the contrast.

She died, he said, in Italian summer, in rich life, in the sensual fullness of nature and man. "The hills and vineyards of the Apennines seemed bursting with midsummer blood." Image after image of the immemorial butchery of nature locates, surrounds, and fixes her death; but the final reaction combined nature with man's sense of it.

Impressions like these are not reasoned or catalogued in the mind; they are felt as part of violent emotion; and the mind that feels them is a different one from that which reasons; it is thought of a different power and a different person. The first serious consciousness of Nature's gesture—her attitude towards life—took form then as a phantasm, a nightmare, an insanity of force. For the first time, the stage-scenery of the senses collapsed; the human mind felt itself stripped naked, vibrating in a void of shapeless energies, with resistless mass, colliding, crushing, wasting, and destroying what these same energies had created and labored from eternity to perfect. Society became fantastic, a vision of pantomime with a mechanical motion; and its so-called thought merged in the mere sense of life, and pleasure in the sense.

It is easy to see the progression from the "tourist" enjoying "the velvet smile of trained and easy hostess" and so putting off the threat of war, to its direct opposite in his sister's death and the collapse of the European system, in the double chaos of individual life and of society; but there is unity asserted here as well as progression: the unity which is the greater the greater the intensity of feeling in the observer: the unity of feeling by which one copes with the under, unrationalizable half of the world: the feeling into which creeps the vital but not quite acknowledgeable notion that true reason is only an awkward and limited sense, like the others. The record of such a feeling of unity is left in the following sentences by which Adams recalls and re-engages a pause in a high place on his trip north from death to Paris at war, thence to Wenlock. The unity was in the response, as always, and by convention: the convention by which revolt becomes restoration and refreshment of mind.

For the first time in his life, Mont Blanc for a moment looked to him what it was—a chaos of anarchic and purposeless forces—and he needed days of repose to see it clothe itself again with the illusions of his senses, the white purity of its snows, the splendor of its light, and the infinity of its heavenly peace. Nature was kind: Lake Geneva was beautiful beyond itself, and the Alps put on charms real as terrors; but man became chaotic, and before the illusions of nature were wholly restored, the illusions of Europe suddenly vanished, leaving a new world to learn.

The reader may note a certain relation between these passages and the recurrent images of dogwood and judas tree at Washington, such as those that surround the account of "Free Fight" under President Grant. Both spring from the same source in insight and both convert the same experience, at different levels in its dominance, to tolerable and rewarding form. The distinctive feature here is that for the first time landscape images are no longer peripheral or contrasting or reminding, but make up the symbol of the central experience itself. Here they become identified with death to the individual as the index to nature's immortality. There is a vast alien momentum to the vast maternity of nature to which oneself is a revolting and contributing part, as day is dark and light.

It was some such sentiment that after death and after Paris worked in Adams as he lay in the sun of memory at Wenlock, a young monk with other monks. "Since the reign of *Pteraspis*, nothing had greatly changed; nothing except the monks." And while he lay there he rejected, in the role of a flattered *Terebratula*, President Eliot's offer of a job at Harvard. *Pteraspis* had withdrawn from the world after a limited contact with change and had managed to survive just the same by seeking a privileged environment; *Terebratula* seemed to have stopped effort as soon as he saw what effort was and survived by sinking steadily to a lower relative plane of sensitivity. *Pteraspis* and *Terebratula* are the two temptations of indolence and sloth, translated, for purposes of mockery, to scientific forces.

It is sometimes possible to exorcise the devil by mocking him. President Eliot was probably not the devil, but the unchanged mind, the mind resisting change by new expedients, was probably still the mind most at home at Harvard College, as at Wenlock. Adams mocked both, because he had no other weapon, even in backward perspective, against the reality of temptation each offered, and in different versions, continued to offer all through life. It was the temptation to surrender the mind, weakened and distraught under the blows it had just received, not to the will of God which required fruits for judgment, but to the will of nature which required nothing and was indifferent in judgment: the temptation of lethargy, of routine, of safety, all the more dangerous when the guise of tradition is newcalled fatality.

What led to Adams' initial rejection of Eliot's offer in favor of its alternative, Washington, came from two sources. One was the fact of character that as experience showed more and more both natural and human forces operating either as chaos or inertia, the remaining margin of free action—of intelligible will—became more and more precious to employ to the full. The other was the conviction, the innate prejudice, that "to his mind, the value of American society altogether was mixed up with the value of Washington." That Washington the office of government was itself slipping into chaos or inertia, that almost no one of intelligence and ability could make a success of Washington, and that Washington plainly had no use for him, Henry Adams, altogether made the value more imperative to assert. *Impavidum ferient ruinae!* remained the imperative in retrospect as in youth. It was the attitude, the gesture, of principle struggling to re-enact itself, in the face of almost certain failure, on its own responsibility. No subterfuge or scapegoat outside the self would do.

"At first, the simple beginner, struggling with principles, wanted to throw off responsibility on the American people, whose bare and toiling shoulders had to carry the load of every social or political stupidity; but the American people had no more to do with it than with the customs of Peking." Perhaps Adams meant that the American people were a complex of energies, and that energies are not susceptible of fault until they have been incorporated into a system of control; in the absence of system only individuals are at fault. But he could not help thinking also of the limitations of character to which energetic inertia drive led. To him the American character seemed ignorant of ignorance, incapable of amusement, and unaware of boredom. Americans thought themselves restlessly energetic; they might be so in New York. In Washington the American was quiet, peaceful, shy, distrustful, awed by money. Work and whisky were necessary stimulants: he had the vice of pursuit, not the virtue of value. In Europe the American was bored and wanted to get home. "He was ashamed to be amused; his mind no longer answered to the stimulus of variety; he could not face a new thought. All his immense strength, his intense nervous energy, his keen, analytic perceptions, were oriented in one direction, and he could not change it." It was the just and tenacious purpose (*Justum et tenacem propositi virum . . .*) of Henry Adams to help make possible a change in direction should it continue to seem desirable, and if not, then to help control the movement under a more intelligent system than the system of patch and tinker to which he felt the country had lent itself. Yet he—or a part of him— went to Harvard for seven or eight years and completed at forty an education to which he ascribed the value of failure.

It is not a question of correct or mistaken judgment but of value. He went to Harvard at the insistence of family and friends, who joined in thinking that Washington meant work, whisky, and cards, and because the editorship of the *North American Review* went with the job. He thought that he might affect public opinion by creating it directly in students and faculty and indirectly through editing. The system of the college under the reforms of President Eliot defeated one half his hope, and the "owlish silence" imposed on him by the task of editing (he published almost nothing of his own while editor) defeated the second half. The failure was that neither institution had any value in framing the actual problems of society, though both had many values by the way. He revolted against the institutions—of which he was a part by nurture and position—by setting up a single man, Clarence King, against them as an individual ideal of the path new institutions should develop. But he took the values with him that he might know, so to speak, the cost of rejecting the institutions in which the values lodged.

There was the value of succession: he lived in Wadsworth, the old President's house where his uncle, Edward Everett, had lived when president of the college; and there was the value, quite beyond practice, of the professional invocation as teacher.

"A parent gives life, but as parent gives no more. A murderer takes life, but his deed stops there. A teacher affects eternity; he can never tell where his influence stops." And there was the special value in teaching history, that it affected the major attitudes of the students. "He makes of his scholars either priests or atheists, plutocrats or socialists, judges or anarchists, almost in spite of himself. In essence incoherent and immoral, history had either to be taught as such—or falsified."

Again there was the value of historical ambition. The man who could bring the Middle Ages into the line of evolution, he thought, would be greater than Lamarck or Linnaeus. These values, attached in their accidents to Harvard College, are dateless in Adams' mind, always affecting its speculations and its elasticity. "History is a tangled skein that one may take up at any point, and break when one has unravelled enough; but complexity precedes evolution. The *Pteraspis* grins horribly from the closed entrance. One may not begin at the beginning, and one has but the loosest relative truths to follow up." These are positive, and represent a commitment which, when he left Cambridge, he took with him.

On the negative side was the inertia of the system, the goodness of the students and their faith in the education they were getting, the need under the politics of the system for every instructor "to shut his eyes and hold his tongue as though he were a priest," and the conclusions, fatal to mass education, that no more than six students can be instructed at once, and that, "nine minds in ten take polish passively, like a hard surface; only the tenth sensibly reacts." Worse, from the attitude of ambition, was the inequality of professors to either civic or social occasions. "American society feared total wreck in the maelstrom of political and corporate administration, but it could not look for help to college dons. Adams knew, in that capacity, both Congressmen and professors, and he preferred Congressmen." On the social side, men who would have been the joy of Paris famished for want of companionship. "Society was a faculty-meeting without business. The elements were there; but society cannot be made up of elements—people who are expected to be silent unless they have observations to make —and all the elements are bound to remain apart if required to make observations."

The two halves of this judgment have different weights,

objective and personal. Harvard College as a faculty of scholars in 1870 stood unconscious of its relations to the forces that were to shape its future and also, more important, was comparatively protected from their pressures; so far as it thought it had a stake in society, it would gain it by a reaffirmation of principles and theory which for the most part, to Adams' mind, no longer applied. Its movements since 1858 were largely expedients further to entrench. Congressmen, on the other hand, though they might be unconscious were buffeted by the new forces and were instruments of change, however balky and distracted. The true failure of the College lay then—as it comparably does now—in that judgment.

The other, or personal, judgment was no doubt in private balance with the first, but it would seem an illusion to maintain that merely "social" values cannot be rich and vital without central connection to society as a whole. There is absolute vitality, socially speaking, even in pure archaism and down through all its gradations into the actual. The point is, such was the richness of Adams' social experience with small intimate groups almost of his own making, that to him Harvard College was official and if perfect was empty; it neither challenged nor struck him, nor drew him out. He made very nearly the same reaction to general society elsewhere; his standard was in his wife's society during the Washington years from 1878 to 1885, the Five of Hearts, and it was a standard that ought not to have been applied except to itself.

Perhaps the reason he nevertheless applied it with unusual rigor to Cambridge at this place in his *Education* was to give him the force of major contrast in introducing Clarence King, the Fifth Heart. King was, like Beethoven in Berlin, education by accident; he touched a limit of human sensibility and revealed, beyond the limit, a human ideal: a mingling metamorphosis of intellect and emotion. It was only by intense contrast that Adams could make the values of his adventure actual; just as, perhaps, it was only by contrast with King that Harvard College and the *North American Review* could be shown as thin. Yet King, as Adams renders him, is real only as an aspiration is real, by the convention of style infused by faith, and by a kind of breathlessness in assertion. King was perhaps the clearest of all the symbols Adams created for himself as lodged in the welling, shifting ambiguity of an individual human being. His figure was human, his stature created out of the human. He stood for what one oneself could do at the utmost and, at the same time, for the riddle of why the effort failed.

The pattern follows that of the old legendary quests of the soul. In the summer of 1871 Adams left Harvard College for the Uintah Mountains, to join the United States Geological Survey of the Fortieth Parallel—leaving the world for the wilderness—because it seemed new truth, and a new sense of nature, might be found there. One morning Adams went fishing alone in the mountain streams and found himself lost when night fell. Giving his mule the rein, he came after two hours to a lighted cabin. "Two or three men came out to see the stranger," of whom one was King, who had himself come up the mountain that day over a hard trail. Adams and King shared a room and a bed and talked till dawn. They were friends "born in archaic horizons . . . shaped with the *Pteraspis* in Siluria." They had the same problems, implements, and obstacles; the lines of their lives converged. "The one, coming from the west, saturated in the sunshine of the Sierras, met the other, drifting from the east, drenched in the fogs of London."

Adams had moved in a series of violent breaks or waves. "King had moulded and directed his life logically, scientifically, as Adams thought American life should be directed. He had given himself education all of a piece, yet broad." King knew America, Art, poetry, professors, Congressmen, women, geology, and the future. "His wit and humor; his bubbling energy which swept every one into the current of his interest; his personal charm of youth and manners; his faculty of giving and taking, profusely, lavishly, whether in thought or in money as though he were Nature herself, marked him almost alone among Americans. He had in him something of the Greek—a touch of Alcibiades or Alexander. One Clarence King only existed in the world. . . . Such a bird of paradise rising in the sage-brush was an avatar." Adams' pattern is religious.

Even his language is beyond the possibilities of Boston and beyond the traditions of Harvard College: an avatar is the incarnation of deity in human form, the renewed experience of which it was the combined purpose of the city and the college to exclude, for it is such experience that re-opens all human problems in full challenge and fascination. Clarence

King, from his first manifestation onward, meant to Adams that a full response to life in his own country and time was possible, and that all assent and revolt and despair were alone meaningful in terms of that possibility; he drew from King, variously, what he put into him. Looking back on that mountain summer, Adams expressed the essence of it in an understatement that still grows in the mind. "History and science spread out in personal horizons towards goals no longer far away. No more education was possible for either man." The impossibility made failure tolerable, at the same time that it made withdrawal inevitable.

CHAPTER SEVEN

The Serpent
and the Golden Calf

When what we hoped for came to nothing,
we revived.

—Marianne Moore

The greatest hazard in the *Education* is the pitfall between the twentieth and twenty-first chapters. Adams was unwilling to represent directly either the fourteen fullest years of his life, the catastrophe of his wife's death which ended them, or the six succeeding years of inward exile and outward flight. Earlier sections of this study* give a makeshift version of these years, and perhaps part of the hazard—that which affects the reader—has been overcome; but the more serious hazard—that which affected Adams in the plot and composition of his book—is not thereby touched. The hazard is that in so foreshortening his perspective he might mutilate his aesthetic purpose. We can partly make up for the missing years in fact and gesture and interpretation, but we cannot either damage or aid the aesthetic unity of the images upon which the whole hangs together or falls apart.

But there was an advantage to the hazard, too, and it shows regardless of whether Adams' decision to take it rested on personal or artistic grounds. It is essentially the artist's problem of how much, for a given effect, to put in, how much to leave out for the reader to put in from his own life, and how much, lastly, to reshape what the reader has been thus enticed to put in. By leaving out the right amount the author joins the reader's stock of response to his own and can then shape both

* Indicated on Blackmur's outline but not found among his papers.—*Ed.*

95

to the same end; the commonest form of this device is under-statement. But Adams, in leaving out twenty years, is not only making an enormous understatement; he is bringing to bear on all his later chapters the force of the unaccountable—the sum of all that had happened which is not recounted—by means of deliberately inexplicit or only partly explicit symbols. The feeling is thus thicker than the prose; the meaning continues after the words have stopped because it was active before the words began. We have thus a recapitulation, here and there in these chapters, of material that was never given in the book and yet refers both the reader and Adams to it with all the more strength because of its deliberate disguise as the shared unaccountable.

There are two efforts at recapitulation, one explict of the career in politics and history and as man of the world; the other a symbolic recapitulation of the inward life and loss and going-on-ness, which is not at all explicit because, in the act of writing, it still pressed and permeated like an atmosphere. By some magic of personality seen as unaccountable—by some power of inward invocation—the inner, lost life has become capital to invest for unequivalent returns in the outer world. There is a kind of earned, saved stock of emotion which instead of producing hysteria—the extravagance of emotion—seems to invigorate *and* criticize intelligence, giving intelligence a kind of reserve wealth in emotion. The consequence in the book, then, of the grand omission becomes both aesthetically and intellectually clear. Though some part of Adams' life had been mutilated, and though that part mattered vastly to him, fur-nishing as it had his direct and daily connection to the world, it does not much matter to us, except as we think that the mu-tilation itself afforded him the strength and courage and necessity to begin a new bout with the world without any direct or daily connection at all, but as it were from a distance and across a gap. It is as if he had been filled, by his emotion, with a new power of response which had now to find a chal-lenge equal to it, at some further and still unaccountable level, in the next fifteen years—1891 to 1905—of the life, not of himself, but of his times.

The four chapters—"Twenty Years After," "Chicago," "Si-lence," "Indian Summer"—are the record of how he found that challenge, told from the vantage of the battle rather than from that of the preliminary skirmishes themselves. It is the story of reaccommodation to old terms and tangles in a new mood. It was not accomplished by a series of new insights and new ideas but by the enrichment of early insights and familiar ideas through emotion which was itself the product of suffering and exile. Hence the reaccommodation was not immediate; was not a jolt back, but a drift; and was never complete, either in actuality or in imagination. There is a kind of truth in Adams' repeated remark—in conversation and in letters—that he lived only posthumously after 1885. But the unclosed gap, by its stress, added intensity to perception—as in a strange place, old eyes.

The title of the first chapter in this batch, "Twenty Years After," is evidently reminiscent of the title of the sequel to *The Three Musketeers*. Dumas' adventurers tried each in his way to react independently to the great causes of their society. It will be remembered that Athos retired, Porthos got crushed under the great stone, and that Aramis became a master of state. The parallel to Adams and his friends is tentative and momentary but is worth reproducing. King, Hay, and himself, said Adams, had tried to count as "force even in the mental inertia of sixty or eighty million people. . . . The combination offered no very glittering prizes, but they pursued it for twenty years with as much patience and effort as though it led to fame and power." The twenty years themselves represented the trial of life roughly on its own terms, with the help only that each of them had been given in the course of normal education through 1872. It was clear in the sequel that the objects of education needed to be redefined, not only with respect of the twenty years just past but also with prospect of the new adventures at hand or the fresh resumption of old risks. The task of redefinition was easy, though it had to be made many times. Education "should try to lessen the obstacles, diminish the friction, invigorate the energy, and should train minds to react, not at haphazard, but by choice, on the lines of force that attract their world." As things stood, only "the most energetic, the most highly fitted, and the most favored have overcome the friction or the viscosity of inertia, and these were compelled to waste three-fourths of their energy in doing it."

How to join purpose to situation, how to combine theory with practice—how to certify the one without falsifying the other—

in terms such as those Adams laid down, required, among other difficulties, that what forces really did attract the world be ascertained, and that a just estimation of the weight or attraction or sink of inertia be made. Both forces forgotten and unforeseen were likely, and there was always the chance that inertia itself engrossed the truest forces of attraction. At the reasoning or conceptual level, this ascertainment and this estimation make up the program of Adams' remaining chapters. It is the level to which he always returns when he has gone beneath it, and the level which he always surmounts when it falls into formula; it is the level of the mind as operative in the daily world, always lacking and always aspiring: the mind as the sum of education. But it was the level, too, that never quite worked; it *had* to dip into the unaccountable, and it *had* to rise into the possible, in order to keep itself alive; and Adams had therefore to use the aesthetic resources of image and tone to give the effect—like that of a wave, a heaving in atmosphere— of the actual motion of experience and the response to it. The problem of interpretation is only relatively less difficult.

The tone is established when Adams tells us that when, after the South Seas, he decided to return to America, it was after a week's reflection in a London hospital, where "the fog had a fruity taste of youth"; and the image is set up when he says that had he had a companion, he would have chosen to go back to the East, "if it were only to sleep forever in the trade-winds under the southern stars, wandering over the dark purple ocean, with its purple sense of solitude and void. Not that he liked the sensation, but that it was the most unearthly he had ever felt."

The conceptual or reasoning level is then deployed in a comparison between the new Cunarder *Teutonic* and the *Niagra* of 1860, which changes instantly from a simple comparison to the expression of a proportion. As the *Niagra* of 1860 is to the *Teutonic* of 1890, so the *Teutonic* is to a future, but not infinitely future, term. Thus there is a conjunction of that which is absolute and instant in the senses, but without reality; that which is absolute in memory and aspiration, and with an infinite reality; and that which is problematic, contingent, speculative, with a kind of immanent, conceptual reality: the fog, the void ocean, and coal as an expression of physical force. So much is clear; but there is perhaps needed one bit of evidence taken from a letter of the season referred to. Adams, coming from exile, had stopped in Paris and there heard Grétry's opera *Richard Coeur de Lion*, with Blondel's song

O, Richard! O, mon Roi!
L'univers t'abandonne

which John Quincy Adams had heard ringing in his ears for days at a time after he had been turned out of the Presidency. The whole impact of the image on Adams' life is explored elsewhere.* Here it is imported only to suggest a nexus between the fog and the void ocean and to explain why in the *Education* he wrote that in Paris his heart "sank to mere pulp." The world was no longer simple and could not express itself simply: a conclusion never so certain as to those who feel a sense of abandonment.

Having set his tone and image and reached his conclusion, Adams "went home as a horse goes back to his stable, because he knew nowhere else to go." His one sure function in life was as "stable-companion to statesmen, whether they liked it or not." It is not surprising, then, that through such a frame he should see society as "slack water," politics as "torpor," and what had been the redeeming energy of Americans for a century—"the creation of new force, the application of expanding power"—as generally running down. Such figures were especially apt since they so well fitted the careers, at that moment of personal *fin de siècle*, of the three friends. Hay had never been given office worthy of his talents and had finished his *Lincoln*; Adams had never been offered office at all and had finished his *History*; King had spurned office and had tried for direct power itself, but "was passing the best years of his life underground." King and Hay were Republicans for reasons that had nothing to do with existing politics; Adams was a Democrat because Cleveland's party contained the "sole remaining protestants against a banker's Olympus." Otherwise the parties had obliterated their distinction in an even balance. In such slack water, such suspense of apparent motion, none of the three friends "knew whether they had attained success, or how to estimate it."

In this, the three friends only reflected the uncertainty of the American people: "They had neither serpents nor golden calves

* "King Richard's Prison Song," pp. 281–336.—*Ed.*

to worship." Here Adams makes what looks like a digression but is exactly a direct approach to his object. It is an illusion, Adams argued, to think that Americans worship money; they waste it without sense of its relative values. Of all that America had built during its century of expansion, only the railways survived. Railways are transportation, stimulus to movement back and forth, channels, in Adams' immediate context, for a kind of reversible pursuit game; railroads set the direction of pursuit without possibility of relative judgment. "The American mind had less respect for money than the European or Asiatic mind, and bore its loss more easily; but it had been deflected by its pursuit till it could turn in no other direction. It shunned, distrusted, disliked the dangerous attraction of ideals, and stood alone in history for its ignorance of the past." To repeat, with neither serpent nor golden calf, only the railroads survived.

The language is strong, and if it were meant as straight history would be too strong to seem truth, but it has a different kind of truth for target, which makes all its strength seem right. Now suddenly the whole chapter is pulled together and is seen to have been a preparation for the salute to the monument upon his wife's grave at Rock Creek. The images of lethargy and slack water are now given their human correlatives by confronting Saint-Gaudens' image with tourist and soldier and priest. Saint-Gaudens held up the mirror: the tourist saw nothing, the priest rejected what he saw, and the soldier objected to having to see it. To Adams, who saw everything he had been or could be, and also all that most men had been or could be, the conclusion was bitter. "The American layman had lost sight of ideals; the American priest had lost sight of faith. Both were more American than the old, half-witted soldiers who denounced the wasting, on a mere grave, of money which should have been given for drink." This is conclusion by art, not history.

But it gives a clue to history, both the unwritten and the unwritable. On the one side Adams invokes as old instances of what his image at Rock Creek might reflect back on the looker, the names of the Sphinx, Christ, Michelangelo, Prometheus, Shelley, and the Kamakura Daibitsu. All these are representative of human energy as imagination, as quest and question, and all gave their meaning not so much in answer as in the process of asking. They represent human life at its highest and most precarious sense of its own meaning—at its highest because in seeming self-created and beyond tampering; most precarious because requiring faith as the medium of appreciation. Without such figures, life slips and becomes a sink, losing half its efficiency even as a machine.

The degree to which Adams held such a feeling is suggested by the stranger in his list of instances—the Kamakura Daibitsu —the great bronze Buddha which Adams and La Farge had seen and photographed during their quest for Nirvana in Japan. In Adams' published letters there is only one reference to it as "the most successful colossal figure in the world," but there are other and better reasons for his having included it in his series of buttresses to the image at Rock Creek. It was something he had not thought of—perhaps hardly knew about—when he discussed with Saint-Gaudens the terms in which the image should absorb significance. It was finished in 1252, at the height of the Virgin's reign in Europe, and it came out of a world that belonged neither to Europe nor to America. Besides, it presided in a ruined and roofless temple over a lost city, sitting fifty feet high and thirty-five across the lap, among sixty-three pillars in open air. The temple and all its buildings had been destroyed by a great sea wave, but the brazed and chiseled bronze figure had endured and grown. La Farge, in his *Artist's Letters from Japan*, published a sketch of it as frontispiece, and wrote four pages of appreciation which will have to stand for the responses of both men, and from which the following sentences are extracted.

Like all work done on archaic principles, the main accentuations are overstated, and saved in their relations by great subtleties in the large surfaces. It is emphatically modelled for a colossus; it is *not a little thing made big*, like our modern colossal statues; it *has always been big*, and would be so if reduced to life-size. . . . Now, freed from its shrine, the figure sits in contemplation of entire nature, the whole open world that we feel about us, or its symbols. . . . All this world of ours, which to the contemplative mind is but a figurative fragment of the universe, lies before the mental gaze of the Buddha. . . . His cognition, undisturbed, envelops and images the universe in final contemplation. . . . One almost believes that the result may be partly accidental: that, as one cannot fathom the reason of the expressiveness of a countenance, or of the influence of a few musical notes, even though one knows the mechanism, so it seems difficult to grant that there was once a choice in the other mind that caused it, that there were once many paths opened before it. . . .

And then, commenting on the accident of the tempest which had left in full light what had been conceived for the shadow of a shrine:

But could anything ever have rivaled the undecidedness of this background of veiled sky and shifting blue, which makes one believe at times that the figure soon must move? As one looks longer and longer at it, with everything around it gently changing, and the shadows shifting upon its surface, the tension of expectation rises to anxiety. The trees rustle and wave behind it, and the light dances up and down the green boughs with the wind; it must move—but there is no change, and it shall sit forever.

Adams looked at his own statue with a similar tension of expectation rising to anxiety, and it was the absence of any token of corresponding reaction in those who brought nothing with which to look, that made him think that the greater part of the American mind was given up to the movement of inertia. "Landed, lost, and forgotten, in the center of this vast plain of self-content," he could see only as a scale for measure the railroads, which grew and grew on a base of coal, and which had only to be completed, but which showed no value, when measured, as education. Railroads showed no economy in reaction and no choice in direction, but were themselves part of the movement of an inertia so omnivorous that it excluded reaction.

That such a conclusion would not stand—that it raised more questions than it evaded—was plain as soon as the particular conviction of sequence upon which it was grounded was laid open to suspicion that it might not be absolute or singular, that it might even be irrelevant to some other sequence or sequences. The sequence of relations in which man felt his own value in a world of ordeal might have to be replaced by a sequence of forces in which, if man felt himself a value at all, he was a value without relation as an individual but only as an instance. The combined experience of Senator Don Cameron, of the money panic of 1893, and of the Chicago Exposition, seemed to suggest the need for conceiving such a new sequence, if not as a replacement then as a parallel to the old sequence.

Senator Cameron enters here as a recurrent and transitional

image. As recurrent he represents the Garibaldi-Grant type in
its final phase: as the political energy which, because it is superior to the *available* intelligence, gets the work of government
done. As transitional, he represents the means whereby the
political energy of the American people passed from one system of society to another. But the transition was in Adams'
mind, too, for it gave him to think that he should find himself—
a man of principle and imagination—in practical alliance once
again, as at every historical moment of American crisis, with
the unprincipled, unimaginative man of blind energy who
acted in the cause of unity and historical purpose because
he was himself a part of them. *Quantula sapientia regitur
mundus!* It was Oxenstiern's phrase, once applied to Sumner,
but the other way around.

The critical point in the change in the American system
came in the political struggle over free silver, and the climax
was in the market crash of 1893. For Adams the struggle was
between silver and the "interests," between morals and necessity; both he and Cameron were on the silver side, but Cameron
expressed his allegiance differently—as supporting the free
money of the common man; but both, according to Adams,
gave up gladly to the necessity of gold when gold asserted its
supremacy as the actual interest—not just of the bankers—but
of the forces that moved the country. It is curious to note that
Adams' own "interests," like Cameron's, were for gold, and that
no one could explain why Cameron supported silver: the *Dictionary of American Biography* says that it was for "some
unknown reason"—which may have been found in his friendship for Adams or some otherwise hidden love for lost freedoms
and the anarchies of the heart.

However that may be, it was Adams' struggle—instinctive,
hereditary, prejudiced—against the supremacy of gold that
made him feel a particularity in the force of gold. But the
particularity was not at once evident. At first, through the
panic of the crash, he felt only that "blindly some very powerful energy was at work, doing something that nobody wanted
done." Since it effected ruin on borrower and lender alike—
that is, all society—"evidently the force was one; its operation
was mechanical; its effect must be proportional to its power;
but no one knew what it meant, and most people dismissed it as
an emotion—a panic—that meant nothing."

This is partly in contempt of those who regard emotion as wrong because emotion is the only overwhelming reality they know, and partly in contempt of those who regard the existing machine of society—which must always be makeshift—as alone right, because they cannot feel the forces which would make them imagine another. Adams could not have denied emotion without destroying his temperament, and he was bound by all his training—all his education—to look for new systems of society in their process of making. At the moment he had been talking with his brother Brooks and was tinkering at Brooks' notion that civilizations followed the movement of the exchanges—local concentrations of monetary systems—along trade routes, which translated meant that societies were unstable and sought new equilibrium. Thus the market crash of 1893 was a convulsion of "disequilibrium between capital and labor, the logical outcome [of which] was not collectivism, but anarchism."

But the outcome, like the human mind that suffered it, was not logical; the two opposed forces were neither anarchic nor collectable, but were two phases of a single force whose total nature and general direction were not yet recognized, and hence had no logic. The Exposition at Chicago, to which Adams addressed himself for information about the outcome, showed both a unity and a break in sequence: it seemed a natural product of the Northwest, but in achieving its character it had skipped London and New York. The art was trader's classicism with a look of unity. Therefore, Adams sat under Richard Hunt's dome as on the steps of Ara Coeli. History persisted in asking freshly the old question about the breaches in its own sequence. Showing the materials in motion, and showing art in arbitrary assertion of inexplicable meaning, "Chicago asked in 1893 for the first time the question whether the American people knew where they were driving."

The art of the Exposition and the mere astonishing fact of its existence were inexplicable, but the industrial exhibits at least suggested a kind of frame for more precise questions, because there it was possible to move from the known to the unknown. To Adams the Cunarder, for example, would reach its limits in 1927, when, along the lines of its present rate of development, force, space, and time should meet. "The ocean steamer ran the surest line of triangulation into the future, because it was the nearest of man's products to a unity." By analogy, the infant dynamo led into unknowable fields of force that could not be taken as unity: "If its progress was to be constant at the rate of the last ten years, it would result in infinite costless energy within a generation." The consequence to the historian was helpless ignorance toward the one unity he had always taken as sure—the unity of natural force. Its sequence seemed still to be mechanical, but the mind no longer kept up with it. If then Chicago asserted unity, as Adams felt, it must be an unconscious drive or drift toward some point of thought, and he decided that "possibly, if relations enough could be observed, this point might be fixed. Chicago was the first expression of American thought as a unity; one must start there."

The problem here is to know in what way Adams meant the word unity as applied to the Chicago Exposition. How ironical was he? how prophetic? how instinctive? Surely there was irony in concluding a description on a tone of unity which began: "Since Noah's Ark, no such Babel of loose and ill-joined, such vague and ill-defined and unrelated thoughts and half-thoughts and experimental outcries as the Exposition, had ever ruffled the surface of the Lakes." But surely there was prophecy, in the sentiment that where there was so much energy there might yet be a form; and, even more surely, it was deep animal instinct to count on actual unity in any mass, however inchoate, which could be seen together, which so to speak *asked*—as the chief exercise of its attractive force—to be thought of in one look. Even a Babel, at a distance, takes on a single tone.

The distance, for Adams, was Washington, the old ideal of American unity by representation, balance, and intelligent direction of the forces of society, politically conceived. Whatever the unity of Chicago was, it was not that of Washington; but it had suddenly become both prior and superior to Washington: it was where, which Washington was not, America was going. The struggle of silver and gold was the conflict of the two assertions of unity, and it seemed to Adams that when late in 1893 the Senate got rid of silver by repealing the Silver Purchase Act, it got rid of its heavy responsibility of maintaining the old unity without assuming responsibility for maintaining the new. "For a hundred years, between 1793 and 1893, the American people had hesitated, vacillated, swayed forward and back, between two forces, one simply industrial, the other capitalistic, centralizing, and mechanical. . . . A capitalistic system had been adopted, and if it were to run at all, it must be run by capital and capitalistic methods; for nothing could surpass the nonsensity of trying to run so complex and so concentrated a machine by Southern and Western farmers in grotesque alliance with city day-laborers, as had been tried in 1800 and 1828, and had failed even under simple conditions."

To Adams this situation represented not only a shift in phase of society but a shift in the kind of force that controlled society; it meant the difference between the assertion of political principle and the submission to economic method—in short, the abdication of politics as value in favor of politics as an efficient machine. How complete the abdication might become, Adams left at this point nearly muted, remarking only that "society might dispute in what social interest" the machine should be run, and that a necessary complement to the new machine was the combination of "trades-unions and socialistic paternalism." In the sequel, other images and other necessities would sharpen the sense of renewed conflict along old lines, but at the moment he was concerned to see, under the image of Chicago, "the whole mechanical consolidation of force, which ruthlessly stamped out the life of the class into which Adams was born, but created monopolies capable of controlling the new energies that America adored." The Babel of Chicago had absorbed the harmony of Washington.

Is not Adams here describing that composite act which is both a surrender and a jumping on the bandwagon, where each, to make itself tolerable, is disguised as the other? The series of images—steamship, railroad, dynamo, Chicago, and the Beaux Arts—are way stations of partial response, virtual recognitions, gatherings of intelligence in accommodation for full response not now possible. Gold overwhelming silver, the monopolies of capital overwhelming politics, inertia overwhelming intelligence, unconscious convulsion overwhelming movement of consciousness: what, faced with such force, could the still conscious victim do but say, *Look what has happened! Well, well, well! Then here we are!*—but all the while the covert under-voice rising to cry, *Where?* and, *How long?* If Chicago was the unity of inertia—drive—drift—instinct, the unity of the uncontrollable, it could only be so in relation to Washington,

which remained the unity of conception—imagination—reason
—tradition, unity by aspiration and control. Torpor and self-
content, like the convulsions which they followed, seem only
to suggest an *unconsciousness* of live forces, a failure in relationship and response; not a failure in being but a disaster from
which it must recover. If Adams seems to say more, it is because he wishes to bring the disaster home, and to explain by
it, too, the prior disaster at Rock Creek.

Thus, in the process of reaccommodation to the actual world
we have images first of the failure of the ideal and second of
the supremacy of the mechanical. Next come, to stage the beginning of the reaction, first images largely personal (in "Silence"), and second images which combine ideal, mechanical,
personal, and aesthetic (in "Indian Summer")—at the conclusion of which the mind discovers that after all it has survived,
and can act, and precisely because it has changed with the
change of society.

Of the personal images, Clarence King comes first and for
the curiously apt reason that he combined in himself the ideal
and the mechanical in such measure that he seemed to Adams
representative, through images of money, of both the old and
the new phases of society. Yet he had not only failed of practical success, he had also suffered a convulsion of his own along
with the convulsion of society, and unlike society he never
recovered from the fatigue in which he was left at the end of
his breakdown. As Winston Churchill once remarked, the test
of a country is what it can do when fatigued, and it is something the same with men. Adams' own language is ambiguous
in the figure at the heart of it. The ideal and scientific education
which had made King seem an avatar in 1871 had been proved
inadequate for lack of money: "Education without capital could
always be taken by the throat and forced to disgorge its gains,
nor was it helped by the knowledge that no one intended it, but
that all alike suffered. Whether voluntary or mechanical the
result for education was the same. The failure of the scientific
scheme, without money to back it, was flagrant."

The idea so impressed Adams that he thrice repeated it in two
pages. "The scientific scheme in theory was alone sound, for
science should be equivalent to money: in practice science was
helpless without money." And again, after remarking that the
successes of John Hay, W. C. Whitney, and Whitelaw Reid were

due not to their education but to the money they married, Adams goes on: "America contained scores of men worth five millions or upwards, whose lives were no more worth living than those of their cooks, and to whom the task of making money equivalent to education offered more difficulties than to Adams the task of making education equivalent to money." And lastly, there was the fact that "wealth valued social position and classical education as highly as either of these valued wealth, and the women still tended to keep the scales even."

The secret of what Adams meant to say—or found in his mind —beyond what he merely said, in these sentences, may perhaps lie in the final clause: the women still tended to keep the scales even. If so, it must remain ambiguous, a mere suggestion that by uniting their social and sexual functions women are able to convert the most disparate values into the form in which they are most needed. In a world, such as the American world, which had become primarily neither social nor sexual, which used avowedly neither the rule of status nor the energy of sex, money had to assume the functions of conversion and choice and judgment at levels where it had never previously been fitted to operate, and where, hence, it operated badly and failed, with some values, altogether. Clarence King, the avatar of ideal education—the man who had most values to convert—was an example of complete failure. Because he had no capital—no creative property in the sense that the money-mind understood—his output could not be converted and payment made, but only stolen. In short, talent could not convert itself into money and seldom into enough social consideration to make up for the lack of money; when resort to other means, such as marriage or business, was unavailable, talent failed and money was wasted. That woman in her sexual and social capacity could still do a better job than money was a possibility around which Adams, as his book went on, composed more and more of the images of his lifetime, but here, as in earlier chapters, it is merely thrown up, a flag in flight.

The immediate flight was with King to Cuba, with Hay again to the Yellowstone, then with Chandler Hale (son of the Senator from Maine) to Mexico, and alone to the islands of the Caribbean. Cuba was conspiracy and rebellion and an "ocean of mischief" and had a special interest; but all served as a contrast to Europe and the United States, and to what Chicago stood for as well as Washington. The torpor of these countries was the torpor, or dead water, of primitive countries, like the islands of the South Seas, that had never shared the general motion. By the time Adams had finished twenty thousand miles of American land and water, he found he had made a choice for action which would exhaust the rest of his life, although he had not yet found the means to implement that choice. He thought "he knew enough about the edges of life—tropical islands, mountain solitudes, archaic law, and retrograde types. . . . They educated only artists, and, as one's sixtieth year approached, the artist began to die; only a certain intense cerebral restlessness survived which no longer responded to sensual stimulants; one was driven from beauty to beauty as though art were a trotting match."

The alternative to art was arithmetic. If art was still good for the torpor of primitive countries outside the general motion, arithmetic was perhaps good for the torpor at the center of motion. If you could not understand, at least you might count and hope that understanding might creep in between your rows of figures. So Adams took up statistics, the cousin and consequence of money, and cast averages backward and forward: "one's averages projected themselves as laws into the future." But "the method did not result in faith. Indeed, every increase of mass—of volume and velocity—seemed to bring in new elements. . . . In principle, according to figures, anyone could set up or pull down a society." Adams reveled through his figures in the ruin of every past and every possible future society, and found a new form of *Impavidum ferient ruinae* to which he ever afterward, as his letters and reports of his conversations show, intermittently recurred. The determined, the positive, the mechanical took on a prodigious kind of reality, along with the arithmetical form, superior to all the unformulable actuality of experience.

The wonderful and abysmal temptation of mathematics, like that of theology to which it is heir, is to credit its mastery of form and pattern and relation with effective control of actual substance. The lure in the temptation lies in the progressive alienation of human values which it appears to make inevitable. It appeals to the suicidal in the individual and the destructive in society—as atheism and war—by making disaster not only certain but predictable. Man is proudest when he stands master-

less and condemned by the inventions of his own mind, when
he has made of his instinctive dread of what is to come a permanent vertigo of numerical sequence. Adams went as far as
any man can along the path of that temptation and still draw
back. But he did draw back; there was still force in him to be
tempted and deflected; which, in this connection, was his sense
of history as actual, apart from any numbers into which it fell.
However he rejoiced in predicting ruin to society, he could not
help pulling up on the consideration that "meanwhile these
societies which violated every law, moral, arithmetical, and
economical, not only propagated each other, but produced also
fresh complexities with every propagation and developed mass
with every complexity."

Here was one test of *mechanicalness* in sequence; for figures
ought to reflect movements which are certain, certainly. If
figures were truth about the motor—what moved—they lied on
the facts—what was moved. There was a lacuna in between to
represent facts. Accordingly, *Pteraspis*, now called shark, is re-
introduced, as representing what survives every moral improve-
ment—any change of law—in society. There had been an interlude of shark education in the South Seas, for there the shark
was divine, and Adams had become a member of the royal, or
Salmon, family, whose source of power was in that divinity. And
there, too, the women had measured like Venus, and Adams
had made himself an image that brought the Greeks on an
argosy there. *Pteraspis* indeed! Venus too! His exile had been
in a strange land, in which numerical sequences, the shark, and
Venus came to have a relation. Failing Nirvana in Japan
(though not giving up) he had found the shark-Venus in Tahiti,
and had there changed his name in deepening his service. Thus
his nieces became *Salmonidae*, and Rodin's *Psyche*, when trans-
planted to the Beverly Woods, became Fishy. On the edges of
life *Pteraspis* was divine energy: in its center, brute.

Some such complex of image and reaction is the background
for Adams' rediscovery of *Pteraspis* after the initial failure of
statistics to account for the survival of stupor and brutality in
the world unchanged and also the survival of man himself.
There was war and massacre all over the world. "Yet impartial
judges thought them all not merely unnecessary, but foolish—
induced by greed of the coarsest class, as though the Pharaohs
or the Romans were still robbing their neighbors. The robbery

might be natural and inevitable, but the murder seemed altogether archaic." Between the contrary habits of the shark and
Venus and mathematical law there must lie some clues to whatever actual faith it was that kept society freshly propagating
itself regardless of past and present ruin both of its plain brutality and the inventions of the mind.

Once again he reached the interim conclusion that had disturbed him so many times. "The object of education, therefore,
was changed. For many years it had lost itself in studying what
the world had ceased to care for; if it were to begin again, it
must try to find out what the mass of mankind did care for,
and why. Religion, politics, statistics, travel had thus far led
to nothing. Even the Chicago Fair only had confused the roads."
As usual with Adams in this conclusion, his terms were ambiguous; nature compelled him to hang on to what he let go;
and rescue was by accident. It was the methods of study, not
its subjects, that were wrong, and what was wrong with the
methods was that they belittled the subjects: the principles got
in the way of the values, and the values made difficulties about
issuing in new principles in direct relation. It was not religion
and politics that were wrong, but what had happened to them
in the regular progress of the substitution of principles for
value; it was not statistics that were wrong, but that statistics
set up to be beyond good and evil; and it was certainly not
travel that was wrong unless it was by the excess of contrary-
spirited values travel provided. All the values remained, and
all pressed, but all were mis-seen: all needed to be seen as
directly as possible, in the direct, combined service of serpent
and golden calf. Here it was that education by accident supervened, with covert and classic violence, cutting convenient
forms away, and discovered the subject itself. If not an end,
Adams had a beginning in view.

The accident was multiple: the discovering of new religion,
new politics, new statistics, and new travel; the new discovery
of the one thing not new in man's mind, the presentness of
history. Mrs. Lodge, but not, as he puts it, the Senator, took him
to Normandy in the summer of 1896 and, looking at cathedrals
through her eyes and her children's, his own eyes cleared, for
it is reported that she had very beautiful large violet eyes
through which anyone could find sight. At any rate, in company
of the Lodges, archaic law and antiquarianism—the defeated

acceptance of *Pteraspis* and the ruined ease of Wenlock—disappeared from Adams' mind, and medieval faith or imagination became an energy with direct relation to present history.

In the fall of 1896 the election of McKinley brought on a new view of politics, partly by dragging some of Adams' friends into the Government, and partly (through Hay's appointment as Ambassador to England) by focusing a new interest in international relations as, at first, an escape from intolerable domestic relations. The two relations were themselves connected in what Adams called a case of true corruption. In order to give Mark Hanna one of Ohio's seats in the Senate, the incumbent, old Senator Sherman, was made Secretary of State. Thus the chief post under the Executive was given to a senile mind merely to placate the greed of a party machine. To Adams this was worse than Charles Sumner's corruption of egotism and principle. "The prospect for once was not less vile than the men. One can bear coldly the jobbery of enemies, but not that of friends." The idea that Hay would shortly replace Sherman only made the prospect worse. "Indeed, had Hay been even unconsciously party to such an intrigue, he would have put an end, once for all, to further concern in public affairs on his friend's part." Thus McKinley not only brought Adams a challenge to a singularly direct view of party politics putting true politics at a complete discount, he also put Adams' personal nest of friendship in peril beyond the mere distractive influence of bringing some of them into office. History was veritably present in relation to current inertia of politics as in the discovery of the old relation of religion, which had also, as Adams found by sampling the religious press, become a kind of inertia.

It is hard to say to which of these blows—the ruin of King, of eighteenth century politics, of the experiment at statistics, or of friendship—Adams was responding in the three-page salute to Silence with which he follows his account of the blows. Again, perhaps, it is the blow not accounted for that had had the greatest effect. Adams' kind of silence is the accumulation of thoughts not spoken, and must eventually build up a head of response that will burst with either inner or outer violence, and sometimes both; and for a talkative and thoughtful man to take to silence—to take to the pursuit of ignorance in silence—requires a good many wounds to lick, and always more than are visible. We can say that under these blows Adams found himself ignorant of what the world cared for, and worse, found himself deprived of what he cared for. Until he could measure and express—and thereby somewhat recover—the values of his own privation, he could not estimate what the world lacked, or cared for, or hoped, without knowing it, to recover. The two tasks, however apparently contradictory, must at some point be interchangeable. That point was the subject, was the object, of the pilgrimage of ignorance in silence. It is characteristic of Adams that in avowing that he had undertaken such a pilgrimage he should call it a hobby: which is the name given those obsessive pursuits where expert values become, in their play, principles at last.

This pilgrim played his hobby in Normandy with nephews and nieces, in London with Hay, in Paris alone, in Egypt again with Hay, in the Near East alone and with Rockhill from 1896 to 1899, traveling not the edges of life but alternately its living and its ancient centers, and traveling in himself, too. In Normandy the great cathedrals drew him on. In London there was a bloodless fear and a press of shadows, as for Odysseus in hell. In Egypt, when news of the *Maine* came, he "leant on a fragment of column in the great hall at Karnak and watched a jackal creep down the débris of ruin." If the jackal was a degraded form of *Pteraspis*-shark, he also "lay in the sands and watched the expression of the Sphinx," which was the non-*Pteraspis* and made even the jackal form less than fatal.

But the wanderings of this pilgrim were not all on even scale or even on the point; there was the unaccountable movement within, that which stirred in the press of shadows and heaved in the bloodless fear; and as that movement pressed in Adams' life, so it occasionally burst palpably into the prose of his book in a sudden sentence beyond the tensile strength of the context to contain. Such is the sentence which interjects itself into the passage in explanation why he could not remain with Hay in the London of 1897. "No wrinkled Tannhäuser, returning to the Wartburg, needed a wrinkled Venus to show him that he was no longer at home, and that even penitence was a sort of impertinence." Except that a few lines down, he calls himself a stranded Tannhäuser. Adams makes no further clarifying reference.

How much interpretation this sentence and its single outrider will bear is questionable, but the reader may be legitimately reminded of one of the Tannhäuser legends and also of the circumstances of the summer of 1897, in the hope that these, taken together, will provide a clue to the singular and powerful rhythmic character of the sentence, which is its true secret. According to one of the received stories, the thirteenth-century Tannhäuser won the love of the girl Lisaura so completely that she killed herself when he deserted her in pursuit of Venus. Tannhäuser, finding Venus, was at first little troubled with his fault and remained enthralled seven years in the Venusberg underworld. At the end of that time he grew repentant and prayed the Virgin Mary for permission to revisit the upper world. This granted, Tannhäuser made pilgrimage to Pope Urban for absolution. But Urban refused. "No," said he. "You can no more hope for mercy than this dry staff can be expected to bud again." When in three days the Pope's staff did bud, Tannhäuser could not be found. No doubt—so the story goes— he returned, though penitent, to Venus. The Virgin had understood the temptation of Venus, through her kinship to that goddess, better than Pope Urban, and had by her miracle imposed a rebuke on official society at the same time that she refused quite to exculpate Tannhäuser, however arduous the pilgrimage in which he undertook to show his penitence. Yet— such was her skill in administration as well as understanding— she had seen to it that he received what was virtually, by official society's own word, absolution *in absentia*. It was, as Adams might have said, a woman's right judgment: Tannhäuser must suffer a little more, until his penitence was no longer an impertinence, before he could receive her forgiveness. He was thus left a stranded pilgrim indeed.

Tannhäuser was not Adams, but Adams was a part of Tannhäuser: a role he could think of himself as repeating by intention of understanding, and also a role others could insist on seeing him play by intention of their misunderstanding. In this play, and equally taken either way, the Virgin was Adams' "creation of her" in the statue at Rock Creek, and Venus was Elizabeth Cameron. There was for years much gossip about Adams' relations with Mrs. Cameron, and at the time to which Adams' lashing sentence refers—the spring and summer of 1897—the gossip and the apparent excuse for it were at their height; for Mrs. Cameron and her daughter Martha traveled with Adams to London, and during the summer when Adams and Edward Hooper took the Pavillon d'Angoulême Mrs. Cameron was nearby at St. Germain. That the territory in between was thickgrass with nieces, made no difference to the talk; the absence of the Senator validated the Tannhäuser role, and only the more so when Hooper and the three younger nieces returned to America, leaving only two nieces and Martha to chaperone a fortnight's tour of the Château Country during which they constantly ran into friends. A playful Venus might well have found herself at home in Elizabeth Cameron; but to Adams, with his dogwood and judas and the stone figure at Rock Creek, the identification could only be symbolic—of a privation and a loss, and of a guilt he had created wholly for himself—which yet pressed the more bitterly because of the talk. His pilgrimage was his own, however conspicuous. "No wrinkled Tannhäuser, returning to the Wartburg, needed a wrinkled Venus to show him that he was no longer at home, and that even penitence was a sort of impertinence." In the sense that penitence must be conspicuous it was impertinence.

The reader may make of the image what his own experience prompts him to; it comes at any rate out of the territory of explosions from within, which batter down our inward protections; the argument here is only that the stress this image stood for has something to do with Adams' role as pilgrim of ignorance in silence, and that it makes more understandable his remarks in summary of the Egyptian scene: the Spanish War, his brother Brooks' notion that civilization followed the Exchanges, the jackal and the Sphinx, and the memory of his wedding trip. "His hobby had turned into a camel, and he hoped, if he rode long enough in silence, that at last he might come on a city of thought along the great highways of exchange." Neither the Roman city nor God's city was enough, until their emotion had been mastered. Nothing was yet enough to bring him out of silence into speech. There had first to be the final flare-up—the harvest—of the old lines of effort and education: with the bloodless fear all intact and at full press; and that is why the next chapter is called "Indian Summer."

"Indian Summer" was an obsessive term with Adams in his letters from the middle of the 'nineties on. Used casually, it had most often to do with the special quality of an aging man's perception and was the aesthetically pleasant twin to what he

called *tussis senilis*—the dry cough of old age. Perhaps we can
say it was the name for that deteriorating climate of the mind
in which understanding replaces rather than crowns experience.
It is in that mild but exciting climate that a man may be said to
live posthumously—after his active life is dead. But in the *Education* the term on its one appearance is used not for the process
or medium of perception but rather as the summary term for
the finished process of life that has happened; it is the situation
in which one sees what is past come to a head and be done before
taking pause and leaping into the future. It is thus a general
term.

"Indian Summer" as a general term comprises the ideas of
Harvest, Final Energy Fling, and Imminent Death. It is also in
phase with the cycle of false or afterlife, where there is a reduced
inner intensity corresponding to superficial added intensity. It
is eccentricity, in Adams' sense, in face of the facts and neither
eccentricity in formula nor eccentricity in perception. Lastly, it
is forerunner—a haunt in advance—of new life. Not all of these
notions were explicit in Adams' mind, and the notion of Harvest
certainly predominated: what is left when the old work is done
and at the point when the new work is not yet begun. Harvest
is of dead things—of things to be stored, or judged, or at any rate
measured, of things that if they change change chiefly by decay
or degradation. Harvest takes the life out of something for the
sake of a different life which is yet to be a repetition of the life
deprived. Every gain is compensated by a loss. A renewal is also
a re-beginning. Thus Harvest is the very essence of the last
preparation for a return.

But if Harvest is the dominant idea in Adams' notion of Indian Summer, the other ideas are, as we see, tacitly present by
attraction—by that vacuum in the waiting spirit which demands them. The sense of vacuum is the very challenge to
creativity, as it is also often, and when the demand is most
deeply felt, the source of ennui, when either the greatest riches
are on the verge or all is nothing worth. The relation is as close
as that of vastation to devastation, or meditation to torpor, still-
ness to death. The difference lies in the point of view, or in the
energy of perception, the shift and degrees of which in the end
make possible or impossible the aesthetic vision which is the
harvest of the harvest, the only possible harvest of Indian Summer.

But the prior harvest is our first concern, as it is the materials out of which the second must be grown; and here Adams obliges, for his chapter falls readily apart into a series of notions which make up a whole chiefly because one mind barned them at one time from one perspective, which is the most dependable if the least eluctable form of composition. There is first what Adams felt as the personal triumph of four generations of the Adams family when, through the skill of Hay and by the bad and unnecessary accident of the Spanish-American War, England acted with the United States as one power against Europe. As Joseph Chamberlain remarked at the time, the Spanish War showed England that all policy was world policy. But the triumph of Hay as diplomat was at the cost of time and energy for friendship so far as Adams was concerned, and at a much greater cost, which had to do with the nature of political power, to Hay for himself. Power triumphed over the individual as poison spreads rigor in the convulsive body; power was obtained only by the invocation of the devil, and to hold great office was to invite death. Perhaps, too, the consequences of power on society were little different from those on the individual: the climax of the American Empire could be best foreseen from Ara Coeli or from Sicily. There, in the old question of Rome, was one corrective to the feeling of triumph, either with or without expense; but a deeper corrective lay in the image of St. Francis who, like the inner half of most direct and sensitive natures, would have nothing to do with official power or official society at all except to fight them.

Then, less a corrective than a jog, there was the old personal image of *Sac* and *Soc*, of justice and the profits of justice, which had been a simplification if not a misconstruction of the human area it had meant to cover: than which it was by nothing shown so clearly as by the new vision of the green pleasure and gray rest in Adams' new profession, the twelfth-century imagination. Then, immediately following, and of course, was the composite and omnigathering image of John La Farge, whose glass was violent and Renaissance and personal as medieval glass never was, but whose human character was wholly otherwise, a reversal of American convention and directness, and a true expression of eccentricity in perception, and who made Adams see why it was that "the mind resorts to reason for want of training."

Next, springing directly, from the sequence of Hay and power and the study of variable eccentricity through La Farge, came the notion—the old notion in intense fresh application—of the failure of principle in politics as seen in England's Boer War. High politics seemed the fruit of luck in the plastic mind; what was known as "politics" seemed to require blindness to facts. On one side, it was plain that only their control of money—personal and social—gave Hewitt, Whitney, and Hay their chance to use their plastic quality; and on the other side, it was plain that McKinley's Pooling Policy was, like the movement to gold, a part of inevitable consolidation in society in which neither luck and plasticity nor blindness to facts made much difference. It was only more evidence on the same line that the friction or conflict of interests as shown in the Senate represented the neutralization of government. Only ignorance —that is, the willful deprivation of the mind of its false formularies, and mathematics—that is, the willing substitution of formulas of relation for formulas of substance, could ever conspire to find unity or direction and so invent the new machinery of government which might control the movement of the new energies. If everything "must be made to move together, one must seek new worlds to measure." That is to say by implication, there must be an imaginative harvest.

Such in brief is the prior harvest of notions in the first stage of Adams' Indian Summer. The series of these image-notions is itself a whole cycle of the way stations of Withdrawal and Return, or rather of a driving out and a new driving in. The reaction is in equilibrium but not equal to the action; and this is true almost even in each member of the series. The new eyes —the deprived vision—had needed time to learn to see; and even the account (Adams' book) was only able to come on itself in the making. Here again is evidence that no man holds all his thought in mind; he may, if he is an author and knows how to compose, know pretty well where he began and what he aims at; but he cannot predetermine the process—the actuality, the experience, the revelation—except as he comes on it while under way. He may "feel" the whole and prophesy the result; but the process is an adventure, and the adventure will modify the result, at least by changing the scale of what had been its expected value.

One does not know a thing until one has put it down to see

what will happen to it in a new medium and what it will attract to itself; what one knows is what one did not put, but what comes otherwise to be there—what was dragged into being by the agency of the language used and by the symbol made. Hence the bias of human pilgrims—men as palmer-worms in the apple of knowledge—toward allegory: partly as a substitute for putting down, better as a means of attracting what was not put down as fuel to the engine of response. The word *pilgrim* is itself a whole school or technique of allegory in Adams' book, and so, for sharpest contrast, is *pteraspis*. We have seen how such terms, becoming allegorical, became obvious incitements to adventure in Adams' mind; so too the way-station image-notions of Adams' Indian Summer; and if we have listed them as a prior harvest, we must now explore some of them as they work among each other on the page and so see the fresh quality of perception they incite in us.

When in 1898 England determined to support the United States against possible intervention by Germany and Russia with regard to Spain, Adams saw the triumph of the long family policy and felt that it had been secured by a combination of Hay's skill and England's fear of Germany. That might seem the expression of personal triumph, but if so it was only secondarily; primarily it was a triumph of policy—of considered judgment and persistent intent and the sense of coming history. As policy, England's action is handled elsewhere; here it need only be said that the Spanish War precipitated a community of Anglo-American interest which had long been held in amorphous suspense. Adams' notion of an Atlantic Combine was the next step. But what Adams really got out of English assurances —what was really his personal triumph—was this: "a sense of possible purpose working itself out in history" which was "true empire-building"—a case of the triumph of Washington over Chicago. Exactly what was meant by "true empire-building" is uncertain, but it may be hazarded as a maxim out of the whole context, that a true empire requires unity of judgment and common action wherever interest is mutual. Such an empire would be Adams' version of what Toynbee calls the *Respublica Christiana*, and would be based on principle in constant but shifting equilibrium with value, of ideal polity with the stress of the actual.

If such was Adams' notion, then the rest of the chapter may

be taken as a demonstration of some of the obstacles—the Boer War and the imperfection of human eccentricity—that stood in the way of its fulfillment, and as a suggestion, by implication of his "new profession" of medieval imagination, of some of the elements needed to join fulfillment and aspiration in a response to them. But pushing a little more softly, there was the joining of law and intelligence in a single action upon which Adams could momentarily rest: "he thought he had a personal property by inheritance in this proof of sequence and intelligence in the affairs of men." He was content, that is, with the joint triumph of his grandfather's policy of intelligence at the hands of Hay and the British Government as he had not been at the triumph of his father against the British Government. It was a partial answer, on the international scale, of his old question whether intelligence could be an effective agent under modern conditions. It may be suggested, to anticipate, that the partly affirmative answer was possible only because modern conditions had not yet made themselves felt as strongly in international as they had in domestic relations, so that men were still able to act along old lines. Even the immediate consequences of the joint action, however, showed some lines of strain as well as intelligence, of convulsion as well as sequence. In Adams' eyes it was appropriate that America should run the West Indies in the interests of Europe and America, but he could not see that it was proper for America to run the Philippines as well, since to take the Philippines was to assume the load of the balance of power in the East at the same time that power itself was shouldered at home. To Adams the risk seemed too great; and he was right.

He was right, prophetically, because the new powers in the world—whether physical or social—would fail to reach balance in the international scene on old lines. But he was also right in a different, closer sense about the effect of old and new powers combined on limited intelligence at home; for he had the example of Hay in front of him. In accepting his promotion to the State Department, John Hay was lost to Adams and to himself, and the reason lay in the heart of a kind of pathological myth. "The amusement of making Presidents has keen fascination for idle American hands, but these black arts have the old drawback of all deviltry; one must serve the spirit one evokes, even though the service were perdition to body and soul." The

cost to Hay was in his own mind his immortal soul, in Adams'
mind his life. In Adams' fancy, "office was poison; it killed—
body and soul—physically and socially. Office was more poison-
ous than priestcraft or pedagogy in proportion as it held more
power; but the poison he complained of was not ambition; he
shared none of Cardinal Wolsey's belated penitence for that
healthy stimulant, as he had shared none of the fruits; his poison
was that of the will—the distortion of sight—the warping of
mind—the degradation of tissue—the coarsening of taste—the
narrowing of sympathy to the emotions of a caged rat." Indeed,
in such language, and to a stranded Tannhäuser, penitence was
an impertinence, no less than to Cardinal Wolsey; no direct
reaction was possible.

But against this excess reaction in one direction Adams had
a middle path and also two further, and ancient, excesses of
reaction in other directions. The middle path was of course the
modus vivendi to which any excess not hysterical reduces itself.
He saw his friend as he could and helped keep things going
through what connections there were—such as the close study
of the pathology of the case; and otherwise permitted himself
to "go back to his own pursuits which were slowly taking a direction. Perhaps they had no right to be called pursuits, for in
truth one consciously pursued nothing, but drifted as attraction
offered itself." The immediate attractions were Sicily and Rome;
not the edges of life but the old centers once again. Syracuse and
Ara Coeli held camel-loads of morals about catastrophe and violence, about the poison of office on the large historic scale. Or
rather, all the world's cities sent their loads of violence—made
their belated pilgrimages—to Rome; and to Adams, at the very
last year of the century, it seemed that New York sent most,
for America had reached the stage of Brutus and Cato—of casti-
gation and conspiracy—and in the Roman light it was clear that
the climax of empire was approaching.

So the middle path of the *modus vivendi* produced in turn its
own excess, and to balance that the third excess at once, and by
nature, came up out of its dark, and not, as fourteen years before,
the dark of Nirvana, but the nearer Christian dark of St. Francis
of Assisi. It is the reserved, oscillating presence of St. Francis in
Adams that explains the violence of his language about office
above; and it must be that in writing it Adams remembered his
violence, as it were, from another place, or even from several

places. It was St. Francis who said that all the structure of society was a pretense of the devil, and it had been Adams himself
who, twenty-five years before, had tried to understand and to
teach the understanding of society in terms of that very aspect
of his society which St. Francis most violently rejected—the complex of feudal and ecclesiastical law. In 1874, at Harvard College, Adams did not think with St. Francis; in 1899, whether
at Washington, Paris, or Rome, he could not think without St.
Francis' alternating from edge to center of his consciousness,
and could not see the law except as one more necessary form of
futility, like politics and religion; it was the difference "between
the twelfth century of his thirtieth and that of his sixtieth
years." But the point is, he still saw both the pressing vitality
and the expressed futility of society; it was the one that gave
poignancy to St. Francis and the other that showed aspiration to
society. Belief and unbelief had a relation of vertiginous reversal; but it was renewable reversal, not extinction. That is
why Adams inserted here his derisive epitaph on the sublime
truths of *Sac* and *Soc*, of justice and the profits of justice; it preserved the problem—a "single thread spun by the human spider"
—which the language about Hay and power had castigated, and
which the language of St. Francis would have anathematized:
the problem of the forces which actually moved men's minds.
"St. Francis expressed supreme contempt for them all, and
solved the whole problem by rejecting it altogether." This
Adams could not do—as the epitaph shows—but he was compelled to adopt St. Francis' rejection as a part of his own new
acceptance of the problem.

If, as it seemed, the contrasting halves of his reaction to society both had their origin in the twelfth century, then the
study—methodical survey—triangulation—of that century might
make up his last profession. That century might then be the
city of thought in which the pilgrimage—however belated, with
whatever penitence—of ignorance in silence might end. This
time he went alone, with neither nieces nor nephews nor friends,
and began to find in deliberate revival of a lost age a sense of
new life in his own. "In the long summer days one found a
sort of saturated green pleasure in the forests, and gray infinity
of rest in the little twelfth-century churches that lined them, as
unassuming as their own mosses, and as sure of their purpose as
their round arches." The accident of drift and the succession of

privation had become, by providing the sense of means, the course of purpose.

The reversal of drift and purpose, age to age, thought to thought, St. Francis to *Sac* and *Soc*, might be sharp, but had to have a medium, and no medium was so likely to show all the forms of reversal known, and to imply others yet unknown, as the experience of an artist in whom the movements of reversal were momentary, continuous, and simultaneous; and for that purpose the image and vignette of John La Farge was at hand and malleable to Adams' own art. The accidents were all apt. La Farge came to Paris at this time. He knew the great glass of the twelfth century and was himself master of a very different art in glass. With the Boer War for nexus he made a good foil to Whistler for the completion of Adams' studies in the types of human eccentricity which had begun with English examples in the Civil War. Thus, with these interests, he could serve to provide new commentary on the old subject of the sequence of intelligence and purpose in history, and could even, lastly, suggest by his own example the *kind* of new training needed for Adams' new purpose in the political world. If each "single thread spun by the human spider," taken separately, showed under stress as futile and broke, perhaps an aesthetic image which took all the threads together, as they were in life, might absorb and even make intelligible the complex of vitality—of instinct and need and restlessness—that made society immortal and fecund, despite the immorality of its history. La Farge was a proximate example of such an image.

Adams begins his rendering in sweeping scale by contrasting general American character with La Farge's special character. It hardly seems necessary to judge the accuracy of Adams' estimate of his friend. The semblance is more important than the verisimilitude. Only the imaginative existence of La Farge is here important; like the supersubtle small fry of Henry James, to Adams a supersubtle La Farge was necessary, and therefore he created him—very much as he had created Clarence King: in order to make actual life more intelligible. As Clarence King was what American minds should have been on early premises, John La Farge was what American minds might be. Both are ideals of possibility. Indeed, part of Adams' point was that he had no standard by which to measure his debt to the actual, processional complexity of La Farge's mind, and that he had therefore to look at it in contrast and together with something else—an act itself aesthetic and creative: making a fiction.

The contrast was simple. With La Farge's mind against it, the American mind seemed extremely uniform, a machine of logic and technical deployment as the English had labeled it in 1867. The American mind approached its object directly and made a direct assertion or a direct denial of fact about it: "all the time loudly asserting its unconventionality," it made a conventional approach, analysis, and conclusion. La Farge reversed all this; his approach was the avatar of indirectness that finds directness out, as Adams' images of description show:

He moved round an object, and never separated it from its surroundings; he prided himself on faithfulness to tradition and convention; he was never abrupt and abhorred dispute. . . . One was never quite sure of his whole meaning until too late to respond, for he had no difficulty in carrying different shades of contradiction in his mind. As he said of his friend Okakura, his thought ran as a stream runs through grass, hidden perhaps, but always there; and one felt often uncertain in what direction it flowed, for even a contradiction was to him only a shade of difference, a complementary color, about which no intelligent artist would dispute.

The distinction between the two forms of approach is radical and is of the one kind that sunders mind from mind in their efforts at communication. The one, serving neither the serpent nor the Golden Calf, having no conventions in the mind by deep agreement and disagreement, is all casual convention—all irritated fact—in the response; the other, having a mind constructed upon convention, is free for full response.

But Adams perhaps made a better figure than he was aware when he said that contradiction was to La Farge only a shade of difference; for it is by such an apprehension that the full sensibility creates, and by such that the listener or reader of good will responds. Yet Adams, when La Farge complained to him that he reasoned too much, had the corrective and inevitable answer: "The mind resorts to reason for want of training, and Adams had never met a perfectly trained mind." This sentence is almost the interchangeably required context for the notion that, when he was a young man in London, he had derived from Thurlow Weed's talk about politics: "Principles had better be left aside; values were enough." There is a twinning here, but of light and dark, not duplication; and if the two notions are taken as twinned—as separable and of different experience, but of the same gestation—they are central to all Adams' thought, are indeed the nether side of that thought, and make up the aesthetic foundation and criterion of it; and Adams' next step is to provide a concrete example with plain distinctions.

The subject is an old one in this work: eccentricity in its relation to intelligence. La Farge and Whistler on the Boer War at dinner make the example; but there is a preface which comments on La Farge's type of eccentricity, the type which marks the mind that runs like water through grass. "To La Farge, eccentricity meant convention; a mind really eccentric never betrayed it. True eccentricity was a tone—a shade—a *nuance*, and the finer the tone, the truer the eccentricity." La Farge's eccentricity, as was usual in the artist, was in his work: that is, in the alterations forced by perception and creation upon the conventions of sensibility. But Whistler, who had a great reputation as an unconventional or an eccentric, showed his eccentricity as a rage of platitude when he made his direct assault upon the world outside his art. "For two hours he declaimed against England—witty, declamatory, extravagant, bitter, amusing, and noisy; but in substance what he said was not merely commonplace—it was true!" Everybody agreed. "Yet La Farge was silent, and this difference of expression was a difference of art." Whistler had *nuance* in art, "but in talk he showed, above or below his color-instinct, a willingness to seem eccentric where no real eccentricity, unless perhaps of temper, existed." La Farge expressed his vehemence in his glass. In talk his mind "was opaline with infinite shades and refractions of light, and with color toned down to the finest gradations. In glass it was insubordinate; it was renaissance; it asserted his personal force with depth and vehemence of tone never before seen." So much for Adams' vignettes on styles of eccentricity in art and personality.

But note how Adams uses these distinctions: first, of course, for their own sake and as bright ornament; second, as aids to understanding the twelfth century; third, as an ironic foil to his own response to the Boer War; and fourth, as a part of his aesthetic image of eccentricity which as symbol combines the triple interest in the forces of mechanics, of intelligence, and of

imagination—that force outside either necessity or intention
which affects both. The first and second uses (the quality and
the accident) are self-evident. The third is clear if we look at
the language Adams himself uses on the Boer War, and the
third leads into the fourth. Most Americans were like Whistler;
their "hostility to England seemed mere temper; but to Adams
the war became almost a personal outrage. He had been taught
from childhood, even in England," that the American Revolution "had settled, once for all, the liberties of the British free
colonies." He objected to proving *again* that Washington and
John Adams were not felons. "He felt obliged to go even further,
and avow the opinion that if at any time England should take
towards Canada the position she took towards her Boer colonies,
the United States would be bound, by their record, to interpose,
and to insist on the application of the principles of 1776."
Adams' language is here official, like that of a State Paper by
his grandfather—his father—himself *manqué;* and among the
shades of contradiction involved lies perhaps the color sense of
his own eccentricity.

Thinking of the three men together, and thinking of principle
and value, reason and training, we may reach a proximate conclusion of the nature and practical uses of Adams' aesthetic of
eccentricity. La Farge's eccentricity was of perception, Whistler's of temper, and Adams', perhaps, of reason that expressed
some admixture of temper and perception. La Farge in glass ran
to insubordination, Whistler in life ran to the commonplace,
Adams in thought to principle, to summarized intelligence. La
Farge left out wholeness, Whistler actual perception, Adams—
did not know what he left out: perhaps action, perhaps the sense
of risk to values involved in action, perhaps the stupidity or
inertia which is an element in decision (since it chooses *against*
the other side). In all three, but particularly in Adams, the
eccentricity of intelligence—that is, the felt attraction of forces
conceived of as other than those in the recognized center—called
for a balancing eccentricity, in the lack of which the whole‘
policy, whether of statesman or man, must be vitiated and drift
until it founder. It is as if Adams in all this passage made a
double plea, both for the consideration of the unaccountable as
such and for a means of estimating, of mastering, of *accounting
for* the unaccountable in images or symbols; the eccentricities

of experience—its true *nuance*—pressed toward such images, and nowhere, for Adams, more inescapably than in politics.

And in politics there lay the immediate example of Hay in his relation to McKinley, the Senate, and the professional politicians. Adams saw that for Hay the chance "lay in patience and good-temper till the luck should turn," while for Adams himself there was the insistent extravagance of the crude contradiction between theory, or education, and fact, knowing all along that the machine had to be run regardless of the eccentricities of both theory and fact. One of the curiosities of the governmental machine was that it had to be run by non-professionals like Hay and Hewitt and Whitney against obstruction by the professionals; the eccentricity was that neither could exist without the impediment of the other: neither intelligence with high motive nor drift with no motive but immediate motion was enough. McKinley, who as much as any President until Harding represented the professionals, made the crucial nature of the relation plain by what Adams called pooling the interests of society under the management of non-professionals like Hay in the hope of efficiency at any cost; and the cost would be more than any President or his public could know.

Adams does not directly account the cost, except to suggest that it was less than the cost of the usual alternative remedy, chaos, but by context and implication the cost of pooling interests under the management of non-professionals and subject to the combined legislation and obstruction of the professionals would be sure to be felt in the reason and training of statesmen's minds and in the principles and values of society, and it as surely had to do with Adams' obsession that office was poison. There was loss and waste all round. In Hay's particular experience in the State Department, there was the cost abroad of the labor in overcoming power-politics and war; which was nothing compared to the cost at home of the incessant and futile labor of overcoming the Senate—or, more accurately, of overcoming one-third plus one of forty-nine or more Senators at any given sitting. That as few as seventeen Senators in an extreme case and never necessarily more than thirty-three in an ordinary case could overcome the will both of the Government and of the majority of the Senate transformed the ordinary waste of politics into the maximum example of government by eccentricity of temper—as if Whistler raging at a Paris dinner table were given the controlling voice on a treaty vote at the Capitol.

Thus Hay's trouble with the Senate was far graver than his trouble abroad; but are not both cases together an example of imbalance in eccentricity? That is, the one does not balance but rather provokes the other, so that in self-defense each asserts itself in the form of principle, whether the principle of national sovereignty or the principle of Constitutional check makes little difference, since each makes but a shade of contradiction to the other seen in relation to the masses of interest either can tilt. It is only that the eccentricity of the Senate is founded upon an obvious eccentricity in principle, which ought to be remediable, and not on an eccentricity of fundamental value, that made Adams turn his feelings about the Senate into a darling phobia. The point of failure lay clearly in the Constitutional provision of a two-thirds Senate majority for treaties. "The fathers had intended to neutralize the energy of government and had suc-ceeded, but their machine was never meant to do the work of a twenty-million horse-power society in the twentieth century, where much work needed to be quickly and efficiently done." With the shift in mass and velocity the principle of reason had grown to be the source of obstruction instead of an anchor of protection. The only excuse for not getting rid of the principle was the belief that Government must be obstructed lest it act badly, which if it applied applied to all society. But this Adams could not believe in face of proof that Government still did well what it was given to do beyond obstructions.

Thus Adams came back, as half his mind always did, to his sense of active politics and to his permanent, if interrupted, role of "stable-companion to statesmen"; and the other half reverted, as it always had since 1870, to the twelfth century and to his role of pilgrim of the imagination. In the new light that shines on every genuine return, the two roles seemed at some level not yet reached to be the same. He knew the waste of politics better than the twelfth century, and it was the older study. To relate the two studies would be somehow to achieve a single role. For this the historical system he had learned and taught in his youth was useless; no such system could either exhaust the vast com-plexities of knowledge in the two studies nor master the new energies that pressed upon the world of the twentieth century or the old energies of the twelfth century that no longer pressed except as they were re-created. He had therefore, as historian, to set up relations which acted like mathematical relations in that they covered his, or any man's, ignorance. The very hostility of such a notion to the old historical system was an excellent reason for trying it. It "swept his mind clear of knowledge" and so made up his mind: "For him the details of science meant nothing: he wanted to know its mass. . . . History had no use for multiplicity; it needed unity; it could study only motion, direction, attraction, relation. Everything must be made to move together."

Such was Henry Adams' harvest at Indian Summer: a final flare-up of purpose achieved by turning memory into the new colors of expectation, but secured no less than memory had ever been in the play of forces through daily life. He had made thus a recapitulation which was also a reaccommodation but he had not done so simply—by giving in, but complexly—by discovering, in the act of perception, that "everything had to be made to move together," so that he had to create, if not an ideal, at least a policy for the play of mind. For to achieve assent to one's society it is necessary to see what it is possible to make out of the forces that activate that society as well as what they make out of themselves. There is an energy as well as an inertia of the mind, a sense of steerage as well as drift. Thus to accept sequence as it shows is not assent but surrender. The impulse to create is involved in the effort at assent, and creation is the underlying form of leadership. The leadership—the teaching— the revolution—that comes from assent is effective precisely insofar as it both transmits and creates images of the ideal in the medium of the actual, the image behind and the image ahead.

That is what things in Adams' book of Education realize themselves at this point as struggling to do: to make everything move together. What was in the beginning a simple tale with several themes, becomes several tales struggling to assert through its images a single theme. It is not that there are several subjects and many distractions which one relates, but that there are many lives and many attractions which one must make into a dominant theme: an effort of which one must suffer the failure. In this respect the individual man is like his whole society, and his society is like him: the effort, and the suffering, can only be made in the great aesthetic images which are the presiding, but inevitably changing, weather of the living culture. Weather is the mystery of climate, which, however we may calculate and map it, we only understand by exposure to it, whether rock or man. There is no truer saying than that all we grow is at the mercy of the weather.

CHAPTER EIGHT

Lancelot on Knife's Edge

Yet the mind cannot—and Adams' mind most evidently could not—help mapping and calculating what it can, for projection and memory, so that it will neither lose nor fail to risk those images it once had or those that remain to be discovered. No mind can be aware of all the currents of its own reaction at once —or, as Adams might have put it, no mind can be so well trained as to be free of the reminding power of logical forms. Maps and mathematics are serviceable reminders that action is necessary short of understanding, just as images and symbols are necessary reminders that even an imperfect understanding touches matters that can neither be mapped nor summed. There is always a recurring point in the mind's motion where logic and image are seen as reversible frail gestures—neither less wayward than the other—that can take validity only from some source outside the scope of either. It was Adams' recurrent actual awareness of the adventure in such reversals that gave his mind momentous power, and it was the momentum of this power that made him peculiarly susceptible to fresh experiences of the unknown outside force; it was this momentum that carried him to his double image of the Virgin and the Dynamo—to the force of symbol and the symbol of force—and made him see himself crawling on the knife's edge between two reversible worlds.

Though twenty years had passed since the writing of *Democracy* and *Esther*, and the sense of motive had richened, the path

was the same in the *Chartres* and the *Education*, and this central
place to which we have now come in the *Education* (Chapters
25 through 29) should show how deep the path was worn.
The two dramas—of man against the society with which he
struggles and which he tries to control, and of man against
the society, or God, or outside force, from which he draws
strength—have for the moment become one. Adams, as he began to feel the fullness of his return, struck a temporary balance
between the eccentricity of what he meant by the Dynamo in
the twentieth century and the eccentricity of what he meant by
the Virgin in the twelfth. The balance was of course not fixed
but shifting: like that of the body in motion, its fulcrum was
invisible, was itself a shifting point on which balancing relations were established and changed, changed and established,
with the succession of challenge, shock, and reaction. We can
see what was balanced if not how the balance was secured, by
merely running over in quick count the chapter titles and the
principal images that come under each of them.

There is first "The Dynamo and the Virgin" in which, as
the general head for the whole group, both are seen as symbols
for occult force, in which both are seen as objects of pilgrimage
for a Lancelot of either age, and in which, under the instigation
of Saint-Gaudens, what is common to the Virgin and Venus
her prototype is seen together; all as of the year 1900. Next
comes "Twilight," which is inhabited by such contrasts as the
value of a Ming vase and the principle of universal war, an
outworn political system and new social energies—which are
followed by the necessary notion of an outside force promoting
and solving both contrasts. *"Teufelsdröckh"* naturally pairs
with "Twilight" (both are dated 1901) as one pairs the area
where illusions are made with the area where the clothes of
illusion—in this case the clothes of energy—are stripped off:
here unity is seen as chaos, and the vast movement of inertia
as typified by Russia is compared with the movement of intensity as typified by the United States. To these are added a
second pair, dated 1902, "The Height of Knowledge" and "The
Abyss of Ignorance," of which the first exhibits man as inadequate to the power, whether of intensity or of inertia, committed
to him by society, and of which the second presents man first as
a victim of the mystery of force, not only of mechanical force
but of force seen as *ennui* or restlessness, and also of lines of

force as direction or movement of will, and then finally, by a brilliant intuition of reversal, makes an image of the Psyche or Thought personified, as itself a force. The movement of the five chapters is thus continuous—as if circular—along the three sides of a triangle, with each angle representing the juncture of two contrasted conceptions of force, the Dynamo and the Virgin, the human machine and its energies, and lastly the human animal and his own force, where at the limit of the third leg of the triangle the end is identified with the beginning of the motion. The force of thought, the trope of Psyche, is itself the outside force, like the Dynamo or the Virgin, and as occult as either. But it is an identity only by dialectic, by reversal, by experience; and the question is how to translate an ambiguity into an ambivalence. If thought is itself the force that moves us, how shall it learn to control itself in its own interests? To which of its two chief autonomous creations—the Virgin and the Dynamo are their symbols—does it bear more the relation known as allegiance? If to both, how then shall the two be united in the third? How can man equal his force in his work?

These are the labors of triangulation and their consequent questions to which Adams came at the climax of his return from exile, and to answer the last question was the task to which he found himself—by the force of his own thought—committed. It was for this that he found he must educate himself over and over to that pitch where the process of education is itself its use; which was why when he came to give an account of himself he called the result the Education of Henry Adams.

But the process continued as dramatic and various and cumulative, so that for its values to guarantee its principles it needs to be explored in its more prominent details; and of these the first is the detail of association clustered around the Great Exposition of 1900 at Paris. Like the Exposition at Chicago, the general impression was chaos, the science unintelligible, the art retrograde, the history either eccentric or dubious, and only the Midway Plaisance plain. But unlike Chicago, which was supposed to make a new leap, Paris represented a continuity: it celebrated the end of nineteen centuries of Christendom, it brought together in one fair all that Europe and America could show in one year at one place, and it marked the beginning of a new century—a new distribution and a new concentration and a new economy of forces; and it did all this, in a sense that

Chicago did not, within the sight and living zone of the great monuments of another effort at the economy of mind which had reached its crisis some seven centuries earlier. The old effort was marked by the cathedrals and churches of the Virgin, by the city of Paris itself with its Saints of the Crusades and its stranger Saints of the Schools. The new effort was marked by the great hall of forty-foot dynamos. Both represented efforts at an economy of force which added to the power of society without adding equally to society's control over the forces it used; each gained its power through the invention of a mechanism for the transmission of occult force—the one biological and religious, the other physical and abstract, from one form to another more available, but no less mysterious, form. The greatness of the Exposition to Adams (as he tells us in the *Education*) was that one mystery not only reminded him of the other but fairly demanded the other, as the left foot demands the right in walking.

To Samuel Pierpont Langley of the airships and the Smithsonian, the dynamo was a motor which was also a channel for converting the heat in coal into electricity; it was a development and economy of force. To Adams the dynamo was also a symbol of infinity, in its remoteness from the coal or water that gave it vertiginous speed and quiet power; therefore, like the Cross, it was a moral force, and prayer was the natural expression before it: the value was in the *occult* mechanism between steam and electric current, between Cross and cathedral. "The forces were interchangeable if not reversible, but he could see only an absolute *fiat* in electricity as in faith"; and if the dynamo were not enough, there were the new rays— or radiations—of the salts of radium, which were wholly new and were therefore anarchic in the absoluteness of *fiat*. That is, the new forces which men so rapidly developed and economized had no equivalent in any existing scale of measure. Man "had entered a supersensual world, in which he could measure nothing except by chance collisions of movements imperceptible to his senses, perhaps even imperceptible to his instruments, but perceptible to each other, and so to some known ray at the end of the scale."

Resuming for the moment his old role of historian, Adams reflected once more that in all the old assumptions about sequence of cause and effect, the unit or standard of measure had been accepted unconsciously and had, when examined, turned out either groundless or incongruous; yet history depended on intelligible sequence and acceptable scale. As historian Adams resolved, therefore, under the impact of two supersensual worlds—the Dynamo and the Virgin—to try the sequence of force: "He insisted on a relation of sequence, and if he could not reach it by one method, he would try as many methods as science knew." Taken as force, the nearest equivalent to the radium or dynamo of 1900 was the Cross of Constantine in 310. Both forces were occult, supersensual and irrational; they did not follow, but they affected the modes of man's thought; they were in Scholastic language "immediate modes of divine substance"—whatever that substance might be; and the second seemed as likely as the first to make a creative revolution in the actual world; that is, in the daylight, sensible, rational half of man's mind. Thus, in making his sequence, he had to treat the rays of radium as the fourth century had treated the Cross—that is, as they had been felt: as attractions on thought; and, for the same reason, he had to treat the Cross as a felt radiation of physical force. To establish the relation between the terms of his sequence, he would "risk translating rays into faith."

The extremity of imaginative risk in Adams' resolve—the risk of *hubris*, of the fatally arrogant and fundamentally unseemly deed—becomes plain when he reveals the second move to which he was impelled. Adams had to choose, as couplet to radium and dynamo, not the Cross but that other version of force which, as Venus, had (so to speak) skipped the Cross and come to rest in the Virgin, and which the Cross had represented partly by contrast, by abstraction and at a remove. What had been felt in the Cross was dead along with its forms; but what was represented by Venus and the Virgin as forms of faith, was still felt, however unconsciously, and whether or not the forms—or, as Adams put it, the women—were dead. So, too, the force of the rays had always been felt, though the symbols through which the feeling became conscious had only just been discovered. No wonder he called this the most hazardous of all educations, with the hazard as great if he slipped either way in estimating the values of his sequence. "The knife-edge along which he must crawl, like Sir Lancelot in the twelfth century, divided two kingdoms of force which had nothing in common but attraction."

It had been Chrétien de Troyes who first told that part of Lancelot's perilous search. As one of his feats in the rescue of Guinevere, Sir Lancelot had to cross a bridge made of a sword as sharp as a scythe, which he did barehanded and barefoot, badly cutting himself, but couraged by love to the sticking point. This was the greatest single hazard that Lancelot had to take, and was so announced to him on every hand: if he crossed that bridge and lived, his whole enterprise would be eventually successful. The general effect in Chrétien's context is that the hazard of the bridge is divine—a concrete anticipation of Pascal's *Divin Hasard*—or at any rate somehow supernatural; no more or less perilous than the human hazards of treachery and battle and lust, it was more significant and more serious. Its risk, like that of Tannhäuser, perhaps combined the values of Venus and Virgin; values which in Lancelot's time, though they were felt and served together by the necessities of the imagination, must have seemed as perilous to combine as to Adams it was to combine, in order to make either intelligible, Venus and Virgin on one hand and the Dynamo on the other.

Adams on his "knife-edge" made progress question by cutting question, and the questions were cries, and the cries the same cry differently voiced as the pilgrim winced in a deeper or a different place, till it seemed that the cry alone kept him in bare balance. What had happened to men and women in America, that though they moved by sex, they did not feel what moved them as a force but only as a waste or scandal of force? "The force of the Virgin was still felt at Lourdes, and seemed to be as potent as X-rays; but in America neither Venus nor Virgin ever had value as force—at most as sentiment. No American had ever been truly afraid of either." For two pages Adams went on to ask why America and American women have been ashamed of sex, seeing in it sin and weakness, never strength, fecundity, the animated dynamo, the greatest and most mysterious of all energies. Sex was "the highest energy ever known to man, the creator of four-fifths of his noblest art, exercising vastly more attraction over the human mind than all the steam-engines and dynamos ever dreamed of; and yet this energy was unknown to the American mind. An American

Virgin would never dare command; an American Venus would never dare exist."

To emphasize by contrast how both Venus and Virgin had been felt as force, Adams quotes from Lucretius and Dante. From the former's *On the Nature of Things* he takes the twenty-first line of the first book, underlining one word: "Quae quoniam rerum naturam *sola* gubernas," to which, because they were so apt to his own case, he might well have added the next four lines. In the Loeb translation these lines read as follows: "Since therefore thou alone dost govern the nature of things, since without thee nothing comes forth into the shining borders of light, nothing joyous and lovely is made, thee I crave as partner in writing the verses, which I essay to fashion touching the Nature of Things." It was to bring things into the shining borders of light that Adams, like Lucretius, invoked the radiant force of Venus and, like Dante, of the Virgin. From the *Paradiso* he takes the tercet beginning with the thirteenth line of the thirty-third Canto; in the English of the Temple Classics, these lines cap the lines to Venus: "Lady, thou art so great and hast such worth that if there be any who would have grace yet betaketh not himself to thee, his longing seeketh to fly without wings"; for Adams knew beyond anything that his longing for grace needed wings to fly. In short, he was making the poet's invocations his own.

This sense of personal invocation Adams expresses lightly, in passing, and by means of a rather curious figure. "Before this historical chasm, a mind like that of Adams felt itself helpless; he turned from the Virgin to the Dynamo as though he were a Branly coherer"—an instrument which he had previously suggested had an absolute value incapable of expression in a mathematical equivalent. According to the textbooks a Branly coherer is one of the most sensitive detectors of electric currents and operates on the principle that the resistance of loose metallic contacts is diminished when struck by electric currents, as one might say that a facial expression eases at the coming of a thought waited for, or that—and this was Adams' case—the mind relaxes as it helplessly accepts the forces it feels coursing through it as thought.

But relaxation is preface to new tension, in which every muscle in the mind cries *Help, help!* The Virgin had been above all a creature of that cry; she gave the help of understanding and worship and piety to the force she represented, both in her role of Venus, the mother of men, and in her heavenly role of Mother of God and men's thoughts; she had been the idea of men's actions. Yet in America the idea survived only as art—and in Whitman only—or as sentiment, never as force. "American art, like the American language and American education, was as far as possible sexless. Society regarded this victory over sex as its greatest triumph." With Augustus Saint-Gaudens, who, being an American artist and in Paris, like Adams himself, for the Great Exposition of the development and economy of force, Adams went to the Virgin's cathedral at Amiens, to see what would happen. It was at once plain that "the art remained, but the energy was lost even upon the artist."

Saint-Gaudens began to seem to Adams one more in the long train of figures—Garibaldi, Grant, Cameron—who, because they represented blind and inarticulate energy and still did the work of the world, made insoluble the relation between intelligence and inertia. Where the previous figures had been men of affairs, Saint-Gaudens was an artist; like the others he was pure act, but his act was an act of taste. "He could not imitate, or give any form but his own to the creations of his hand." Although "no one felt more strongly than he the strength of other men, . . . the idea that they could affect him never stirred an image in his mind." Adams thought of Gibbon, who in his own phrase "darted a contemptuous look on the stately monuments of superstition," and reminded himself that Gibbon brought on the French Revolution; and he thought of Ruskin, who had lectured on the same monuments in reaction against the Revolution. "One sees what one brings." Saint-Gaudens brought himself and admired the monuments as taste, the art apart from what had compelled its existence. Saint-Gaudens had lost, not his strength, but his knowledge of its source. "He writhed and cursed at his ignorance, much as Adams did at his own, but in the opposite sense. Saint-Gaudens was a child of Benvenuto Cellini, smothered in an American cradle. Adams was a quintessence of Boston, devoured by curiosity to think like Benvenuto. Saint-Gaudens's art was starved from birth, and Adams's instinct was blighted from babyhood. Each had but half of a nature, and when they came together before the Virgin of Amiens they ought both to have felt in

her the force that made them one; but it was not so. To Adams
she became more than ever a channel of force; to Saint-Gaudens
she remained as before a channel of taste."

Here again Adams had a private source for his conclusion:
a feeling which, when examined, proved unaccountable and
so could not directly be put in the context, but a feeling the
eddying quality of which is roused in the echoes of the context.
May not that quality transpire if it is remembered that all the
relation between Saint-Gaudens and Adams over the monument
in Rock Creek showed Adams as in an unusually creative position and Saint-Gaudens in an unusually plastic position, and
that Adams afterward referred to the monument as "my creation" of the Virgin? With such considerations tacitly framing
his mind, Adams, in the *Education*, merely remarks that Saint-
Gaudens instinctively took the horse as the channel of power,
adding: "The attitude was so American that, for at least forty
years, Adams had never realized that any other could be in
sound taste." But it was not only that the American naturally
translated his notion of power into horsepower, but that the
instinct that led him to do so was faulty: it kept him from making live images of the steam and electric power with which he
was really concerned, or at least it lighted up his inability to
do so. To conceive twentieth-century man as on a horse was
as fatal as conceiving him a king: it was an outmoded and
blinkered role, except socially; or, to make the best of it, it
made a lesser power pass in symbol for a major. Yet Saint-
Gaudens, or the American, was not alone; Matthew Arnold at
the Grande Chartreuse was no better. "Neither of them felt
goddesses as power—only as reflected emotion, human expression, beauty, purity, taste, scarcely even as sympathy." Arnold
and Saint-Gaudens were precisely, as Adams had been when
he wrote his novels but was no longer, "wandering between
two worlds, the one dead, the other powerless to be born"; and
the difference between them and Adams lay in Adams' effort
to *feel* both Virgin and Dynamo as one force. The effort of
feeling is aesthetic.

To Adams it had become a necessity of mind that these forces
acted interchangeably on men, and it was to him a fact that "by
action on man all known force may be measured"—and the
force was measured in symbol. More important: "The symbol

was force, as a compass-needle or a triangle was force, as the
mechanist might prove by losing it, and nothing could be
gained by ignoring their value. Symbol or energy, the Virgin
had acted as the greatest force the Western world ever felt, and
had drawn man's activities to herself more strongly than any
other power, natural or supernatural, had ever done; the
historian's business was to follow the track of the energy; to
find where it came from and where it went to . . . its values,
equivalents, conversions." So, once more, Adams laid out his
work.

That symbol was force is a conception plain to him who first
sees a watch or is first wounded by a gun; it is also plain enough
to those who have a disposition to create new symbols; but to
those merely familiar the force may seem watered and the
symbol sickly. The question is how far we can say that the
mariner's compass is not only a symbol but itself the force that
opened up the overseas world. It is the question whether radium
is the symbol, or itself the force, of matter breaking down—
of which the process permits (and is itself identical with)
work to be done, change to occur, life to happen. It is the question whether the triangle (as the model or armature of an
enclosed area) is the symbol or itself the force that permits
the management of plane surfaces. Or it is the question—to
take a more nearly irrational abstraction—whether π is the
symbol or itself the force that permits the management of
curved surfaces, and so on.

All these images of the mind have complexities and con-
vertibilities and shifting channels as they symbolize or perform
work. So does the Virgin. All might work on man, but none
would perform man's work without their symbolic form;
neither help nor heal is possible without the image of intent.
That is, in both sets of cases, the energies at work are occult,
can be tapped only through symbolic form, and can be tested
only through a kind of imaginative empiricism, a kind of spiritual pragmatism. The degree of imagination or spirit at which
one feels one's expression change—a new look come into the
eyes, or an old waver—is the standard of understanding. The
degree of experience or practice at which the felt expression
becomes a skill in the fingers is the test of truth. If these stipu-
lations seem uncertain, it is at any rate certain that neither

mere articulateness—the open formula, nor mere inarticulate-
ness—the stress of blind intuition, is a satisfactory test of any
relation in the realm of the occult. Only the shifting clusters
of unaccountable meanings which attach themselves to what
we call the symbols of that relation give them vitality and
resourcefulness. Thus the symbol almost always expresses more
force than it seems to, and commands rather less than it pretends to; so that when one is actually setting up relations
between symbols, or between symbols and the forces they express, one had better both look for more than appears and cut
down on practical expectations: as in love or the atom.

In the effort of relating radiant powers which had occult
sources—the effort of translating rays into faith—all these questions and considerations raised themselves and made a kind of
general motion in Adams' mind which drove him to depend
more and more upon the Virgin for each point of departure
and termination. The Virgin, of all available symbols of radiant energy, had both the richest cluster of unaccountables
and the most familiar attributes; she attracted the mind most
and stirred most responses; she was the most human; therefore
she seemed easiest to handle; because one could bring more to
see her with, one could feel more surely the force she represented. To find an equivalent symbol in the dynamo required
an equivalent state of awareness, a congruous sense of the unaccountable and a comparable sense of the familiar. Being inhuman, the dynamo offered little help.

Reaching some such conclusion, Adams fell back on those
modes of the mind which had created, or discovered, the symbolic force of the Virgin—that is, those aesthetic modes which
may include even the most abstract algebra among their means
to the concrete and their avenues to the occult, just as they
insist that the most concrete or dramatic images, once they are
put in motion, force themselves into the abstract. These are
the modes that seize an identity and feel an energy; it is not
the means that count, when they are the means of science, but
the dominance of the mode whereby the value rather than the
development and economy of energy is seen. To the impasse of
the Dynamo and the Virgin, the aesthetic image is Adams' offered solution, and it is offered because the aesthetic image is
itself a force—unaccountable, occult, wayward; but also instinc-

tive, immediate, and familiar, in long good standing. "In such labyrinths," Adams begins his commitment to the aesthetic modes,

the staff is a force almost more necessary than the legs; the pen becomes a sort of blind-man's dog, to keep him from falling into the gutters. The pen works for itself, and acts like a hand, modelling the plastic material over and over again to the form that suits it best. The form is never arbitrary, but is a sort of growth like crystallization, as any artist knows too well; for often the pencil or pen runs into side-paths and shapelessness, loses its relations, stops or is bogged. Then it has to return on its trail, and recover, if it can, its lines of force. The result of a year's work depends more on what is struck out than on what is left in; on the sequence of the main lines of thought, than on their play or variety.

There is a kind of deep pluralism in this paragraph, a reversal of values and principles, a dialectic, in the Hegelian sense, of mind and theme, which issues in a quivering shapelessness that is the critical point in any invoked metamorphosis from one phase of thought to another. It asks the question: Does the mind bring itself to its theme or does the theme absorb the mind? Do the helps to which the mind resorts—its currents of algebra and its formularies of emotion—transform the theme or the mind? Does one write what one wills, or does one write to discover—to see and feel its crystallization—the will to which one must assent?

The answers, like the questions, are all double, and if choice is cast either way it only makes the duplicity deeper. But Adams was not trying to give answers, and he was only implying the questions: he was exemplifying the process by which he wrote and the idiosyncrasy of the special difficulties with which he had to cope. The process had to involve a good deal of ad-libbing, of trial and trial and subsequent discord, because the symbols or forces he was trying to triangulate exerted pressures which could not be articulated by any means short of crystallization—by unforeseeable, precipitated growth. The process, the difficulties and the growth become plain enough if a *résumé* is made of the chapter which the passage quoted concludes. The essence of the chapter lies in the phrase, *Symbol was force*, and its exegesis is when it is crystallized with that other phrase, *One sees what one brings*. Langley and the Dynamo, Gibbon, Saint-Gaudens and Amiens Cathedral, the notion of symbol and the notion of style, are the whole story. Lodgment is secured by the opposition of Lucretius and Dante (Venus and Virgin) to sex in American society, with the extension in which the idea of sex is seen as surviving only as art, and the art surviving only as taste.

When what has been felt as a primary force and cultivated as a symbol comes to be felt only as art and cultivated only as taste, then, by so much, have the values of life lost their edges in settling twilight. If some such course had been run in the treatment of sex as a force, what had happened to the treatment of other forces and to the values that clustered about them? Adams, being in Paris when the Boxer Rebellion broke out, found that history and society combined to show that even in the City of Light twilight was settling in, and he had only to use the standards of those parts of society which still effectively held power to find images to measure the shift of light. If standards were of price, a picture by Sir Joshua or a chair once sat in by Mme de Pompadour was the peak of interest. "Society seemed to delight in talking with solemn conviction about serious values, and in paying fantastic prices for nothing but the most futile." Though the struggle over China seemed in 1900 as once again in 1945 to involve control of the world, "the value of a Ming vase was more serious than universal war." Thus Adams repeated the judgment forced upon him thirty years before when English duchesses fawned upon the red capote of Garibaldi and the nobility of both sexes could only crane like boors in response to the beauty of Mme de Castiglione and together made up Motley's idea of the Perfection of Human Society.

But in repetition judgment took in more territory and made satire sharper. It suggested that society had become sure only of its arbitrary or gamy values, which are the elements of an arbitrary style, and that the symbolism of bric-à-brac is mutilating: representing pure restlessness and excluding creativeness. Society that behaves like a museum is indifferent to the present and contemptuous of the future. Decorative values when made dominant preclude desperate values. Porcelain is surest when its source is forgotten. The Rosary can replace the Rose, and does, whenever serious attention flags.

Adams does not connect social and political values but he puts them side by side; to the value of the Ming vase in Paris

he adds the values estimated in the European chancelleries
and the American State Department. Here the point is that men
seemed to know their way no better in politics than in physics
or sex even when, unlike their social friends, they had to act and
to invite action: the ignorance and the need to know were as
great in one field as another. What perhaps made the example
more instructive was that it gave America occasion to show its
new strength in its initial imposition of Hay's Open Door policy.
That it was more strength than insight showed in the quick
collapse of the Door under the combined impact of European
greed and Senatorial obstruction at home. The symbolism behind the Door was weak and afforded no means to look either
through or ahead. There Adams drew his lesson. Practical men
saw no further ahead than the next election; corporations sometimes saw ten years; the historian—and particularly the historian Adams—ought to look forward fifty years. "His object is
to triangulate from the widest possible base to the furthest point
he thinks he can see, which is always far beyond the curvature
of the horizon." But if he tries to do so he finds himself in a
new form of twilight: "his walk soon becomes solitary, leading
further into a wilderness where twilight is short and shadows
are dense."

This new twilight was the oldest of all, the twilight of the
gods and of human catastrophe; and Adams was alone neither
in walking through it nor in the means he took to protect himself from it. He had the company of Hay, who staggered, and
King, who dropped in illness. All three friends played stoic, not
because they believed in the role but because they had been
taught to assume it; because, also, penitence was a sort of impertinence, and because by pretending not to care each could
feel intensely what he cared for most. All his life, stoicism had
been to Adams an obsession: a boy's pride, a man's will, a
prison and a refuge, an incentive and an aggravation. Marcus
Aurelius seemed to him sometimes a hero because of his stoicism, sometimes stoicism seemed moral suicide. At best it was
an alternative to values not bearable, at worst it denied life by
obliterating the sense of what had given life meaning. Here,
thinking of the three friends in their last twilight playing
stoic as it were for love of each other, Adams made the bitterest
judgment of all: "The affectation of readiness for death is a

stage rôle, and stoicism is a stupid resource, though the only one. *Non dolet, Paete!* One is ashamed of it even in the acting."

Here as with the aged Tannhäuser and wrinkled Venus the fury in the words is in excess of their apparent context. There is a reversal in it, too: where as a younger man projecting life he had thought of his grandfather and quoted Horace—*Impavidum ferient ruinae*—as an older man he thought of something unaccountable and quoted the third Epistle of Pliny the Younger with a background in the thirteenth Epigram in the first book of Martial: *Non dolet, Paete!*

But the context needs to be redeemed. Paetus having been ordered to kill himself because of cowardice is shamed by his wife Arria who, after stabbing herself, holds out the knife to him with the cry: "It does not hurt, my Paetus!" So in Pliny; in Martial the fable is more bitter still. "When chaste Arria was offering to her Paetus that sword which with her own hand she had drawn from out her breast: 'If thou believest me,' she said, 'the wound I have inflicted has no smart; but the wound thou shalt inflict—this, for me, Paetus, has the smart.' " The distinction in "smart" seems plain enough; to a man of Adams' sensibility, Arria's self-willed act was a kind of full response, while that of Paetus was forced by shame and as near as possible a stage-act devoid of moral content: either an affectation or moral suicide or both. *"Non dolet, Paete!* One is ashamed of it even in the acting."

The reference was classical, but the memory welling in Adams both in the act of 1901 when King disappeared and in the act of writing four years later was of his wife as well as of King. The whole passage exemplifies one of the recurrent shocks—the rebirth of an old shock in a new and inevitable shock—by which Adams finds himself driven to greater effort. King goes west to die, the prairie darkens: the old pursuit is the only pursuit: of some light at the end of the passage: of the lighted cabin in mountain night: "the last and only log cabin left in life" where he might again fall into the arms of King: King the Avatar. "Time had become terribly short, and the sense of knowing so little when others knew so much, crushed out hope."

Out of the old stoicism and its new transcendence came a kind of restless ripeness that had to itch until it burst. The

triple sense of helplessness, urgency, and attraction that inhabited him during the time of waiting, he made into an image of
the mystery of magnets—as he saw them competing on his desk
and as he felt them competing in history. They represented
lines of force as old as gravitation and as contradictory and
as unknown; yet they had suggested no idea—had never raised
the intensity of their force beyond that of a toy—until someone
conceived the mariner's compass sometime between the middle
of the thirteenth and the middle of the fourteenth century. But
even the magnet as compass did not become reliably accurate
until Lord Kelvin's time, when it had begun its new career as
a "pump, supply-pipe, sieve, or reservoir for collecting electricity."

That the development of the magnet had been for so long
so slow and equally that it had suddenly become so rapid, and
that neither rate of movement was changed except by the
accident of new reaction, brought Adams up on man's fundamental squirming ignorance: the helplessness of mind before
the commonest forces. Thus "he could imagine no reason why
society should treat radium as revolutionary in science when
every infant, for ages past, had seen the magnet doing what
radium did; for surely the kind of radiation mattered nothing
compared with the energy that radiated and the matter supplied for radiation. . . . He figured the human mind itself as
another radiating matter through which man had always
pumped a subtler fluid." It was Adams' itch to estimate the
force of that fluid; and whether he had to do so by translating
rays into faith or faith into rays was the urgent question; for
in making either translation there was a reversal not only
of one's own thought but of thought itself. What made for
helplessness was that by the tradition of the Western mind
choice was cast in a simple opposition either pole of which
was untenable to a mind sensitive enough to feel the attraction
of the other.

The magnets were supposed to remove the question from
personal sensitivity, and so they might have done in their
original form of lodestone or in their earlier development as
mariner's compass; for then they stood for unity of position or
direction or attraction; but in its new development as dynamo,
the magnet "staggered his new education by its evidence of
growing complexity, and multiplicity, and even contradiction,

in life." The physical symbol of unity became in fact a symbol of complexity the moment it developed new powers. In politics as in science the powers were running ahead of choice, and choice was beyond control. Henry Adams felt as if he were still Adam "between God who was unity, and Satan who was complexity, with no means of deciding which was truth." That he could see President McKinley as Adam and the Senate as Satan was no help in seeing God in any form, which was what Adam and Satan required. In the past the sight of God had always proved to be the sight of unity, but unity was now a multiplicity beyond the power of the mind to *see* as unity.

The question becomes sharp as to Lancelot on knife's edge. Was unity then a condition of mind?—a limit of approach? "Maundering among the magnets" whose lines of force he could not see as one, Adams reread the piece on Lyell with which he had begun his intellectual career and concluded that unity belonged to the young; the old tended to see multiplicity. It was another case of the difference, in Adams, between the attitude of *Impavidum ferient ruinae* and *Non dolet, Paete!* The difference was not in substance but in the degree of self-consciousness, was between an integrated and a relatively disintegrating response. "Unity is vision; it must have been part of the process of learning to see. The older the mind, the older its complexities, and the further it looks, the more it sees, until even the stars resolve themselves into multiples; yet the child will always see but one." How then, under what conditions of mind, could unity again be achieved?

Once again *Pteraspis*, the unchangeable and uniform, is introduced, but this time with a new attribute, as if to represent a new agency or at least an element of self-contradiction. It is called here the ganoid fish—bright-scaled, enameled, nacreous —a fish covered with pearl, a creature which, though itself unchanging, takes fresh energy, or pearliness, from outside. So attributed, the ganoid fish *Pteraspis* is used as an incentive for a fresh adventure of the mind in the long labor of conceiving itself. Adams "wished to be shown that changes in form caused evolution in force; that chemical or mechanical energy had by natural selection and minute changes, under uniform conditions, converted itself into thought. The ganoid fish seemed to prove—to him—that it selected neither new form nor new force, but that the curates were right in thinking that force could be increased in volume or raised in intensity only by help of outside force."

The curates were right. Geology was in the same predicament as religion and reacted in about the same way: being unable to encompass either its source or its direction, requiring some source and conscious of many directions, it divided in heresies that had in common only dogmas that asserted ignorance. "In thought the Schools, like the Church, raised ignorance to a faith and degraded dogma to heresy. . . . Evolution was becoming change of form broken by freaks of force, and warped at times by attractions affecting intelligence, twisted and tortured at other times by sheer violence." As pantheism had been the logical consequence of the Schools of the Church, anarchy was the logical consequence of the Schools of Science. The remedy proposed was a larger synthesis. But to Adams as an historian the larger synthesis was, like stoicism, a form of suicide: a confession of inability to react. To him the curates were right. "Politics and geology pointed alike to the larger synthesis of rapidly increasing complexity," but to react to it required a change of intensity in the mind that did the reacting. The mind itself, if it could not see the complexity, might yet raise itself to feel the forces, new and old, that underlay the complexity and made them one. Though the forces already existed, they would, in the sense that the curates were right, be felt as new forces imposed from outside; as the mind feels always at its height of work that it draws on power not its own but its object.

The nature of the change in intensity required was of course not new, but only the use to which it was put, and even that was less new than out of fashion. Adams expresses it by indirection, and what he says comes to a plea that the mind use the powers of reaction it does not know that it has, upon the knowledge that it does not know that it knows: in short, a plea for the perfectly trained mind. "Any student, of any age, thinking only of a thought and not of his thought, should delight in turning about and trying the opposite motion, as he delights in the spring which brings even to a tired and irritated statesman the larger synthesis of peach-blooms, cherry-blossoms, and dogwood, to prove the folly of fret."

The language is lyric and of the essence, a plea for evolution of the mind by play within itself, to which the alternative was only the necessary opposite: "to begin afresh with the *Limulus* and *Lepidosteus* in the waters of Braintree, side by side with Adamses and Quincys and Harvard College, all unchanged and unchangeable since archaic time." But "what purpose would it serve? A seeker of truth—or illusion—would be none the less restless, though a shark!" The alternative might be desirable, and to most minds at the end of the tether was the natural slackening; but to Adams, "devoured by curiosity to think like Benvenuto," it could be only an alternative, one more inconsequence of the Boston mind, and so could be most the added incentive of temptation summoned in order to be met. The shark was a pearly fish, the Psyche within; and Adams had to go on, in effort after effort till effort was single, to make his mind delight in turning about.

The most complete turning which Adams ever made, and which gave him perhaps the most delight, was that in which he inverted the instinct for order that leads men to make syntheses into the instinct for, or insight into, the anarchy that results from syntheses. In making his inversion, he worked on the theory that if a larger synthesis is only large enough, it *is* chaos, unity *is* anarchy; and he called his theory Conservative Christian Anarchy. The reader may take the theory at any level that suits his habits of mental play, but he will get most out of it by playing with it in suspense, to see, as Adams did, what profit in values it might yield as a venture of the mind which has just left the twilight of taste and is about to enter the twilight of the Gods. If the Ming vase or Mme de Pompadour's chair stood in practice for universal order in a world verging on universal war, and if the scientists broke up the order of their world for the sake of larger and larger syntheses, so that statesmen and scientists alike found themselves either helpless or irresponsible, then surely no extravagance which, even if only for contrast, combined conservatism, Christianity, and anarchy could produce a more frivolous illusion. The combination might even, by irony, produce a relation which touched truth, and smarted.

The Paris of the summer of 1901, the music of Wagner, and the society of the two poets Trumbull Stickney and George Cabot Lodge, together touched off the adventure. Paris was for Adams, now that he had rediscovered the Middle Ages, the supreme teacher for variety of direction and energy of mind, and was so "in any jumble of time . . . but the effect was one of chaos." One of the proofs of the vigor of Paris was in its reaction to Wagner. At Bayreuth, Wagner became musical dilettantism—a taste without relation. But at Paris or New York the music was alive because of the anarchistic ferments there. Wagner's music meant catastrophe, and "Paris coquetted with catastrophe as though it were an old mistress . . . while New York met it with a glow of fascinated horror, like an inevitable earthquake, and heard Ternina announce it with conviction that made nerves quiver and thrill as they had long ceased to do under the accents of popular oratory proclaiming popular virtue. Flattery had lost its charm, but the *Fluch-motif* went home."

The reference is to Milka Ternina singing Brünhilde in the *Götterdämmerung*; Adams had heard her in New York, Philadelphia, and London, and had thought of her in Paris; she was much in mind, too, because his friend Sturgis Bigelow had for years a conspicuously more personal infatuation for her; she was nature and art—an art of nature. Thus her singing of Wagner stood in the same contrast of reality to stodginess to the singing at Bayreuth, as universal war stood to a taste in chairs and vases, or as sex to sentiment; she made of music the curse of nature upon all that false order that exists in man only by self-flattery. She appealed to Adams because through her Wagner spoke with the voice of the twelfth century, and because, thereby, she could embody successive waves of an emotion so close to Adams that he could only express it by seeing it in some embodiment, personal or intellectual. There are two sentences in a letter to Spring Rice which make the nexus to the present discussion. "I remember how I came up from the wilderness ten years ago, and what a consternation and horror I felt at seeing so-called civilization again. That emotion was the source of the C.C.A."

This is the nexus under which it becomes intelligible that the two young poets, Lodge and Stickney, abetted by Adams, who was young in the special sense of Indian Summer, should reject the spirit of socialism as "hopelessly bourgeois" and form "the wholly new and original party of Conservative Christian anarchists, to restore true poetry under the inspiration of the Götterdämmerung." What Stickney and Lodge and Spring Rice meant by true poetry may be seen by implication in their poetry; the

first two died young, and Spring Rice at fifty-nine. None of
them but Adams ever reached that full prose of Indian Summer in which things usually thought alien to poetry become
its true heart; and none certainly but Adams was ever truly a
"Conservative Christian Anarchist." Whoever originated it, the
party was his own creation; the triad of oppositions which were
its life could only be worked up together in a single sensibility,
though others could follow suit at a remove. Adams both fur-
nishes a high model in the chapter called "Teufelsdröckh,"
and himself looks on a removed model, a thought not his own.

Diogenes Teufelsdröckh—that is to say, Born-of-God Devil's-
dung—it will be remembered, is the Professor of Things in
General whose life and philosophy are rehearsed in *Sartor
Resartus*. The first or autobiographical part of the book is, like
Adams' *Education*, told in the third person, and was actually a
version of Carlyle's own life. The only biographical parallel
that need concern us here is that both Teufelsdröckh and Adams
suffered a shock in middle life, of which the result was bitter
disillusionment and withdrawal; but there is an intellectual
parallel much more significant in the three principal philosophical chapters. In the first, disillusionment develops into the
Everlasting No; in the second, the mind dwells in the Centre
of Indifference; and in the third, the meaning of the world becomes plain as the Everlasting Yea. The reader will see how
the *Education* makes a loose application of this scheme both
in the book as a whole and especially in the chapters beginning
with "Twenty Years After" and running to the end. Teufelsdröckh, like Adams, was a tourist or a wanderer on the edges
as well as at the centers of life, and much might be expected to
be in common between a pair of wanderers who were also
professors of Things in General. But there are two passages,
both in "The Centre of Indifference," which would alone legit-
imize Adams' adoption of Teufelsdröckh as title to his chapter.
Each man came up from his wilderness after an experience of
initiation and each produced a philosophy only half playful,
based on a triad of opposites. The first passage is the opening
sentence of Carlyle's chapter.

Though after this "Baphombetic Fire-baptism," our Wanderer sig-
nifies that his Unrest was but increased; as, indeed, "Indignation"
and "Defiance," especially against things in general, are not the
most peaceable inmates; yet can the Psychologist surmise that it was

no longer a quite hopeless Unrest; that henceforth it had at least a fixed centre to revolve round.

The passage goes on to the effect that baptism equals freedom.

Aside from the word "Baphombetic," which Carlyle appears to have made up on the basis of "Baphomet," an old name for Mahomet, applied to the false idol the Templars were supposed to have worshiped—aside from that word, the entire sentence could have been written with justice and discernment of the whole later stage of Henry Adams' life; it fits, and not by any accident except the accident that Carlyle and Adams converged upon a fundamental level of experience, to which they brought enough so that they could respond to it. Whether Adams was conscious of the particular sentence quoted is irrelevant; it presides in its own right, it controls, without participating in, the emotions of Adams the Wanderer searching to discover what is the fixed center he revolved around. The other passage, of which there is no doubt Adams was conscious, is not relevant generally but only to a particular place, as will be seen when the place is reached; meanwhile return must be made to the course of the chapter itself and to the principles of Conservative Christian Anarchy, of which the resemblance to those of Teufelsdröckh, once noted, may be ignored—just as the emotions of Ternina singing Brünhilde, once grasped, must be remembered.

Adams' principles are exhibited in the following order. From Hegel and Schopenhauer rightly understood comes the principle that thought needs to contradict itself in order to find its true nature; but there must be provision for limited agreement in order to reach, through the "larger synthesis," ultimate contradiction: "In the last synthesis, order and anarchy were one, but . . . the unity was chaos." The mind's job, therefore, was to "accelerate progress; to concentrate energy; to accumulate power; to multiply and intensify forces; to reduce friction, increase velocity and magnify momentum, partly because this was the mechanical law of the universe as science explained it; but partly also in order to get done with the present which artists and some others complained of; and finally—and chiefly —because a rigorous philosophy required it, in order to penetrate the beyond, and satisfy man's destiny by reaching the largest synthesis in its ultimate contradiction." No party could have principles or objectives more demanding.

Against them lay the course society seemed actually to be taking as illustrated in extreme form by the collectivistic anarchism of men like Kropotkin and Reclus. To Adams, Kropotkin represented sentimental Russian inertia, and Reclus French order and inertia, both based upon the priestly conception of society which each inherited. "Neither made a pretence of anarchy except as a momentary stage towards order and unity." With them and with all collectivists, "the mind that followed nature had no relation. . . . The conservative Christian anarchist could have no associate, no object, no faith except the nature of nature itself; and his 'larger synthesis' had only the fault of being so supremely true that even the highest obligation of duty could scarcely oblige Bay Lodge to deny it in order to prove it." This is to say that Adams' principles led after all to a philosophy of order which, like that of the Christian Church, accommodated itself to all known disorder, and which, unlike the Church in practice, was prepared to fit in new disorders as they were felt. Order was how man put together his reactions to the disorders in nature; and where the Church tended to rearrange received reactions—the sum of a finished revelation—Adams tended to believe that reaction or revelation were one with continuing experience. Thus it might be that what seemed the chaos ensuing upon his "largest synthesis" of disorders should turn out to be order after all. Until experience was perfect, even chaos had to be denied. The quandary was difficult, but it intensified the energy of reaction.

There seemed, for example, to a man biased by his role of historian and "stable-mate to statesmen," two areas of human society where his doctrine reigned in practice, America and Russia; and the forms in which they reigned were so sharply different as to constitute each a proper denial of the other. Senator Lodge took Adams to Russia across the Polish plain, and Adams brought enough of America with him to see a division in the order of social nature that seemed, as it grew, to halve the world. "In America," he wrote, "all were conservative Christian anarchists; the faith was national, racial, geographic. The true American had never seen such supreme virtue in any of the innumerable shades between social anarchy and social order as to mark it for exclusively human and his own. He had never known a complete union either in Church or State or thought, and had never seen any need for it. The freedom gave him courage to meet any contradiction, and intelligence enough to ignore it." The complex American variety was "Nature—pure and anarchic as the conservative Christian anarchist saw Nature—active, vibrating, mostly unconscious, and quickly reacting on force." Russia was as near as possible the opposite of all this, and the opposite of all European experience, too. "Russia had nothing in common with any ancient or modern world that history knew; she had been the oldest source of all civilization in Europe, and had kept none for herself." Studied under Adams' principles, "Russia became luminous like the salt of radium; but with a negative luminosity as though she were a substance whose energies had been sucked out—an inert residuum—with movement of pure inertia." Her people, who had been nomadic, "had lost the means of motion without acquiring the habit of permanence. . . . Their country acted as a sink of energy like the Caspian Sea, and its surface kept the uniformity of ice and snow."

On this comparison ends the only sketch Adams seems to have made of what he meant by Conservative Christian Anarchy. It is in one sense a primitive and ambiguous sketch with deliberate extravagance of detail, and it leaves formally unresolved the contradiction that it nevertheless composes between the two types of energy, American and Russian. We can say that the point of view behind it is *conservative* because it holds hard to what survives in man's mind, *Christian* because it feels it must encompass in a single piety even the most contradictory of the values which survive, and *anarchic* because all the values and every act of encompassment are products of an order of forces that are beyond the scope of the mind to control and that are perhaps alien and ultimately destructive to it.

The depth at which Adams held this point of view and his need to express it partly in the form of a play at an impossible political party, may be better understood when it is remembered that Shakespeare and Michelangelo were charter members of the party. The nub of the position seems to be that the mind ought to follow nature and pay attention to the forces that press on nature, whether as fresh action or as resistance to fresh action. America and Russia are given as extreme cases of different kinds of attention and different susceptibility to the forces of nature. America *reacted* because her organization was less committed, more sensitive, and perhaps more superficial than Russia's. Russia *resisted* because, fully committed to herself, her organization was profound and obliterated at the edges. But both reaction *and* resistance were forms of movement to some extent outside intelligent control; each, rather, obeyed different intensities (or inertias) of concentration. Both could be understood only in contradiction; each was perhaps the outside force that affected change in intensity (or inertia) in the other.

If the contrast of Russia and America as a step in Conservative Christian Anarchy ceased to interest Adams, the problem in the contrast itself interested him greatly; it was the major shaping consideration in his conception of foreign relations because it gave him instantly a fresh incentive to estimate the causes of universal war; it affected also his philosophy of history, and it provided new images in which to focus the contest of the forces of nature and the force of thought as it both developed and attempted to control the forces of nature. The contrast gave, in brief, new and objective form, by the change in the relations considered, to both his old questions: as to the meaning of history and as to the possibility of intelligent action in affairs of policy.

The most radical way of expressing the Russian half of the contrast was to identify the forward momentum of the great mass of Russian people as inertia of race: motion which persisted by resistance on collective instinct to either the choice or the attraction of change; just as the American half was expressed by identifying the random and various speed of the American people—who were, so to speak, by choice not a race but were bent on becoming one—as the accelerated energy change in coal: motion by conversion of and reaction to physical forces in the interests of change, with minimal regard for instinct. To Adams it seemed that the major political conflicts of the future would occur between these forms of social energy, and that, should either form be converted into that of the other —should Russia become a different America, or America become a different Russia—the conflict would become intensified until unity or chaos supervened. Adams looked from America on Russia much as America and Russia today may expect to look on China and India so soon as those peoples genuinely seem on the point of shifting from one phase of energy to another. Put otherwise, Adams looked on Russia as the Western

World seriously began to look upon Japan in the 'thirties—as threatening to combine the inertia of race and American or coal-power intensity. Still otherwise, Adams looked generally, not just at Russia but at the world, as furnishing the monstrous and fatal possibility that the kind of force he called inertia of race might digest into itself the intensity of accelerated physical force, when thought as an attractive force would become ineffectual and would survive only as taste—the high price of Sir Joshua or Picasso—or as the technical servant, the engineer, of the forces of infinitely accelerated inertia. No doubt final light and final dark are much the same, but man's mind fears blinding light less than blotting dark, and sees what he fears.

These possibilities did not show all at once, nor any one of them. In the first phase Adams asked merely whether Russian inertia of race could be broken up or take a new form. The primitive races, like *Pteraspis*, seemed to deny evolution. A new and outside power might change them, but otherwise they were unlikely to raise their racial energy—the residuum in them of what had once been the impact of new powers—to a higher level of intensity. The development of new ability to react seems to depend often on an increase of hardship accompanied by the accident of insight to discern and seize the challenge of survival by a change in form. Russia was not a primitive race but she was very near collapse when, as a race, she did determine and seize the challenge in 1918, at the moment when the old momentum seemed lost. What enabled her to seize the challenge was the simultaneous seizure of techniques of higher intensity already prepared for her through nearly a century elsewhere in the Western World. It was not special insight on Adams' part, but the exercise of his theory of sequence in history—his requirement that the historian look a generation ahead along alternative lines—that led him to determine the challenge Russia would later meet and the means by which she would meet it. Russia herself in 1907 thought she would meet her right challenge if only she could recoup herself as a military power: the very effort which in its failure was to make acceptance of the later challenge imperative.

That Adams saw right, ironically and as an alternative, does not soil the virtue of his theory; irony is the third point of view—the view of the constructed possible—which occasionally triumphs over both ignorance and assurance. Adams asked

Lodge how long it would take Russia to catch up with Western movement, and when the Senator wanted better than two generations, Adams had nothing to say: "For him, all opinion founded on fact must be error, because the facts can never be complete, and their relations must be always infinite." Then he evoked his ironical possibility: "Very likely, Russia would instantly become the most brilliant constellation of human progress through all the ordered stages of good: but meanwhile one might give a value as movement of inertia to the mass, and assume a slow acceleration that would, at the end of a generation, leave the gap between east and west relatively the same."

The irony is that both things have happened: the jump and the slow acceleration, the leap and the lag; and Adams was right in thinking that his two powers—coal power and inertia—might equally apply to Russia. "As inertia, if in no other way, she represented three-fourths of the human race, and her movement might be the true movement of the future, against the hasty and unsure acceleration of America." But it was also clear that Russia was exposed to coal—to the dynamo, the Daimler motor, and the X-ray—to all the successive intensifications of mechanical energy that were transforming the conditions of Western man; and being exposed to the contagion, she might catch it. Adams was justly afraid in 1902 of the political consequences of a hundred million American steam horsepower; by 1940 the American figure quadrupled, and somewhere in this process whereby coal truly became the dynamo, Russia caught on and began her own process of combining the new powers with her own old power of inertia. Though she still lagged absolutely with relation to America, Russia had by 1934 risen from fifteenth to third place in the production of electrical energy; and for the period 1929 to 1937 the acceleration of the Russian dynamo was at a ratio of one hundred to one compared to America. The political acceleration, after the first forward burst, would appear to have been retrograde.

However you look at it, Adams was right in remarking that "Russia was too vast a force to be treated as an object of unconcern." He had himself three ways of looking at it: through the eyes of La Fontaine, through those of Teufelsdröckh, and through those of a statesman of coal power. In his late years Adams read La Fontaine and carried him in his mind much as in his middle years he had read and carried Petrarch, as mirrors of intention and standards of reaction: Petrarch for the personal life, the fabulist for the public. So when he got to Stockholm he looked back at Moscow with the eyes of the monkey in the fable of the Monkey and the Bear, and talked first like the one and then like the other. He was not so sure of satisfaction as La Fontaine's monkey was. The American was the monkey with a motor; Russia was the bear, who might or might not acquire a motor; "but so much was sure; the monkey and motor were terribly afraid of the bear."

Teufelsdröckh was such a monkey, and he too had been afraid of Russia when like Adams the Wanderer he had turned up on the North Cape or World Promontory. As he stood alone asking "futile questions of the silent infinite" there came threateningly against him a Russian smuggler of great stature—a very hyperborean Bear, Carlyle called him. It was only the Russian's size that bothered Teufelsdröckh, but size gave him uncertain momentum and a kind of general unpredictableness; at the critical moment, Teufelsdröckh turned him back by drawing his best Birmingham horse pistol. Pistol Adams had none, only the dubious force of thought, which gave him more curious courage than strength to pretend to hold his own; for his own force of thought made him see—in the electric lights and telegraph, the newspaper and steamer—that the new forces had penetrated to the very edge of the archaic ice, and so united Hammerfest and Trondheim in the same system that contained New York and Chicago; but it made him see, too, that the new forces had penetrated no farther—that they had touched neither the ice nor Russian inertia. The ice and the bear still moved, but the bear, because incalculable, was the more frightening. The new forces could balance the ecliptic with artificial light at the North Pole, as they could ignore the division of sexes in America; but they had not yet shown they would not be victims of a force almost as old as the ice, the force of inertia of race.

With race Adams could do nothing but make it a mystery deep in experience; it was what, thinking of it, made him understand the Virgin in Normandy and feel at home in Scandinavia as in New England; it was a watermark like Harvard College which set one apart without marketable value; it was also what was alien to him in the bear, Russian or other, because he was a monkey; but it was much else besides, it was an unaccountable element that had something to do with the lack of unity in Russia while it evidently also had something to do with the unity of the coal-burning races; it remained a mystery which if solved would provide a missing clue to history.

Meanwhile it was possible to ask what controlled the lines of unity that were projected from New York to Hammerfest, and how far that system of control differed from the system—or inertia of race—that worked Russia. The acceleration in the lines of unity that brought Adams the news of McKinley's death was "marvellous, and wholly in the lines of unity. To recover his grasp of chaos, he must look back across the gulf to Russia, and the gap seemed to have suddenly become an abyss." Adams let that abyss become a division in the lines of force by translating it from intuition to the map. "From the archaic ice-barrier to the Caspian Sea, a long line of division, permanent since ice and inertia first took possession, divided his lines of force, with no relation to climate or geography or soil." Adams' passage through Germany on his way home gave him a means of marking what made the division. Germany had become a coal country. In 1858 she had been rustic, medieval, and military. In 1901 Cologne's cathedral had "an absent-minded air of a cathedral of Chicago." In 1858 only trade had united Germany to the world. In 1901 "Coal alone was felt . . . and the stamp was the same as that of Birmingham and Pittsburgh. The Rhine produced the same power, and the power produced the same people—the same mind—the same impulse. . . . From Hammerfest to Cherbourg on one shore of the ocean—from Halifax to Norfolk on the other—one great empire was ruled by one great emperor—Coal. Political and human jealousies might tear it apart or divide it, but the power and the empire were one. Unity had gained that ground. Beyond lay Russia, and there an older, perhaps a surer, power, resting on the eternal law of inertia, held its own." Teufelsdröckh's horse pistol had turned dynamo and become the symbol of unity.

The unity, then, was in the attractive force of coal, and the unity was superior to and indifferent to political and emotional unity in the sense that neither politics nor emotion could now manage it in their interests, and in the further sense that both seemed bent on managing it *against* any of their own interests that went beyond the day. Coal seemed an independent force of nature that attracted other forces to it which had previously themselves been independent and attractive, but which now reacted more or less violently to their own anarchy. The unity of coal transposed, in attracting them, other forces to chaos and would continue doing so by reason of the superiority of its mechanical manifestations; it would make the non-mechanical forces of emotion and politics—sex and war—act *as if* they were mechanical. It is not surprising that the new dominance of such a force should first arouse and then foster arbitrary reactions: *Realpolitik* and militarism; precisely after the fashion of the old force of inertia. Against the intense force of coal which attracted was the mass of inertia which absorbed other forces; either force tended equally to obliterate the force of thought whenever thought was unable to recognize with conviction, and assert in aspiration, its own primacy over its own interests.

Adams felt that such a condition prevailed potentially and was virtually sure to prevail actually, and in response to his feeling he used the figure of Teufelsdröckh, Philosopher of Clothes and Professor of Things in General, as a fixed center around which he could revolve in his own efforts to resolve the contradictions in the experience of thought into an affirmation of faith in it. Teufelsdröckh, if you like, was a necessary form of positive reaction, deliberately ironic and remote, from the Conservative Christian Anarchist's negative reaction. It was because Americans were unconsciously Conservative Christian Anarchists that they were at once singularly ill-equipped to master the force of coal and relatively safe from annihilation by it. They could be saved, but they could not save themselves; they were as much the victims of their own hurried reactions as if they had succumbed to inertia of race; the intelligence, by developing itself in parts only, was in as great danger of whole stupidity as the mass which was aware only of its own momentum. Intelligence in either case was illusion. Teufelsdröckh was the embodiment, in the fact of that recognition, of the courage to persist in the attempt at whole intelligence, even if every step in the attempt bogged in illusion; at least the illusion was intelligent.

As if to prove the paradox in the role, Adams as Teufelsdröckh at once set about stripping the clothes of illusion from the Height of Knowledge in order to find himself in the Abyss of Ignorance, where he might at least make a fresh start. Thus the chapter called "The Height of Knowledge" begins with the American illusion that tragedy, like sex, can be ignored, whether the tragedy of three political assassinations in forty years: which meant the substitution of violence for law and reason and popular will; or the tragedy of the individual such as Clarence King: which meant the substitution of lesser and blind values for greater and conscious values in the management of society short of violence. These themes, once announced, are followed by portraits of Theodore Roosevelt as a limited mind beset by unlimited power resorting to pure act, and of Henry Cabot Lodge as a man who, because his life and education conflicted, shifted from leg to leg and could act on large occasions only from small motives. Then two more themes of power are resumed: the theme of how to control those who control the powerhouses, compared to the theme of how to see lines from the powerhouse working in international relations. The underlying theme of all these themes can as usual be put doubly. New powers were disintegrating society and setting independent centers of force to work which even money—man's old institution for the equilibration of forces in the social interest—could barely hold together. So one statement of theme; the other might be this: No man can be trained to wield the powers inherent in great office, and the more energy he has with which to try, the more likely he is to make a blind surrender. Adams did not invent these themes: he felt them at work, and like Ternina singing the *Fluch-motif*, they announced catastrophe.

It is as if Adams should have said: The obstacles to a renewal of such success as at rare moments man has had are in the lack of institutions, symbols, and intelligence adequate to respond to the forces under the impact of which he must make his renewal. No doubt man has never been actually equal to the forces that press him; the forces have always shaped his purpose or limited its range, but it has never been necessary that they limit the height of his aspiration, and that they should seem now to do so reflects new weakness in the man, not supremacy in the forces. By so much, is man giving up his role.

As if to make his negative thesis stronger, Adams begins with a swan song for Clarence King, the one man in his crowd strong enough and equipped with the right skills in the right measure, the man with a scientific education such as one might think fitted to the actual society of his generation; and who yet failed not only for want of money, bad luck, and weakness of one sort or another in his opposite number the American people, but for some unaccountable reason besides—perhaps because he was the only one of a kind. One hesitates to risk it, but it may be that when King withdrew in his breakdown of 1893, the strength he gathered in his asylum was good only on the periphery of society, in the West Indies, among Negroes and the dispossessed generally; it was a recapitulation of strength for a *different* society, not ours; it was no good for the new capitalism and hidden socialism of 1900. His death in a California tavern may yet have been a new and just avatar; very nearly did Adams throw himself into the arms of that justice and that King, at the end as at the beginning of their generation. Maybe the house on Lafayette Square, the tie to Hay, and the family go-cart saved him; maybe dogwood and judas and the figure at Rock Creek preserved him; maybe the combination of thirteenth and eighteenth century—of emotion and principle, of image and reason—not only saved and preserved him but compelled him to make, with their backing, one full effort to master the terms and identify the purpose of the new powers and the new society. His great insight into his own effort was that it was to have its effect posthumously, like a monument of repair; just as King's effort had its effect in its gathering, its inception, like a spring to haunt always those who once drank of it before it sank and the sand dried.

At any rate, King was the image of that which once was, and Adams the image of the thing that returns and will again return, precisely because of the contrast in their abilities to meet society at its living center. No doubt King was himself the joy of life and never shared it; Adams could see and image and make the joy of life of which he only rarely partook; the tragedies of both men were equal—the one of full birth or revelation, the other of slow growth or discovery.

King, as Adams gives him, may never have existed; perhaps in reality he was only Adams' other half—the half that failed, the half in all of us which constantly recurs that might *once* have been. If so, we may by taking King as a point of departure see how Adams' book adds to our own stature by creating drama in terms of growth and motion which are not yet done, though as they move they sometimes move from the known point and behave—in Eliot's phrase—as the wind behaves. The portraits of Roosevelt and Lodge, to which we now come, make clear examples not just for themselves but in the context of theme with which Adams supplies them through the force of the image of the dead King working from behind.

A friend in power is a friend lost is the motto for both portraits. Deduced historically from Seneca's fatal relations with Nero, it predicted a different degree of death when applied to Adams' relations—or Hay's—with Roosevelt. Hay as well as Adams had not to commit suicide but to become supernumerary when faced with Roosevelt in his new or Presidential torrential role of pure act. Where King *ought* to have been the "height of knowledge," Roosevelt *was*. That is, Roosevelt symbolized how far beyond knowledge action went. Adams shows him as belonging in the series of Garibaldi–Grant–Cameron–Saint-Gaudens, and as perhaps the last member of the series yet possible to conceive. He was irresponsible to his power because identified with it. He wielded "unmeasured power with immeasurable energy," but the power was greater than the office and the office was greater than the man; and the effect was tragic:

No mind is so well-balanced as to bear the strain of seizing unlimited force without habit or knowledge of it; and finding it disputed with him by hungry packs of wolves and hounds whose lives depended on snatching the carrion. . . . The effect of unlimited power on limited mind is worth noting in Presidents because it must represent the same process in society, and the power of self-control must have limit somewhere in face of the control of the infinite.

Roosevelt broke down, in Adams' judgment, by resorting in crisis to arbitrary action; and as he made most conditions take on the air of crisis, he broke down rather frequently. He could be explained as representing the extreme case of that mind which is so energetic that it ignores as much as possible all institutional aids to policy and acts directly; he was the *lusus naturae*, and almost wholly unpredictable except as the rough equivalent of the force he wielded.

Henry Cabot Lodge was very different; not a *lusus naturae* at all, he was the demonstrable product of education, environment, and ancestry; even his inconsistencies could be explained, even his lapses predicted. The essence of Lodge lay in the same cause that made Roosevelt unpredictable. "New power was disintegrating society, and setting independent centres of force to work, until money had all it could do to hold the machine together. No one could represent it faithfully as a whole."

Roosevelt represented the disintegration along with the power, which was what attracted Lodge to him; but Lodge had also his formulas for reaction from his past—social, educational, historical—which made his reactions uncertain, and his convictions rather than his acts arbitrary. If Roosevelt was absorbed by the new powers that shaped him, Lodge was swamped in a cross-slop of new powers and old because he could neither be absorbed by either nor find a third position—the position of imagination and statesmanship—outside both. Lodge could never, Adams wrote, "feel perfectly at ease whatever leg he stood on, but shifted, sometimes with painful strain of temper, from one sensitive muscle to another."

One knew what disturbed Lodge: tenacity without purpose, suppleness without conviction; he needed a leader and submitted to an energy; self-righteous obstruction and the licensed piracy of the political caucus were his chief weapons. Like Webster and Sumner before him, but from a smaller mold, he was a high type of timeserver. With so little certainty in him, he could be nothing else. Adams for a moment lets himself gingerly into the same boat. "Only Bostonians can understand Bostonians and thoroughly sympathise with the inconsequences of the Boston mind"—that is, with the difficulties of reacting to a background of such conflicting and highly idiosyncratic elements. Double standards, like those of Shakespeare, are necessary. But, said Adams, if "double standards are an inspiration to men of letters . . . they are apt to be fatal to politicians." In the political game played by Roosevelt and Lodge there was for Adams nothing but "the amusement of the pugilist or acrobat." The blind energy of Roosevelt and the uneasy shifting of Lodge left them, and "the larger study" of politics, "lost in the division of interests and the ambitions of fifth-rate men."

With that, Adams pulled himself out of the boat. If Roosevelt and Lodge and domestic politics were lost, Hay and foreign affairs were left, making room and need for the larger study: "foreign affairs dealt only with large units, and made personal relation possible with Hay." There the wolves were bears, the hounds lions, and the carrion the world itself. The personal relation with Hay and the parallel development of Adams' theory of foreign policy have been studied elsewhere.* Here foreign

*Blackmur's three chapters entitled "Foreign Affairs," not included here. See Editor's Introduction.—*Ed.*

affairs need be present chiefly for their value as a symbol to draw a spirit of intent into the general problem of politics. In that light, Roosevelt and Lodge disappear because neither of them was able to act purposively in domestic politics, and Hay survived because he could at least attempt to act purposively in foreign affairs. The size of the unit handled made the difference and would continue to do so until new skills—and new institutions—were developed. That is, in point of fact, the old skills and institutions were still able to handle the new powers through the procedures of foreign affairs—and only through those procedures.

Put the other way round: the force of thought in foreign affairs, though, and perhaps because, a popular subject, had developed rather faster than the force of thought in domestic affairs, and, if not adequate to its task at any one moment, was at least used to great sweeps of conflicting powers. It could, because it must, and at any risk of error, forecast shift, and concert, and collapse of the masses of force that made complexes of themselves under the names of nations and groups of nations. So much—outside the Senate—was beyond debate: the forces were real, whether understood or not; but in domestic affairs—though the forces were as real as, and no doubt resembled, the forces in the international field—nothing was free of debate, in the Senate or out of it. One question for following generations was whether the management of domestic forces could achieve the large scale of foreign affairs, or whether, on the contrary, the management of foreign affairs would in its turn lose all horizon larger than the arena.

It is such values and such prospective questions that Adams engages around the nuclear notion that "modern politics is, at bottom, a struggle not of men but of forces." The men "become every year more and more creatures of force, massed about central powerhouses. The conflict is no longer between the men, but between the motors that drive the men, and the men tend to succumb to their own motive forces." The problem of domestic politics was how to make the men who control the powerhouses public trustees, when the power "will then control society without appeal." This is Adams' twin to his contention that the problem of international politics was how to realize the fact of the coal-power empire which skirted the Atlantic. These twin notions were potentially one. But in 1902 it was possible to work by political methods toward the recognition of that empire only in its international units, and impossible to do so in its domestic or national fractions. For Adams, unless still newer forces should crystallize, the fact was determined, the quality of the recognition of it still indeterminate. How far he was right in his determinism is less important than that his attitude of determinism gave him a frame for theory and action where, with respect to an over-all policy for society, each made the other seem inevitable within the scope of reasonable alternatives.

Theory and action—that is, policy—required a combination of America, England, France, Germany, and Russia for the development of that energy, coal, which made them, or might make them, one. Such a policy, in the guise in which to Adams it seemed to be forming itself, was antipathetic to his eighteenth-century notions of reason, intelligence, and freedom and even more antipathetic to his thirteenth-century notions of emotion, imagination, and aspiration: "This capitalistic scheme of combining governments, like railways and furnaces, was in effect precisely the socialist scheme of Jaurès and Bebel." But in the conditions the effort to apply such a scheme was inevitable, since its only likely alternative was the death of all policy. "Either Germany must destroy England and France to create the next inevitable unification as a system of continent against continent—or she must pool interests." There must be either a coal-power combination or a gun-power combination as terrible waste preface to the coal-power combination. It was, on the great scale, the story of silver and gold all over again. Just as in America gold—as concentrated capitalism—had won in 1896, so its *alter ego*, coal, would in the end win, unless the competitors first destroyed each other, in the world of the Atlantic.

These notions look on the surface like a train of thought—a conception of policy—but they are not so at bottom; their authority is in the emotion and aspiration which as policy they would destroy. These notions are the representative contenders in an imagined drama: the horror in the shapeless mass, the stalking joy in the possible form; and they mount to an aesthetic image by means of which reality is, not escaped, but accepted. One can assent to the worst actuality—as damnation or crucifixion—if one can fuse its repulsiveness and its inevitability in a single image. One assents to what one works against.

The image here is of tragic pride: the Height of Knowledge.

The whole world had conspired since 1860 to bring every gift of knowledge and comprehension of the springs of international action to Hay and Adams—or to any minds intently watchful. It was the story of King in a further field. To Adams, at that pinnacle, "the proportions of his ignorance" had never "looked so appalling. He seemed to know nothing—to be groping in darkness—to be falling forever in space." He knew only "the relative intensities of his Coal-powers, and relative inertia of his Gun-powers"—one or the other of which must surely and intolerably overwhelm him.

But one works against what one assents to in an image by making other and opposite images out of the same actuality, differently seen. There lies the great power of the aesthetic mode of the mind, that by equilibrating the opposed pressures of paradox it is freed of the burden of resolving them; and the equilibrium is in images. Thus, if King was dead, Hay tottering, and all three minds a tragedy because coal and guns—not knowledge and will—were to ruin-rule the world, then Adams, who had made King an image out of a real man, might make another, this time a Queen, and out of a real goddess if not a real woman. But goddesses do not crown the heights of knowledge, they span the abyss of ignorance. The King was dead; long live the Queen!—Such is the battle of attractions in men's minds, and such the consequent habit of emotion, that when a King dies and a Queen follows there seems more of a break than a succession. All the other thing, that was hidden, comes new-blue with a sense of balance almost unmanageably risky and almost dizzily reversible. So for Adams, Teufelsdröckh became Lancelot again and swayed on the knife's edge.

The Queen was of course the Virgin Queen of Heaven, and her court another Ara Coeli where all the old lines of will and sex and imagination converged, and all the new lines of force and mathematics and psychology merged, and both discovered themselves to have been asking different forms of the same questions. Lines of will became lines of force, and lines of force became thought. The force of the Virgin was love and acted as an attraction on thought and pulled it together. Against the force of the Virgin was the force of nature, a *vis a tergo*, which acted as a propellant on thought and kept it moving, with the effect of restlessness, as it were against itself, defeating, denying, duping itself at every turn. Yet through the restless chaos of the mind must the mind's unity be approached, just as the Virgin must be approached through the philosophy of the Schools which had laid claim to be the science whereby the force of the Virgin could be better understood. Where the Virgin had been concerned only with man, the Schools had been concerned with metaphysical forces exactly as if they were twentieth-century physical forces. As the Church had paid enormously in blood and treasure for its unity of Virgin and Schools, so the unity of twentieth-century science paid even more; for the unity science asserted was chaos for man. Even the new science of the psyche—the study of man as a unit in his thought—came out with multiple personalities and saw only dissolving mind ahead. Psychology saw thought as one force, without institutions, equal in human terms to zero: to psychology man was a unit in chaos. The thirteenth century, on the contrary, saw man as a unit in unity. Thus were opposed man's lowest and highest ideas of himself, in each case conceived in terms of force beyond himself. How could the two ideas be brought into relation?

Such in summary is the course of thought run through the Abyss of Ignorance, and such is the question asked at every pause or breach of sequence as well as at the end of the course. With the summary and the question in mind, some points in passage can be examined; and of these the first is the point of the fresh role Adams assumed to mark his fresh start. This is the combined role of the student poet in the Paris attic and the cuckoo in "the nest of a better citizen." Student poets commonly regard themselves as outside if not inimical to society, as archaic anarchists, and as masters of true meanings which society has forgotten. Your cuckoo is very different in externals; he is so content with society that he is unwilling to add to it by his own efforts, and he insists on what he loves by irresponsibly stealing it; the cuckoo is the bird of spirit that must live in some nest other than its own but that ends up by finding its own nest through some other's building. The role suited Adams so well that he thought himself at last carried away in it. "After so many years of effort to find one's drift, the drift found the seeker, and slowly swept him forward and back, with a steady progress oceanwards." So ends the long train of images about slack water, torpor, deadness in motion; and it ends aptly with an image of ocean progress right to the facts. If a straw, even, is thrown into light surf off rocks, it will work gradually seaward, a direction contrary to the apparent motion of the swells.

There is real connection between this image and the following statement that he began to see "lines of force all about him, where he had always seen lines of will"; and the connection shows in the implication that lines of will had always been lines of force, that will *was* force, and that will and force were interchangeable expressions. The point is worth attention. "Perhaps the effect of knowing no mathematics is to leave the mind to imagine figures—images—phantoms; one's mind is a watery mirror at best; but, once conceived, the image becomes rapidly simple, and the lines of force presented themselves as lines of attraction. Repulsions counted only as battle of attractions. By this path, the mind stepped into the mechanical theory of the universe before knowing it, and entered a distinct new phase of education."

The mechanical theory of the universe seems to have meant to Adams a system of forces that, once set in motion, were self-operating, but with a margin of play between their attractions and repulsions, and with a permanent uncertainty as to the balance, or imbalance, of forces to which a man might respond at a given moment; which thus allowed for a radical variation in the quantity and intensity of known force. Further, the system seemed to him capable of deep alteration, from the human point of view, by the application of fresh force from outside—though the fresh force might afterward turn out to have been only an old force that, by entering a new phase, as water becomes steam, altered the relations among all the forces. Thus when thought entered its mathematical phase in the seventeenth century it set up a new system of relations and released new intensities among the physical forces, and by a kind of inadvertence of new ignorance tended to invalidate the relations between the forces of will and imagination and the physical forces.

Not "knowing" mathematics, Adams could not surrender to the formalism derived from mathematics by which that invalidation had come about: which was the advantage of his ignorance; but being alert to the values which created mathematics—the mapping of lines of force, the plotting of relations of motion—he retained what the mathematician loses in the intoxication of abstract skill, the sense of the reserved dominance both of the forces measured and of those that remained

unmeasurable; and he could see the identity of system and
resemblance of effect in the very incommensurability of all the
forces taken together. Images were as good as figures—perhaps
both were phantoms—as their tide coursed in the "watery mirror" of the mind. Whether forces repelled or attracted or con-
certed each other, if either image or figure could be made of
them together, then they must have a common feature, and that
feature characterized the mechanical theory he held.

If mathematics led to a mechanical conception of force, then
so, to the student poet in his Paris attic, did the Virgin of
Chartres. Mathematics and the Virgin, taken in the lump, were
each beyond management; each was symbol and each radiated
action and formulas to substitute for action; each absorbed action. What they had in common was their occult character,
which was measured by its impact on one's ignorance. Force
had always been felt as occult attraction. To the imaginative
mind the attraction was God, the power not now and not known
but at work and to be reached. With the decline of the imaginative mind the attraction of God declined—was differently distributed; and the conception of *vis a tergo*, the force from behind—no less occult but requiring the invention of a symbolism
that tested the facts of abstraction rather than the facts of sense
—took its place, with the effect that the experience of God was
pushed further and further back from the symbolic grasp of the
imagination. The intense knowledge of mystery in force became
the dispersed unknowableness of God; and each made claim to
the virtue and sufficiency and unity of the other.

The truth, particularly in the mechanical theory of the universe, no doubt lay in the relation between the two; and the
relation was man's mind, attracted or pulled by both, and unable to resist the feeling that each was, not the equal, but the
reversal of the other. During the experience of such reversals,
there is, and always will be, in the life of the individual and
in the pattern of culture, an interim state, when the motion of
pure and all-absorbing restlessness in body and spirit super-
venes, to become the source and end-all of conviction. How could
a mind be but restless, which had become dissatisfied with
knowledge because of its mystery and outraged by ignorance
because it made mystery a mere sink? Adams, as cuckoo "in
the nest of a better citizen," quotes Pascal as showing that *ennui*
is the master-motor of man, and between the halves of his quo-

tation inserts his own phrase, "Mere restlessness forces action." Then to Pascal he adds George Herbert's lines from "The Pulley":

> If goodness lead him not, yet weariness
> May toss him to my breast.

The distinction between the two notions is polar: that is to say, identical at a maximum remove. The language of Pascal is modern and descriptive of all men's experience when the sense of occupation is low and the sensibilities are exacerbated; Pascal draws on and complains of a universal reserve force in man's heart which "fills the mind with its venom." It is curious that this particular conception of restlessness as *ennui*—as diabolical—does not seem to have matured until the seventeenth century, and in France, as a kind of accompaniment to the rebirth of mathematical method. Whether Adams had it in mind does not appear, but Herbert's lines are indebted to a very different conception of restlessness, pre-mathematical and imaginative. According to the poem, God poured every blessing on natural man except one: the blessing of Rest was reserved for heaven, where its attractive force would serve as a mechanical device—a pulley, as we should say, a block and tackle—to bring man to worship God and not his gifts. Herbert's weariness is a climax of motion where Pascal's *ennui* is in the desire not to move. What they have in common is the attractive force of the state of rest in God. Both experiences—both roles—are common, and when they are undertaken at the same time, the "battle of attractions," pulling differently in the same direction, brings on a burst of energy which may be imaginative. "Mere restlessness forces action" was not an idle connection on Adams' part, but an assertion of motive.

It led him, as he says exactly, "straight to the Virgin of Chartres" to ask her to show him God—or Force—"face to face, as she did for St. Bernard." But Bernard had not come burdened either with weariness or *ennui*, either exhausted or envenomed, but brimming with the energy of faith; therefore Adams' answer could not be Bernard's. The Virgin, though she welcomed Adams, told him that she, with Christ, had only the personal force of Love, and that he had better ask St. Thomas of God's other and infinite energies. The distinction was familiar and brutal. Love should be sufficient for human wants, but the mind which has become conscious of itself—conscious not of faith but of the need of faith—is too restless and too much addicted to logic to be capable of receiving love simply: it wants other things at once; it wants unity, and at any cost. Logic and *ennui* —the sign and the energy of the imperfectly trained mind— carry man intolerably beyond his own wants, producing, for example, whether by the thirteenth-century Schoolmen or the twentieth-century scientists, a pantheistic deity conceived as "the ultimate energy, whose thought and act were one."

The Schoolmen depended on the notion of infinite gradations in the Great Chain of Being: they were metaphysicians; the scientists depended on the notion of infinite gradations—or degradations—of energy: they were physicists. Both were mechanical. Each compelled the assumption of a unity that could not be experienced. Society and particularly the Church had always adopted the assumption and had always asserted unity at any cost of blood and treasure, and furthermore had always seemed to know what was meant by the assertion. Adams, thinking of the Virgin and the personal force of love, insisted on his experience and felt compelled to deny the name of unity to any conception either beyond that experience or which did not take account of the immediate—personal—unity he felt in the Virgin: "but no teacher would know how to explain what he thought he meant by denying unity. Society would certainly punish the denial if ever anyone learned enough to understand it." All the forces of logic and *ennui*—of science and inertia— all the contagion of habit and violence, all the resources of the mind—which stand for want of training in full response—almost, one might think, all that could be called the institution of the mind—conspired against either the denial of ultimate unity or the assertion of immediate unity which made the denial valid.

Yet Adams stuck to his experience, willing to stretch it, to add to it, to put it in parallel to other scales and schedules, but unwilling—as cuckoo or poet—to blot it or any way renege. If to him "the scientific synthesis commonly called Unity was the scientific analysis commonly called Multiplicity," why keep it? The scientists and metaphysicians all seemed to agree that the universe "could be known only as motion of mind, and therefore as unity. One could know it only as one's self; it was psychology." There, in the force of thought, might be the secret of a unity which was not a further synthesis, which did not analyze as multiplicity, but which was vision, discovered in the act of seeing and feeling and preserved in the act of imagination. The degree of human unity of which the force of thought was capable would depend, therefore, on the idea one held of its position and attractiveness relative to other forces. In the form of the Virgin the force of thought had become the supreme act of imagination and therefore the supreme vision of unity, the helper and governor of art and life, as had been Venus in the age of Lucretius. What had happened to the status of the idea, and so to the unity itself—what had happened to the force of thought—when studied in the twentieth century along the lines that other forces were studied?

Looking into the science of psychology, Adams found that it had atrophied his power of thought. The psychologists could not decide whether or not the Psyche was a unit—Adams gives the term in Greek, ψυχή, to assert the distinctness of the idea— but had discovered new multiple personalities "whose physical action might be occult in the sense of strangeness to any known form of force. . . . Thus the compound ψυχή took at once the form of a bicycle-rider, mechanically balancing himself by in- hibiting all his inferior personalities, and sure to fall into the sub-conscious chaos below if one of his inferior personalities got on top. The only absolute truth was the sub-conscious chaos below, which everyone could feel when he sought it."

To Adams as historian, concerned with the force of thought, the question that this view raised was startling. "If his mind were really this sort of magnet, mechanically dispersing its lines of force when it went to sleep, and mechanically orienting them when it woke up—which was normal, the dispersion or orienta- tion?" This was another form of the question of the relative values of the high and low view man took of himself; but in either form the question could be asked only by the man who felt himself oriented to the high view at the moment of asking but who also felt the risk in the situation: who knew that he did orient chaos, that he did somehow unify multiplicity, by the force of thought alone, but that the force of thought might at any moment, finding itself unequal to its task, slip into the chaos, the multiplicity, the complete dispersal below. The task was rational and self-chosen, but needed outside help; and the psychologists' picture of dissolving mind brought the need home.

"Sanity," said Adams, "sanity was an unstable artifice," and went on to make an image of his own sanity. "His artificial balance was acquired habit. He was an acrobat, with a dwarf on his back, crossing a chasm on a slack-rope, and commonly breaking his neck." The dwarf was the inferior personality who got on top; the dwarf was the unrecognizable, unclaimable, irreclaimable other self, the restless devil of the unaccountable: the burden of Lancelot on knife's edge, felt by usage as the twin pressures of logic and *ennui:* actually, the dwarf on the back.

The dwarf grew heavier; for if the new psychology was right, and there was indeed nothing but dissolving mind ahead, then the mind could depend on no force but the restlessness which envenomed it. Only chaos and the higher synthesis—the logical display—of chaos were in order. It is as if Adams had quoted the language Shakespeare gave Othello at the moment when the struggle of faith and restlessness most disconcerted him and he felt his mind, losing the personal force of love, dissolving.

> Excellent wretch! Perdition catch my soul,
> But I do love thee! and when I love thee not,
> Chaos is come again.

The dwarf grew heavier, and the labor of balance a more desperate balance than ever. Adams thought of Gibbon and Buckle and Comte; believers in reason, driven by *ennui* to rigorous thought; and felt himself, as an historian, like them, "driven back on thought as one continuous Force, without Race, Sex, School, Country, or Church." The dissolution of mind seemed final, the dispersal of energy complete. The dwarf was real.

But to understand the reality of the dwarf—man in present motion—he had to be put in scale with the reality of man in what had seemed a different motion. Psychology, said Adams, meaning the ψυχή herself, suggested a unit—"the point of history when man held the highest idea of himself as a unit in a unified universe": the cathedrals and philosophy of thirteenth-century unity. For the other or opposite unit he took the complexity of himself. The first unit—from 1150 to 1250—was the century in which men's minds were ruled by the Virgin through Race, Sex,

School, Country, and Church; and to conceive entry into it from the attitude of "dissolving mind," and with an intensifying drive of restlessness to deny in fact the imagination of unity it stood for, was indeed to begin from the bottom of the abyss of ignorance. Ignorance is the deepest emotion knowledge can reach when confronted with the mystery of its own force; for in ignorance, fully felt, is the faith of what we know and do not know that we know; ignorance is the final name we give to our plunder from experience at that raised level where it is again its own meaning. In turning to his saints and cathedrals and women of the thirteenth century—to their philosophy and mechanics and the personal force of their Virgin—Adams was deliberately turning to an old and chief attempt to image the force of the human mind at the raised level of its own meaning in the hope of renewing that elation in his own mind and for his own time. To him, as historian, such images were the substance of history. Particular failure was nothing. "When what we hoped for came to nothing, we revived."

CHAPTER NINE

The Revival

Est ergo animae vita veritas, sensus charitas.
—Bernard, *Sermones de Diversis*, 10, 1

The youngest stars are heaviest and generate most
energy, irrespective of temperature and pressure. This
would not be so if they were made entirely of terrestrial
atoms, which radiate more as the temperature and
pressure rise. Such evidence again indicates that the bulk
of the energy for radiation comes from types of intensely
active matter unknown to us, which vanish as the star
ages, probably by the coalescence of positive protons and
negative electrons, their consequent annihilation as
matter and their conversion into gushes of electro-
magnetic radiation.
—Dampier, *History of Science*

The two quotations above are meant to point directly at the two
chief themes that interweave throughout *Mont-Saint-Michel
and Chartres*, and, taken together, are meant to suggest a third
theme which transpires only gradually and which must transpire differently for different readers. The sentence from St.
Bernard if paraphrased to read, "The life of the soul is truth,
its content—the actuality of its experience—is love or charity,"
declares its own theme: the nature and intensity of the difficulty
when man undertakes in imagination a high view of the aspirations he finds in himself and feels in others, and the need of love
—of radiant emotion, and whether taken as sex or as understanding—to express the aspirations. The sentences from Dampier
illustrate in the terms of twentieth-century physical science the
kind of relation that such aspiring minds must feel toward the
universe. In both cases the radiant energy—of love, as of electromagnetism—seems to come from outside any experience articulable either in the emotions or the machines which it infuses.

Men as a rule tend to rely predominantly on one or the other
form of energy and consequently to ignore the other form;
either the universe or the emotion disappears from the human

equation, and gradually one or another form of determinism replaces rational or imaginative faith. But there are some ages when there is no clear dominance on either side, when, rather, a double effort is made with such intensity that a kind of vital, shaking balance is struck where both imaginative and rational faith make a single, and full—if perilous—equilibrium of the energies that man uses and the energies that drive him along and which together express his possibilities and shape his fate. To some, Athens in the fifth century B.C. is such an age. To Adams, reacting between the purple voids of his Southern Pacific and the clutter of the Chicago Exposition—between private nihilism and public self-satisfaction—the Norman-French state during parts of the twelfth and thirteenth centuries seemed in its religion, art, love, and philosophy to strike a human balance between man and the universe, which was alone for fullness in the Christian world. The effort was as intense as it was various and showed the fullness of its unity most clearly in the Cathedral of the Virgin at Chartres. How that happened—how the Virgin of Chartres could represent both the energy of love and the energy of matter in a single radiance—is the third theme which transpired for Adams from the study of the other two and which, as it got into his book, makes its substance.

So much for general purpose; in postscript to which it may be repeated that Adams meant to use his chosen age as one point in his effort to triangulate the movement of thought as a force. If successful he would feel a sense of relation, and thereby of direction, to the movement and force of his own mind which had been subject to so much nineteenth-century education. And on the possibility of finding such a relation may be hitched a secondary purpose (which might be major in the event) of finding in a parallel example the conditions and limits and necessities under which man in the twentieth century might again bring his aspirations and his fate into full and perilous equilibrium. But only if kept secondary could that intent be perfected.

No one knew that better than Adams, and whether in his role of artist or of historian. Barring two or three paragraphs, to which we shall come, he never let his secondary intent become explicit; only the tone, the rhythm, and the selection of image witnessed the use to which in the last chapters of the *Education* he meant to put the *Chartres*; otherwise the *Chartres* is straightforward aesthetic-historical criticism, moving from

point to point, resuming itself from time to time to take care of
increasing complexities, and in the end returning on itself for
summary and conclusion and a kind of open resolution of conflicting themes. It may be useful to set down the skeleton of
straightforwardness with extreme possible simplicity. Adams
begins by posing the conception of God common to the Normans
of the eleventh century against the conception which they developed in the twelfth and thirteenth centuries. The earlier conception is symbolized in the church of Mont-Saint-Michel,
where the saint is the defender of man in peril of the sea—of
all perils from without, and the later conception is symbolized
in the Cathedral of Our Lady of Chartres, where the Virgin is
the living intercessor between mankind as individuals and the
perils of law, whether divine or human. The one was Romanesque and military, the other Gothic and intuitive; the one was
a matter of struggle and survival, the other a matter of understanding and aspiration. Each conception was imaginative and
each gathered to it the highest art of its time. But Adams' interest is in the second rather than in the first, and in the transition between the two.

So much for the first part of the book, ending with the fourth
chapter. Chapters 5 through 9 make different specific approaches to the significance of the Virgin in the building of her
churches, in their ornament, light, and color. The third section
of four chapters deals with the power of the Virgin as Queen
in the Church, in the Courts of Love, in poetry and romance,
and through her miracles: all in terms of love and sex. The last
three chapters place beside the Virgin images of Abelard as the
extreme of intellect, of St. Francis and St. Bernard as the extreme of emotion, and of St. Thomas as the extreme man of
reason and emotion held, like the architecture of Chartres, in
perilous and unstable balance.

In short, Adams tries to give a serial account of the imaginative stage of Christendom when it was in transit between the
age of terror from without and the age of terror from within,
and perhaps the fullest image of accomplishment—aside from
the cathedrals themselves—is that of the Hive of St. Thomas,
which needs its small preface of contrast with our own age to
be felt in its fullness: "An economic civilization troubles itself
about the universe much as a hive of honey-bees troubles about
the ocean, only as a region to be avoided. The hive of St.

Thomas sheltered God and man, mind and matter, the universe and the atom, the one and the multiple, within the walls of an harmonious home."—Only the hive that is the image for Adams' book has a richer and more complex harmony than that of St. Thomas' system, for it is the harmony of the things which made his system possible and of which he never took whole stock, as well as the harmony of the system itself. Adams' bees ventured widely, and the harmony—or unity—within the hive is because the honey of imagination is brought together from so many familiar flowers, not all sweet, some wild, but all human.

It was not the architecture of the hive alone. It was the honey in the comb: the honey of generation which has in it the anguish of aspiration and is itself the expressed essence both of the energies that move man and of his response to them; and this is so whether the energy—that is to say, God—is conceived as a prime motor infinitely distant, as the direct radiance of creation, as the dialectic reversal of thought, or as the direct apprehension, in the human terms of the Virgin's miracles, of maternity and love. But it is most so when all these conceptions are felt together and are single in their radiance; and this is what Adams tried to feel. He felt all these conceptions as a single act of the radiant force of faith which moved the great Christian age. Himself lacking faith, he so ached with the want of it that he possessed himself imaginatively of man's reach when faith was live. His book is the story of that imagination, and that was honey, too. If we keep the image of the hive, the honey, and the making of the honey all in mind along with the simplified structure of the book outlined above, we shall have something like an adequate means of approach to the actual, or aesthetic, composition of the book and how its elements are kept in tension.

We see at once that there are four levels of tension. There is the tension of the relations of the transition age felt for their own sake; there is the tension felt when thirteenth-century determinism is taken as a foil or background for twentieth-century determinism; there is the tension of Adams' plea for unity as vision in human terms; and there is the tension of Adams' own spiritual autobiography. The first and second, as they become one, make possible the third, and the created presence of the fourth is what fuses, as it was the incentive of, the other three. Although it will be impossible either to follow through each tension separately or to take them wholly together at any one time, both attempts must be made—each, so to speak, keeping the other as the next thing in mind.

We must do this through seeing by what gestures Adams moved his thought about. In a sense, one goes up into a high place in order to be cast down, looks into the sun to be blinded, plunges into the pit to be raised; so it is with the conduct of an author and his readers toward a serious book: positive acts of creation and appreciation are undertaken in order to bring about their reversals. Large gestures of this order are the discoveries sought for, small ones are the conventions by which the large are set off and by which sometimes they seem almost to be generated. Thus Adams set up the conceit that his book is written only for nieces, and young ones at that, still capable of cherishing dolls and of playing with other forms of naive perception—such as light and color, hope and woe—without presumptuous objection to the incongruous and the contradictory. The use of this device permits free gestures of emotion; and as it were creates in the willing reader the conditions of uncommitted response, the recklessness of true feeling, beyond what the merely committed mind can afford.

But against this, Adams sets the convention of historical form. The nieces—and the uncle, too—could transform into emotion only what the story gave as actual under the deepest scrutiny; if the play was to be real play it must find itself playing with real things: genuine extravagance was of real wealth, and real wealth had to be earned. What the nieces stood for was generative sensibility, the appeal to which limited effrontery of intellect; and, similarly, historical form limited effrontery of emotion. The effort to balance the two gave the book motion; and the motion was that of Adams' own mind striking balance after balance; for the historical form represented all that had been trained and made public in his life, and the nieces represented all that could not be trained on any known method and which would die if made public. It is the two striking together that achieve the gesture of discovery—of pilgrimage finished— by which the book moves us.

A clear example of how the two smaller and conscious gestures could be balanced to make the larger gesture may be found early in the book. Adams has been describing in detail the Norman and eleventh-century part of Mont-Saint-Michel, and has just declared that its size did not matter but that its style "is the starting-point of all our future travels." How, he asks, does it affect the nieces?—and proceeds to answer for them. "Serious and simple to excess! is it not? Young people rarely enjoy it. They prefer the Gothic, even as you see it here, looking at us from the choir, through the great Norman arch. No doubt they are right, since they are young: but men and women who have lived long and are tired—who want rest—who have done with aspirations and ambition—whose life has been a broken arch —feel this repose and self-restraint as they feel nothing else." Then, after a little development, he goes on—or back—with the history. Though there was repose in the emotion, especially when felt with nieces, the thought in Mont-Saint-Michel was perhaps "the most unreposeful thought ever put into architectural form." It is the eleventh-century Norman idea of the Church Militant threatening heaven itself and setting about meantime to conquer the world at hand in the first stage of a great outburst of united human energies. But the idea is nothing to the purpose of the book—and the history is nothing—without the response of a man, to his nieces in wishes, to whom life might seem a broken arch.

Thus our example reveals all the levels of tension we expect to find separately both running together and running on; but it also serves to show in what way Mont-Saint-Michel was "the starting-point of all our future travels"—why, in short, its name made half the title of a work in which it took up only a minor fraction of the space. It was a starting point found in the middle of the flux and had to carry the sense of all the momentum from behind and to suggest all the dangers ahead when the present adventure should be done.

The eleventh-century part of Mont-Saint-Michel was the simply and directly felt unity of God; the thirteenth century was the full and plastic expression of man's multiplicity as unity; and the later additions of the fourteenth and fifteenth centuries gave the Mount "the modern expression of war as discord in God's province." To Adams the fifteenth-century gate of the châtelet "forebodes"—and we shall see why—"wars of religion; dissolution of society; loss of unity; the end of a world." The arch between was the life that had been broken: "the catastrophe of Gothic art, religion, and hope." And the living arch could better be understood in terms of the Church Militant from which it sprang than in the terms of the Church discordant in which it lapsed; for the earlier age gave an effect of having stopped, while the later age seemed still to be going on, its discord and violence and multiplicity still spreading, the felt stain of catastrophe in one's own twentieth-century life—felt, of course, as the obsessive ache that led Adams to write his book.

The earlier age had a unity forced upon it from without and was expressed in action; it stood in peril and concentrated its energies in the simplest, most direct, most naive known forms: the conquest of England and Sicily, the abbatical economy, feudal rule, the fortress Church of St. Michael, the *Song of Roland*, and a religion exclusively of God the Father. All stood together for survival, and survival was both the measure of unity and its limit. It was an age of absorption in the immediate task, but a hard task that called for intensity of effort; it lived, so to speak, on the subsistence level of imagination. It is that kind of work out of which great imaginative civilizations are sometimes made when the immediate necessities of the task are overcome and there is an unwonted release of energy already unified. It is not so much Toynbee's Challenge and Response in one age; but a challenge overcome in one age and a response released, or created, in the next age. There is a connection between the two but it is of sequence, not identity; it is the connection, at closest, of transition, and the transition itself must have another term which always seems bound to fall again under the rule of necessity. Adams' age of transit was the Gothic Transition—the moment of release between the singly militant and the violently discordant, the moment of imaginative balance between the mastering of the challenge and the disintegration of the response. In human terms, as only the struggle for survival could raise enough energy for its beginning, so only some catastrophic inadequacy of the raised human spirit to its own ends could account for its lapse.

But let the energy which Adams found in the *Song of Roland* do for an image of eleventh-century single militance; for the song was, in Adams' argument, the feeling which was not only built into Mont-Saint-Michel but was also kept alive there—as sung or recited—for centuries after the Archangel himself had ceased to be representative. So close—so single—was society that what seems to us a military epic was then also a means of prayer and religious celebration; it was the religion, and the society, not the poem, that changed; and the poem becomes, therefore— as it was sung in the wars of the Conquest, on the Crusades, and after dinner—the clue to the kind of unity and energy that were lost with the change. The poem was military, monosyllabic, direct. "The words bubble like a stream in the woods," and in the words "the action of dying is felt, like the dropping of a keystone into the vault." Death in battle, on crusade or pilgrimage, was the keystone to Church and Society, for death was the right true act of homage due to God conceived as a feudal seigneur who absorbed the Trinity and excluded the Virgin. Nothing could be plainer, simpler, or more absolute; it was how eleventh-century men found themselves feeling about themselves when they built a church or made a poem; and Roland's own sword Durendal is an epitome of that feeling and shows what was concentrated in that singleness of feeling and how much of the living man went into the homage of death. The sword contained in its hilt relics of St. Peter, St. Basil, St. Denis, and the Virgin Mary, any of which "would have made the glory of any shrine in Europe." But so martial was religion, so religious Roland's war, "the relics serve the sword; the sword is not in service of the relics."

So much for Adams' image of predominant masculine energy. It rings in the Norman Salle de Chevaliers, in the conquest of England and of Sicily, and in the first Crusade; the impulse that set it ringing was the impulse of supreme Western energy and unity to create a universal state which should range from Norman England to Norman Jerusalem. But above and on the north face of the Mount, in the great pile called *La Merveille*, built in the late twelfth and early thirteenth centuries, stands both the proof that the single masculine impulse was not enough, and the development or flowering of that impulse to the point, in the human terms it had to meet, of defeat. It is as if men can unite and succeed only when the complexity of their ambitions remains unfolded; unfolded, the passion that united the ambition flowers and falls apart. For the Merveille was a great Gothic hall of the twelfth century and, with the eleventh-century church and the thirteenth-century refectory, showed the rise, flowering, and end of the impulse to unity: the whole Gothic Transition, seen here in simplest concord. The marriage of the Romanesque to the Gothic made "a union nearer the ideal

than is often allowed in marriage. . . . What the Roman could
not express flowered into the Gothic; what the masculine mind
could not idealize in the warrior, it idealized in the woman;
no architecture that ever grew on earth, except the Gothic, gave
this effect of flinging its passion against the sky. . . . When
men no longer felt the passion, they fell back on themselves,
or lower."

The assertion of force was simple; the assertion that followed
and was the flowering of the first, the assertion of the supremacy
of love over force, whether in the architecture of the cloisters
on the Mount or in St. Francis' Sermon to the Birds, was perhaps simpler but beyond man's power to endure. Mont-Saint-
Michel had in its architecture solved the problems of the universe: God reconciles all. But architecture remains true only as
example—as art—beyond the time of building; a rule Adams
knew by heart, for it is the beauty of his examples and the
pathos of his thought that he tries to keep everything out except
what went into the building. The building at Mont-Saint-
Michel had changed utterly at the beginning of the fifteenth
century, when a gate of the châtelet was plastered over "the
thirteenth-century entrance called Belle Chaise." Adams goes
on: "It frowns in a spirit quite alien to the twelfth century; it
jars on the religion of the place; it forebodes wars of religion;
dissolution of society; loss of unity; the end of a world. Nothing
is sadder than the catastrophe of Gothic art, religion, and hope."
A châtelet is a small castle, and is a term sometimes used for a
court of justice and prison. Thus the Mount had moved from
a fortress of safety to a fortress for prison, from an energy which
was concentrating to an energy which was dispersing, from a
form of life to a formula to impose on life, from age to age; but
it was also, taken together, and building by building, a *pons
seclorum*, the bridge between the ages; which is why it is with
justness Adams calls his chapter "The Merveille."

The next chapter, "Normandy and the Ile de France," is a
bridge of a different order, a little bridge of genealogy and
commentary between Mont-Saint-Michel of the eleventh century and Chartres of the twelfth. The genealogy is partly art
and partly personal, and like all genealogy is a little arbitrary
in its selection of family heroes and heroines and in the values
asserted of them. Adams was interested in the ancestors of the
Virgin of Chartres. But though he allows her a tree running

from Jerusalem through Byzantium and Italy and grants her close relations with France, he is most emphatic about her Norman connections, partly because it was in Normandy that he had first seen her transform fortress churches into her shrines and palaces, and partly because Adams felt himself Norman for artistic purposes—"an English scholar of a Norman name"—and even went farther, and felt that Normandy was a kind of New England in Europe.

Thus, so far as the twelfth-century Virgin was Norman, she was also New England and some part of his own inheritance. Indeed, in reading the chapter anyone familiar with the letters must constantly expect Adams to make positive claim of kin. "I am sure," he wrote Gaskell, "that in the eleventh century the majority of me was Norman,—peasant or prince matters nothing, for all felt the same motives,—and that by some chance I did not share the actual movement of the world but became a retarded development, and unable to find a place." To his brother Brooks he makes the claim closer still: "I have rarely felt New England at its highest ideal power as it appeared to me, beatified and glorified, in the Cathedral of Coutances." To Mrs. Cameron he presents a kind of generalized claim: "All true imaginative art belongs to the imaginative period which must be religious and military"; and on that we can return to what he did publicly have to say about Coutances some eight or nine years later. It was, he said, a fortress altered into a church. Outside it was the church of God the Father who never lied; within, it was the church of the Virgin; but there is no transition between the two; the bridge is a jump come on, as Adams says, unexpectedly:

Among the unexpected revelations of human nature that suddenly astonish historians, one of the least reasonable was the passionate outbreak of religious devotion to the ideal of feminine grace, charity, and love that took place here in Normandy while it was still part of the English kingdom, and flamed up into almost fanatical frenzy among the most hard-hearted and hard-headed race in Europe.

Adams never argued whether his Norman universal state was in essence military and imaginative or religious and imaginative; the one broke out of the other and the two were in fact inseparable, as in himself the new and especial Norman reflowering of New England: the flowering of Quincy and

Beverly granite in loving form. Adams is himself the true
ecumenical propaganda: he wished to make universal the relation he felt as truth between himself in twentieth-century
Paris and Chicago and the twelfth-century Virgin of Chartres
whom his 250 million arithmetical ancestors had created. To
him the true movement of history lay between, and his own
access to that movement he could best find, for personal reasons, in Normandy. It was there that he could find himself in
a central and stirring passage of the human adventure; and
we should never, in presuming to enlist ourselves in his adventure, forget how much of it is in emphasis his own creation,
and how it therefore enjoys the rights and limitations of foreshortening that go with the work of art.

The next chapter—"Towers and Portals," which brings us
to Chartres—provides us with two examples. In comparing
the old twelfth-century tower and flèche with the later sixteenth-century tower and flèche, Adams says the old tower
belonged to the Virgin—that is, to the "ideal of feminine grace,
charity, and love" expressed by the twelfth-century Virgin;
but the later tower, in Adams opinion, belonged rather to
Diane de Poitiers—that is, expressed a feminine ideal lower
by three and a half centuries of history. The point of difference
is clinched, for Adams, when he complains of the French word
adresse used as a term of praise for the means of transition between the square tower and the octagonal flèche; he prefers the
more Norman term *droiture*—rightness, justness, honesty—to
any term that means cleverness or mere technical skill. It is a
matter of temperament, but it is the temperament built into the
whole mind of the book; there is an echo in the final chapter,
when in praising the system of St. Thomas for its transition
between God's power and man's free will, Adams concludes by
remarking that, "in a result so exquisite, one has not the heart
to find fault with 'adresse.'" Again, mere technical skill—
which may be had in any, and even the worst, age—will not
do. What Adams felt in the spire of the Virgin's Church and
in the aspiration of Thomas' system came from a depth and
fullness of being that belonged to one age only; and in the firmness of his feeling he could let himself go in the details of
sentiment. The new tower was Gascon, decorated, jeweled,
laced to hide its age. The old tower was Norman, austere,
belonging to the Crusades and St. Bernard. The distinction was

arbitrary in assertion, fundamental in feeling, a dogma in faith.

It was also a means of teaching nieces, a means of teaching what to exclude, what to look for, and what to anticipate: a means of teaching the first steps in achieving the conditions of faith—with faith being thought of as the actual experience of the occult force that keeps us going. Adams, having come on this means, pursued it without too much care for consistency. If the towers were not persuasive in their plain contrasts, perhaps the porches would do better. "If the spire symbolizes aspiration, the door symbolizes the way" to eternal life as seen by the Church and art of the First Crusade. On the North porch, which was twelfth century, in the sculptured life of Christ there is no crucifixion, no misery, no judgment. You "are entering the Court of the Queen of Heaven who is one with her Son and His Church, . . . the greatest of all queens, but the most womanly of women." The North porch was the Virgin's and human; there she is Queen Mother—"too high to want, or suffer, or to revenge, or to aspire, but not too high to pity, to punish, or to pardon." But the South porch was Christ's and showed not the promise but the stigmata which prove salvation. Power is from Christ, and Mary supplicates him. "The whole melodrama of Church terrors appears after the manner of the thirteenth century, on this church door, without regard to Mary's feelings." Where the sculptures on the North porch were warm and of persons, those on the South porch were of "a maturity which chills the blood" and were anonymous, masculine, and of the religion that reflects the sword rather than the cross.

For fifteen of his large pages, Adams elaborates his initial assertion, as persuasively as his stone figures will let him, that for something like two centuries, whether as Byzantine Empress, or French Queen, or Queen of Heaven, there was a divine right in the Virgin, "apart from the Trinity, yet one with It," that overcame all other rights, divine or human, official or piratical, which came into competition with it. To Adams, the halves of the story were as black and white as, in the early chapters of the *Education*, Boston and Quincy, Winter and Summer, City and Country, Law and Sensation, Man and Nature had been; and as Boston had triumphed over Quincy when the Pilgrim impulse was run out and turned on itself, so when the response to the Virgin had weakened, the Church

Militant of the eleventh century became a new and suicidal orthodoxy, which, free from outward peril, turned inward, lashing.

But it is not only the towers and portals, it is, so to speak, every stone he can name that Adams uses—or, as he says, the Virgin used—to build his deity. Historically, it was a religion from beneath—a feeling of needed force; in Adams, it was a religion from above—an imperative felt *as if* from beneath. Adams was looking for the force which on the evidence of the society must have existed and must have been felt, a force which was compassionate as well as supreme, and a force which, if there should be a similar society, must exist and be felt again. As the force was unorthodox—beyond the control of reasoned rightness and its corrective—the effort to discover and rebuild it was all poet's work: true autobiography, with composition.

In historical and religious poetry as well as in the personal lyric, composition suffers from the tendency to say everything at once; formal history and religion have discipline and order of service; the informal, like direct love, are besieged defenseless; and Adams' next chapter, "The Virgin of Chartres," shows both how resourceful and how defenseless he was. He laid out a plan as formal as a ladder, with historical rungs, but he did all his climbing by his poetry and got no higher in the end than where he began. What saves the chapter is its musical aspect: its repetitions and variations intensify the theme, until at last its simplest statement seems a revelation that continues after the words have stopped. Both processes are worth following, and indeed both must be, for neither can be unraveled.

The idea of the chapter is to show the degree, and the scope, and the quality, and the actuality of the power of the Virgin; and to suggest too, perhaps, how so great an exaltation could have only a tragic fall. But it begins—the nieces are now supposed to be entering the church for the first time—it begins with a few remarks to one side while the eyes are getting used to the light, the light of the church, and the light of the age, both Gothic. To some there is darkness and mystery, age and fear; always, of all the styles in which man has worn his mind, the Gothic gets away—to some in its darkness, to others in its light. To Adams it is light: the twelfth-century light of exuberant youth or, to bring it closer home, the kind of light of "the eternal child of Wordsworth, over whom its immortality broods like the day"—the light of an age which "loves so many toys and cares for so few necessities." Over such an age the Virgin reigned, and the age built her churches, like that at Chartres, to be, as she saw fit, her palaces or her toy houses; at any rate it built what it conceived would please her, "to charm her till she smiled"—that is, till the age itself felt rewarded in its expression of its aspirations. That was the light in which the Gothic got away.

Whatever it was, that light, as expressed in the Virgin's palaces, it was the light of the seven liberal arts, and of all the affairs of love and taste and ordinary life as well; it was the light of man's best vision on earth of the heaven to come. A cathedral like Chartres "expressed an intensity of conviction never again reached by any passion, whether of religion, of loyalty, of patriotism, or of wealth; perhaps never even paralleled by any single economic effort, except in war."

So much was assertion of poetry, and if Adams knew that he must return to it, he knew also that he must lay out also some of the steps—the rungs on the ladder—which faith took in gaining its intensity of conviction. To do so would give him, as it had given his ancestors, something for the poetry to move through, and in response might give the poetry speed and density in motion, solidity and spaciousness of impact; and the best way to do so was to assume a process going on, not where man created the Virgin to symbolize and unite his aspirations but where the Virgin created a new kind of man who would in the actual world work toward her ideal. At least Adams seems to have thought such an assumption best fitted the work he saw done in the twelfth and thirteenth centuries, and it is certain that by such an assumption he was better able to feel man's relation to the Virgin as the effort to control and approach an occult force, and as parallel to his own feelings about the twentieth-century dynamo. Men become known by the quality of the force they dream or fear as dominant in the age they live in, and forces that go out of fashion have not always gone out of existence; and who should say, who lives not in the stone but the atomic age, that Adams might not qualify a part of the age of faith as the age of the Virgin of Chartres?

At any rate that is what Adams does. He shows us man investing in the force of the Virgin and investigating its aspects, and he shows the Virgin attracting men to her and compelling them to reshape themselves nearer her heart's desire. The only two singularities of the process were that the force of the Virgin seemed more human than any other force felt in Christian terms and, by consequence of the first, that she raised to divinity above law the inconsistencies of human needs by shedding favor on them all. That is why men gradually saw that all true law lay in her grasp and why, for a time, they were able to know themselves totally her creatures. The perfection of Chartres Cathedral is only one evidence of the passion of that knowledge, but in terms that, as Adams says, must appeal to the practical American mind, the cost in money of the Virgin's palaces in France alone corresponds in cost to that of the great nineteenth-century effort in covering the land with railway systems. Both were uses of force and monuments expressing relation to that force maximum at their time of creation; and both showed what moved the men that made them. But the difference between the two centuries makes the force of the Virgin more striking.

The force that made the railroads made little else except by accident of attraction and agglutination; the railroads were not occult. The force that made Chartres Cathedral not only made many other things but also united them into a single society so long as the "latent scepticism which lurks behind all faith" in that force did not emerge to choose new surrenders and more narrowly human relations to force. The Virgin made St. Bernard and the whole Cistercian Order as reflections of her force as mysticism; she made also Abelard and the Schools; she made a great deal of the Crusades; she made the battle cries of every contending army; and she made the Court of Love. And she did all this in a blaze of light, a luminousness of faith, with a symbolism as simple as literary realism.

To the poets she was the whole Trinity in tolerable form, the "Templum Trinitatis, the Church itself with its triple aisle." The Trinity "was absorbed in her." Thus she was royal, with all the powers and privileges and all the human values now forgotten as belonging to royalty. But she made nothing so small of herself as to keep aloof: "not even the weakest human frailty could fear to approach" her. "Her attribute was humility; her love and pity were infinite." And Adams quotes a prayer the Church still uses: "Let him deny your mercy who can say that he has ever asked it in vain." That is why—the practical availability of her force—she made whole populations her creatures, so that the whole countryside of Chartres joined in a single movement, as surprising then as now, to build her church, working in silence and devotion and tenacity amounting to a miracle. Her presence, says Adams, was felt by the architects "in every stone they placed, and every touch they chiselled." And the miracle occurred three times, in date with the Crusades. Everybody worked and gave, from top to bottom of society, each equally to please the Virgin and in obedience to her commands. Adams is as emphatic as that; then, having made his emphasis one way, reverses it to see if it will not be stronger made the other way. The reader is meant to keep both emphases in mind; for Adams, in his reversal, is only imposing from above what was felt from beneath.

The twelfth-century mind worked along a pattern which required the presence of the Virgin for thought to move or churches to build: "Without the conviction of her personal presence, men would not have been inspired; but, to us, it is rather the inspiration of the art which proves the Virgin's presence, and we can better see the conviction of it in the work than in the words." It is in that sense—the sense that the art of the Cathedral of Chartres was inspired—that Adams continues: "Every day, as the work went on, the Virgin was present, directing the architects" to do things which, without the inspiration, they did not and could not do elsewhere.

The next four chapters are devoted to commentary and praise and elucidation of this direction under the generalized heads of "Roses and Apses," "The Twelfth-Century Glass," "The Legendary Windows," and "The Court of the Queen of Heaven"; and in every instance Adams tries to show how—judging by other examples elsewhere where the full inspiration of the Virgin was wanting—the Virgin overruled the best practice of architects and made them perform a series of impossibilities which stood and still stand today through the divine supremacy of her taste. What is perhaps most important in this part of Adams' story is the recurrent resort to that taste as an animating principle in architecture. The great Rose on the breast of the church is off its axis and ought to be awkward; instead it is superbly placed. The apse has no unity of style and ought to annoy the eye; instead it unites vision, a boudoir built for light. The pointed arches ought to collapse, and are certainly in constant peril; but they not only stand, they leap. In fact all that is built into the church is a perilous balance of incongruities, anachronisms, and contradictions of law and feeling; but the force of the Virgin's taste—the multiple inspiration of the artists in line and space and color—as the shifting fulcrum under the balance, makes it seem all a single creation. Its unity is that you are compelled to know it all together, in a kind of cumulative but single act of vision, seen now on the sanctuary, now in the nave, now from the portal—in the glass, the sculpture, the spire: all so many versions of one force, and thereby all one style.

These, as he gives them, are so many rungs in Adams' ladder; but the reader can no more climb than Adams himself could without the aid—given by the assertion of the full mind—of what is called poetic insight, the insight which creates the thing it sees. The insight is into the emotion of living religion, the deepest, Adams calls it, "man ever felt—the struggle of his own littleness to grasp the infinite." Adams saw that struggle generally in the whole external church and emphatically in the pointed arch. For the outside he takes the sequence: "the broken arch, our infinite idea of space; the spire, pointing, with its converging lines, to unity beyond space; the sleepless, restless thrust of the vaults, telling the unsatisfied, incomplete, overstrained effort of man to rival the energy, intelligence, and purpose of God." Again, and more briefly: Because the round arch could not rise, leading the mind upward to where the mind was, the Virgin's architects broke and pointed their arches. "In this church the old Romanesque leaps into the Gothic under our eyes; of a sudden, between the portal and the shrine, the infinite rises into a new expression."

And to that may be added a characteristic expression of Adams' generally, though here fastened to the whole miracle of the church: "True ignorance approaches the infinite more nearly than any amount of knowledge can do." He goes on to say that the nineteenth century was indifferent to what it could not understand, while the thirteenth century "cared little to comprehend anything but the incomprehensible." That may be so in a humorous sense but it is worth remembering, because it applies to the whole problem of poetic insight what he meant by true ignorance: a present sense of the "unknown" other than in the consciousness that uses words and ideas. Ignorance is surely a meaningless term for Adams' purpose unless it is limited to cover the absence of articulable knowledge in the presence of another and positive skill of knowing. One has to possess one's ignorance like knowledge. On another page Adams clinches his notion of the difference between the nineteenth and thirteenth centuries by saying that the one expressed its sense of unity by the commerce of goods and the other in the commerce of ideas: particularly the ideas of philosophy, poetry, and art: all efforts to make use of "true ignorance."

With this distinction in mind—which Adams carried so far that he insisted modern man had lost the color sense which was one of his twelfth-century glories—we can better understand the effort at articulation behind the language chosen for the concluding passages to the chapter on "The Legendary Windows" and that called "The Court of the Queen of Heaven." They are prayers, one to clarify, the other to redeem, the sense of true ignorance as felt in the force of the Virgin. The first of these prayers is prepared for by a consideration of some of the non-religious windows, the windows put in for color and ornament—put in, in short, to *please*, in the highest and fullest sense of that full act, to please whoso might be pleased. It is an occasion when the unofficial, the unregulated, becomes the act of pure piety, natural and necessary as breathing. Such an occasion, to the wholly devoted mind, may well be desperate; and Adams conceives the artist who is striving to please the Virgin as in his desperation praying to her for guidance and choice, praying, that is, for inspiration. So great is the need of inspiration when it is felt as lacking or uncertain that the whole of life—quite beyond any knowledge of it—is at stake. "Gracious Lady, what ought I to do?"—So Adams ends his imagination of the artist's prayer. "Forgive me my blunders, my stupidity, my wretched want of taste and feeling! I love and adore you! All that I am, I am for you! If I cannot please you, I care not for Heaven! but without your help, I am lost!"

What he had done was to give what a man might say in the thirteenth century as prayer who had felt as a lifelong condition of being the emotion that a nineteenth-century man—or a twentieth-century niece—might only hope for as a moment's revelation. Adams played with the emotion he brought until it became the emotion he found and gave him a kind of re-

served—a not quite released—eloquence of supplication. He
then turned—the place in the page almost bodily turns—to the
reader, to the most favored possible niece. Sensation has reached
the limit of its range.

You [he says], or any other lost soul, could, if you cared to look and
listen, feel a sense beyond the human ready to reveal a sense divine
that would make the world once more intelligible, and would bring
the Virgin to life again, . . . and anyone willing to try could feel
it like the child, reading new thought without end into the art he
has studied a hundred times; but what is still more convincing, he
could, at will, in an instant, shatter the whole art by calling into it
a single motive of his own.

This is the language of love when it becomes the religion of
love without ceasing to be what we all mean by love—when it
wishes to clarify its sense of itself as creation at its highest
pitch. This is the "bodiless creation ecstacy is very cunning
in," and this is the foreboding of that chaos that comes again
when love—that made the world intelligible—is gone. And it
is language like this which helps explain why he should have
called the Figure on his wife's grave his creation of the Virgin.
Adams' withdrawal from the world had been very remote, and
the spiritual autobiography of his return led him through the
emotion of Chartres. That he had come on the need and the
capacity of such language proved that his pilgrimage had been
an actual adventure, where indeed a part of him still wandered. The language at the end of "The Court of the Queen of
Heaven" is in the same sense autobiographical, representing
only a different form of the same discovered need and the same
achieved capacity. Where the first passage clarifies true ignorance as the artist's inspiration, the second pushes so far into
true ignorance that it seems an experience truly universal, and
is therefore a form of redemption, and a means of return. The
emotion is again love.

And again Adams comes on it by the intensity of his own
re-creation of, response to, and use of, the force of the Virgin;
and again he reaches the critical point of poetic insight after
an effort at formal explanation which failed, by itself, to
satisfy the conditions but demanded also what Adams could
himself bring. It is no limitation of reality or of divinity to say
that men see only what they bring, know only what they make,

feel only, in the end, their own emotion. Here Adams is concerned to understand the beauty and unifying power of the great windows of the sanctuary over the whole church, but he is careful to say nothing, actually, about the sanctuary until he has covered—and re-covered—a great deal of other ground first. Yet since he begins by saying that the artist is at home in the sanctuary because he built it for God, whereas the nave was built for the people, it is possible that the first two-thirds of the chapter are more an *ad-libbing*, a means of getting himself going, than deliberate preparation. Something else *might* have done as well, which makes all the surer that what is given does excellently. What he does give is another version of the old story of the particular disunity and incongruous variety of the parts of Chartres. This time he points the story with the memory of the great churches of Sancta Sophia and Monreale which had theological unity and were built with single, brief, intense efforts. Chartres, on the contrary, was built in a series of intense spasms over a period of hundreds of years, in different styles, by a society which was rural, feudal, and royal, but never concentrated; and such unity as it had was in plain fact the unity that it could be seen altogether in the same place under the dominance of a single relation, itself shifting, waxing and waning: its relation to the Virgin.

When the question is asked what that relation is, it "seems to answer itself like an echo": it is ten thousand people on their knees, who "knew the Virgin as well as they knew their own mother." Every room, every bed, every neck, every street corner had its image or emblem of the Virgin; she was present "in every act and almost in every thought of life"; and she was present because everyone felt "her boundless sympathy" instantly available. That answer, so stated, was indeed no more than an echo of the question, and was hard to take if one compared, say, as Adams is compelled to do—though with the echo warm in his ears—the Rose windows of Blanche of Castile and Pierre de Dreux opposite and opposing each other in the transepts. Let alone that the enmity of Blanche and Pierre in life very nearly wrecked French society, their Roses represented very different conceptions of the Virgin to whom they bore common relation. The Virgin of Blanche was feminine and the Virgin of Majesty, with powers the Church never conceded; the Virgin of Pierre was masculine in conception and the Virgin of Theology, with her rights as Christ's mother but no more. Where in one the Virgin was regent, in the other Christ was King. How, then, could such opposed conceptions be united in the Virgin of Chartres? The seven windows of the clerestory which lighted the sanctuary, Adams argues, make the meaning of the echo clear. And he strengthens his argument by reminding the reader that these windows, forty-seven feet high in their own dimension and rising a hundred feet in air, make the full vista seen when entering the church three hundred and thirty feet away, and that they therefore dominate, and were meant to dominate, the whole church.

There, in the seven windows, quite out of sight of the war in the transepts, and of the other war in the world, is a single composition with the Virgin Queen in the center and her Court filling the windows at her either side. She dominates, but by neither majesty nor theology nor passion: her figure is too retiring and too calm for any of these. The Virgin of Chartres, says Adams, is in this her central image the Virgin of Grace. She is at home among her people, and her Grace, it may be risked, is the humanity in man that compelled him so to portray her that her presence "calms our excitement as that of a mother calms her child. She is there as Queen, not merely as intercessor, and her power is such that to her the difference between us earthly beings is nothing." It is the power of common humanity felt as supreme. To people in trouble "this sense of her power and calm is better than active sympathy. People who suffer beyond the formulas of expression—who are crushed into silence, and beyond pain—want no display of emotion—no bleeding heart—no weeping at the foot of the Cross—no hysterics—no phrases! They want to see God, and to know that he is watching over His own." Then Adams presents the image of the mother who has lost her baby, praying. "The earth, she says, is a sorry place, and the best of it is bad enough . . . but there above is Mary in heaven who sees and hears me as I see her, and who keeps my baby boy till I come; so I can wait with patience, more or less! Saints and prophets and martyrs are all very well, and Christ is very sublime and just, but Mary *knows!*"

Such knowledge is the ultimate reserve power to meet the conditions of life—the very reserve of grace abounding—found at the very bottom of ignorance. It could be known, so to speak, only directly; yet only by the extreme indirection of art could it be commonly known, and the meaning of the art had to be identified with religious faith; it had to seem, what it was, the divine in the human, and it had to be, in the actuality of faith, what it seemed in symbol, God's grace touching man. Such truth—such knowledge, such ignorance—was emotion. A society which undertook to express itself, as French society tried to in the twelfth and thirteenth centuries, in terms of that emotion, ran constantly the risk—and regularly succumbed to it—of excess, hysteria, insanity, not only in the field of the emotion itself but also in other fields infected by it. Rural, feudal, royal such a society had to be, for no other society was loose enough and heedless enough to have stood the strain; yet it may be that only the truth of the emotion made the facts of the society tolerable. So far as the emotion triumphed, all the machinery of society was reduced to the personal relation, including the machinery of God, at least as a matter of faith and imagination, where the personal relation is substance itself. But the triumph failed to last; it could not be maintained even as art; society could not afford the cost as its excess of energy disappeared.

It may be the tragedy of man, not that he cannot cope with the physical or intellectual energies that confront him but that he cannot build a society—only, for brief moments, a religion or an art—appropriate to the emotion which alone freely expresses him. If it is not tragedy it is something both better and worse: man's chief undeclarable possibility. No wonder, when they came closest to declaring it, men looked chiefly to Kingdom Come, and made in this world chiefly art. No wonder then, looking at the art, and thinking of the men and their effort to equal the emotion they felt, Adams saw the Virgin who had represented the whole—herself the emotion—as "looking down from a deserted heaven, into an empty church, on a dead faith."

That is Adams' first—but not final—farewell to the Virgin of Chartres; and as the order of syllables closes into its final spondee, they clinch what died as a living memory into Adams' sensibility. Those who complain that he romanticizes a fantastic or an eccentric impulse have not thought from what depths that impulse came, nor how ancient and universal its human history is, nor how hollow is the pretense of denial that it still exists, which is the chief obstacle to its expression today. As if to defend himself against the charge, when it should come to be made, Adams expressly lodges the source of his image of radiant compassion in the force of sex, and places the Virgin as the end-form—so far in Western society—of the impulse which had created Astarte, Isis, Demeter, and Aphrodite.

The force of sex is the force of creation: is Woman. In American society sex is taken, apart from personal experience, as a sentiment, as feminine in the weakening sense, and is commercialized as Mother's Day; sex as force is still to be seen in the nearest beehive, where it is concentrated in the queen bee with an exaggeration beyond man's practical capacity. In the twelfth and thirteenth centuries a balance was struck between pure sentiment and naked force which still affects the language of courtship and minor poetry, where the sentiment gave ideal form and standard for response to the force. We have the tradition and regard it as a plaything, the ballad of some other time, not ours even when we sing it. Adams, thinking of the Virgin and of the Court of Love at the same time, knew the tradition was firm in its source and that the ballad—or *roman* or *fabliau*—was true song and passed into reality beyond the form of the words. He was no more afraid of the symbols men used than of the emotion the symbols made real. "Tradition," he remarks, "exaggerates everything it touches, but shows, at the same time, what is passing in the minds of the society which *tradites*."

When the Crusaders found the game of chess in the East the king was attended by a minister, but when they played the game in France the minister became the place now called queen (then sometimes called also the Virgin), and assumed the most arbitrary and formidable role in the game. Sex—whether Queen, Virgin, or Woman—was, as men played with their sense of it, supreme. As woman, sex made her the equal of man in the affairs of the world and the heroine—as a rule surpassing the hero at every turn—of the adventures in which, so far as he was poet, man evidently preferred to pass his life. As Virgin, the creation of sex gave a sense of control and a feeling of acceptable authority by filling, through the Church, the whole of society, both of this world and the next. As Queen, particularly as Queen Eleanor and her two daughters, sex ruled the manners—the meaningful game—of society by creating the complicated passion of love which rests on the story of Tristan and Isolde no less than on the authority of the Virgin, and which still gives the brutalities of the flesh reality and their scandals beauty. The equality of women, the worship of the Virgin, and Courteous Love were all in recognition and expressions of the force of sex; all were ideals of that force made actual in the concern felt for them; all were parts of the same thing, a human creation out of non-human force.

Adams knew perfectly that the effort was imaginative and that what is in heat imaginative reality is in cold imaginary phantasm. "While the Virgin," he says, "was miraculously using the power of spiritual love to elevate and purify the people, Eleanor and her daughters were using the power of earthly love to discipline and refine the courts. Side by side with the crude realities about them, they insisted on teaching and enforcing an ideal that contradicted the realities, and had no value for them or for us except in the contradiction." The best proof, to a modern mind, that the poets who established the tradition of Courteous Love understood the extent and value of the contradiction lies in the fact that a common language was used (Adams gives two poems by Thibaut) in addressing Queen Blanche and Mary Queen of Heaven. The fact was a convention, and the convention made art.

French art [says Adams] starts not from facts, but from certain assumptions as conventional as a legendary window, and the commonest convention is the Woman. The fact, then as now, was Power, or its equivalent in exchange, but Frenchmen, while struggling for the Power, expressed it in terms of art. . . . Illusion for illusion, courteous love, in Thibaut's hands, or in the hands of Dante and Petrarch, was as substantial as any other convention;—the balance of trade, the rights of man, or the Athanasian Creed. In that sense the illusions alone were real; if the Middle Ages had reflected only what was practical, nothing would have survived for us.

The practical does not survive, and when we find it in the dustbin of history we do not know what it is until we have lent it the life of what has survived—either in the existing common tradition, or in the art once made out of the substance, in a different stage, of that tradition, or by what seems the accidental access to universal experience. What survives is what can be seen as having once expressed the practical intensely, because in the present mind it seems still, however less intensely and at whatever new remove of loss or hope, to do so.

To estimate survival is a primary purpose of education, as to appreciate it may be its final value. Adams' whole intent in these chapters is to estimate and appreciate the thirteenth-century French effort in the social and poetic arts—by the Three Queens, by the court poets Chrétien and Thibaut and William of Lorris, by the Bourgeois poet Adam de la Halle, and by the anonymous poets—to express practical life, and by expressing to change it, so as to make it tolerable. (King Richard's Prison Song Adams deals with here, too, but it concerns us, and Adams, more seriously in another context and is dealt with at length elsewhere.) The estimate comes high, for the remove is very far off; we undertake no longer, except as superficial manners, the moral that love makes gentle equally the knight and the boor; yet that moral is what survives. The appreciation comes higher still, for it involves the notion, which we have almost totally discarded, that all the kinds of love which move us are in the end one and are, as one, religious.

What we have discarded is of course neither the love nor the religion but the modification in our notions of each which their identification makes necessary. There, at that point, is the sharpest difference between the Middle Ages and their successors. Taking Lorris' *Romance of the Rose* as the end type or at any rate the final form of the poetry of Courteous Love, its special character is clearly that "the Rose is any feminine ideal of beauty, intelligence, purity, or grace—always culminating in the Virgin—but the scene is the Court of Love, and the action is avowedly in a dream, without time or place." Lorris, coming at the end of his period, as Adams says, "made epoch"; the action—whether of woman or Queen or Virgin—by being avowed a dream no longer enjoined reality but made desperate escape from it. The Rose was rose water. "The Woman and the Rose became bankrupt. Satire took the place of worship. Man, with his usual monkey-like malice, took pleasure in pulling down what he had built up." It was not a question of fact but of feeling; the facts were the same; yet where man had felt he lived to be saved he now began to feel that he died to be lost—to be damned. "For the first time since Constantine proclaimed the reign of Christ, a thousand years, or so, before Philip the Fair dethroned Him, the deepest expression of social feeling ended with the word: Despair."

This is Adams' second farewell to the power of the Virgin; and the student of Adams' sensibility may rejoice to note how much this time the sense of history both redeems and supports the excess of emotion which culminated in the closed spondee, "dead faith," of the first farewell. The first was prayer, and a matter of poetry; the second is history and might have been written by Adams' master Gibbon in a new Ara Coeli, but by a Gibbon converted, who had learned, in the twentieth century, what the eighteenth could not see, that there had been a new decline and a further fall in man, worth a deeper despair, because more was lost, than in the old.

One loses what one is. Despair comes when hope is seen to be vain without any lessening of the intensity with which it is felt, until at last the sense of fate descends upon the sense of hope, and a new hope is born. Adams stood himself in shifting balance between the two senses, at least after the sixth of December 1885, and as he grew older inclined more and more to see both the sense of hope in himself and that in his age succumb to a sense of overriding fate. The balance shifted far and the little hope that survived had need of a mighty lever: despair, the lever of what is felt as lost. Adams could have found no better way of seizing that lever than the one he chose at the beginning of his next chapter, "Les Miracles de Notre Dame." There he prints side by side prayers to the Virgin by Dante and Petrarch, and then, refusing to translate them except by sidelong phrase, says that he has not brought them in for their beauty, "but chiefly to show the good faith, the depth of feeling, the intensity of conviction, with which society adored its ideal of human perfection."

Dante wrote when the power of the Virgin had begun to wane, and Petrarch wrote later still, but the intensity with which they invoked what they hoped for had if anything increased; the power of the Virgin seemed more real by being less available. Perhaps great literature differs from the other great arts by always being a little posthumous to its actual inspiration: it celebrates, as in epic and tragedy, exactly what survives out of what has been lost: what is still real, however desperately held. So Dante and Petrarch in their prayers; Adams, at a greater remove in time and emotion, had the different and more tentative task of bringing his readers—his nieces in wishes—back to what Dante and Petrarch could still take for granted, and had to do so by appealing to what still survived of the old impulse, however changed, in them and us. After prefixing with great poetry the notion that the Virgin

was the ideal of human perfection, he had to proceed to re-
awaken the sense of what that ideal once chiefly comprised.

What better clue to those elements could there be than in the
miracles—the arbitrary transformations of the real into the
actual—which the ideal performed in those who were faithful
to it? Miracles are what men always want, and in the Virgin
it was the ideal itself that became the miracle because by her
presence, constantly assumed, she provided a human—an actual
—escape from everything less than or greater than the human
ideal: from the law of Church or lord, or God's logic and justice.
She was the necessary human consequence of the rigorous and
implacable conception of God as Trinity. The Virgin was the
ideal of man as he was, and made tolerable both the living
world and the world to come. With her help, with the miracle
of her presence, it was possible to suffer both the consistency
of Caesar and the inconsistency of God. Without her, says
Adams in a remark involving a question which we cannot yet
master, "Without Mary, man had no hope except in atheism,
and for atheism the world was not ready."

If Adams' sentence may be pushed a little further, we find
in it the reason why he called himself a Conservative Christian
Anarchist; without some human ideal resembling the ideal of
the Virgin no society can make tolerable the virtual atheism
into which, without her, the world seems gradually—rather less
gradually after 1945—to have fallen. Adams wished to keep,
because he felt the need survive in himself, he wished to con-
serve the Christian anarchy—or, if you like, the over-all compassion—which he had seen in the Virgin act as a binding force,
where the Trinity failed, then, as later, over a society otherwise
disorderly and deeply disconcerted. We see here, too, pushing
a little further, why he thought all Americans were naturally
Conservative Christian Anarchists, for to him what kept American society together and plastic was the fact that deep in its
unconscious feeling for the human ideal it had never committed
itself to any single version of the good as supreme. He would
have been delighted, could he have believed it, when in 1945
the Pope declared the Virgin Empress of the Americas, but he
would have legitimately objected when the Pope's legate ascribed a particular policy to the Virgin Empress in Mexican
politics. To the Virgin Adams knew, all politics were the same,
as all humans were sinners, without distinction or degrees. The

acts by which she expressed that attitude were the sum and substance of her miracles.

Perhaps Adams carefully selected what miracles to recount with that attitude in mind; certainly after twenty pages and as many miracles he seems to have earned for his feeling of that attitude the stature of judgment:

Mary concentrated in herself the whole rebellion of man against fate; the whole protest against divine law; the whole contempt for human law as its outcome; the whole unutterable fury of human nature beating itself against the walls of its prison-house, and suddenly seized by a hope that in the Virgin man had found a door of escape. She was above law. . . . She knew that the universe was as unintelligible to her, or any theory of morals, as it was to her worshippers, and she felt, like them, no sure conviction that it was any more intelligible to the Creator of it.

Her secret was positive compassion; she was what might be called the Buddhist element in Christianity, for with her as with Buddha compassion is, as Adams' friend La Farge wrote, "the first of all virtues, and leads and is the essence of the five cardinal virtues, which are—note the sequence—pity, justice, urbanity, sincerity, *and* wise behavior." So with the Virgin and, in Adams' portrait, her order of virtues; prudence was necessary, but as a kind of afterthought. To Kwannon the Compassionate One and to Mary the Mother of God, compassion included the idea of sorrowful contemplation.

How positively Adams felt compassion as dominating the Virgin's character, he tried to make plain in the record of its long endurance. "The convulsive hold which Mary to this day maintains over human imagination—as you can see at Lourdes —was due much less to her power of saving soul or body than to her sympathy with people who suffered under law—justly or unjustly, by accident or design, by decree of God or by guile of Devil." Men feared justice and distrusted law; they wanted favor or compassion depending on the quality of their need, but they could find neither dependably at merely human hands as they could find neither at entirely godly hands.

They longed for a power above law—or above the contorted mass of ignorance and absurdity bearing the name of law; but the power which they longed for was not human, for humanity they knew to be corrupt and incompetent from the day of Adam's creation to the day of the Last Judgment . . . they yearned for protection, pardon, and love.

This no form of the Trinity, though omnipotent, could give.

The Mother alone was human, imperfect, and could love; she alone was Favour, Duality, Diversity. Under any conceivable form of religion, this duality must find embodiment somewhere, and the Middle Ages logically insisted that, as it could not be in the Trinity, either separately or together, it must be in the Mother. If the Trinity was in its essence Unity, the Mother alone could represent whatever was not Unity; whatever was irregular, exceptional, outlawed; and this was the whole human race.

The order of these last quotations has been reversed and the text pruned so as to come back cleanly on what seems the central and underlying question of Adams' book, in order to ask which emphatically, so far as the reader is concerned, he may be said to have written; for as we ask it of ourselves and in our own immensely pressing terms, it gathers together almost all that is questionable in our own society and shows us an image of the peril of what loss in which we stand. Why did Catholic Christianity subordinate the compassion of the Virgin to the personal realm and condemn her to small miracles, and why did Protestant Christianity exclude her altogether? Why should society drive out the one divinity that made tolerable the burden of justice and law, whether God's or man's? But let Adams ask his own questions.

Why were all the Protestant churches cold failures without her help? Why could not the Holy Ghost—the spirit of Love and Grace—equally answer their prayers? Why was the Son powerless? Why was Chartres Cathedral in the thirteenth century—like Lourdes to-day—the expression of what is in substance a separate religion? Why did the gentle and gracious Virgin Mother so exasperate the Pilgrim Father? Why was the Woman struck out of the Church and ignored in the State? These questions are not antiquarian or trifling in historical value; they tug at the very heart-strings of all that makes whatever order is in the cosmos. If a Unity exists, in which and toward which all energies centre, it must explain and include Duality, Diversity, Infinity—Sex!

Adams does not answer any form of his question; rather he continues to ask it in differing forms as if in some final form it might, like the Sphinx, be its own answer, and he himself be a part of the question; but at least we can now see why he took so much trouble to show both the reality of the conception of the Virgin and the universal felt actuality of her presence. Without both taken as proved, the question could not meaningfully have been asked at all. Perhaps if he had written the study of the Reformation he at one time thought of, the answer would have emerged—would have been secreted—under the pressure of what happened between 1300 and 1600 over against what happened between 1600 and 1900; for in the first period what was meant by the Virgin grew to seem unnecessary through pride of intellect, and in the second period both what was meant by the Virgin and what was meant by the intellect —as prime movers in men's affairs—grew to seem unnecessary through surrender to pride in the mastery of natural force, what Adams called the dynamo. Where the dynamo absorbed the intellect, the intellect first tried to come into balance with the Virgin and then, in a rash of pride, excluded her except as a mechanism.

To Adams' exposition of the dynamo we shall return, as it was his object that we should do, and returning we shall find that the dynamo was only the most intense frame Adams could find for his question: "Why was the Woman struck out of the Church and ignored in the State?" Why, that is, at the very moment that he got most help from the Woman, did man suddenly think himself able to stand on the feet of his own intellect? Why did he assume for himself an omnicompetence in Church and State exactly equal to that very omnipotence of God from which the Virgin had been created to protect him? Why, since then, did man follow one broken omnicompetent state with another? Why, now, at the first sign of breaking of his only political aspiration founded, like the Virgin's, on a balance of actual emotions, does he rush again into the practice, and virtually the doctrine, of a new and brittly rigid—what is called fatal—omnicompetence?

If this extension of Adams' question is legitimate we have all the more reason to try to recapture in a single perspective his portrait of the Virgin who led him to ask it; and this is what we may call the godwardness—the divine waywardness—the blessed uncommittedness—the pure grace taken as untrammeling free will—which the men of the twelfth century attached to their most human creation of supreme force. It was perhaps the presence of the uncommitted, wayward, godward good—as shown by the Virgin and St. Francis—at the center of the twelfth-century universal state that made it relatively success-ful; as it was perhaps the absence of the leaven of the uncom-mitted that broke the omnicompetent universal state of the thirteenth- and fourteenth-century papacy. The Virgin repre-sented, expressed, the will of the people as individuals; she represented not only the anarchy to *be* ordered, she also repre-sented the forces, anarchic or not, which were *not* to be ordered but to be included, heeded, supplicated. The Virgin was to Adams the force that could by love create order out of the actual.

But it is only Adams' form of expression that can be dis-missed as that excess of devotion known as Marianism or Mari-olatry. His true interest lay as always in the determination of a force outside himself, and outside any possible self, which yet rejuvenated—even re-created—the self in the form of works not otherwise, apparently, possible. The self without the aid of a great outside force becomes intolerable to the self; as we see in lechery without the force of sex. (Not sex without love; it would be truer to complain of love without sex, love without the strain, and the demand to respond, of the stream of crea-tion.) What happened to the Church, to Christian society, when the Virgin stopped building—and when St. Thomas and St. Francis stopped building—was the loss to it of the greatest out-side force it had ever known: the only force capable of over-riding with good—with health—the tendency of that society to self-mutilation and the relevation of all good to the "other" world. The Puritans did not get rid only of Woman, they got rid of imagination and charity, too, the three forms in which they had so long drawn on outside force; but the woman—sex—Mary Virgin—summed them all.

The Virgin of the twelfth and thirteenth centuries had not only the powers of Eve and Demeter and Venus; she was also the mistress of all the arts and sciences, was afraid of none of them, and did nothing, ever, to stunt any of them. Under her rule, so far as it ran, what corruption they showed was their own, and reflected men's ignorance in her praise; and during her reign, therefore, great things were done—at least in Italy and France. She was Queen by divine right and compassion and understanding, not by law and formula. Those who owed

her fealty were compelled to do their best whether their best
followed law or not. No woman could be more divine; no
divinity could be more human; no human ideal could more
surpass human weakness and bring to men so near their full
human strength.

Discovery of this sort of balance in the Middle Ages was the
limit of Adams' Marianism, just as the conception of its ana-
logue in the smaller field of politics was the limit of his
eighteenth-century Americanism. The Virgin was the practice,
through all the interests of society; more than the principle she
was the practice, of the true balance of powers, with the individual always tilting the balance. Thus she was felt, by individuals singly and collectively, as personal presence: as the
unaccountable other thing wholly there; and what was felt was
the saving grace. All the exceptions she made to the minor
interest were redeemed by adherence to the major interest of
the law; thus she was on all sides of all quarrels, and rightly
on all banners. She was the personal equation at the heart of
law and justice; but never the personal equation all by itself.
Adams says she was in effect a separate religion, and that may
be the story; but she never ought to have been made so; and
it is our fatal lost chance that the Roman Church should have
absorbed her by particularizing her rather than centralizing
her. She was the one practice (*not* St. Thomas, *not* St. Francis)
which, kept as a reservoir and source of central principle, might
have made the good society possible—and possible at something
like full strength; for it was her practice to bear all burdens.
Instead, she was put to minor miracles, such as make ill society
tolerable, and healed mere breaches of order; whereas what
was possible and wanted—and of which in her cathedrals and
poetry she had proved herself capable—were fresh creations of
order: those fresh creations of order which can alone make
room and home for the new disorders the world flings up as it
changes its direction and its pace. It is that possibility we still
work on, without her help; and it is in part Adams' sense of the
continuity of that effort which led him to insist that America
had never committed herself exclusively to any one form of the
good, but rather, at least by implied question, to uncommitted
goodness itself.

The Virgin made the world intelligible by divinity that took
second thought; Americans tried atheism in the guise of free

factions—for which, as Adams says, the Virgin's world was not ready. The great question is whether Americans are—or even were in a simpler context—ready either. Adams never outright asked this question; but, thinking of all "those others" who groveled in desperation of faith, he asked *Why not me?*—just as he asked whether the compass moved man or man moved the compass. No single man alone is ever capable either of deciding his relation to the forces which move him and which he moves, or of choosing which of the forces he greatly feels will suffice his allegiance. Thus Dante, writing after 1300, chose three—the Virgin, St. Bernard, and St. Thomas; and out of these three extremes of force developed the fullest imagined order any single mind in the history of Christendom has ever seen.

So it was with the whole age that preceded Dante. Neither to the twelfth nor to the thirteenth century was the Virgin enough. The very extremity of her lodgment in the heart of mankind— the extremity of the waywardness with which she stood between man and God—required that men addict themselves also to other extremes: the extreme of intellect self-willed and anarchic as in Abelard, the extreme of the direct intuition of God as in Bernard, who held the world in contempt, or as in Francis, who loved all God's first creations, and the extreme of intellect architectural and hierarchic as in the reason of Thomas. So, in his last three chapters, Adams turned to the study, or rather to the dramatization, of these extremes in the astonishing relation by which, at least in perspective, they seem parts concerting into a whole. Irreconcilable if their positions were taken in reaction to each other, they yet had a common relation which kept them, for a time, in perilous balance; and that, in Adams' language, was their relation to the Virgin—or to the Church filled with the Virgin who, from each point of view taken separately, was not enough, but who, if all the points of view were to survive in harmony, was all the more necessary. The harmony was of true liberalism:

A Church which embraced [wrote Adams] with equal sympathy, and within a hundred years, the Virgin, Saint Bernard, William of Champeaux and the School of Saint-Victor, Peter the Venerable, Saint Francis of Assisi, Saint Dominic, Saint Thomas Aquinas, and Saint Bonaventure, was more liberal than any modern State can afford to be. Radical contradictions the State may perhaps tolerate, though hardly, but never embrace or profess. Such elasticity long ago vanished from human thought.

Adams could have added, to complete the full federation of faith, kings, dukes, and knights, the courts and communes—not to mention the dual empire—which with whatever conflicts the Church also embraced; but let us force attention simply on the individuals as Adams orders them. The sequence of dominant qualities attached to these names might be: The Human; God as emotion; the intellect as machine; the humanistic; the love of God as creation; orthodox balance in the Church; intellect as architect; intellect as intuition. Society—the Church—did not force these contradictions, though it did those of the Albigensians; nor did it unite them; it tolerated and embraced them. So thinking, we may without serious risk ask whether so wide a unity of contradictions did not come about rather through some underlying movement of inertia than through any policy made by charity of understanding or by any deliberately kept sense of self-elasticity in the presiding mind. At any rate consciousness turned soon enough to omnicompetence, and faith to *plenitudo potestatis* when the furies of fanaticism reigned everywhere. Becoming exclusively conscious, the age made the terrible mistake of trying to balance *only* congruous forces, seeking to destroy the incongruous forces which weight so much either side of any true balance.

Faith, to work, cannot be exacerbated; and yet, to work, Faith seems always either to have persecuted the unfaithful or put them beyond the pale of faith's benefits. This was relatively true of the twelfth and thirteenth centuries; absolutely true of the following age; it is only on balance and on a chosen fulcrum of the impossible ideal that Adams could see his Church universal as housing and succouring a liberal society. It may be risked, thinking by choice only in admiration of Adams' chosen age, that the beautiful pang of great aspiration striking on great tolerance was possible because that age found itself merging in a *series* of commitments which only made a conviction when felt together. The unity was in the convergence of straight lines in the *general* mind and was most likely never unity at all in any single mind—unless in St. Thomas.

Certainly the commitments to which Abelard—Adams' first example of an extreme—lent himself hardly reflected unity at all. That apostle of the Holy Ghost saw little comfort or grace in any mind but his own. His function was chiefly that of irritant, innovator, anarchist as rebel, and his power was that of the unaided intellect everywhere passionately equal to itself, everywhere calamitously unequal to the world in which it found itself. He was rather a John Randolph of the Schools: his ultimate weapon was temper; and the source of temper was much the same, for each felt, as the self-willed mind must, that official society cheated him of the use of half his talents. But the differences, once the type is recognized, are greater than the resemblances.

Abelard was master of the common technique of the intellect of his time—the kind of dialectic formalized in the syllogism— and the trouble he got into came from the fact that he pushed his technique a century ahead of what his time was prepared to accept and did so, so to speak, entirely on his own authority; he made theology the creature of dialectics and made dialectics human. St. Thomas, a century later, made dialectics the servant of theology and made theology angelic—at least in presumed authority. Abelard made anarchic hash of official theology by introducing the human concept into the irreconcilable conflict between Realism and Nominalism: he knew that that was what men did in practice, or at least that it was the practice of his own mind. St. Thomas knew that the human concept was necessary if the official theology was to succeed, and therefore built it syllogism-by-syllogism into the aspiring architecture of that theology. Abelard failed; Thomas perhaps succeeded—later, when he was canonized, officially and against all comers. But their enemies—those who were against the Schools, against dialectic, against the supremacy of any form of intellect—were differently disposed. Abelard ran into the emotion and pride and intemperateness of St. Bernard when Bernard was at the height of his power, having made a Pope and a King his own. St. Thomas ran into the emotion of the Franciscans after the death of St. Francis when his friars had become learned with a kind of school system of their own.

Abelard was silenced, though imperfectly. Thomas, when he died, left his doctrine in living controversy in which it was at length changed so far as time could change it, and for purposes he could not have envisaged, made official. Abelard was the victim of political jobbery; he was promoted into positions of power in which he lost his freedom; but what else was he asking for when he invented, under the title of *Sic et Non*, the trick of setting up inconsistent or contradictory statements of the authorities in the obloquy of parallel columns? Perhaps St. Thomas, too, asked his own fate; for his great effort was to compromise objectively, not to sharpen subjectively, the irreconcilable problems of the mind, and that is the type of effort official society always looks on with interest and adapts to its own uses, with or without the aspiration which made the compromise a viable balance.

But it was not only the triangle of Realism, Nominalism, and Conceptualism that interested Adams in Abelard's mind. Despite or because of his celebrated affair with Héloïse, which left her an Isolde and him much less than a Tristan, Abelard was a Catholic-Puritan prototype of those reformers who destroyed, among other things, the divinity of the Virgin. On the one hand an early workman on that version of the Great Chain of Being which by the eighteenth century left man dangling entirely free—or guyed only by threads of reason—on the other hand he attempted to replace man's actual relation to the Virgin with an intangible relation to the Holy Ghost. The temptation to do so had been by logical necessity always present in the frame of the Trinity, and it was perhaps chiefly the popular faith in the Virgin that had kept the temptation down. A Trinity of Father, Mother, and Child was natural, intelligible, and traditional: it was the infinite series of the human family and was by instinct felt as parallel to the family—to the mystery —of heaven. How otherwise could God show his Oneness as Diversity understandably to man, and yet keep the mystery of it actual, within the power of man to rehearse? Christianity had worked for some centuries on a tacit compromise between the Official Trinity and the Natural Trinity, and the bridge between had been in the shifting, multiple role of the Virgin. The Virgin, as the center of something like a separate religion, had, so to speak, triangulated the two versions of the Trinity; she was the access to the understanding of either without loss of mystery.

Abelard, a philosopher who dealt with theology as if it were a part of the study of law, seems to have resented the human need for the Virgin and to have insisted that the Trinity could be explained in conceptual terms alone; castrated, he had become a lover of the abstract; the mystery disappeared because he could no longer feel it. But he had on his side the strength of future history—much stronger than the methods of logic and law—and even though the Church condemned him and compelled him to burn his book with his own hands, he was able with the support of the Abbé Suger to retire into the Church itself and built an oratory of reeds and thatch, dedicated to the Trinity but called Paraclete, to which his scholars followed him in great numbers, so that he became the chief contender with Bernard for leadership in popular intellectual opinion. Though Bernard won at the time, by political means, Abelard would seem to have won in the end; for certainly the concept, shorn of some of its Scholastic logic, won over emotion, shorn of its faith. The novelty of what came to be called the Monastery of the Paraclete was only less shocking than the novelty, as applied to Scripture and theology, of the critical principle of parallel columns, and it was on the second novelty that he was sentenced to silence, than which, with the paranoiac energy of his mind, there could have been no judgment harsher.

But between intellect presumptuous and emotion presumptuous, what choice? Abelard made God logical and necessitarian, to be known in the abstract, and touched by the pointed arch of conceptual thought. Bernard felt God as mystery and emotion, to be known by revelation, and touched through the Virgin. Each was exemplary in his certainty of authority, where the arrogance of faith was no less than the arrogance of reason. Each thought that because the other led wrong he himself led right, and without alternative. Each therefore condemned the other without a hearing, the one from the depths of experience, the other from the heights of possibility. To those not caught up in the precarious grandeur of either position, there is no choice between them, only a perpetual stress of alternation.

How extreme the alternation is may perhaps be seen if we plant between the figures of Abbot Bernard of Clairvaux and Abbot Abelard of Saint-Gildas the very different figure of Abbot Suger of Saint-Denis; for it is right, in this labor to understand the ideal force of the twelfth century, that we should see the humanist and patron of art set between the Schoolman and the saint. Adams makes a dozen references to Suger, to his exquisite Abbey Church and to its glass for the Virgin in which the figure of Suger himself appears prostrate at Mary's feet, and to the political power by which he intervened between Bernard and

Abelard, and Bernard and Queen Eleanor. Perhaps Adams' sharpest reference for our purpose is when he remarks that the flèche on the old tower at Chartres does not represent Bernard, who assumed leadership of the Second Crusade under it, but does represent Suger, Peter the Venerable of Cluny, and Abelard. With that reference in mind we can consult the portrait of Suger drawn by Erwin Panofsky in the introduction to his translation of Suger's essays *On the Abbey Church of St. Denis and Its Art Treasures.* After observing that Suger was that Patron of Art who, alone among patrons, described his intentions, Professor Panofsky goes on:

As the head and reorganizer of an abbey that in political significance and territorial wealth surpassed most bishoprics, as the Regent of France during the Second Crusade, and as the "loyal adviser and friend" of two French kings at a time when the Crown began to reassert its power after a long period of great weakness, Suger (born 1081 and Abbot of St.-Denis from 1122 until his death in 1151) is an outstanding figure in the history of France; not without reason has he been called the father of the French monarchy that was to culminate in the state of Louis XIV.

In short, Suger not only stood in the middle between the extremes of Bernard's emotion and Abelard's intellect, he stood also in the middle of what we now regard as society: in the middle of its art, politics, and economics. A good business man, ripe with the sense of practicable equity, and strong with the sense of his own rectitude, he secured a relation between the Crown and his abbey which was without conflict. Perhaps he took advantage, in this relation, of the fact that his abbey harbored the relics of the "Apostle of all Gaul," and was therefore a royal abbey, the tomb of kings; certainly he took advantage of it as a means of uniting all France under the Oriflamme of Saint-Denis against the threat of invasion by the Emperor Henry V. The force of the abbey was the residual strength by which he developed the prestige of the Crown and by which, also, he made himself the "mediator and tie of peace" with local counts, with England, and with the Empire. He abused his power, as Adams might have said, only for legitimate ends: the aggrandizement of the crown and the beautification of his abbey according to his own lights and temperament.

Both lights and temperament were to Bernard's mind presumptuous, nor were they safe from the attentions of Abelard's

intellect. Bernard and Suger were at opposite poles as to the
conduct of religious life and perhaps as to its object as well.
To Bernard proper monasticism meant blind obedience and
self-denial, to Suger discipline and moderation. Bernard made
a cult of silence, Suger of conversation; one was glad of fasts,
the other delighted to find cause for feasts. Bernard would have
kept the people out of Clairvaux, Suger made more and more
room for the crowds at Saint-Denis. Bernard distrusted every
splendor of the senses. Suger thought nothing "would be a graver
sin of omission than to withhold from the service of God and
His saints what He had empowered nature to supply and men
to perfect: vessels of gold or precious stone adorned with pearls
and gems, golden candelabra and altar panels, sculpture and
stained glass, mosaic and enamel work, lustrous vestments and
tapestries": exactly what was to Bernard detestable. Yet Suger
represented perfectly a source or nexus of spiritual life in the
great fraction of men which Bernard did not understand at all.
As Panofsky puts it:

If the spiritual pre-eminence of St.-Denis was Suger's conviction, its
material embellishment was his passion: the Holy Martyrs, whose
"sacred ashes" could be carried only by the king and took precedence
over all other relics however much revered, had to have the most
beautiful church in France.

Bernard left a treatise in intense prose on the Steps of Humility,
Suger left a record in elegant and Euphuistic Latin on the
beauty and dignity of his abbey church. To Bernard art was a
temporal snare—and a great risk to faith and spirit. Suger
found in the philosophy of light transmitted from the Platonists
to Christian terms by the Pseudo-Dionysius (whom he took to
be the Saint-Denis of his own Abbey) permission "to greet
material beauty as a vehicle of spiritual beatitude instead of
forcing him to flee from it as though from a temptation; and to
conceive of the moral as well as the physical universe, not as a
monochrome in black and white but as a harmony of many
colors."

Suger was a proto-humanist, and no more a Scholastic than
he was a saint. Where he thought it prudent to make and keep
friendly terms with Bernard, he also found himself generous
enough to protect Abelard from Bernard and to tolerate, even
when aimed against himself, the most irritating habits of

Abelard's intellect. For when Abelard, after his mutilation, became a monk of Saint-Denis, he did a small piece of scholarly research which demonstrated that the patron saint of the abbey could not possibly be the Dionysius the Areopagite mentioned in Acts. This was treason to the Crown and Abelard was jailed; yet when he escaped, Suger seems to have made it possible for the affair to be overlooked providing Abelard kept out of monasteries. Later, when Abelard first got into trouble with Bernard, it was Suger who arranged the jobbery whereby Abelard's "punishment" was to be made Abbot of Saint-Gildas. Protection of the independent and intransigent intellect against the authority of intransigent emotion could hardly have gone farther. It was men like Suger and like John of Salisbury (himself a pupil of Abelard's, clerk to Thomas à Becket, and at the end of his life bishop of Chartres) who kept the extremes of twelfth-century intransigence in a relation of balance. Suger as well as John might have said, "I prefer to doubt, rather than rashly define what is hidden." But perhaps they spoke as statesmen and artists must, between good and evil; the one wanted beauty, the other charity; both wanted peace and order in the world they dealt with.

But they could only have it so, if at all, in terms of some extreme ideal or of some balance of extreme ideals—some Bernard and Abelard, some Francis and Thomas, some Pascal and Newton, each pair making extreme poles of emotion and intellect. One of the curiosities in studying such extremes is that the relation often becomes clearest in the art that lies between; for it is art that shows what happens to the extremes when actually experienced by minds otherwise ordinary. Art, in any fixed relation, is always the extreme of the ordinary. So Adams seems to have found; the emotions expressed by the artists, whether in architecture or poetry, gave him illustrations of what mystic and philosopher, what act and thought, must humanly have meant; the next step was inevitably to treat mystic and philosopher as themselves artists, only greater than the others—which was precisely how Adams had treated the Virgin; and the last step was by a little stretch of his nature to become himself an artist treating his own actual experience as material for his art. There was no other way Adams could master his material in detail or feel it together as unity; it was solely as artist that he could bring to his material what he had and take from it what he needed. He brought his feelings and experienced an emotion.

It is only with the sense that there was some such scheme in Adams' mind in the last three chapters of the *Chartres* that we can understand what he is doing there or make any use of it for ourselves. How otherwise can we accept, as a preparation for considering St. Francis, an implied comparison of Bernard to Voltaire, and a positive comparison of Bernard to Bacon, the one having regard to a measure of skepticism, and the other having to do with contempt for schoolmasters. Voltaire distrusted those excesses of human reason which confounded human dignity, and Bacon repelled those which prevented direct response to direct experience. Both, together with Bernard, depended on revelation, insight, intuition, and on the observation of these. Each gave a path to human emotion and concentrated its force as an image of salvation; only in their sense of revelation did they differ fundamentally, and the nature of revelation was determined for each by the drift of his age—in their skepticism, which was governed by their faith in emotion, they were one. They were skeptical of what prevented access to reality. Each grasped reality directly, by authority. Authority, when used, is authorship, and the product of authorship is art—whatever else it may be at the same time. As if to forget whatever else it might be—as if to come on it plain—Adams inserts into his discussion of French mysticism text and translation of hymns from the School of Saint-Victor which if not pure authorship were pure emotion, and inserts also, just beside the hymns, what he calls the true Promethean lyric of Pascal, a passage put together from the *Pensées* expressing the pure emotion of a man who cannot tell whether to deny God or the validity of his own mind. The emotion of incertitude is put against the emotion of conviction. And what Adams says about each reaches into his own experience and becomes part of his autobiography. Let us put them side by side.

Of Pascal: "The mind that recoils from itself can only commit a sort of ecstatic suicide; it must absorb itself in God; and in the bankruptcy of twelfth-century science the Western Christian seemed actually on the point of attainment; he, like Pascal, touched God behind the veil of scepticism." Adams had a closer relation to Pascal than is here apparent, and we shall come to it shortly, but can we not at this point assure ourselves that

Adams was pointing to part of his own experience in the figure of Pascal? Ecstatic suicide is the recoil of a mind given, as Adams' mind in part was, to logic. Love is the recoil of the mind given, as another part of Adams' mind was, to faith and the poetry of faith, as in the Victorian hymns. "The art of this poetry of love and hope," writes Adams, "which marked the mystics, lay of course in the background of shadows which marked the cloister. 'Inter vania nihil vanius est homine.' Man is an imperceptible atom always trying to become one with God." But he does not stop there; he adds as if in direct consequence to his image of mystical poetry a digression out of the concern of his own imagination. "If ever modern science achieves a definition of energy, possibly it may borrow the figure: Energy is the inherent effort of every multiplicity to become unity." It is no digression; it is the thing that was there all along, and in the personal sense it was to see it in terms of the twelfth and thirteenth centuries that Adams had made his whole study.

It is such an apparent digression and true central stroke as this that makes us see how little Adams went to his Middle Age for escape and withdrawal and how much for backing and renewal. He had to read his need in another language to understand it in his own. Thus he writes of the French mystics: "The human soul was an atom that could unite with God only as a simple element"—the element of their own sinfulness, and then, to bring the idea back to himself, remarks that they "showed in their mysticism the same French reasonableness; the sense of measure, of logic, of science; the allegiance to form; the transparency of thought, which the French mind has always shown on its surface like a shell of nacre." The French saints were not extravagant; their aims were high but not beyond reaching; and they expressed the paradox that the French mystics were not mystical, neither as mystics proper nor in philosophy, the arts, and religion. The drama was in balance, the climax in reserve, the substance in humanity. It was not Bernard and Abelard (nor Suger and John, at their easier levels) who could show the ultimate extravagance of the forces that were balanced, but rather Francis and Thomas, beside whom Bernard was practical and Abelard timid and their quarrels trivial; yet it is in the dramatization of the extremes of emotion and intellect which Adams makes of Francis and Thomas that we can understand the unity he saw in the Virgin, and the kind of unity he hoped to create for himself and for his own world; not the unity of Francis, not the unity of Thomas, but the unity of both with what had necessarily to come in between to make either tolerable. By this treatment, Adams seems to imply that the Virgin was a little nearer Francis than Thomas, but perhaps he meant only that Thomas stood in a little greater credit than Francis in the twentieth-century mind as he did in the thirteenth, so that Francis needed the extra support.

Certainly no man ever stood more fully on the strength and purity and risk of his own emotion than Francis does in Adams' portrait of him. He knew what he wanted and he knew what was possible; precisely what was visionary and beyond what had been hitherto possible. He wanted, in absolute poverty of self, to love equally every created thing, from the grass and flowers, the birds and men, to fire and death, and to praise what he loved without taint of desire, and so love God. This the intensity of his faith not only allowed him to do; it also, for a time, swept thousands after him; his example gave shape and humanity to a great popular emotion by which the world might be denied without loss but a rise in love for all that God had created in it. The emotion did not last Francis' lifetime; but as an ideal of essential Christianity, an ideal of a deep recurrent state of the human heart, the example of Francis has never disappeared. It persists in the feeling we have as to what manner of man Francis must have been each time we reread the Sermon to the Birds and the Little Song of the Sun.

Francis inflamed the substance of religion with its spirit. For when Francis denied the world he denied chiefly human pretensions—and particularly institutional pretensions—about the world; and he did so in order joyously to affirm the world and human life and all life at every level that had not reached pretension. Francis was a troubadour, a finder and worker at the great role of saint, or else a saint playing the role of poet. To him poverty was the riches of freedom from the pretensions of wealth; poverty alone had accompanied Jesus on the cross and afterward to His borrowed grave, and it was therefore that he invoked our Lady of Poverty: "O poorest Jesus, the grace I beg of Thee is to bestow on me the highest poverty." As with poverty, so with chastity and obedience. To him chastity was the riches of freedom from the pretensions of lust; obedience was the riches of freedom from the pretensions of power. And it was these riches with which he praised Sister Fire as dancing and warmth and radiance; the birds as the carol of creation; the flowers and grasses as creation itself; and Sister Death as the angel of return to the creator. All creation, loved, was its own meaning.

All this, to Francis, was science and philosophy as well as religion. To him humility, simplicity, and poverty were true science and led to heaven. To him fire and air and trees and birds had rational beings as well as men; and man no more than a thrush needed a psalter to praise God, and no more than a brook did he need logic. One of his friars once answered a series of theological arguments, says Adams, by a tune on a rustic flute. Such attitudes were certainly heretical to the official Church, very much like the attitudes of the Virgin as the architects and poets had seen her. Adams puts it that "the Virgin was human; Francis was elementary nature itself, like sun and air; he was Greek in his joy of life," and goes on to quote in proof the Sermon to the Birds; with which fresh in mind he is able to explain why the heresies were accepted: "The immense popular charm of Saint Francis, as of the Virgin, was precisely his heresies. Both were illogical and heretical by essence. . . . The charm of the twelfth-century Church was that it knew how to be illogical—no great moral authority ever knew it better— when God himself became illogical. . . . Both were human ideals too intensely realized to be resisted merely because they were illogical." Thus Francis was able, when asked to control his order more in conformity to the general rules for religious orders, to answer in a great public convention including St. Dominic and many Schoolmen, that he had to reject all rules but his own, which God had "mercifully pointed out and granted" to him. Then he concluded: "And God said that he wanted me to be a pauper and an idiot—a great fool—in this world, and would not lead us by any other path of science than this. But by your science and syllogisms God will confound you, and I trust in God's warders, the devils, that through them God shall punish you, and you will yet come back to your proper station with shame, whether you will or no."

The effect of these words, as reported in *The Mirror of Perfection*, was that "the Cardinal was utterly dumbfounded and answered nothing; and all the brothers were scared to death,"

to which Adams adds his own imagination: "For a single instant, in the flash of Francis's passion, the whole mass of five
thousand monks in a state of semi-ecstasy recoiled before the
impassable gulf that opened between them and the Church."
It was to such an image Adams had been leading up, and he at
once made the best of it. "No one was to blame—no one ever is
to blame—because God wanted contradictory things, and man
tried to carry out, as he saw them, God's trusts. The schoolmen
saw their duty in one direction; Francis saw his in another."
Apparently both were failures, since after five hundred years
society could adopt neither, though neither has yet been finally
judged, and no alternative has been proposed.

Adams exaggerates the gap between intellect and act; he
could not only afford to but was compelled to, just as the Church
could not afford to and was compelled, for its life and the life
of society, to try both paths and ignore the gap between. The
stress of that effort was perhaps the stress of life itself in the
institution of the Church, so that it is no surprise to note that
the Church moved first one way, then the other. But it is even
less a surprise that Francis should have felt antipathy to that
half of the Church represented by the Schoolmen. "If 'nostra
domina paupertas' had a mortal enemy, it was not the pride
beneath a scarlet robe, but that in a schoolmaster's ferule." For
the rest Francis accepted the Church without qualms or question as necessary for the ministry of the sacraments, though
otherwise he did not make much use of it. That is, Francis
felt only the inevitable conflict of the Ideal of the Gospel and
the Actual of the Church.

Just as Francis was the extreme to which the Church (under
Innocent III) was willing to go toward the ideal gospel, so the
Church was the institution which made his gospel possible. The
Church was faced with spiritual and lay revolt; Francis needed
both spiritual and institutional support. They needed each
other, to purify hysteria and to humble authority. Each was the
extreme the other could tolerate. But the toleration was precarious; shortly before his death, the Church refused his primitive rule and afterward, though she canonized him, denied the
validity of his testament. The Church only recognized the fact
that Francis' Order itself had split into various degrees of rigor
and relaxation. The Church accepted Francis as she accepted

the Virgin—as effects of popular will which could not be controlled until they could be, first, institutionalized and, second, formalized. Where the Virgin and Francis gave vigor in actuality to the life of the Church, the Church responded by turning the vigor into machinery: mankind was incapable of so much actuality for more than a few years. The interim period of imperfect control—of unstable balance—was the high point of aspiration, and, more than that, the maximum reach of actuality in the history of the Christian Church.

But Adams is all the more right for being a little wrong in exaggerating the gap between Francis and the Schoolmen. The Church was heritage and opportunity which alone made his energy take form and achieve more than exemplary significance. The lesson for modern institutions should be plain: that balance is better than control, that responsibility is better than rule, that risk is better than security, and that stability is death. But the stability and security here spoken of are not the opposites of anarchy and starvation; they are the opposites, rather, of flexibility and variousness. The institutions of society must, to survive, be kept flexible and various enough to receive and react to new impressions. This perhaps is the lifetime argument Henry Adams makes, directly in *Gallatin*, implicitly in the *Chartres*, and in the compositional process of the *Education*; if we can feel the arguments and follow the process we have learned Adams' lesson.

Just the same, there is little use in the lesson of the Unstable Balance as illustrated in Francis, unless we think of it in terms of something Adams was well aware of but which he hardly touched on in his book—namely, the ferocious and single-minded brutality which was the complement of every aspiration in the balance. The brutalities balanced too: those done for God, for Church, for simple aggrandizement, or for their own sake were somehow of equal weight and pressure in the general turbulence of society. Man is most violent in asserting and imposing order when his society is least capable of receiving it. The instance that comes to mind here has to do with the persecution of the Albigensians, which ran from the beginning of the eleventh century through the fourteenth century but which reached its height in the twenty years between 1209 and 1229, when under the name of Crusade great numbers of heretics and others were massacred and burned, the authority of the Church was perfected, the House of Capet absorbed the south of France, and the Provençal civilization was destroyed.

If the Crusade began in 1209, also in that year Francis collected his first eleven disciples. To Innocent III the Crusade was necessary to the safety of the Church; having protected himself, he could afford, seven years later, to sanction another and milder form of the same heresy in the ragged barefoot Friars Minor of Francis. There remains a wonder. The Albigensians, hating the world, effected some reform in the Church—in the conduct and celibacy of the clergy—and were exterminated. Yet the Church digested, transformed, and relaxed to more nearly normal monastic practice, the Franciscans—who loved God's creatures—and did so before Francis' death, as preparation for his canonization. The wonder is in the double act of slaughter and sanction; in that double act is the dreadful balance of denial and assent on which human identity is perched, and on each arm of which hangs, seesawing, fruit of pure Eden line. It is against the background of such a double act that Adams justly quotes Francis' *Cantico del Sole* as "the last word of religion, as it was probably its first," and turns then to grapple with its alternative in St. Thomas Aquinas.

Adams does not argue precisely that Thomas was the last word of human intellect, but he certainly treats him as if he were the archetype for whatever that last word might turn out to be: some form of forms, some system, in which every need and interest of man, if he accepted the authority of the system, would find itself harmoniously at home. One of the great temptations of the mind is to accept such an authority for the sake of the harmony without regard to the mutilations and suppressions and violent frivolities thus imposed on what is harmonized; the only worse temptation, in this direction, is to accept the mutilated harmony for the sake of the authority. Thomas found himself in an age when both these temptations were open and had been indeed succumbed to, in part, by a hard-set papacy and a series of rising national states. Political and cultural unity were gone; emotional and religious unity were shaken. Thomas, under the authority of reason, had to rearrange and balance the disparate forces; whether consciously or not, his work tries to make the new assertions of authority tolerable by the force of intellect alone. Like Francis, he remains as example and inspiration, until a different theology or a different world arrives to make intellect alone an adequate force.

For Thomas' task the times were wrong, though he could not have known it; he came just after what Adams calls the moment of equilibrium in 1215, when his thought would have given additional strength to social movement rather than mere expressive perfection, had the equilibrium only endured; but not again till perhaps the middle of the nineteenth century did an equilibrium of conflicting forces capable of absorbing his thought recur in the form of a liberal, scientific, and determined society. All that was needed was translation of that thought to the terms of economics, biology, and physics. The Church, in making Thomas official a little after the Franco-Prussian War, moved in the opposite direction and tried to translate modern society into the old terms. Adams, accepting the society so far as he could understand it, tried to see what St. Thomas would be like as an expressive part of it, with the result that he sees him putting into balance the laws of science and the needs of man.

The appeal of Thomas was for Adams and the Church the same, that his decisions were miracles, logical conclusions in advance of knowledge, which self-evidently added to the fund of positive knowledge. The method of the syllogism was human (Bernard thought it was presumptuously so) but in Thomas' hands it obtained what seemed superhumanly authoritative results, with an ease, assurance, and absence of effort as remarkable as was the apparently methodless method of Francis. On the face of it, Thomas merely selected between disputed opinions and rendered decisions; what gave his decisions the effect of miracle was the early maturity and elegance of form now associated with mathematical thought. His thought did not need to be immediately implicated in experience because it built on what had been abstracted from previous experience by previous minds using earlier forms of his own method. In such a system, if the form were elegant enough, one thing *truly* led to another. Thus the power of decision was immensely energized, as in poetry or architecture, by the sequence of formal relations. Conviction was inescapable so long as the forms held.

"Beginning," Adams writes, "with the foundation which is God and God's active presence in His Church, Thomas next

built God into the walls and towers of His Church, in the
Trinity and its creation of mind and matter in time and space;
then finally he filled the Church by uniting mind and matter
in man, or man's soul, giving to humanity a free will that rose,
like the flèche, to heaven." In such a structure God—the foundation—could not be taken for granted, but had to be proved a
concrete thing by the senses: *nihil est in intellectu quin prius
fuerit in sensu.* The simple assumption of realists like William
of Champeaux would not do, any more than the even simpler
assumptions of conceptual-minded nominalists like Abelard;
the one led to pantheism, the other to materialism, neither to
the God of the Church, who had to balance both. Adams presents Thomas' situation by comparing it to that of a modern
mechanical physicist. Thomas saw motion and inferred motor:
the mechanic saw motion and inferred energy everywhere at
work. Thomas inferred at the end (going backward to the beginning) an intelligent, fixed motor; the mechanic saw the
possibility but held it incapable of proof. To Thomas the notion
of form—elegance of articulation of thought—required unity,
and that requirement was to him adequate proof. There the
mechanic—though Adams does not say so—must have confessed
himself as dumbfounded as the Cardinal to whom Francis addressed his plea for freedom from control by the Schools.

At any rate to think so is one way of seeing the gap between
Thomas and Francis, and the greater gap between both and
the twentieth century Adams knew. Both the fullness and freshness of Francis' faith and the ageless authority of Thomas'
reason seem far from the center of twentieth-century movement—so far that they seem, as Thomas meant them to seem,
very close together. To Thomas faith was not personal, what he
believed he believed as a proposition; revelation was to him new
knowledge rather than new life, and he appealed to the fount of
revelation through the Fathers and the Scriptures just as he
appealed to the fount of natural knowledge through Aristotle
and Plato. The mysteries of faith and the truths of reason were
distinct forms of knowledge, the first taking priority over the
second but both capable of being handled in much the same
way. Theology and philosophy were two branches of the same
subject, capable, so to speak, of receiving the same form. Thus
the real question for him was always: How shall we reach a
predetermined conclusion in which the forms of revelation and

of reason shall be united? The answer his work made was: By architecture, the art in which stability of forms in their most daring use was proof of truth and manifestation of intent or need. One hardly knows whether it was the analogy to architecture or that to physical science in Thomas which appealed to Adams most; the ideas of imagination and of law were equally near his heart; and the envisaged results, in a liberal state and a predetermined mind, left him equally at home.

Doubtless Adams made no choice; doubtless the essence of Thomas' attractive force was that by the authority of his form he composed the dualism of fate and freedom, mechanism and vital purpose, anarchy and organization, order and chaos, in a single assertion of unity. By in some sense assenting to both at the same time he achieved the perilous balance of Christian theology. God was the metamorphosing margin between pantheism and materialism: the transforming act which created both law and contingent freedom of choice within the law: so that a criminal might choose "between the guillotine and the gallows, without infringing on the supremacy of the judge." The solution fitted needs, not facts. The needs were in man's nature.

[Man] insisted that the universe was a unit, but that he was a universe; that energy was one, but that he was another energy; that God was omnipotent, but that man was free. The contradiction had always existed, exists still, and always must exist, unless man either admits that he is a machine or agrees that anarchy and chaos are the habit of nature, and law and order its accident. The agreement may become possible, but it was not possible in the thirteenth century nor is it now. Saint Thomas's settlement could not be a simple one, or final, except for practical use, but it served, and it holds good still.

The mystics, skeptical of themselves, doubted the worth of Thomas' man-god relation; as Adams says, the mystics got into the Church by breaking the windows and had no use for what was to them the lock-step of the syllogism: "But society at large accepted and retains Saint Thomas' man much as Saint Thomas delivered him to the Government; a two-sided being, free or unfree, responsible or irresponsible, an energy or a victim of energy, moved by choice or moved by compulsion, as the interests of society seemed for the moment to need."

Such a theology—such a philosophy—could not help becoming art and ending in aspiration, like the spire on a church.

Conceiving God as having the merely original freedom to
create out of nothing the intent of his own will, Thomas gave
man the contingent freedom to be wicked or absurd, and thus
gave him more than the State ever did: some choice, a place
in the Church and in the life to come, and a sense of holding a
seat at the center of the universe. That is, the square founda-
tion-tower of God's Act of Creation, which was the normal
energy of God, the façade of the Church, "suddenly, without
show of effort, without break, without logical violence, became
a many-sided, voluntary, vanishing human soul." As with the
old flèche at Chartres the transition was perfect, "and neither
Villard de Honnecourt nor Duns Scotus could distinguish
where God's power ends and man's free will begins."

It will only strengthen our conviction that Thomas' system—
whatever we think of it as philosophy or theology—was great
art, the formal expression of man's actual needs and responses,
if we try to assess the practical situation which it met. Thomas
came just after an age—1115 to 1215—in which thought and
emotion flowered in unusual balance, and at the beginning of
an age when the dominant thought and the dominant emotion,
being out of balance, became equally fanatic. Where the institutions of society had been relatively free—that is, in some sense
mutually responsible—they seemed now drawn once again into
the panacea of absolutism where claims of power were made
without mutuality or intent of balance, as we would say today,
unilaterally. The horror more than the glory of human institutions began to become manifest. Thomas labored to give the old
balance a new form on the old or inherited model, and so far
as what was inherited was actually transmitted he succeeded,
both for his own and later time. But the dominant powers of
the time had hardly more than ancestral piety for the old model
—as we can see in the degeneration of the Crusades and the rise
of the commercial spirit, in the multiplication of heresy, and
in the substitution throughout the political world of arbitrary
for representative power.

Here is a sentence written of the papacy of Thomas' time,
which shows how far that institution had gone and why its new
position, by inspiring both rebellion and imitation, precipitated
insoluble conflicts. "In the Popes of the thirteenth century this
plenitudo potestatis, legislative, administrative, financial, and

almost doctrinal, was undenied; and in their omnicompetence, so long striven for, they had the opportunity of making their gravest errors." Beside that sentence, here are three more, comparing the attitude toward the papal power of Gregory VII, who began this part of the history of the papacy in the eleventh century, and Innocent III who brought the papal power to its zenith in the thirteenth. "[Innocent III's] spirit was never dismayed by the gulf lying between the high Petrine theory of sovereignty and the historical and more limited practice of the Roman bishop. It could be bridged, if one went carefully enough. It never affected him as strongly as it had affected Gregory VII, with his finer intuition and darker sense of conflict" [*Cambridge Medieval History*, Vol. VI].

In such a situation it is not surprising that Thomas should have failed of pervasive influence in his own time. His thought in part moved with the time, in that it attempted to balance the new assertions of power, but in part it moved against and ahead of the time in that it anticipated an intellectual rigor for which the time was not prepared. His contemporary influence was controversial, and his system became a question of university politics at Paris and Oxford. The Franciscans especially attacked it for its presumptuous Aristotelianism and its usurpation of rational access to authority. Adams' own school of Chartres (as it disappeared) was anti-Aquinam, as was Robert Grosseteste in England. Thomas was *the other and impossible thing* to many minds, for there remained still a strong anti-authoritarian flow in thirteenth-century thought. And there was besides widespread conservative distrust of Thomas' means of supporting the universality of the Church on the Creed by setting up another and parallel authority in reason. The actual triumph of Thomas came in the nineteenth century when he was used to supply the authority in reason which the Church needed to encompass modern science and the combination of popular and dictatorial (non-Christian and anticlerical) nations into which Western society was breaking apart. As art, Thomas' triumph was the greater in that the skill of his solution (of the problem of balancing Faith and Reason) did not transpire until his system was used against a worthy opponent.

But his system would have been art even less than truth if

it had not also been made in response to a radical problem of his own time. Here is the judgment of W. H. V. Reade in *The Cambridge Medieval History:*

The heroic attempt of Aquinas to define a sphere for philosophy without detriment to the sovereign rights of theology was simply one expression of the whole medieval struggle so to adjust the temporal power to the spiritual as to create a dominion of political freedom within the higher sovereignty of the Church. The project, we may hold, was impossible. It is certain, at least, that it failed. . . . Yet this failure was the last and greatest achievement of medieval philosophy. . . . The air of finality that hangs over the weighty pages of Aquinas has a prophetic significance. For the work of Aquinas, consummate in its kind, had exhausted the materials then existing for the edifice of philosophy, though not the ingenious art of arranging them in new patterns. The great age of dialectic had vanished with the rebirth of Aristotle; the age of Aristotelianism was to perish in still greater revolutions. Alike in politics and in science more portentous questions were soon to be uttered: whether a society founded on an immutable gospel could find room for the modern State, and whether a *scientia experimentalis* beyond the dream of Roger Bacon could be reconciled with an infallible Church.

The notion will not bear too much pushing, but judging by Adams' response to him, Thomas anticipated these questions; for they concerned any State not wholly theocratic but with a tendency to become so, and any body of knowledge in peril of thinking itself complete; and it was Thomas' intent to keep Faith and Reason open except as to origin and conclusions. That he has been used otherwise does not invalidate the intent, any more than the misuse or amelioration of Francis' Rule invalidates the *Cantico del Sole*. What the nineteenth-century Church saw (from an immutable gospel and an infallible Church) was the need for an order which would "place" the parliamentary state and a body of inclusive, inconclusive knowledge in an over-all architecture of aspiration and authority. The twentieth-century Adams, from the *other* point of view, saw the need which an immutable state and an infallible knowledge had for a gospel and a church. Both saw the need expressed in Thomas. Where the Church saw authority, Adams saw art: as objective and conventional in the *Summa* as in the glass of the Prodigal Son, but also as personal and human as the Court of the Queen of Heaven.

Thomas, that is, did not stand alone. Like the cathedrals, Thomas was the result of two hundred years of experiment and discussion. The art and the science—the religion and theology— were one because they represented a complex balance of effort by many debating minds around what Adams calls "the despotic central idea" of organic unity. The system of St. Thomas and the great cathedrals was possible only to minds in which that organic unity was a vital dogma—minds, that is, in which it operated both as energy or will and as the unfailing standard of criticism. That was how the truth of the universe looked to the thirteenth-century mind, as an organic unity to which all roads and all lines of work necessarily led. Truth was not a relation, as it tends to seem in the twentieth century, but the source of the relatedness of things; and the difference is the difference between two kinds of universe, that in which unity is grasped precariously by faith and that in which centraliza- tion is imposed by incessant, and always inadequate, measure- ment of relations. Adams seemed to feel that it was not man who had changed the universe but that it was the universe, by showing a different aspect as it moved, which had changed man's mind. But he also seemed to feel that the consequent weakening of intensity in man's mind was relative rather than absolute, and that therefore the work was all to do over again under new and more difficult conditions. Some kind of organic unity was his own ideal, and he had come on it by having grasped it imaginatively, in its last apparition, at the height of the Middle Ages. *Mont-Saint-Michel and Chartres* is the record of the imagination.

To his effort to grasp the ideal actually in his own age we shall return shortly, when the study of the final chapters of the *Education* is resumed with the fresh energy with which we, like Adams himself, have been charged in the study of the *Chartres*. It is the same study; in each, by the risk of faith, "the equilibrium is visibly delicate beyond the line of safety." But before making that move, indeed before quite finishing the study of the *Chartres*, let us make a kind of small digression ahead of time on Adams' *Life of George Cabot Lodge*, for in that book Adams made his only explicit remarks on the artistic mind of his own age and place. Adams saw that mind as in the fullest possible contrast—in temper, scope, and environment— to the artistic mind of the Middle Ages, and yet saw the two minds as almost identical in intent. Contrast and identity are equally edifying, and especially so if Adams' *Lodge* is read as a footnote to his *Chartres*.

Formally, the book is a memoir of a poet who died young, at the height, not of his powers, but of his possibilities. Informally, so to speak, it is a tribute of friendship, written at the request of the poet's parents; a task for which no one was better fitted than Adams, since he and young Lodge had stood in the relation of uncle and nephew to each other and since the shaping of Lodge's imagination had been part of Adams' conscious work: Lodge had been the other member of Adams' political party, the Conservative Christian Anarchists. Actually, the book is something more than either a memoir or a tribute; it is also an essay in the criticism of the poetic imagination and the predicament of poetry and poets in the last quarter of the Bostonian nineteenth century and the first years of the twentieth; and it is with this emphasis in mind that we see the book forming a natural part of Adams' work. It was written in 1909 and 1910 (Lodge died in 1908) and published in 1911, which were the years in which Adams both finished his speculative essays on history and prepared his revision of the *Chartres*. With the imaginative energy of the twelfth century firmly in mind as man's highest standard in such matters, he could not help concluding that in the twentieth century poetic energy was, like Nirvana, out of season. Let us see along what lines he reached that conclusion.

He begins by letting Boston stand for the universe, because for a Lodge or an Adams nothing else claimed the right, but better because the claim served as a point of departure from which the counter claim for poetry—for imagination—could best be asserted. Boston believed it stood apart because of its complexity and refinement. But to a poet born in Boston in 1873, the city showed a society "which commonly bred refined tastes, and often did refined work, but seldom betrayed strong emotions." The true movement of society had become scientific and mechanical, with "a steady decline of literary and artistic intensity." Hence Boston could not inspire a taste for poetry, and if a poet appeared he must have been one innately. Existing society showed the absence of what history and poetry found at the heart of earlier societies. "The sense of poetry had weakened like the sense of religion." The story was not new, only the emphasis was heavier. In New England, loneliness and reserve were natural from childhood, and so made latent what ought to have been instinctive expression. "The latent contrasts of character were full of interest, and so well understood that any old Bostonian, familiar with family histories, could recall by scores the comedies and tragedies which had been due to a conscious or unconscious revolt against the suppression of instinct and imagination." Poetry had become suppressed instinct: a reaction against society rather than, as formerly, the favorite expression of society itself.

Poetry as revolting instinct had made the poet a rebel everywhere in English, but had put, Adams thought, a special character on poets who rebelled in Boston. As in his own case he had drawn the opposition between Quincy and Boston, summer and winter, life and death, so to explain Lodge he drew the opposition between Nahant (the cape or spit of long beach ending in tumbled ledges across the bay from Boston harbor, where the Lodges lived) and Boston, where Nahant, as the sea, meant everything to Lodge that Quincy had meant to Adams. The presence of the sea, Adams thought, helped Bostonians break away from society to a unity with nature, with a resulting underlying simplicity of mind. Thus, the more Lodge's character spread, "the more simply he thought, and even when trying to grow complex—as was inevitable since it was to grow in Boston—the mind itself was never complex, and the complexities merely gathered on it, as something outside, like the sea-weeds gathering and swaying about the rocks." That simplicity, that feeling of unity with nature, so affected a mind like Lodge's that "man became an outrage,—society an artificial device for the distortion of truth,—civilization a wrong. Many millions of simple natures have thought, and still think, the same thing, and the more complex have never quite made up their minds whether to agree with them or not." To the older Romantic poets, revolt was natural, "but to the Bostonian absorbed in the extremely practical problem of affecting some sort of working arrangement between Beacon Street and the universe, the attitude of revolt seemed unnatural and artificial." Life had been hard, and the Bostonian "felt he ought not to be reproached for the lies that the world, including himself, had wrought, under compulsion, on the exceedingly rough and scanty parchment of God."

The Bostonian's special difficulty, as Adams saw it, lay in the fact that for him the gap between the poet and the citizen was impassable. There was not a pair of hostile camps, as there had been in the slavery question, with men changing sides and consolidating opinion so that society was convulsed in the process. There was rather indifference: the situation of the man who has something to sell which nobody wanted to buy—namely, the poetry of revolt, and who is, as a poet, ignored. "Society was not disposed to defend itself from criticism or attack. Indeed, the most fatal part of the situation of the poet in revolt, the paralyzing drug that made him helpless, was that society no longer seemed to believe in itself or anything else; it resented nothing, not even praise. The young poet grew up without being able to find an enemy."

This is the generalized background against which Adams thought the young American poet had to play his role about the year of the Spanish War; Lodge in particular reacted at twenty with a combination of philosophic depression and intense ambition, from the first of which he never recovered and the second of which was never satisfied; both, rather, were deepened in the dozen years of his writing life. He published too soon to a small and unwilling audience, and his chief works—the two poetic plays *Cain* and *Herakles*—had as their characteristic theme the very nexus of his own situation: man lifting himself by his will, which he asserts to be the Will of God. Adams thought it was a theme impossible to enact in modern life except as insanity. "All Saviours were anarchists, but Christian anarchists, tortured by the self-contradictions of their rôle. All were insane, because their problem was self-contradictory and because, in order to raise the universe in oneself to its highest power, its negative powers must be paralyzed or destroyed. In reality, nothing was destroyed; only the Will—or what we now call Energy—was freed and perfected." The theme, Adams went on, had "the supreme merit of being the most universal tragic motive in the whole possible range of thought."

It was no wonder that he thought so; it had been the thematic background against which he had raised his own twin towers of Energy—or Will—in the *Education* and the *Chartres*. It was no wonder, either, that in discussing Lodge's poetic dramas he should have gone on to gloss the failures in execution with the glories of the aspiration. Least of all is the wonder that he saw Lodge's failure tacitly not in his work but in the society which he addressed but with which, as poet, he could not cooperate. The point is that without cooperation poetry cannot achieve its intention, with the looming implication that without poetry society cannot continue to exist for long. Point and implication are both focused in what happened to Lodge personally after the death, at the age of thirty, of his friend the poet Trumbull Stickney. He tried to spread his circle and failed, and the failure was the same as that of his poetry: it could spread only where it was not felt, in a sea of indifference. "This consciousness of losing ground,—of failure to find a larger horizon of friendship beyond his intimacy;—the growing fear that, beyond this narrow range, no friends existed in the immense void of society,—or could exist in the form of society which he lived in,—the suffocating sense of talking and singing in a vacuum that allowed no echo to return, grew more and more oppressive with each effort to overcome it. The experience is common among artists, and has often led to violent outbursts of egotism, of self-assertion, of vanity; but the New England temper distrusts itself as well as the world it lives in, and rarely yields to eccentricities of conduct." That was all; Lodge yielded rather to death.

Adams in writing passages like these, was what Hay once called "at his most royal." Neither Lodge's poetry nor his printed letters warrant the strength of Adams' expressions; he wrote rather from the larger context of his own work and temperament, not with judgment but with mimetic imagination, as if he himself had tried the role he thought Lodge ought to have undertaken, but of which both were somehow deprived by the conditions of their lifetimes. The difference between them was that Adams never yielded to death, and that when he yielded to eccentricities it was not to those of conduct but to deep eccentricities of being, and yielded only to make a balance between them. In that, he resembled Abelard, not St. Thomas; he was himself the balance between the twin eccentricities of the *Chartres* and the *Education*, where the stress or attraction of each redeemed the eccentricity of the other, but not of its own. His theme was Lodge's theme, to raise man to his highest idea of himself; and how close he felt Lodge's difficulties were to his own we may see for ourselves by returning now to the pertinent passage in the last chapter of the *Chartres*. If we remember that Adams saw Lodge as revolting against a society so indifferent that it did not believe even in itself, we shall the more acutely judge Adams' own burden.

Modern science, like modern art, tends, in practice, to drop the dogma of organic unity. Some of the medieval habit of mind survives, but even that is said to be yielding before the daily evidence of increasing and extending complexity. The fault, then, was not in man, if he no longer looked at science or art as an organic whole or as the expression of unity. Unity turned itself into complexity, multiplicity, variety, and even contradiction. . . . A straight line, or a combination of straight lines, may have still a sort of artistic unity, but what can be done in art with a series of negative symbols? Even if the negative were continuous, the artist might at least express a negation; but supposing that Omar's kinetic analogy of the ball and the players turned out to be a scientific formula!—supposing that the highest scientific authority, in order to obtain any unity at all, had to resort to the Middle Ages for an imaginary demon to sort his atoms!—how could art deal with such problems, and what wonder that art lost unity with philosophy and science! Art had to be confused in order to express confusion; but perhaps it was truest, so.

Omar's kinetic analogy perhaps needs, at this late date, to be refreshed on the page; Adams' life almost exactly spans the time when Fitzgerald's version of the *Rubaiyat* was an effective part of almost every mind, a book of most common prayer:

> The Ball no question makes of Ayes and Noes,
> But Here or There as strikes that Player goes;
>   And He that toss'd you down into the Field,
>   *He* knows about it all—He knows—HE knows!

To the last line of this Fitzgerald added a note that in the original it was a very mysterious line, "breaking off something like our Wood-pigeon's note, which she is said to take up just where she left off." Against the wood-pigeon's note of knowledge expressed by lyric salutation, Adams places for analogy a very specifically nineteenth-century scientific image, not of expression but of manipulation. The imaginary demon sorting atoms in this passage was quite certainly inspired by Adams' favorite image in Clerk Maxwell's *Theory of Heat* (1872), in a passage quoted by Adams' favorite scientific commentator, Karl Pearson:

One of the best-established facts in thermo-dynamics is that it is impossible in a system enclosed in an envelope which permits neither change of volume nor passage of heat, and in which both the temperature and pressure are everywhere the same, to produce any inequality of temperature or of pressure without the expenditure of work. This is the second law of thermo-dynamics, and it is undoubtedly true so long as we can deal with bodies only in mass, and have no power of perceiving or handling the separate molecules of which they are made up. But if we conceive a being whose faculties are so sharpened that he can follow every molecule in its course, such a being, whose attributes are still as essentially finite as our own, would be able to do what is at present impossible to us. For we have seen that the molecules in a vessel of air at uniform temperature are moving with velocities by no means uniform, though the mean velocity of any great number of them, arbitrarily selected, is almost exactly uniform. Now let us suppose that such a vessel is divided into two portions, A and B, by a division in which there is a small hole, and that a being, who can see the individual molecules, opens and closes this hole, so as to allow only the swifter molecules to pass from A to B, and only the slower ones to pass from B to A. He will thus, without expenditure of work, raise the temperature of B and lower that of A, in contradiction to the second law of thermodynamics.

Thus expanded, it ought to be plain how in this single alternation of figures—of Omar's ball and Maxwell's demon—Adams is making a trial balance of the two halves of his problem: the reconstitution of the sense of unity in religion and science, philosophy and art: and how, in doing so, he speaks in the double voice of the Virgin and the Dynamo.

As usual—for it was his constant intention and inevitable risk—his means of discourse were aesthetic. The problem of unity always turned out, for him, a problem of aesthetics, of appreciation, of seeing—not of seeing the surface simply, but of seeing the flux fully—of seeing the surface with its depth and opposite. That is why he closed the passage we have quoted with the remark that "art had to be confused in order to express confusion; but perhaps it was truest, so." He did not mean, as Yvor Winters among others has thought him to mean, that the artist as artist had to be confused, or that his art could resort to confused or spontaneous forms; there is nothing in his practice that evades clarity and distinctness of form. He meant

rather that there must be an underlying equivalence between
the art and the complexity of what the artist, as man, had seen.
The artist had precisely to put chaos in order, with what aids
in form he could muster and with as few cheats in perception
as possible. The general analysis of the *Education* and the
Chartres which this study has made should be amply illustrative of the kind of chaos and the kind of order he was committed to and the relations between them. Taken together, they
make the unity of his vision and the attractive force of his
aspiration: to raise man, by past example confronted with
present condition, to his highest intensity. His arrogance is the
aesthetic necessity to see imagination as the will of things.
Luckily, there is in this last chapter of the *Chartres* a short
passage which will do as both past example and present condition—as both chaos and the order with which it can be seen.

Those who have an ear for rhythm—for that meaning in
music which persists after the words have stopped—will perceive to what extent this passage has influenced the choruses of
T. S. Eliot's two plays *Murder in the Cathedral* and *Family
Reunion*, just as the same passage and also Adams' images of
dogwood and judas influenced the same poet's "Gerontion." It
should be remembered that Adams frequently refers to himself
in the letters from 1891 to 1911 as either a poet or a student in
the Latin Quarter. Adams' reference here is to the technical
means by which Thomas saved God's free will—and man's too
—from Abelard's logic. Adams, as by nature of the Latin Quarter, refused the cheats in perception.

This philosophical apse would have closed the lines and finished the
plan of his church-choir had the universe not shown some divergen-
cies or discords needing to be explained. The student of the Latin
Quarter was then harder to convince than now that God was Infinite
Love and His world a perfect harmony, when perfect love and
harmony showed them, even in the Latin Quarter, and still more in
revealed truth, a picture of suffering, sorrow, and death; plague,
pestilence, and famine; inundations, droughts, and frosts; catastrophes world-wide and accidents in corners; cruelty, perversity,
stupidity, uncertainty, insanity; virtue begetting vice; vice working
for good; happiness without sense, selfishness without gain, misery
without cause, and horrors undefined.

It would not be easy, because of the great length and patience
required, but it would be wholly possible to make a valid

analysis of this passage and its music on the model of the remarks just made about Omar's ball and Maxwell's demon, but it is simpler and perhaps more effective, instead, to quote another passage in which Adams played the same tune. He was not satisfied with his first attempt and when in the *Education* opportunity again provided, he played it once more, in a different key. The nexus is again the effect of the universe as it changed in man's experience of it, here called a multiverse; but the passage about to be quoted is not so much a part of Adams' conscious argument as an aesthetic explosion in the course of that argument.

He could not deny that the law of the new multiverse explained much that had been most obscure, especially the persistently fiendish treatment of man by man; the perpetual effort of society to establish law, and the perpetual revolt of society against the law it had established; the perpetual building up of authority by force, and the perpetual appeal to force to overthrow it; the perpetual symbolism of a higher law, and the perpetual relapse into a lower one; the perpetual victory of the principles of freedom, and their perpetual conversion into principles of power; but the staggering problem was the outlook ahead into the despotism of artificial order which nature abhorred.

It is explosion, not argument; Adams knew better than anyone that law, whether of old universe or new multiverse, never explained the fiendishness of man or any other really pressing question. It is aesthetic, not hortatory, not only because of the litany on the word *perpetual*, but because it is an image, that he could not keep out and was compelled to force in, of the actual human process which underlay all law and to which all law was inadequate, but which was the actual situation—the aesthetic was always the actual—the law had regularly to grasp at. It is with this sense of the pressure of the actual and the need to grasp it—both to hold it off and be tormented by it—that we can best read the last sentences of the *Chartres*, and it is with this sense, too, that we must read these sentences back into the whole book with whatever of ourselves we can bring with them.

The peril of the heavy tower, of the restless vault, of the vagrant buttress; the uncertainty of logic, the inequalities of the syllogism, the irregularities of the mental mirror,—all these haunting nightmares of the Church are expressed as strongly by the Gothic cathedral as though it had been the cry of human suffering, and as no emotion

had ever been expressed before or is likely to find expression again.
The delight of its aspiration is flung up to the sky. The pathos of its
self-distrust and anguish of doubt is buried in the earth as its last
secret.

Pathos was with Adams always secret; and it was the special
power to perceive that secret—to perceive what Henry James
would have called the secret of the secret—but without requiring it to be articulated, that Adams brought with him. To him
it seemed a simple power, part of the appreciation of common
fate but in his own day and country adulterated and quite lost,
except among artists and children. Therefore he wrote *Mont-
Saint-Michel and Chartres* as an artist and addressed it to
nieces, and thereby objectively revived that power in a kind
of permanent renewal and deep preparation for a full return
to life at its highest intensity. It is in this sense that the book
may be called spiritual autobiography: the true or real biography which, as he realized it, gave him the strength to cope
with his biography in the actual world and make that true, too,
in the guise—itself with its pathos and its secrets—of Education.

Before returning to that actual biography, there remain for
a little consideration certain habits, aspects, traits of mind
which, infecting both biographies, made a bridge between them
possible. One of these is introduced in the name Pascal. The
only long quotation in the *Chartres* not bearing directly on the
twelfth and thirteenth centuries is a pastiche from the *Pensées*
which Adams calls the "true Prometheus lyric" and in which,
he says, Pascal "touched God behind the veil of scepticism."
Both this passage and that quoted in the *Education* come at
crucial points and have a peculiar force over and above their
plain content: they represent a part of what Adams brought
with him. Let us see if we can illuminate—for certainly we
cannot explain—the affinity between the two minds. The conception which Adams found in the *Pensées* of positive *ennui*
has something to do with it. The discipline of Pyrrhonism has
something more, along with its consequent "natural" pessimism. The passage quoted in the *Chartres* introduces Pascal as
a figure excruciated, four centuries later, by the problem of the
relation between intuition and reason which St. Thomas had
solved, and no doubt in that capacity Pascal gave Adams an instance of his own excruciation.

But perhaps more important than any of these, there is the

example in Pascal of an intense levity in both style of language and deportment of mind: as if the depth of his doubt gave him an orthodoxy, and the force of his *ennui* gave him a security, that permitted the mind to play while it rancored, and even encouraged it to frivolity in all but the most severe rackings of desperation. It is this levity of style that shows best the multiple powers of Pascal's mind and the firmness, however unknowable its substance, of its foundation. Such a man if uprooted carries the world with him in the very fury of his mutilations. More equable spirits may feel that he lacks mountain laughter— which is perhaps the need expressed in the levity; but Pascal read his Montaigne, from whom his laughter might have come, with his other self only; and the two selves attacked each other. Adams does not seem to have read much Montaigne either, enough to bow and claim distant kin, but he understood in himself the commotion underneath Montaigne, and he made a juncture with it in Pascal—in the style of Pascal. *Such a man am I!* he cries, *and with such a difference!* It is in thinking of Pascal, with Montaigne behind him, that Adams' own style is understood. In the intense levity of Adams is his own Pascal: the anguish of self-distrust and doubt. Pascal is part of his spiritual biography: the great creative labor in which men have to make use of others in order to see demonstrated the truth of that which in themselves alone they cannot believe, though they suffer it.

Among the differences between Pascal and Adams is Adams' reticence and its consequences. In men of reticent habit—of the indurated New England exterior—it is the spiritual that is reserved even more closely than the emotional. Mere temper, any of the products of irritation, might be permitted freely to air, but spirit and emotion had to be forced out and through channels that offered the look of remoteness. For Adams, twelfth-century imagination was such a channel, and Pascal provided, at halfway point, a kind of viaduct to it, with levity and *ennui* the means of access. But the extremes of difference count heavily in making identity. Pascal in his last years would not allow the beauty of a woman to be praised in his hearing. Adams loved the beauty of women and girls and children. One of his most remarkable levities is in his memoir to Clarence King where he adverts to brown girls and black; but until the last years of his life he made no open mention of his dead wife.

Again, Pascal carried in his bosom his amulet of fire, written in his own hand; Adams carried his Prayer to the Virgin, folded in his wallet. The difference is not in appropriateness but in the ideals themselves. Each, to use Baudelaire's language about Pascal, had his gulf which he carried within him in the blackness into which each looked, Pascal to see the fire of consummation, Adams to see the radiance of the Virgin; Pascal to die, Adams to live. Pascal had a revelation—a stigmatization—of death in life; Adams had a revelation of life in death. The difference is utter and nothing; it is only a difference in phase, as in the water that may alternate from ice to vapor.

Another trait, which when understood serves as a portal to the mind Adams created for himself in writing the *Chartres*, lacks a name like Pascal—lacks indeed any name at all—but may be illustrated in certain lines of the poem "Among School Children" by W. B. Yeats. Yeats wrote it after his experiences as Senator of the Irish Republic, serving on a Committee to inspect the schools. The nuns and children together remind him of mother and child, child and old man, and of the nature of human aspirations.

> Both nuns and mothers worship images,
> But those the candles light are not as those
> That animate a mother's reveries,
> But keep a marble or a bronze repose.
> And yet they too break hearts.—O Presences
> That passion, piety or affection knows,
> And that all heavenly glory symbolise—
> O self-born mockers of man's enterprise.

In his poem Yeats breaks off, which is right: there can be no formal close to such cries, they come in the middle, they break the flux. And that is so in Adams—as in the sentence where the Virgin looks down from a "deserted heaven, into an empty church, on a dead faith": a sentence which comes at the end of a chapter, as a stanza close, not at the end of the book. But just the same, in Yeats and Adams, the cry reverberates: *O self-born mockers of man's enterprise!* They are not mockery; they are ourselves mocking ourselves, as we fail to keep grasp on the power of our own imagination.

The peculiar bitterness of this perception comes, not from the absolute growth of knowledge in the last century, but from a change in habit toward a particular knowledge which was always as open to us as to Plato or Lucretius. Plato knew the gods were mythical, and Lucretius addressed in Venus a natural force. What has changed is concentrated in the recognition that the gods are fictions; and the bitterness comes from the incapacity to make the necessary renewals of recognition. In asserting that access to the supernatural, both in history and now, is through the imagination, we have not digested the supernatural but only put it further off and made it unavailable except as spooks and fairies. Fictions of the supernatural ought properly to correspond either to our experience of the actual world or to our aspirations to the ideal world; but there is no propriety in forcing correspondence to the concrete or logical worlds, and the attempt to do so is exactly what puts the supernatural out of reach. No god was ever made of the concrete; no god was ever made uncritically. The gods are made—discovered or revealed—rather out of the most intense possible mutual criticism—the engaged sense of the concert and the conflict—of the highest values of the society concerned.

The twelfth-century Virgin was a very critical product indeed, and Adams' book shows the process and detail of the criticism. The materials were actual, the criticism valid, the result a real fiction; it had the force of reality and the humanness of a fiction. That the Virgin was supernatural—that she ruled and attracted the forces of nature from without, and by occult means—goes almost without saying. Consider against her such characteristic twentieth-century American gestures toward the occult as Charlie Chaplin the little fellow set upon, Krazy Kat the illimitably loving, and Mother Eddy the healer; the twelfth-century Virgin, who had all these concerns at heart, envelops them without a quiver or a shiver of her radiant energy, for their fictions degrade the very actuality of life and the reality of aspiration that the Virgin affirms. It takes only a modest power of criticism to see that much: they are such mockery of man's enterprise as cannot even break our hearts—which Adams' Virgin surely did. It is the difference between escape, puerilization, denial, and assent, maturity, faith; between the Paramount Theater and Chartres Cathedral.

Here perhaps we can begin to feel definitely—like the tug of a rising tide on the anchor line—hitherto unrealized strains that were yet constant in Adams. It is as questions that they are most definite. Why does Adams remark that the universe offers

us aspects different from those it offered St. Thomas? Why does
he quote from Pascal the passage about the desert isle? Why
does he see all his saints (except perhaps Bernard) as heretics?
Why does he feel the Virgin as a "separate" religion?—Well,
Adams saw chaos where Thomas saw order; Adams lived tem-
peramentally just ahead of—or just before—collapse: it was the
next and precedent stage, with both shadows encroaching. He
had been on a desert isle and had become a member of its royal
family: he had been invested with rights in the special loneliness of deserts. Lastly, with regard to the saints, it was only
as heretics that he could see their force as saints. He knew by
what extremity alone images of faith were made and destroyed,
and he had himself his separate religion at Rock Creek.

All these traits were outlets for each other and had reversible relations; the process of reversal was the living condition of
strain, and the effect of it comes through in the book—though
only so much as its readers can bring with them to recognize.
Adams felt himself, as if he were a reader, an outsider at the
heart of things; an exile already translated to the prodigal
at home; an alien because he *knew* his own identity; a man
who had need to perfect his loneliness in company as he had
to refresh it in the pilgrimage of flight, and who knew so, both
ways, how deeply he was engaged in the common enterprise.
Within that enterprise he perhaps never felt he could play his
right role. He could not even name his role, but its very name-
lessness rode him. His role played him, and in playing racked.
He is, as we look at him, the play of the force of thought:
responsive, gallant, free to the limit of his conditions. For
what did he call himself?—a pilgrim, an uncle, a teacher, an
artist, a companion. He sought Nirvana out of season, deliberately. And what title did he accept?—the Angelic Porcupine;
and how translate it?—as a 'possum asleep, as a kitten in wal-
nuts, as a mandarin of a new class: *impavidum ferient ruinae:*
nameless, but a true image.

CHAPTER TEN

The Full Return

Whatever Adams' role is to be called, it has one constant element: it makes terms with his times; and one constant motive, to make the terms expressive both of himself and of the times. At the end of every flight he made, whether in act or thought, whether to Tahiti or to the twelfth century, he found himself in closer contact with twentieth-century America. His pilgrimage was prodigal and its riches were in the return. What he brought back became a part of the way to understand what he discovered at home; it had become a trait of personality—the *result* of a lifetime—to express new terms of relation with each return; and a full return would be composed when to formulate the universe was identical with the task to formulate the self. As Yeats says, it is in the full moon, when the maximum is reflected, that the self is lost. Adams' return seems to have approached the full during the period in which he wrote his chief imaginative pilgrimage, *Mont-Saint-Michel and Chartres* —that is, during the three years ending in 1904. The pilgrimage and the return showed simultaneously; where the later chapters in the *Education* move backward into the *Chartres*, the actual text of the *Chartres* moves forward into the *Education*. Either book renews the questions and the insights of the other under different occasions, each put in terms of the other.

Nothing illustrates this better than the three chapters in the *Education* now under study—"*Vis Inertiae*," "The Grammar

of Science," and *"Vis Nova"*—for it is here that the crossing
is made between the Virgin and the Dynamo, that the force of
the one is seen as a phase of the force of the other. Adams made
the crossing in pursuit of the question that must lie at the
bottom of all efforts toward formulating the universe: What
were the forces that moved modern society, how did they
hang together, and how was a self-respecting mind to respond
to them? Adams' working answers were simple. There were two
old forces, the inertia of race and the inertia of sex, and one
new force, the intensity (which might become inertia) of artificial energy. The new force was in conflict with the two old
forces and seemed likely to predominate. The mind able to
respond to this conflict of forces—able to see them in concert
and so control them—did not exist; it must be born from contact
between the old forces and the new. The mind geared to either
set of forces alone would be helpless to respond to the other;
geared to both sets, the new man might create, or secrete, a
new universe. Response was creation.

The working answer was simple because it corresponded to
Adams' experience and the permanent bias of his mind. Adams'
symbol for inertia of race was Russia, and he set it up at one
pole in the conflict in foreign affairs. Through the accident of
his close friendship with Hay, with the special advantage of
the *necessity* of looking ahead which belongs to all foreign
offices, he had acquired a direct sense of the mass of society in
motion. Adams' effort to create an American foreign policy
vis-à-vis Russia has already been examined as the struggle
between intensity that had to be intelligent and inertia that
had merely to roll. But all societies had inertia of race, and
Russia was only an example. Beyond that, Russian race inertia
may be thought of as a foil for Adams' streak of genealogical
obsession: his search for ancestors, for seed forms, to establish
identity amid change and variety. Adams was a man of family.
Adams on Russia should remind us of Tahitian girls and Greek
goddesses; on Normandy and New England; on the South Sea
islands and the Scandinavian mountains: all of which, for him,
showed forces of inertia to which he felt deeply kin. Inertia of
race was vital instinct without necessarily vital purpose or vital
aspiration: vitality in mass.

If inertia of race stood out as the mass of Russia, the intensity
of the new artificial forces stood out in American railroads and

powerhouses, and in the American response to Russia. Thus the intensity of the new forces focused once in terms of the Atlantic system of which America was at the center, and again in terms of the physical sciences which, at that very moment, with radium and X-rays, turned from the affirmation of rational order as supreme to the assertion of man's helplessness before the forces of a supersensual chaos. It was a return, in new phase, to the helplessness of twelfth-century religious society before the forces of a supersensual order. The difference in phase was critical, and made the forces seem to point in a different direction. Where the order of religion had heightened man's sense of individuality, the chaos of science heightened his sense of mechanical relationship in a mass society, with individuality an eccentric accident. The old conception of the Great Chain of Being, like the older conceptions of rank and degree, had entered a new phase, through the laws of science, of fortuitous determinism. Nobody asked favors or pled privilege of the dynamo. The fortune of the individual had become desperately determined, as the railways determined the sites of towns; it disappeared beyond the scope of his will without chance for a wish—or would have done so were it not for the inertias of race and sex.

The inertia of sex—Adams' third force—had the graces of three symbols: the Virgin of Chartres, the Venus of Lucretius, and the immediate American woman. The force of sex still existed in all three phases, but the American woman could use none of them to the full, not even her own phase. Her sexual function to maintain the family had been put in abeyance— she had been liberated from it—to provide cheap work in factory or office. Where she had once been the victim of the Church she was now the victim of the machine. Yet her sexual function was necessary to *any* society, and the question was how far the sexual function could be made merely mechanical and still renew its impulse. It was another form of Adams' older questions about women: Why had the Protestants struck the Virgin out of the Church? Why had the Puritans struck the woman out of State Street and the City of God alike? Was it not because the Protestant and Puritan movements got their impulse from early forms of the new mechanical forces? After Calvin and Bacon, God had become the great mechanic. If anything needed architecture to express mechanism, it was sex.

These forces—two of inertia, one of intensity—were the forces Adams had to triangulate into the future. Race was military, mechanics was industrial; sex was the family—the provider of soldiers and workers. The Church, and other forms of religion earlier, had put race and sex in equilibrium; but the twentieth-century Church was not equipped to balance either race and sex alone or race and sex in the pressure of the new mechanical forces. Unless new mental power was created, there was no tolerable solution of the conflict of forces. Socialist (which is to say mechanical) or military Caesars stood in the offing.

Caesars—the state for no sake—was what these forces pointed at: the mechanization of race inertia: the collectivized, bureau-cratized, urban-industrial state centralized in a despotism of artificial force. Only new mental power, only a new incarnation of religion into culture—T. S. Eliot's language—could prevent it. Before such a prospect, Adams' mind both rebelled and assented. The assent was to the force stronger than the self; the rebellion was in the hope of deflecting the forces, however little, by setting the mind's own force against them. Rebellion against inevitable forces consisted in seeing their combined necessity in terms that more nearly fitted the human will. If the mind felt the contact between the old and the new forces deeply enough, the mind's reaction would itself be a result—a new movement— of those forces. So to feel and so to react were the conditions of full response; a task which Adams had long since begun, but which he had now to make final, if only in the sense that he had himself come to a stop. The *tussis senilis*—the cough of old age—which had troubled the grandfather's *Diary*, now troubled the grandson's *Education*.

It was this point of view—this feeling that it was necessary, if possible, to modify necessity—which governed Adams' reac-tion to his three forces. Naturally, as the three forces worked simultaneously, they had in fact to be considered together. It was only in the forms of study that they could be separated, and even so they had a tendency to run together. Russia as race, American woman as sex, the laws of physical energy as mechanics, were Adams' deliberate artifices of study, as far apart as his mind could conceive; yet any one of them brought the others to mind.

Thus race called for sex and both were called by steam and electricity. Looking at Russia as the force that demanded action in American foreign policy, Adams concluded that Russian expansion would continue by racial inertia until its mass met a force equal or superior to it by reason of its greater intensity, when it would either give in or conquer. Part of the reason for this conclusion was the inability of Germany to decide whether to ally with the West or to merge in Russia. Germany stood on the exposed European edge of the expansion. Another part of the reason was the absence of responsible government in Russia: Russian movement seemed independent of government and an effect of racial mass. Russian government had been Europeanized time and again but had never been able to govern by European methods. A third part of the reason for Adams' conclusion was historical. For two hundred years the convulsions of Russian expansion (in northeast Europe, in the Near East, in Asia and latterly in central Europe) had been the chief cause of European convulsions. By 1903, the expansive movement of Russia seemed to have acquired enough momentum to overcome the combined European and Asiatic continent—unless a *vis nova* could be found to hold its own against this *vis inertiae*.

At this point Adams asked what was inertia, as he might have asked what was a five-dollar bill? How good was the name for the energy dealt with? Inertia in physics was the property by which matter at rest, rested, or in motion continued to move in a straight line. But Adams was concerned with movement of mind, not of matter. To him, the mind was never at rest, "but moved—when normal—about something it called a motive, and never moved without motives to move it. So long as these motives were habitual, and their attraction regular, the consequent result might, for convenience, be called movement of inertia, to distinguish it from movement caused by new or higher attraction; but the greater the bulk to move, the greater must be the force to accelerate or deflect it."

It seems probable, on the basis of these sentences, that Adams regarded race and sex primarily as forces of inertia moving the mind to action in the social world. What else they might have been was not part of his story, except for its foundation or genesis. His story was history, prophesying or "triangulating" history to come. He was thus a revolutionary Augustinian against the classical scientists of his time. Having converted physical inertias into mental inertias, he asked at once if inertias could be overcome. History suggested that perhaps race inertia had been overcome by destroying the race, "but surely sex inertia had never been overcome at all." Sex, said Adams, "is a vital condition, and race only a local one. If the laws of inertia are to be sought anywhere with certainty, it is in the feminine mind." Unlike the subject of race inertia, which was everywhere in history, woman was hardly touched by English and American history. "But if the problem of inertia summed up the difficulties of the race question, it involved that of sex far more deeply, and to Americans vitally. The task of accelerating or deflecting the movement of the American woman had interest infinitely greater that that of any race whatever, Russian or Chinese, Asiatic or African."

It will be remembered that, at the time Adams wrote, Slavic immigration, the "Yellow Peril," and "White Supremacy" were all extremely acute questions on the American scene; Adams merely converted the race question to a more universal and more potent level, as a part of history past, passing, and to come. But to him the sex question was vital to history itself, and was serious enough to be joked about and rolled as a regular conversational ball. "Without understanding movement of sex, history seemed to him mere pedantry." So he asked his partners at table why the American woman was a failure, and regularly got the answer, "Because the American man is a failure!"

The answer was less frivolous than anyone but Adams would have at first thought. The American woman had failed to hold the family together; to create a new society; to hold her own in Church or State; to find use for her freedom or a stage for action, when, at forty, motherhood was over. If it was a serious question what would happen to Russian race inertia under the impact of new artificial energy, it was a much more serious question what would happen to America when much greater artificial energy is turned over socially, as was the fact, to women. The Russian answer did not yet show; but Adams wrote with the feeling in his language of an acceleration and deflection of Russian energy beyond possibility of control. Only the exact nature, never the massive result, was in doubt; upon the exact nature, and how to control it—or how it could control itself—everything hung. The American answer was self-evident only in terms of the directions in which American women were moving: the butterflies at the resorts, the tourist trade, the Colonial Dames and the Daughters of the American Revolution.

These were the surface directions. Behind them moved the industrialized and urbanized working woman. "All these new women had been created since 1840; all were to show their meaning before 1940. . . . The problem remained—to find out whether movement of inertia, inherent in function, could take direction except in lines of inertia. This problem needed to be solved in one generation of American women, and was the most vital of all problems of force." Where she was really moving was, like the man, toward the machine. Where her force had been the "inertia of rotation" on the axis of "the cradle and the family," she seemed now about to find a new field, where she would be a victim of artificial force rather than, like Venus, herself the perfection of physical force. "So far as she succeeded, she must become sexless like the bees, and must leave the old energy of inertia to carry on the race."

The "old energy of inertia" would presumably resemble the energy of sex degraded, from the human point of view, to the relatively mechanical sexuality of the bees, at any rate to a sexual force which was not also a mental force. On such a prospect, the American woman, following the man, could see before her "only the future reserved for machine-made, collectivist females." That she did not rebel, as she had always done in the past against masculine victimization, was because she had now "nothing to rebel against except her own maternity." The Church, to Adams' mind, had possibly "been made by the woman chiefly as her protest against man." With the Church gone—overthrown by the man because it was feminine—she had only man's refuge, the machine. "Already the American man sometimes felt surprise at finding himself regarded as sexless; the American woman was oftener surprised at finding herself regarded as sexual." She had given up more than she was aware, and had become a new thing without knowing it. What she had given up was her rational force and her imaginative possibilities. What she had become was an obscured and automatic reproductive function at a level Adams thought less (since the relative birthrate was falling) than the optimum. What she had yet to become was doubtful, but was evidently something mechanically responsive rather than creatively expressive.

Looking ahead, Adams had to use a literary metaphor out of the past. He could not discuss his problem with young women, he said, "because Faust was helpless in the tragedy of woman. . . . The Marguerite of the future could alone decide whether she were better off than the Marguerite of the past; whether she would rather be victim to a man, a church, or a machine." Marguerite, it will be remembered, was seduced at fifteen by Faust, killed her baby, was imprisoned, and went mad. Faust wanted her to escape; she refused, died, and went to heaven. If, then, we think of Adams' American woman as a Marguerite unconscious of her rôle and the man as a Faust who did not know how to make her see her rôle we can see why the American woman explained her own failure as part of the failure of the man. The implication is that the force of sex—its inertia and function—had always been manipulated by man; deflected differently for different purposes. His failure, and hers, came because he now proposed to do without that force in the belief that his new forces made it superfluous. The consequences to that habit of mind which tried to see the future were plain.

Between these various forms of inevitable inertia—sex and race— the student of multiplicity felt inclined to admit that—ignorance against ignorance—the Russian problem seemed to him somewhat easier of treatment than the American. Inertia of race and bulk would require an immense force'to overcome it, but in time it might perhaps be partially overcome. Inertia of sex.could not be overcome without extinguishing the race, yet an immense force, doubling every few years, was working irresistibly to overcome it.

Thus sex resembled race. To overcome the inertia of race, it must be destroyed and reconstructed by a superior force; and the case was the same with sex. In former times the superior force was either military or religious. In modern times, in both cases, the superior force was artificial energy.

Adams was right in choosing the inertias of race and sex as the chief probable victims of artificial energy; though neither, as he tackled them, was a scientific subject but were both still parts of the old Roman *scientia*, both might someday become more scientific. One critical reservation to Adams' point of view would be that modern industrial countries do not *need* as much sex as older societies needed for survival or even for optimum expansion. New resources and new techniques, and the absence, for the first time in history, of pretty continuous plague and starvation in the whole area of Adams' Atlantic system, put a discount on the value of sex—a discount, not a bankruptcy. Adams was tacitly thinking in older terms—of the waste of nature and her "reckless maternity"—of the wilderness of judas and dogwood; terms which the new artificial energies had already altered as they applied to his chosen inertias. Their absolute values remained, but their relative values had changed more than he was aware. To preserve the absolute values in the new relation was his true problem, and he was right to insist on it even if his view of the new relations was prejudiced and erroneous. It would have altered only his exaggerations and nothing of his judgments, had he seen how the population problem of India and southeast Asia under the impetus of a mild injection of artificial energy in the absence of Western resources suggests the *need* of a mechanization of sex there. Even war, in itself, no longer cuts population much in areas dominated by new forces, and its effect on race in Russia is doubtful. Further, inertia of race among the decimated Jews seems to have intensified. Thus Adams was righter than he might have thought. The conversion or reconstruction of the inertias of sex and race have become even more exigent problems for 1950 than they seemed to him in 1900; and the greater exigence is, as he foresaw, the direct result of accelerated artificial energies.

What then was man's relation to the new energies and how did it change, from a relation of confident mastery and service, to a relation of helplessness and blind, or chaotic, reaction? How did it come about that the growth of the new energies seemed to destroy both the classical conviction of creative politics and the Christian conviction of creative peace and creative progress? The second question Adams does not explicitly ask but it is implicit in the way in which he asks the first: as a question touching the quick of the fundamental question of unity. Race and sex had always been forces of inertia which led to convictions of unity at times of crisis. If the new energies converted or degraded the old, could the new energies themselves either create a conception of unity or teach man to make a tolerable secular society without such a conception?

These grave questions Adams took with him as a Pilgrim of Power as he had taken earlier versions of the same questions with him as a Pilgrim of the Virgin; and as he had gone to the cathedrals of the twelfth and thirteenth centuries as the highest expressions of the Virgin's power, he went now to the architecture of scientific law as the highest expression of the new energies. There he betrayed his eighteenth-century prejudice for exclusive order and his nineteenth-century education in inclusive scientific law. But what he found, in 1900, was not unity but chaos. He found the unity of science destroyed and lawgivers chased from the Temple in the interests of improving science by limitation. After the discovery of X-rays and radium and with the development of the laws of heat, the unity of science was only its unity of method, and held only if the method was limited in application to the field of the senses.

The argument is ambiguous; there is again the old conflict between the classical *scientia* of common sense, order, and justice and the "science" of hypothesis and law, the conflict between the idea of a universe ordered by man and the idea of a law which ordered man in a universe which was not necessarily his. The Christian solution, from Athanasius to Augustine, had solved the conflict by imposing upon it, through the conception of the Trinity, the revealed laws of God. The nineteenth-century mind thought that science could re-establish the old claims of *scientia* along new lines of positive law. But at the turn of the century the dogmatism of the new law collapsed, and along with it collapsed the possibility of positive dogma understood as the expression of vital purpose. Against this solution, Adams presented the picture of a mind escaping from a rigidity but holding on to the determinism which made the rigidity possible. At the same time Adams showed himself working to gain from de-dogmatized science renewed contact with occult or religious energies, not in a spirit of obscurantism but in the search for illumination. That was his necessity as the Virgin was the necessity of the twelfth century. Each wanted unity, and each knew that unity must somehow be descriptive of man's relation to chaos. If the future was to be a despotism of artificial order, fostered by artificial energy drawn from the chaos of unknown forces, so, too, it had been with the Virgin, who had saved the City of God by making a world against nature in the image of her own fecundity.

What Adams seemed to argue was that the great human efforts to deflect movements of inertia need not follow the known laws of nature, though it must be imagined that they transcend nature. The illusion that they do so, being thought truth, is a form of energy and a form of movement of inertia until some new deflection becomes necessary. Such an argument rests on the assumption that the imagination creates tolerable orders—human orders—of society because it finds intolerable the order into which nature had lapsed. Creation is by revelation or divination. To Adams it seemed that the imagination of woman—the inertia of sex—had commanded a higher level of conception than the masculine inertia of power and logic. Women—as illustrated by Venus and the Virgin—had alone made the world tolerable to man.

But the requirement in 1900 was evidently beyond the command of woman's imagination. Neither unity of the lump—the unity of race inertia—nor the unity of the existing structure —the unity of sex inertia—was capable of administering the new forces in a tolerable order. The requirement of the twentieth century was new mental powers—*Vis Nova*—to control the new supersensual forces. "If this view was correct," Adams wrote, "the mind could gain nothing by flight or by fight; it must merge in its supersensual multiverse, or succumb to it." The mind must establish a relation of authority and will—choice and purpose—to the forces that move it; it must remake itself in integrity out of those forces. It had to handle what it knew, in despite of what it did not know.

It was with something like this point of view that Adams made conclusion to the chapter called "The Grammar of Science," and indeed from this point of view his own new grammar followed instinctively. But let us see how he came to it before we examine what he did with it. Partly, he reached his conclusion by the rediscovery of chaos and the rediscovery that all order is artificial or human, when the gods have left it, and apt to be contrary to nature in a larger field than that in which it was congruous to nature. That these discoveries were scientific rather than moral, physical rather than political, only aggravated the need for new mental powers in the new fields of morals and politics—history in action—which the discoveries laid bare.

The shock of these discoveries came to Adams through the

self-questionings of the leading scientific authorities Adams
could find, and he only called his chapter "The Grammar of
Science" because that was the title of Karl Pearson's book,
which first successfully communicated some of that questioning
at a lay level. Adams said that his friend Langley had prepared the way, in his Smithsonian Reports, with papers on
psychical research, the X-ray, and radium, which foretold the
overthrow of nineteenth-century dogma. These papers "had
steadily driven the scientific law-givers of Unity into the open;
but Karl Pearson was the first to pen them up for slaughter in
the schools."

It should be emphasized that Adams made little use of Pearson's work in detail but rather let his argument serve as a point
of departure for his own response. The part of Pearson's argument that Adams used was that the claims of science had to be
cut down to the field of the senses. There conceptions of law
must stop, since laws can neither be inferred nor projected
beyond sense impressions. Adams' response was that in that
case the mind must go on without conceptions of law. After
quoting Pearson that "briefly, chaos is all that science can
logically assert of the supersensuous," Adams continued: "The
kinetic theory of gas is an assertion of ultimate chaos. In plain
words, Chaos was the law of nature; Order was the dream of
man." What Pearson wanted to avoid was anthropomorphism,
myth, hypostasis, and false hypothesis in science, in order,
exactly, to maintain standards in scientific work; he wanted
to keep science from becoming metaphysics, and it was at the
tendency of science to become metaphysics without knowing it
that he aimed his polemic. The effect on Adams was the conviction, which he held with varying degrees of speculative uncertainty, that Pearson's very reduction of the claims of science
to go beyond its phenomena, made metaphysics once again
necessary. Science, by stopping short, revealed the subject matter of metaphysics. Adams, as an historian, knew that the mind
would always try to know the unknowable, and that he himself
"would be forced to enter supersensual chaos" from which
Pearson meant to exclude him.

Common practice, whether in theology or physics, had been
to call the field of study Unity and the knowledge of it Order.
The revolution of 1900, as Adams called it, reversed the relation. The field of study was chaos, and order was an artificial

convention interposed between the mind and the chaos that rushed in upon it. The act of revolution was the creation of artificial forces: the X-ray, thermodynamics, radium, in the use of which knowledge was unnecessary and the sense of help-lessness was perhaps an advantage. For the new forces were not a mere extension of knowledge, but a fresh creation; they did not throw man into Unity or the arms of God, but made unity and God superfluous. The astronomers of 1600 had merely upset the world; the scientists of 1900 had convulsed the world; to Adams, it was like "the convulsion of 310 when the *Civitas Dei* cut itself loose from the *Civitas Romae*, and the Cross took the place of the legions." In the new revolution the "metaphysical bomb" of radium took the place of the Cross and of reason and nature as well.

That is to say, the continuity of thought had snapped for the first time in history. Where Constantine and Galileo had united thought the new revolution cast it loose. Its truth, or its unity, had become, as the Germans said, an abstraction of the unknowable, or as the French said, a convenience, or as Karl Pearson said, "a medium of exchange." Thus the historian— thus Henry Adams—"must not try to know what is truth, if he values his honesty; for, if he cares for his truths, he is cer-tain to falsify his facts. The laws of history only repeat the lines of force or thought."

It is at this point that Adams' thought made one of its imaginative releases. It appears in three versions, all of which are resorts to the underblows of the human mind in which experience finds actual response and actual repudiation and in which the actual risks of life are undertaken. In these under-blows lies the strength of enterprise. The first version is con-tained in that great litany on the perpetual reversing dualism of man's self-destruction and self-creation (quoted in Chap-ter 9), which ended on what there may have seemed an afterthought: "But the staggering problem was the outlook ahead into the despotism of artificial order which nature abhorred." Here it is no afterthought, but the ejaculation of insight to which the litany led. When the mind uses unknow-able forces and does not believe in the possibility of "truth" in the old sense, then its action will be despotic in fact, and its motives will be lies told in feeling. What is despotic is arbitrary, what is arbitrary is accidental; and a policy of successive accidents is a surrender to the chaos of artificial order, which nature, if she existed, would surely break down into her own, deeper chaos. It was the rising sense of that deeper chaos which, as Ovid says, came first, that contributed the rhythm and forced insight in Adams' language.

Early also, not in nature but in Adams' manhood, was the trope of the oyster secreting a pearl upon the irritation of a grain of sand. In 1867 Adams had written his brother Charles a declaration of independence: "I am going to plunge under the stream," he began; and ended: "I shall probably remain under water a long time. If you see me come up, it will be with an oyster and a pearl inside. If not, why—so!" Thus the young man meant to go pearl-fishing. In 1907 the effort of fishing—of living—had itself become the pearl, and was more the work of the woman than the man, of sex and imagination than of war and thought.

As history unveiled itself in the new order, man's mind had behaved like a young pearl oyster, secreting its universe to suit its conditions until it had built up a shell of *nacre* that embodied all its notions of the perfect. Man knew it was true because he made it, and he loved it for the same reason. . . . The man's part in his Universe was secondary, but the woman was at home there. . . . She conceived herself and her family as the centre and flower of an ordered universe which she knew to be unity because she had made it after the image of her own fecundity; and this creation of hers was surrounded by beauties and perfections which she knew to be real because she herself had imagined them.

Here Adams interrupted the second version of his release— and the interruption is the third version—to cite authority from what he calls the noblest verses of the greatest philosopher, two fragments from the invocation to Alma Venus at the opening of Lucretius' *The Nature of Things;* he quotes, as it were, by the book, without name or place. The Rouse translation of the second fragment runs as follows: "Since therefore thou alone dost govern the nature of things, since without thee nothing comes forth into the shining borders of light, nothing joyous and lovely is made, thee I crave as partner." There Adams stopped: *Te sociam studeo!* Is not fellowship a better word than partner? And if *studeo* means *crave*, surely it is with the senses also present of zeal and close striving; for Lucretius wanted the help of Venus, as Adams himself did, in writing the hard verses to come. In any case *Te sociam studeo* is a personal cry, a prayer for the restoration, the resumption, of the faith which makes possible the creation of a tolerable society.

Such prayer is in response to the under-tug of the total human obligation, the tug which is onward—for it is the tug of repetition—the more it seems backward. Having made it, Adams returned with that further incentive of pathos to the trope of the oyster and the pearl which had beset him his whole adult life. "Neither man nor woman ever wanted to quit this Eden of their own invention, and could no more have done it of their own accord than the pearl oyster could quit its shell; but although the oyster might perhaps assimilate or embalm a grain of sand forced into its aperture, it could only perish in face of the cyclonic hurricane or the volcanic upheaval of its bed. Her supersensual chaos killed her."

The personal pronouns in the last sentence have no antecedent. Perhaps it is woman or sex or the *Te* in *Te sociam studeo!* Venus herself. There is at any rate a parallel in what Adams immediately develops. He was himself, said he, according to all the masters of fact he could find, he was himself, "henceforth to be a conscious ball of vibrating motions, traversed in every direction by infinite lines of rotation or vibration, rolling at the feet of the Virgin at Chartres or of M. Poincaré in an attic at Paris, a centre of supersensual chaos."

Adams was not thinking here by reason; thought lapsed, rather, and re-emerged in images and invocations; but he had nevertheless to profess reason along with the images; he had to identify his waking life with what he had dreamed and so to make himself responsible for what had begun there. History and image together instructed his reason that to all the old forces the mind had made adjustments adequate for survival. It had learned how to assimilate chaos through whatever channels of force it had appeared. The fresh burst of chaos, the "new avalanche of unknown forces" of 1900, "required new mental powers to control." If this view was correct, "the mind could gain nothing by flight or by fight; it must merge in its supersensual multiverse, or succumb to it." It must either take unto itself the new force—which meant the creation of a fresh political, moral, religious, and metaphysical universe; or it must strip itself of all personal and purposeful powers—choice, judgment, motive—and disappear into the chaos itself. The universe had changed its aspect; the question was, Could man's mind change to agree with the universe, or must it—in terms of anything traditionally conceived of as the mind—disappear?

Individuals might take a decision as an act of criticism; but individual decision was worthless unless it individualized what society was actually doing or might be attracted into doing. The question of decision always became a question of vision and of statesmanship. Where was society going and how could one bridge the difficulties by which it got there? When Adams tried to envisage what choice between *Vis Inertiae* and *Vis Nova* was implicit in the action of his society, he could not see singly; like the society itself, he inevitably saw double; and what he saw was of course stained—like the light in the Virgin's churches —by his own obsessive images; so that he found, he saw chaos, violence, anarchy. What he saw in mere fact is simple: a struggle for world political power in the Russo-Japanese war, where Russia moved by inertia and Japan by a kind of mechanical, chess-like intensity, and where, by contrast, America showed extraordinary new force, exemplified by the steam engine and the dynamo and personified by President Roosevelt —but a force which she was as yet powerless to use for a vital purpose whether at the St. Louis World's Fair or at the President's table in Washington.

Russia, Japan, and America together "made a Grammar of new Science quite as instructive as that of Pearson" and left Adams a Pilgrim of Power as well as a Pilgrim of the Virgin. "The new American, like the new European, was the servant of the power house, as the European of the twelfth century was the servant of the Church, and the features would follow the parentage." (Indeed Adams was right; by 1940 the American Catholic called the authority lodged in St. Patrick's in New York the powerhouse.) For Adams the two roles, and the two forms of force, were joined by the fact of the automobile, which swallowed the centuries minute by minute, from church to church, in France, and in America by the fact that although the Virgin could no longer open World's Fairs she could shut the one at St. Louis on Sundays. The automobile only emphasized the degeneration of the motive power. Where had the power gone to? The question was only the question asked backward of what could be done with the new power to give it, like the Virgin, the effect of human motivation, either as accumulation or as reservoir and source. How could the brooked capacity for belief become a possibility?

Quite as if the actual process of thought were interrupted by it, Adams broke off his questions to introduce the fact of the bomb that killed Plehve, Russian Minister of the Interior and defender of despotic inertia, on the 28th of July 1904. In the fact lay a temptation to conclusion: that though speculative education might proceed by trial balances, practical education came by bomb; and the temptation was all the greater because Adams got the news in Troyes, where he was studying stained glass. "Martyrs, murderers, Caesars, saints and assassins—half in glass and half in telegram; chaos of time, place, morals, forces and motive—gave him vertigo. Had one sat all one's life on the steps of Ara Coeli for this? Was assassination forever to be the last word of Progress? . . . The Conservative Christian Anarchist had come to his own, but which was he—the murderer or the murdered?"

The temptation was just; it was the right temptation for the historian who had sat thinking of Gibbon, and dreaming beyond him, all his life on the steps of Ara Coeli; it was right because it called on all his powers, and all Gibbon's powers too, to refuse, and more than that, it was right because, once refused, he was compelled to take the hardest of all intellectual decisions for a mind much used and disappointed: the decision that the intellect is truly a force which the individual must use though the world fall on his shoulders—*impavidum ferient ruinae*. It is not a fact but a choice: the intellect, like the society of which it gives an account, is an imperative enterprise. It goes forward by the incentive of its own horror, which pursues it. What else is Adams saying here?

The stupendous failure of Christianity tortured history. The effort for Unity could not be a partial success; even alternating Unity resolved itself into meaningless motion at last. To the tired student, the idea that he must give it up seemed sheer senility. As long as he could whisper, he would go on as he had begun, bluntly refusing to meet his creator with the admission that the creation had taught him nothing except that the square of the hypothenuse of a right-angled triangle might for convenience be taken as equal to something else. Every man with self-respect enough to become effective, if only as a machine, has had to account to himself for himself somehow, and to invent a formula of his own for his universe, if the standard formulas failed.

This is the policy of the old human intellect suddenly conscious of its task; and Adams was only affirming its full import when he went on to say that he wanted no absolute truth, "only a spool on which to wind the thread of history without breaking it," only "to shape after his own needs the values of a Dynamic Theory of History." Absolute truth would be useless and probably fatal to living society as it has been fatal to all those fragments of society which deluded themselves that they had it. All Adams wanted was what society always required, a means of giving an account, in its own terms, of what it actually was. What had happened to Adams, on his return to society, was that as an individual he had identified himself with, and assented to, not American society, not Christian society, not *any* society, but society itself. How deep and sharp that identification was we can see in the plea to his colleagues in history for a like identification, which he made in "The Tendency of History."

This was the eight-page communication which Adams sent in lieu of a Presidential address to the American Historical Association in 1894. The paper reads in one respect like an earlier version of the three chapters in the *Education* which we have just been studying; but in another respect it differs from them. It is an argument for action or for setting up a basis of action by historians and teachers of history; and if it did not expect approval or adherence, it would at least keep the official records of the American Historical Association clear. The argument was, that as history had tended to become a science of those forces which controlled man, it made no difference whether the science was accurate in detail: historians would find themselves at the focus of action and would "be compelled to act individually or in groups" on public opinion. The paper laid out the possible coming situation in which such action would be required and the probable alternatives of action that might be taken. The situation would be the state of shock following "the establishment of a fixed science of history." It would no longer be harmless, but would act with the kind of force exerted by Rousseau, Adam Smith, or Darwin. "What shape can be given to any science of history that will not shake to its foundations some prodigious interest?" Any science of history would profoundly affect the vast social forces which struggled for control of the contemporary world: Church, State, Property, or Labor. A science of history which fixed the path society must follow could not possibly help both Church and State, property and communism, science and religion, trade and art.

Suppose history pointed toward a communistic triumph, "would property, on which the universities depend, allow such freedom of instruction? Would the state suffer its foundation to be destroyed?" Suppose, on the other hand, "the new science required us to announce that the present evils of the world—its huge armaments, its vast accumulations of capital, its advancing materialism, and declining arts—were to be continued, exaggerated, over another thousand years, no one would listen to us with satisfaction. Society would shut its eyes and ears." To listen "could lead only to despair and attempts at anarchy in art, in thought, and in society." The third possibility would be for the new science itself to commit suicide by proving that society must revert to "absolute faith in a personal providence and a revealed religion."

Thus, no matter where history showed society as bound to move, it would arouse hostility. Yet, if history was a science, it must accept what was provided by its hypotheses. The Historical Association must therefore answer either Yes or No "under the pressure of the most powerful organizations the world has ever known for the suppression of influences hostile to its safety. . . . If such a crisis should come, the universities throughout the world will have done most to create it, and are under most obligation to find a solution for it."

It would seem to matter little to us, in assessing the burden of these remarks, whether history can be a science in the sense Adams used the term, or whether it can be a science at all. Some of the attraction of the study of history today is felt in the possibility that it might not be a science after all, at least in the limiting sense. In either case it is a study having to do with the relation between men's conception of the ideal and their actual experience; it belongs in the school for statesmen who, as Adams taught, must lead society where it must go; and it belongs especially in the school for that statesman—whether

potential or manqué—who inhabits each of us and who must
be taught to gainsay both repudiation and acceptance and to
practice critical assent to whatever it is that is our actual experience. Under such a point of view, Adams' plea to his colleagues takes on the weight here wanted: it illustrates his effort
to make a trial balance between *Vis Inertiae* and *Vis Nova* and
exemplifies, before it was made, his identification with society
itself, and his resolution to find some formula to account for
himself to himself, "some spool on which to wind the thread of
history without breaking it."

No matter how far Adams got into a theory of force, he never
forgot to attend to the mannikin who made the theory; the
mannikin might be liver than the theory. So it is here. "Among
indefinite possible orbits, one sought the orbit which would best
satisfy the observed movements of the runaway star Groombridge, 1838, commonly called Henry Adams." Adams had the
right star, but gave it wrongly the number of the year of his
birth. The runaway star is Groombridge, 1830, and is so-called
because of its unusually large proper motion. It is in *Ursa Major*
and is of that magnitude only doubtfully visible to the naked
eye.

Why should he not, in so hopeful and human an effort, make
use of the characteristic patterns of thought created by the conspicuously new forces of his time? If he could do so, he might
feel a little confidence that he thought on the same impulse
that he acted and might gamble a great deal that his thought
would turn out as live as the act—if only so long as the pattern
was in fashion. Why should he not, then—why must he not,
rather—set to work on a Dynamic Theory of History with its
accompanying Law of Acceleration? It was his obligation in the
university in which he taught.

CHAPTER ELEVEN

The Full Response

At any rate, the effort to conceive a dynamic theory of history brought Adams as near full response as his mind, working in its calling, could come. A dynamic theory would be a way of looking at forces operating together, and the test of the theory would be how far it promoted the habit of reaction to those forces. That is what the words mean: to have a dynamic theory is to behold forces at work, to be a spectator reacting to what is happening. That is to say, finally, a dynamic theory of history is how we take a human part in the play of natural forces.

Thought, in a mind like Adams', was never much less anthropomorphic than the Greek language from which the thought sprang; he had always the compulsion to put a human shape and a human relation upon the forces to which, as he reacted to them, were themselves part of human experience. There was as much of Lucretius in him as of Gibbon, and Lucretius was most in him when he sat on the steps of Ara Coeli. He accepted the materials and patterns of twentieth-century thought as the decorum for his poetry, but his story was the old poetic story of how man sets a value upon life and how he struggles to make that value actual.

No decorum could be more difficult for a poet to accept, and still keep his story in sight, than that of twentieth-century thought; for it is a decorum that alienates and oppresses if it does not exile the greater part of what had formerly been meant

by the human, and more than that, it is a decorum that appears
to take over the human for purposes of its own. Just the same
for an historian—if you do not believe Adams' kind of history
to be a form of poetry: the thought of modern physics alienates
or exiles the history of Gibbon or Thucydides and substitutes
its own lines of motion for the old play of human motive and
tragic creativity. In any case, it is just the same for Adams,
whether you call him poet or historian or a special type of
imaginative layman. That is why he begins by jumping into
the enemy's camp, adopting his weapons, following his tactics,
and apparently fighting his war. He makes man his victim, like
the modern novelist, and drives him into total exile, like the
modern substitutes for religion; he prepares for his return by
giving him such a blow that he can recover from it only by an
explosive act of will or perish; and in all this Adams gives him
no quarter but the quarter that goes with a sense of urgency,
and shows him no mercy but the mercy of the accelerating rush
of time. That is, he draws a picture of man as the almost
mechanical creator of energy and the more than mechanical
victim of the energy he has created.

His dynamic theory of history begins by treating man as
physics treated nature: as the development and economy of
force. The sun, man, a mathematical point, were all forces, since
all did work; therefore, the same laws applied to each. Thus
Adams reversed the common assumption that man captures
forces, and made the dynamic assumption that the forces cap-
ture man: man, he said, "is the sum of the forces that attract
him." By such a theory man is reduced, like nature herself, to
the movement of inertia: which may be deflected, intensified,
accelerated, but must in the end be degraded, according to law,
and come to nothing; or at any rate must reach the extinction
in man of everything hitherto held human, including the power
to envisage and react to his fate.

The predicament of the mind still capable of setting up the
dynamic theory of its own extinction is difficult but not intolerable. Curiosity is never livelier than about the cruelty of
the mind to itself; nothing is of such vital interest as the means
of death, nothing so terrifying as the means of rebirth, the end
of what passes and the persistence, through new phase, of what
always was, the dreadful mortality in the pursuit of the immortal. So it was with Adams. In the last three chapters of the

Education, as in the last three of the *Chartres*, he united the curiosity and the interest into a legacy of life and metaphysics by a gesture of poetry. To that gesture we shall come; but let us look first at the two papers Adams left behind him, called "A Letter to American Teachers of History" and "The Rule of Phase Applied to History."

In these papers we see the cruelty of mind to mind pursued with the liveliest possible curiosity into a kind of desperate dogma. Here Adams plays with his dynamic theory as if it were fact, and in his play shows that combination of frivolity and seriousness which the man of the world and the stoic both think go best with surrender to the inevitable. In these papers physics is *all* physics, and everything else is physics, too; there is no metaphysics, no poetry, and no gesture—only the murderous sweep of law reaching, aspect by aspect, into the life of man. It is the other and lesser thing Adams might have done to finish his *Education*; it is the same thing that he did do, but at a lower, more polemic, more practical, less meaningful level: at that level of play which is the breakdown, rather than the completion, of the mature mind.

It is not certain when these papers were written; they were finished by 1910, three years after the *Education*, and as the Preface to the "Letter" says, purport to be a report written fifteen years later on "The Tendency of History," which he had sent to the Historical Association in 1895. It is a report, he says, of an effort to calculate the values of coordinates in the different fields of the movement of inertia. Actually, these papers are something quite different; they define an extreme form of determinism, whether mechanistic or vitalistic, as the next inevitable conception of the human mind, and then derive the consequences of the definition as if they had the force of absolute law. It is the circular argument in which the circle narrows to nothing.

Let us see how he gets there. It is always interesting and sometimes a triumph of illusion (Nirvana is always out of season) to watch a mind force itself to the condition of nothingness as if it were an access of sensibility. Adams begins by reminding his colleagues the American historians that the reign of unity by the will of God ended about 1600 and was followed by the reign of the unity of indestructible energy. The Law of the Conservation of Energy administered that unity until about

1850 when a second law appeared, contrary to the first from a human point of view, which said that although energy was indestructible it necessarily dissipated itself like a cloud of free steam until, for any effective purpose, it was lost, forever unavailable. That is to say, all energy tended to reach the condition where further transformations were impossible.

Adams liked best Clausius' definition of this second law: The entropy of the universe tends to a maximum. The time was coming when there would be no more tropes of energy: no more lively transformations, fresh idioms, new twists of expression: in short, no more poetry—and certainly no more unity. What kind of unity was it when the energy united dissipated before your eyes? The question had only to ask itself to be thrown out of court; no answer could be competent or relevant; the law of dissipation did not affect the law of conservation. Nevertheless, the question continued to ask itself in one form or another, and still does, and asks itself most painfully in terms of the trope of vitalism, which those who objected to entropy immediately invented. Vitalism said that social or biological energy was not physical energy at all; and historians felt at once that they were vitalists and wrote the story of processes that operated independent of mechanical law.

What Adams was anxious to point out was that vitalism was no help to the historian. He cities Anton Kerner on the vital energy that inhabits protoplasm, and concludes that it "had a way of coming and going in phases of intensity much more mysterious than the energy itself. Catastrophe was its law." Death was such a change of phase, an irrecoverable dissipation. Presumably then, since social energy was a kind of vital energy, then social energy must dissipate, too. And again, if history knew the law of that dissipation, history was a science, and a science in a fix. To join the fate of biology and physics he quotes Andrew Gray on Lord Kelvin. "All work is done by conversion of one energy, or intensity, into another, and a lower: if the conversion is prevented, all processes which involve such conversion must cease, and among these are vital processes." And against this, metaphysics, as illustrated by Eduard von Hartmann, provided small consolation in the doubt whether "the world-process will work itself out slowly in prodigious lapse of time, according to purely physical laws; or whether it will find its end by means of some metaphysical resource when it has reached its culminating point."

The emphasis of argument is all the sharper because Adams wanted to show that "Darwin's Evolution" contradicts both Conservation and Dissipation. Nineteenth-century society was no different from twelfth-century in its rejection of law. Society took to evolution as it had taken to the Virgin, for the sake of an assured future. Society decided that evolution must be upward and made for itself its own third law of energy, the Law of Evolution: "that Vital Energy could be added, and raised indefinitely in potential, without the smallest apparent compensation." Faced with this third law of energy, the historian is compelled to decide either that "society does work by degrading its energies," which is what physics teaches him, or that society in the form of vital energy does work in defiance of physics, which is what popular evolution permits him to believe; and if he leans toward evolution he runs the risk that he has joined society in looking one way and working in another, all the while moving with society in shifting direction and at an uncertain rate.

Adams comments on the historian's predicament from the point of view of physics: "The acceleration of movement seems rapid, but the inertia, or resistance to deflection, may increase with the rapidity, so that society might pass through phase after phase of speed, without noting deflection in its thought"—very much as if society were retreating upon an island in a rising ocean, with each tide a form of unifying force until the last which was obliterating. So it had been in history through the sequence of the classic gods, monotheism, Scholastic philosophy, and Newtonian physics, where the older gods were popular and the newer developed compulsory force, but all were forms of inertia. "Inertia is the law of mind as well as of matter, and inertia is a form of instinct; yet in western civilization it has never held its own." The inertia of thought was on a washing ledge without knowing it; the law of degradation was "already enforced in every field excepting that of human history."

At this point Adams ends the first phase of his argument with the remark, for clincher, that Darwinian Evolution had gotten its success and its effect of science from Sir Charles Lyell's theory of Uniformity—a theory which had perforce given way to a

theory of catastrophe, jumps, revolution, according to which
Evolution proceeded by a series of leaps which were irreversible
and limited, and which developed a degree of specialization that
certified extinction. Thus if the professor of history accepts
physics he will keep silent; if he fights and turns to Darwin he
will find not the survival but the extinction of the species. The
law of degradation has crept into the biological citadel without
notice.

The next twenty pages play with the gay ferocity of a kitten
at the evidences of degradation: the narrowing jaw, loss of hair,
inability to suckle, the general enfeeblement of the race and
diminishing vitality in a world itself moving toward the heat-
death of final equilibrium: to "a useless light and a barren
heat." Thus the business of society had become protection, not
against the enemy without, but against the enemy within: its
own deterioration. What is called social legislation exercised
powers like the powers of war. So, too, what are called philosophers built systems on the failure, not the survival, of society;
not only the professional philosophers, but also "the anarchist,
the esthete, the mystic, the revolutionary socialist, even if they
do not despair of the future, agree with the pessimist in the same
sentiment of hatred and disgust for whatever is; in the same
need of destroying the real, and escaping from it." The language quoted is not Adams' but his translation of a passage from
Emile Durkheim's *Le Suicide*, in which the title is the theme:
that everything in society leads toward voluntary death; and
it is by means of this passage that he makes his transition from
physics and biology to thought. As a transition it promises
poorly.

Which is what Adams wanted. Thought is only a loophole;
but that loophole is the only escape from the barriers of physics
and biology, the escape into a conception of man which has as
little as possible to do with physics and biology, and centers
itself in a disembodied spirit. There vital energy will be not
animal but intellectual. But—and this is why Adams wanted a
bad transition—intellect or reason "can be only another phase
of the energy earlier known as Instinct or Intuition," which was
itself a category of Will. Will was a name for energy. Hence
man, since he is specialized beyond variation, is an example of
enfeebled will. By this conversion of metaphysics into a branch
of physics, history becomes the science of human degradation.

The alternative is the assertion that man's energy is supernatural, something no longer made by nature; and in the lack of which man became helpless and turned increasingly to thought, to the form of consciousness called intelligence. Thought is man's struggle with the helplessness of the enfeebled will. "As far as he is animal, the thinker is a bad animal; eating badly; digesting badly; often dying without posterity. In him the degradation of vital energy is flagrant."

At this point Adams resorts to Bergson's contrast of intelligence and intuition to deepen the helplessness and emphasize the enfeeblement of thinking man; and again the metaphysics corresponds to the physics. Intuition is a lesser but even more necessary loophole than reason, for intuition has been sacrificed to intelligence, and has become vague and discontinuous, a waning light rising only at hazardous times but, in Bergson's language, "a light which pierces, none the less, the darkness of the night in which our intelligence leaves us." It is Bergson's intuition that reminds Adams of man's savage loss: the direct, aesthetic perception of the light that might have been shining on what has happened. The language is of the judge adding his personal fury to the judgment otherwise made. It is nature, in whose bosom man has never been entirely comforted, who is the culprit mother; it is nature who has produced "this one-sided Consciousness, this amputated Intelligence, this degraded Act—this truncated Will." That is, nature produced thought through the agency of man, and "the function of man is, to the historian, the production of Thought"; and he must treat it, in parallel to the other sciences, and since its incentive in instinct is gone, as "the history of a more or less mechanical dissolution."

The historian must, but again he must not. He must both teach according to what the formulas of energy discover and predict, however alien to the independence and even the life of the mind that made the formulas; and he must teach according to his sense of himself as somehow supreme, in his very identity, over what moved him, wore him out, and kept him going. He must teach, whatever thought was in reality, its own conception of its role. He must teach that "the flower of vital energy is Thought, and that not Instinct but Intellect is the highest power of a supernatural Will;—an ultimate, independent, self-producing, self-sustaining, incorruptible solvent of all earlier or lower energies, and incapable of degradation or dissolution." If he abdicated that pride he abdicated what seemed in history the sole motive for existence. Yet abdication was what the sciences presented; already Intellect was turning into mathematics so far as it expressed itself and otherwise into "a passive instrument of a physico-chemical energy called Will;—an ingenious economy in the application of power; a catalytic medium; a dynamo, mysteriously converting one form of energy into a lower."

In short, man's intellect, the flower of his vital energy, studied every field of energy except itself as subject to physical law, and the problem was whether or no the intellect that studied was also so subject. The problem was old; it was another form of the problem of faith and reason; it was an emphatic form of the problem of unity: one way or another Adams had been rehearsing the problem all his thinking life, and when he came in his layman's study of the physical sciences upon a promising new form of the old problem he could not help pushing it for all it was worth. Here was physics with a Law of Conservation and another Law of Entropy which was consistent enough with the first law so far as physics went but which was either contradictory to everything human or destroyed it. Where was faith and where was reason? What sort of unity of man in relation to the universe was possible in the new world where entropy did its work on conservation: a world where nothing was lost and nothing renewed?

Such was the statement of the problem in Adams' "Letter to American Teachers of History"; in his second chapter he aggravates the problem under the title of "The Solutions." He had already, in point of time, made his serious effort at a solution in the *Education*; here, in the "Letter," he had to emphasize the obstacles and the incentives to the solution in the hope of aggravating others to come to his own version of the problem; and he had also, perhaps, to see whether he could undermine his own solution. He had to see whether abdication was not in fact in the order of things; to see whether, after all, man was the "creature, not the creator, of the social organism." There is nothing a mind of Adams' type trusts so little as the thoughts by which he saves his life; yet he must come back to them: like death they will either end him or save him, or both. The thought which Adams distrusted because it saved him was as old as the problem which raised it and as complex, as teetering in its balance, as elusive of any set form.

History, this thought says, must make a provisional decision—a fiction taken as warrant for action—a convenient statement—about the relation of man to his environment. The statement, the thought itself, is interrogative. Is man bound by the laws of the environment? how much? Does he add laws of his own? and, if so, how do they jibe or mesh with natural law? What is the constitutionality between man and nature? Here the thought teeters and comes up on the other side, the side of the old arrogance of intellect, and again it is interrogative. Must man not, rather than conform to some deduced constitutional notion, must he not reconsider his view of the scope and run of natural law? If laws are conveniences for the descriptive ordering of discourse and the prediction of behavior, had man not best make certain of their convenience? What is the nature of necessity in natural law? What is the nature of rationality in nature? What is the nature of nature that it prompts such human questions?

Something is known of the nature of reason in man: that it is human and that its exclusiveness is pretentious; and what is known of reason suggests that it can at best only partially apply to nature. Yet if it runs at all in nature it seems it must run at least that far in man—precisely to the extent that man is part of nature. This is to suggest that reason is a phase of nature, that will, instinct, intuition are other phases of nature; and the question is how far shifts in phase shift the rules. Do ice, water, and steam—do geology, biology, and electricity—obey the same rules? But to ask such questions is to have presumed that knowledge may be absolute. Is it not safer to presume that though there may be an identity of rule, the very conditions of experience prevent its discovery? Nature in its different phases may operate by rules which, to the single and limited phase which is man's mind, may seem contrary or at least inconsistent. Yet man is condemned by the law of his own history to the permanent labor of making his phase "see" the other phases as consistent. He must make a theory of himself in nature.

It is because Adams felt so acutely the need of that theory, both in history and in the immediate experience of his own mind, that he persisted in setting the human problem in terms of the agreement or contradiction of the two laws of conservation and entropy. Since he came before the time of the non-rational (in the human sense) mechanics of the atom and the even more non-rational developments in topology, he also persisted in the provisional attempt to submit man's mind to mechanical law. He took as if seriously the gospel of the Dynamo as total replacement of the gospel of the Virgin, in order to see what would happen if he made that substitution with real seriousness: that is, with a theory of full abdication. The prospect reached through full surrender to intelligence turns out as dismal, and much like, full surrender to instinct, or intuition, as will: "The vast majority of minds, educated or not, are invited to live in a complex of anarchical energies, with only the privilege of acting as chief anarchists," and with the only function, as he captured and controlled other forms of energy, of accelerating the operation of the Law of Entropy in armies and wars, in drinking and lunacy, in deforestation and agriculture, in every characteristically disproportionate human wasting of the earth. It is to further that waste that "civilization and education enfeeble personal energy; *emollit mores:* they aim especially at extending the forces of society at cost of the intensity of individual forces." The individual disappears into the solution of society, and the solution does work he could not, and would not, have done. "The social Organism is the cause, creator, and end of the Man, who exists only as a passing representative of it, without rights or functions except what it imposes." Such a society is peculiarly subject to the degradation of energy, and indeed requires degradation in order to survive.

Here Adams says nothing of his private theory or way of beholding called Conservative Christian Anarchy, but it should seem plain in the face of such a society—our own society looked at as physics—why his only refuge lay in that invention. He says nothing; instead he concludes that the historian, that man, can no longer close his eyes to his society, and must set up some common formula or figure to study vital energies. The assent of physics would be needed to the formula, but the humanities would require some abandonment of the second Law of Thermodynamics in order to assent to the physics. Neither physicist nor humanist could get his work done by a formal exception of Reason from the field of the formula. "Either the law must be abandoned in respect to Vital Energy altogether, or Vital

Energy must abandon Reason altogether as one of its forms, and return to the old dilemma of Descartes."

That is to say, Adams would return to a fresh formulation, unacceptable to Descartes, of the aspiration and denial of free will. What Descartes could not have accepted was what Adams himself could never accept as a way station in argument: namely, that the decision rested with the physicists and physico-chemists, even if these were all Newtons. Adams' mind ran always to metaphysics; that is, lacking the theology, the craving of his mind for full theory ran always to the poetry of reason, and depended for concrete support neither on the reason nor the formula of physics, but on the reason and the form of poetry. The polemics against reason and poetry in "A Letter to Teachers" and "The Rule of Phase" were perhaps only a penalty and scrupulous corrective—the brief of the Devil's Advocate—applied because of too great a metaphysical craving, and because of a legitimate and tormenting doubt that perhaps, after all, the history of man had passed beyond, had dropped beneath, the phase when thought could represent either his meaning or his intentions to himself. With Adams the torment of that doubt came in the years between finishing the *Education* and the second version of the *Chartres*; it might well have tormented him every second instant had he lived to 1950, when the regular lapses of public thought seem to release fresh bursts of vital energy turned suicidal or puerile by turns.

Indeed it is as a text or prophecy for that prospect that "The Rules of Phase Applied to History" (1909) can be read. It is one of the temptations of the human mind, whenever it reaches a certain pitch of energy, to see that energy converted into something else: into some slavery to the goddess Fortuna, to the movement of the stars or astrology, or to some other hypostasis of mechanical law. That is, the mind, on the sudden, desires to give in to one of its mature aberrations, and in these moments the aberrations seem to correspond both to its experience and to the light that shines in experience; so that the aberration puts on the look of the necessary next step of reason, or vital energy, or law, or whatever aspect the universe happens to turn up: some old story in an aggravated form. It is what happens when under the torment of self-doubt the reason in the mind turns to anger without losing the form of reason. This is the secret of Adams' speculative pessimism; it springs from an anger lodged

in the mind itself, an aberration of its own nature, the supplication of a special, but momentary, tyranny, like that of a
poem which, because in itself it craves to be free, must be
written in strict form.

"The Rule of Phase," then, is such a poem written to celebrate
the ardor of thought by transforming it into such conditions of
tyranny that thought is impossible. In the very center of the
essay lies alpine ice: the chill of being, of thought itself, and
this icy thought is taken as a solvent. The language is very
strange: it is short of style, but all the elements of style are
there in turmoil not quite in solution. "This solvent, then—this
ultimate motion which absorbs all other forms of motion is an
ultimate equilibrium—this ethereal current of Thought—is conceived as existing, like ice on a mountain range, and trickling
from every pore of rock, in innumerable rills, uniting always
into larger channels, and always dissolving whatever it meets,
until at last it reaches equilibrium in the ocean of ultimate
solution."

The ice image is serious and it runs back at least as far as
Adams' review of Lyell's *Principles of Geology* in the October
1868 *North American Review*, where he wrote of "the world's
great ever-recurring winter"; and it runs too, both backward
and forward, to the vision of glacial chaos he saw in the Alps
after his sister's death. Ice for Adams, in one mood of his mind,
was both the all-beginning and the end-all; it has that kind of
seriousness here, it is thought striking the senses from outside.
But the senses themselves have their own thought, striking
within, a steady experience of motion which Adams never forgot and of which he makes one of his finest declarations in the
sentence next before the end of this essay—just at the point
where the Rule of Phase no longer applies either to history or
to the mind that construes history. We shall see shortly what
the declaration makes plain in Adams' speculative pessimism:
here they are wanted naked as an example of the human spirit
—of Henry Adams' laboring and buoyant Psyche—recovering
itself in the midst of metaphysical dismay. He has been speaking of the perplexity of the mind confronted with external
forces of which the only knowledge is in the names given them.
The perplexity is the same, he says, "as before the common,
infinitely familiar Fluctuations of his own Thought whose action is so astounding on the direction of his energies."

Between the ice-thought and his own Thought lies the tyrannical poem of "The Rule of Phase Applied to History." All tests are tyrannical, in some sense made in the anger of doubt or the anguish of distrust. In this poem the action of thought is submitted to the tyrannical test of mechanical law, in this case Willard Gibb's rule of phase for theoretical or prophetic chemistry. Under this test we see thought put through a ballet of contortions never previously, and even now unwillingly, part of its performance. Poor thought not only dissolves; it is forced to disappear into the absolute which cannot be grasped by any sense, like a construction in mathematic form of physical force. It is thus a dramatization of the impulse to suicide or destruction. Dante would call it one of those great catastrophic effects man creates when he submits his understanding to the tyranny of a single mode of the mind. Freud might have said that this was Adams' version of *Beyond the Pleasure Principle*, which explains how it is that men do not wish to get well but prefer to nourish their diseases and despairs as the one certain road to the stability (equilibrium, Adams would say) which is death. Yeats, if he read it right, could have observed of the whole essay, "Man has created death."

What Adams actually does is to force that infinitely familiar fluctuating thought of his, so full of aspiration and dismay, to take forms and avow allegiance to laws, which would certify its accelerating destruction. This has often been done before, in incantation, in theology, in war: none of which taken exclusively cover the action of man. In Adams' time the same diabolical and gratuitous destruction was found in an arbitrary metaphysics of science: that is, by identifying the observing mind both with its theory of observation and with the facts observed. This is to identify ignorance with the force of truth, which is both a practical and an emotional necessity, but not valid after the impulse is gone; which is why those of us who did not, or do not, have the impulse cannot apprehend the necessity. Comte is now no more welcome to us than Buckle, Spencer than Nordau; and Adams when he is in their moods is no more welcome than they are if we take them as truth instead of drama. Here we want Adams' drama of thought as energy with its acts exposed in successive stages of history. Nothing could be more ambitious and more tyrannical than the assertion of history as the science of thought, and nothing could sink the last buoyant figment of thought deeper than the confession that historical energy was identical with the energy of matter; yet this assertion and this confession were the avowed intentions of Adams' essay. After we look at what he did with the intentions we shall then look at how he got away from them.

The look at what he did need not take long: the grasp for fortune is instinctive, whether fortune is called fate or unconscious determinism; and like other instinctive actions it has a kind of violence about it. Adams grasped at everything he could lay hands on in chemistry, physics, and astronomy which seemed to suggest that the energy of the universe was running down, or was running into a solution: "an ocean of discontinuous particles." Having grasped what he could from the sciences, he proceeded to take thought as an energy which was also its own final solvent. History was the account of how thought hurried to its last end, phase by phase, with an increasing acceleration. It was as if Thought cried: *Everybody does it, why not I?* If in the natural sciences the three important variables are attraction, temperature, and volume, in history they must be pressure, acceleration, and volume. In history, then, thought passed like a current through a series of critical points determined by these factors, always "conceived as a solvent, acting like heat or electricity, and increasing in volume by the law of squares." And this current, this solvent, said Adams, "is conceived as existing, like ice on a mountain range, and trickling from every pore of rock, in innumerable rills, uniting always into larger channels, and always dissolving whatever it meets, until at last it reaches equilibrium in the ocean of ultimate solution."

It is this poetic conception of the force of thought which leads Adams to surrender history to mathematical physics. The surrender, like the conception of it, was accomplished by poetic means: by a series of images of Adams' actual experience of the change in direction and form of the force of thought during the Renaissance under the laws of mass. Man's mind felt the attraction of mechanical rather than religious force—both occult—and changed sharply. "As each newly appropriate force increased the attraction between the sum of nature's forces and the volume of human mind, by the usual law of squares, the acceleration hurried society toward the critical point that marked the passage into a new phase as though it were heat impelling water to explode as steam."

This is not only poetry, but speculative poetry, proceeding with the intense levity of the desperate theologian to the application of a rigorous artificial form. The rigorous form is here the law of squares as geometrical progression. Surely there is both intensity and levity if the mind cries, as Adams' mind cries here, What happens to the force that moves me, what happens to my experience of it, if it is submitted, both backward and forward, and with every possible formal decorum, to the law of squares? What happens is an intolerable extension backward into the original perfect ignorance of butterfly or beetle and a fatal extension, truncated by the square root to immediate zero, forward. It is by analogous means always that man has wooed occult force in the exigence of the moment. The form chosen dictates the direction found throwing the experience—the sense of the force felt—into new perspective or into new dogmatic intelligence. The beginning and the end are equally arbitrary.

Adams' arbitrary beginning was the assertion that the three hundred years 1600–1900 marked clear limits to the mechanical phase of man's mind in attractive relation to force. Proceeding backward, the square of three hundred is ninety thousand years for the religious phase; and proceeding forward, the square root of three hundred is seventeen (and the year 1917) for the electrical phase; and the square root of seventeen gives the year 1921 as the practical culmination of human thought in a familiar universe. But like most religious poems of a speculative character, Adams' arbitrary form had double application. If the numerical value 1296 is assigned to the mechanical phase, to present volume of thought, "the preceding religious phase would have a value of only 36 as the average of many thousand years, representing therefore nearly a straight line, while the twentieth century would be represented by the square of 1296 or what is equivalent to a straight line to infinity." It is hard to say which application of the law of squares represents the over-plot and which the under-plot; and perhaps the choice can be made only by temperament . . . [*end of manuscript*]

KING RICHARD'S
PRISON SONG

I

By January 1912, Adams had brought out two hundred and fifty copies of the revised version of *Mont-Saint-Michel and Chartres*, and by February 8 three dozen copies had been sent to colleges all over the land—especially women's colleges, since the book was addressed to nieces. He still insisted that the book was inadequate, incomplete, and partial, for all the time and care and collaboration that had been levied for it. The consent to reprint which had been wrung from him was an embarrassed consent; given because it was, in the circumstances, "less Adamsy to consent than to refuse," as he had written Ward Thoron—and so more "Adamsy all round." Furthermore, consent once given, and the book having appeared, there remained the author's emphatic dread that, for the very reason that few could ever read and respond to his book, thousands might make of it a text, or worse a guide—a possibility that made Adams swear he would burn Chartres itself first. But the book was out, and regardless of all else was ready for use as Adams' headstone, with his *Life* of George Cabot Lodge as a footstone.

Footstone and headstone—so he said himself; one more repetition of the theme that had beset him through half his waking moments since December 1885, the theme that had driven him with singular vitality and variety of effort to travel half the existing world and to ransack most of its history in search of a meaning appropriate to the theme: the theme that he was already dead in everything except the accomplished fact. With any luck at all, accomplishment at seventy-four could not be long delayed. The *Chartres* was the headstone, the best monument Adams could raise to the "Light Ages" of the aspiring imagination; and the *Life* of young Lodge—Thomas Aquinas Lodge, as Adams liked to refer to him—made the footstone, because in the broken promise of that poet's death Adams saw the tragic fable of the aspiring imagination in his own darkening age. The circle had come round. Seen together, the two images guaranteed the sentiment that he had expressed to his brother Brooks in another context years before—the mere practical context of political and economical instability: "The worst of it is that we have no imaginative race left to reconstruct a faith or an art."

The circle had come round in everything but fact. The event hung back, for both Adams and his world, from its necessary duty. The old Adam quite refused to die, and the world of Adams refused with frivolous desperation to succumb to its last convulsion. Tenacity of life had always been a feature of the worst ages, whether in individual man or his society, and Henry Adams followed his type. Back in Washington from six months in Paris, he could no more help occupying himself than the beetle he felt himself to be, and could no more help expressing himself than the active imagination he actually remained. Waiting was one of the fuller forms of life, especially if you waited for death. Beetle and man wrote with one pen to Boston asking to have the nieces packed up in regular order and handed over to Adams' Express two at a time; he would supply the gruel. One niece was with him, well-disposed and good, but when she went others would be needed in succession without fail, for society and stimulation and affection. But the mood was bad, even with nieces to help. The young, he wrote, are too old to die, and the old also were too old to die; and as for himself, "I've got to go, to go, to go to bed." The obsession was there like a nursery rhyme that will not stop its private refrain in the head; it was there in the weather, too, for the next day he reports the worst blizzard since the 16th of February 1838—the day of his birth—adding that he couldn't bear it a moment longer.

Perhaps also there was ironical food for the obsession of death in the photograph he had just received of what he called his thirty-thousand-year-old baby, which had been dug up for him, saved, and called his own, under the direction of Professor Hubert in the excavations at Dordogne. The food was of ironical delight. Adams had subscribed to the fund for the excavation on the stipulation that such a baby be found for him, and here it was, or at least its photograph; and Adams was deeply pleased at his vicarious paternity and always referred to it with affectionate emphasis on the full thirty centuries of its perspective. An apartment must be arranged for it in Paris (actually the bones went to the Musée de St. Germain), and when Hubert suddenly got a twin for it, so much the better: the sense of symbolic juvenescence was redoubled. Here, in a dying age, and to a dying man, was a preserved and ancient infancy. For once and at last Adams had got appreciably nearer "his earliest ancestor and nearest relative, the ganoid fish, whose name, according to Professor Huxley, was *Pteraspis*, a cousin of the sturgeon, and whose kingdom, according to Sir Roger Murchison, was called Siluria."

Except for the nieces, who "flowed in like dividends," the age was observably dying, and Adams' hope was that "his universe would last as long as his eyesight." Meanwhile, one held one's tongue except to one's friends; but to them, since it was what they were for, and since one always had something to say if only for relief and gesture, one let go. Society was flat and politics was worse. Roosevelt was a flailing fool and soared above the storm if you can call such a wreck a storm, but no matter what he was or what he did he was no substitute for the characters in the *Chanson de Roland*. Adams' reaction to society in the winter of 1912 was excessive and personal. The joy of excess is its own best corrective. Of Champ Clark, who then seemed the likely Democratic candidate, he wrote that he "seems to be a primitive, like my thirty thousand year old baby on a hairy elephant with the Southern statesman manners of a hundred years ago." Again:

The X that rather amuses me is the value of progressives. I take it that Theodore valued himself very seriously as Napoleon at Elba. He had every reason to think that he controlled opinion. . . . I am therefore the more interested to see that the public shows no kind of interest in his ideas. With its usual bread-and-butter instinct, the public cares only for the tariff, which is in fact the root of the situation. . . . More people, more noise. Down with the tariff! They will soon

strike a snag there! Lord, how I would like to join them in downing
the tariff if I dared, and how quick our Theodore would drop his
Judges if he dared be honest for once, and strike at the laboring man.
No human being cares a damn about the Judges or anything else but
their plunder.

These sentences come from a letter to his brother Brooks. An
earlier letter, also to Brooks, fills in the background.

If the process of social revolution is to continue with the acceleration
of the last three years, my limit of 1917 is too far off. The year 1911
saw the dissolution of the old society in several very great empires.
We shaved it closely in Europe. In order to escape it, Italy plunged
into war. France is always on the verge of it. Germany has raised
its socialistic force to the highest power consistent with the old order.
England is believed to be facing the issue this very day, and is to
pursue it in the case of Ireland, without a moment's delay. A continuous belt of dissolved society now stretches round the world, from
Sicily eastward to Pekin, and throughout Mexico. At the same rate,
the disease should reach the heart of sociey, Central Europe, within
this year, unless it is already there.

Nor can I see any corner of refuge. On the contrary I feel rather
safest in the centre of the whirlpool. Your inquiry about Roosevelt
leads me to this conclusion. Politically Roosevelt merely reflects the
general dissolution, and in that sense, has no more interest to me
than Lloyd George or Juarez or the German who is momentarily at
the head of the dissolving energies; but socially and personally Roosevelt touches us all very closely, and affects our happiness. Not only as
a political force is he a reflection of the degradation of energies; but
still more as a social example. His mind has gone to pieces, and has
disintegrated like the mind of society, till it has become quite incoherent and spasmodic. . . . Of course the people who follow him
are of the same neurotic and morbid temperament, and it matters
little whether they are few or many. If a majority, they prove that
my theory of the dissipation of energy has proved itself.

The reader should remind himself here of two things. Nineteen twelve was a Presidential year, so that opinion, even the
best of it, ran strong. The other thing is that the belt of "dissolved" society took in nearly the whole world within two years.
What dissolved was the remnant, as Adams saw it, of his ideal
society: that of the rational imagination whether as witnessed
in late eighteenth-century republican democracy or as in
twelfth-century Christianity. The extracts are made here, however, to show the general tone of Adams' response, and may be

capped by two more references to the correspondence. To Louisa Hooper he wrote in the spring of the year that life had poisoned him with an *idée fixe:* Everyone was loony. Mrs. Gardner and the John Lodges were alone sane. Even his thirty-thousand-year-old-baby was insane. The sentiment is only another phase of the sentiment expressed in a letter to Brooks from Paris in the summer of 1911. He is commenting on the public reaction to the great drought that then threatened the bread of Europe. "The average man of the highest education is a greater imbecile than the old-fashioned boor, who at least recognized an inexplicable phenomenon when he saw it. Our educated classes will not recognize the day of Judgment, until they are resting in hot oil."

To entertain such sentiments frivolously is fun; to entertain them seriously is more fun—and a form of liberal education—but it leaves the sensibility wrenched and pained and commonly rather taut. So it was with Adams in the winter of 1912. Although he saw no refuge for himself as a representative of social energy, degraded or not, he had a double refuge for himself as a private imagination. There were the nieces and nephews as always—he had six tenants from January 23rd to February 22nd, and others to follow during the spring, with all the small things that turned up for flavor: he notes that a Boston niece got her brooch and seemed pleased, though you can never tell if a Bostonian is really pleased.

That was half; and there was besides his continuing interest in the Light Ages. The new *Chartres* being out, and distributed, there was the pleasure of awaiting responses. He was especially interested in the Catholic response, and threatened, if he was not made a Cardinal, to speak a word against them to Notre Dame la Haute. He was not, however, so far as appears, even rebuked, which rather disappointed him. More positively, he was working in two fields, that of tenth-century architecture and that of the medieval romances or *chansons*. We hear of long labors in textual criticism, a critique of German scholarship, many suggestions to his pupil Ward Thoron, then in southern France, for his work on the manuscripts of Turpin, and lastly of the work he was himself doing daily on a verse translation of the *Chanson de Willame*, which came rather earlier, Adams thought, in the Charlemagne Cycle than the *Chanson de Roland*. The translation, of which he attempted a page a day, was his stint of work and his flywheel of interest. It was meant to keep him going. Characteristically, in a letter to Professor Luquiens, he both belittled and magnified his intention. "Although this is a mere plaything, and I have no thought of publishing, it is so fascinating an amusement that I hope to make it last the rest of my life. It involves upsetting pretty much all French history in the 10th and 11th centuries." Nothing, of course, would suit Adams better than to upset a couple of centuries of French history in terms of a *Chanson de Geste* in which a woman—Guiborc by name—was important.

Such was the winter, its obsessions, and occupations, its responses and its pleasures. Spring brought again the sight of France close enough to count, and the letters are full of references to sailing. Rooms were engaged for passage on the *Titanic;* there was work to be done, which must be got at; there was relief from Washington that must be had—relief from that modern world which Adams felt mostly as increasing strain; and for these a twelfth-century attic—his apartment in the Bois de Boulogne—was best. But as he waited, the *Titanic* struck its iceberg and went down, together with the Republican Party. The shock was great and shook the nerves of memory and expectation. Society for once seemed as pessimistic as Adams himself; which made Paris, for normal behavior, all the more necessary. The *Olympic* was substituted for the *Titanic*, and on the 22nd of April he wrote to Louisa Hooper, who was to accompany him along with other nieces, that the right rooms were engaged, and that the Henry Whites were installed in their new and magnificent eighteenth-century house. Then, a day or two before sailing, Adams sat in his library and read how the sailors on the *Olympic* had struck because of insufficient life-boats.

That news coming close and a consequence upon the tragic blunder of the *Titanic* brought on one of those high floods of feeling, drenching the sensibility and loosening all the nerves, which we call burning indignation; and the indignation, in this case, brought on physical shock. Adams keeled over. For six weeks he lay, partly delirious, his house his hospital, three doctors and a student in attendance and three nurses in residence. What had occurred was an apoplectic shock to the left brain which affected the right hand. The family apparently grew doubtful of the treatment Adams was receiving in Washington and especially doubtful of the prohibition against moving him from the heat of a Washington summer. At any rate Dr. Worcester was sent for from Boston. William, Adams' colored servant, expressed his opinion of the Washington medical regime by whispering succinctly to Dr. Worcester as he took him in: "They're living off Mr. Adams' terrapin and champagne." Doubtless William lied on the facts; but his master, who never taught facts as such, must surely have appreciated the intention, the spirit, and the form of William's whisper. Dr. Worcester disagreed with the Washington view of Adams' condition and its treatment, and saw nothing but good in moving him. Adams' intermittent delirium he held to be less integral to his condition than an effect of an excessive dosage of bromides which had been given to abate the "restlessness" of the patient. Adams had never been anything but restless.

Dr. Worcester was evidently right. When Adams seemed well enough to move, toward the end of June, there was some difficulty, because of the then adjourning Congress, in obtaining a private car. Senator Lodge finally got one, and with an interne and a nurse aboard, Adams was carried to Lincoln, Massachusetts. The train was met by Dr. Worcester and an ambulance. Adams walked off the train, refused to look at the ambulance, and rode with Dr. Worcester to his brother Charles' house in South Lincoln. He also refused emphatically to have a nurse, insisting that the houseful of nurses he had had in Washington had been palmed off on him when he could do nothing about it. As a matter of fact there was no need of a nurse in South Lincoln, and relatively little need of medical attention; Dr. Worcester came frequently but more because Adams insisted on it than for medical reasons. Adams wanted to get well—as long as he was going to live at all—as well as possible; and it gave him a sense of security in progress to have Dr. Worcester on hand.

So began his first summer and his first full year in America since 1889. Lincoln, like its neighbor Concord, is New England at its quietest, and, in an earthly sense, most opulent: a rural, not a manufacturing, town and township, part residential and part farming, a rolling, well-watered country with green fields and green woods. Charles Francis Adams had moved there in

1893 to escape an urbanized and cheapened Quincy; and the move brought him, he said, out of a tomb into sunlight and living air. The effect on his brother Henry was as exhilarating. The day after his arrival he walked over a mile in the woods and walked there regularly thereafter. He grew and felt robust, and there was no noticeable enfeeblement of either wit or memory. He did not suffer for company outside his immediate family; Louisa Hooper spent three days a week with him; Mrs. Cameron came later; there were other nieces and friends. It was, however, all nieces and no men.

By the end of July he had resumed a good part of his correspondence, and his interests of the winter were fully resumed, though not, naturally, in full activity. On the 27th he is already hoping to get down to Dordogne and his thirty-thousand-year-old baby, is anxious for Ward Thoron to publish his edition of Turpin, and is commenting on the campaign. Mrs. Roosevelt, he hears, has lost her sense of taste, which must be dreadful; but he is afraid to write to her in sympathy because, in that summer of the Bull Moose, she might think him joking. In October he is having a masseur and feels more robust than for twenty years and proposes to sail for France on the 18th of February with Louisa Hooper.

To his brother Brooks he was slightly more candid, or was on the 18th of October more distrustful of himself. He was trying, he wrote, to return to Washington in apparent health. "Of course," he went on, "it is only apparent. The right side is, and always will be, partially disabled; but the damned thing kills only at its leisure, and meanwhile I want to seem human." Later in the same letter he adds, perhaps an effect of the Lincoln landscape, "but I wish Washington were as countrified as it was sixty years ago."

II

Washington presented other difficulties besides its loss of rural quality, and besides even its staring evidence of social degradation. If Adams was to return to his own house, alone, partially disabled, and always liable to another shock, someone must be found to keep him company, keep him alive, and keep him supplied with such contacts with the outside world as he either could not or did not care to make for himself. The supply of nieces, however copious and regular, might yet show gaps; for even nieces had lives of their own. What was needed was a permanent niece in residence—which may be a very general and ambiguous title, but which represented a constantly heavy if widely variable duty. How much care and thought went into the search is immaterial; no search could have produced more satisfaction than the event showed. Miss Aileen Tone, a young and charming woman, and already a "niece" of sorts, not only performed the full function of niece in residence to perfection, but also by the accident of her private talent gave Adams' sensibility a new vent and his imagination a final and extraordinarily apt form of expression. She brought him what he had apparently not dreamed of, the music of the Middle Ages. As music is the ultimate art, the purest or the most primitive, the most formally sophisticated and incredibly the least committed to any prejudice or experience except itself; so it provided Adams the only form of expression he ever found that could unite all his aspiration and all his interest without distrust and anguish and doubt. Despair itself, in music, and even at seventy-five, could be a *Vita Nuova*.

Miss Tone, tall, slender, dark-eyed, Catholic by faith and training, and of a robustious feminine vivacity, had besides the accomplishments of personality, a trained and lovely voice and a taste for singing such few old French songs as she had come across. When she came to Adams' house from New York she felt instinctively that her singing days were over for the time. However, she brought her music with her, including a new anthology of old French songs. That was Adams' stroke of luck, coming late but all the more lucky for that. He apparently remembered that she sang, and brought the subject up himself. *Sing?* he said to her. *Why not? Open all the doors in the house, and sing.* She showed him her new anthology and told him that there were a few songs in it of the twelfth century. He showed astonishment and doubt; it had not occurred to him that there might be music for the poetry he had loved and worked on for so many years; and when he actually heard the words sung he was tremendously excited—to what degree and extent is shown by the following letter to Ward Thoron, who was still in the south of France.

13 Dec. 1912
1603 H Street

Dear Ward

Your letter of Nov. 30 arrives this morning. Since my last I have dug deep in new 12th century holes which needs, as digging, much help.

The new vein was opened by Miss Tone, when she came to make me a visit a month ago. She brought music, and especially a publication by J. B. Wekerlin, "Echos du Temps Passé," Vol. I. quite lately published, which began with a Chanson of the Chatelain de Coucy, who (Wekerlin says) died in 1192 in battle with the Saracens, on Richard's Crusade. Wekerlin says he himself copied the musical notation from Ms. 63 fonds Paulmy. When I saw that—just calmly written and printed as though it were figs,—I had three more paralytic strokes in straight sequence. Can such things overcome us like a winter's cloud, I cried. No! it can't be! and I begged Miss Tone to sing it, which nothing loth, she did. To our delight, it was as good as the 12th century glass at Chartres,—but quite that! The Tree of Jesse, blues, greens, and all. It was a misericorde,—*Merci Clamans,* —in face of death. Quite exquisite! Full of 12th century style and feeling! and quiet and simple as Richard's Prison-song.

Then we turned the page and found a song of Thibaut, also charming; and references to 63 Chansons notées of Thibaut's. Then two lovely songs from Robin et Marion, with references to the *fonds Lavallière* and *fonds Cangé.* For years I have pined for *Robins m'aime, Robins m'a,* and there it was! I had more fits—many more!

I set to work, and wrote to everyone on this side to help; but of course I must get the work done in Paris, and everywhere. There is no reason why I may not find this music anywhere. No one has touched it, or only to print it for cursed modern ears. I must search all over Europe for the music of Richard's Prison-song, which I want above all. It was and is the greatest historical monument possible to discover. My only wish is to live long enough to discover it.

I want you to take up the job, and have every bit of 12th and 13th century music now to be found, photographed or copied for me as soon as possible. I have not a minute to spare. If able to do it, I shall come over to Paris in March to help, and bring Miss Tone. We shall set up a college of the 12th century. Meanwhile if you will help, give orders at once. You can start on fcs 5000 to begin with. We shall have to do much travel, and I am a mighty poor wreck to travel or work, far feebler than anyone knows; but this interest will keep me on, Looly will be in it, and I hope Elsy Adams, and later Mrs. Keep.

I write in a hurry to catch Saturday's steamer. If necessary use the telegraph. The printed books are no great good. They are chiefly

Tarbé, "Chansons du Chatelain de Coucy," and of Thibaut de Champagne, Francisque Michel, 1830 (musical arrangement by Perne). And Lieder des Castellanes von Coucy by F. Fath, Heidleberg, 1880.

Good luck! Yrs in haste

H.A.

I will send you my new edition or anything else you want.

Mr. Thoron went to work with such great success that by the 5th of February Adams had his copy of the Prison Song and cabled as his first thanks the single word *Beautiful*.

Neither Adams' surprise that the music existed, his delight in it and excited further search, nor his special desire for the score of the Prison Song, should seem in the circumstances anything but natural. Almost nothing of twelfth-century music was known in 1912, and what little was known was either unreadable or misread; the notation was in the commonly misunderstood old modes; the monks of Solesmes were then at work on the Gregorian modes, but nothing had been done at all for the secular music; one man's guess was hardly better than another man's gross mistake, and only the wrong people had done any extensive guessing. Yet the few songs Miss Tone brought with her, with the help they got in reading them from Father John La Farge, who was stationed that year near Washington, and from Jean Beck, whom they brought on precisely to help them, showed at once the pure strength of grace and directness. It was a matter for Adams almost of instinctive taste; if the twelfth century had any music at all it was bound to be great music; and the more one got of it the better off one would be. Adams was always a collector, and the passion of pursuit, and discrimination, was among his continuing pleasures.

The pursuit of the Prison Song of Richard Coeur de Lion was instilled with a deeper passion than pleasure, and amounted indeed to the expression of a consciously inherited bias on a parallel and personal plane. The pursuit, that is, was of pattern, almost of composition. That the element of pattern or composition in question was personal to Adams' sense of his own life, and in a way equivocal or ambiguous, should heighten its interest for analysis: it is the style of the man himself, the quality of his imagination outside his works, of which we grow aware, and so learn to feel the slow cumulus of its pressure holding the works together.

The evidence should tell the story, and fancy need only see

where the fragments fit. John Quincy Adams made an entry in his Diary for November 7, 1830, from which the following sentences are extracted.

No one knows, and few can conceive, the agony of mind that I have suffered from the time that I was made by circumstances, and not by my volition, a candidate for the Presidency till I was dismissed from that station by the failure of my re-election. They were feelings to be suppressed; and they were suppressed. No human being has ever heard me complain. Domestic calamity, far heavier than political disappointment or disaster can possibly be, overtook me immediately after my fall from power. . . . In the French opera of *Richard Coeur-de-Lion*, the minstrel, Blondel, sings under the walls of his prison a song, beginning:

> O, Richard! O, mon Roi!
> L'univers t'abandonne.

When I first heard this song, forty-five years ago, at one of the first representations of that delightful play, it made an indelible impression upon my memory, without imagining that I should ever feel its force so much closer home. In the year 1829 scarce a day passed that did not bring it to my thoughts.

It should be observed that this entry is made a year and a half after the time to which it refers, and that no entry in 1829 mentions Richard at all.

When Henry Adams first read his grandfather's Diary for 1829 is uncertain: his father began publishing it in 1873 and ended in 1877; the first printed reference is in his introduction to his *New England Federalism* (1877). The next reference is in a letter from Paris to Elizabeth Cameron, December 29, 1891.

I hurried off to the Opéra Comique [he wrote], to perform an act of piety to the memory of my revered grandfather. Some people might think it a queer place for the purpose, and the association of ideas may not be obvious even to you, but it is simple. . . . He was so much attached to Grétry's music that when he was turned out of the Presidency he could think of nothing, for days together, but *"Oh, Richard, Oh, mon roy, l'univers t'abandonne"*; and as I had never heard the opera, I thought I would see it now that it had been revived at the Opéra Comique. Nothing more delightfully rococo and simple could well be, than the music of Grétry. To think that it was fin de siècle too—and shows it in the words—and led directly to the French

Revolution. . . . Unluckily the Opéra Comique, which used to be the cheerfullest place in Paris, is now to be the dreariest, and poor Richard howled mournfully as though time had troubled him.

Rococo and simple and *fin de siècle* were not enough for Adams —or only enough for piety; the sentiment was sound, the occasion dramatic, and the tone enduring—for King Richard, for John Quincy Adams, and for his grandson—but far short of the great level of imaginative actuality that a king, a president, or a more memory-ridden man deserved. King Richard's own words, when he found them, were "a true cry of the heart, such as no other king ever approached," and he inserted his paraphrase of them, together with the text, on page 222 of his *Chartres*.

The reader who is curious, or who needs to be satisfied of the long pains Adams took on this poem, may be referred to three letters he wrote to Frederick Bliss Luquiens on the 5th, 15th, and 21st of March 1911, when he was preparing the 1912 edition of the *Chartres*. They are included in "Seventeen Letters of Henry Adams," edited by Professor Luquiens in the *Yale Review* for October 1920. The poem doubtless remains what Adams called it, "one of the chief monuments of English literature," and its verses show the "direct energy, simplicity, and intensity of the Chanson of Roland." Here we are concerned primarily with the use Adams made of it as an objective and actualizing symbol of his own suffering—an element in the symbolic pattern of acceptance, rejection, and expression in which he could not help composing his sense of his own life. The reader may find the texts as easily in the *Chartres* as elsewhere. Here the beginning, the end, and an emphasis on one or two facts should suffice.

> Ja nus hons pris ne dirat sa raison
>   Adroitement s'ansi com dolans non;
>   Mais par confort puet il faire chanson.
>
> . . . .
>
> Comtesse suer, vostre pris soverain
> Vos saut et gart cil a cui je me claim
>   Et par cui je suix pris.
> Je n'ou di pas de celi de Chartain
>   La meire Lowëis.

No prisoner can tell his honest thought
  Unless he speaks as one who suffers wrong;
  But for his comfort he may make a song.

. . . .

Countess sister! your sovereign fame
May he preserve whose help I claim,
  Victim for whom am I!
I say not this of Chartres's dame,
  Mother of Louis!

The paraphrase is rough and some of the words lose force because of the exigencies of English rhyme—Adams' accomplishment as a poet was not equal to his instinct—but it should help the reader feel his way into the old French and find something of what absorbed Adams there. *Pris*, for example, which is the end word of every stanza except the last, where it is the center word, is a strong, almost a physical word for the condition of being a prisoner; for being confined, isolated, and, as it may be emphasized here, *deprived*. For that is the meaning that may best be associated with the following phrase, where *adroitement* surely means more than with *finesse d'esprit*, means surely something nearer its old sense of uprightness and justice, so communicating to *dolans* the sense of a wrong justly felt as grievous. So, if you like, John Quincy Adams, who was certainly a man deprived as well as abandoned, may have been imagined by his grandson as feeling. John Quincy turned to a Providence in whom his faith wavered and kept on with his work; his grandson, deprived by a Providence in whom he did not believe at all, turned like Richard, at least by indirection, to the half-human and wayward deity of Our Lady of Chartres, in whom he did not believe either except imaginatively, and also kept on with his work.

The music, when it came, the translation from verbal sound with all its accidents and barriers of sense and commitments to place and person, to pure and uncommitted emotion, only heightened the actuality of the Prison Song as symbol. As sung sound it meant *all* that it meant, and nothing else; hence it could bear infinite repetition, as in the condition of poetry it could not, and Adams had it sung to him and his friends many times in his last years without ever having to explain to others or troubling himself as to its particular meanings. Perhaps he did not know them, except as music.

Possibly it is necessary to point out that there is nothing peculiar and certainly nothing mystical about Adams' relation to the Prison Song. It is only the instance, the particular, that is limited to Adams; as human behavior it is universal—and as for the instance, it was only, as his friend Henry James would have said, an extraordinary case of the normal. The imagination gives itself to music as to nothing else without awkwardness or embarrassment or any sense of violation. People sing hymns or love songs; dance in public to music; attend opera or symphony or chamber concerts; and by a great and decent convention share and express the most terrible or most fundamental emotions, and do it over and over again, without feeling or even considering the necessity of wearing any mask other than that the music provides—which is no mask at all, but a voice. Adams with his Prison Song did no more than his neighbors; only he may have done it more deliberately, as an act or art, than is usual even among sensitive men.

It is only one more illustration of the difference between the nondescript imagination and the representative imagination. The first we may say administers its experience without altering it and almost without suffering it. The difference is not in vitality but in response; for the representative imagination is driven constantly to force its experience to the crisis of expression. By expression we mean the achievement of external or objective form, where as a rule the experience becomes impersonal in just the degree that it is expressed, however personal its origin. The first paradox is that in that objectivity is our only sight of unanimity; and the worse paradox is that in even the best—the most objective—expression of private emotion there is an arbitrary or willful element which makes the moment of crisis the verge of collapse or emptiness. Hence we turn as Adams turned in his Prison Song to the support of some existing form or convention of the general imagination, as if merely by existing and because we share it, its own profoundly arbitrary character might virtually lose itself in the exacting actuality of form. All that we are truly capable of believing in is what we can put into our gesture, our buildings, our images, or our song; and we know best what it is that we be-

lieve when we respond as well as act, sometimes when we do
not act at all but only respond, when we participate as spectator
or audience: which is to say, when we take account of the
infinite complexities in the simple guise of objective form, the
flèche on a church, a bar in a song. So Adams took his Prison
Song, as deliberate art, hardly veiled gesture, to focus his
sense of life. So we may take Adams, and know him best, at
the remove of those forms in which he found himself.

III

It is the essence of the normal to become extraordinary when
looked at. The normal is what we all fall short of; it takes
chiefly a kink of sensibility, a freak of evil luck, and a kind of
studious, even quizzical attention to details to bring it out. It
is there, but never shows till dragged out; and when it does
show, it shows as queer or terrifying or mad, often as cold or
foreign, and is frequently for a long time unrecognizable—
sometimes doubtless forever. The instinctive taste of the human
mind, once it reaches an intellectual, a spiritual, or an imaginative level, is always for the eccentric, the confused, the excessive
—as we see in religious myth. Thus it is the great business of
art and the necessary ruse of good sense, since neither can keep
silent, to correct that failure of taste on the part of the expressive imagination by infusing its vision of the normal with every
homely twist and routine eccentricity, every humdrum oddity,
it can manage. We see the pursuit of divinity terminated in a
garden and arranged by money; it is tried by law, condemned,
and thereby proved—than which nothing could be more eccentric, or seem more "natural." It is what is called bringing things
back to earth.

Adams was no divinity, only a prime example of representative imagination in America—as representative as foreigners
tell us our beautiful women are. He was no more rapt in his
music than the women in their beauty. He was busy about it
in a variety of ways and with a number of persons: as scholarship, as a limit for restlessness, and as a reliable mode of social
expression. He wrote letters about small details, he collected
texts and scores and tried to work out historical sequences in the
new perspective to go with his old studies, and in the evenings

he made people listen to the singing whether they liked it or not. The results, brought back to earth as we are now trying to bring them, were unpublished. *Tussis senilis* got in the way —not in the way of work, appreciation, imagination—but in the way of composition, partly by shortening time and diminishing energy and partly by emphasizing to an unusual degree for Adams the personal and precious aspect of moments in passing: that they had, willy nilly, to be filled. So the old President, as his grandson remembered him in the 'forties, who had in his dressing closet a row of tumblers inverted over caterpillars which "were supposed to become moths or butterflies but never did." At either end of life, one's garden may be cultivated with all the more intensity because the crop is not in view.

At any rate there was no second *Chartres* left for publication. What powers of composition Adams had left were concentrated on his own life, which had after all, as long as it lasted, still to be rounded off. Without an active sense of composition Adams, being an artist, would do nothing. It is a pity, as Professor Luquiens observed. "If Mr. Adams had lived a few years longer, it might have meant as much for the mediaeval lyrics as his having lived long enough to finish 'Mont Saint Michel and Chartres' had meant for the 'Song of Roland.' " The Professor hit it just right; Adams would have told him, had he asked, that beginning in April 1912 he was already dead and existed only in a kind of pre-posthumous limbo in which serious work was impossible: a statement which might have been authenticated in historical parallel. Almost, but not quite at the end of the last volume of John Quincy Adams' Diary, the entries are brought to a formal close. The old President had suffered a shock, on the streets of Boston, and had been carried to his son's house on Mount Vernon Street. When he recovered he regarded his life as over and so marked his Diary done. The further entries—a few pages for a few months —were to his mind posthumous and were made, so to speak, in another place.

The results were not only unpublished but personal; as we said, the greatest result of the music was that it gave him something to do that had charm as well as efficacy, something that absorbed him as well as roused a response, and on every level, and in every situation—yet without ever *overtly* seeming a substitute for what was really wanted. Such is the strength

of the human animal, even when crippled and dying, that
it can impute values where it must, and if the values are felt
as fresh, life itself is in thought renewed. The words are simple
and make the action seem easy; but there were barriers, breaks,
and failures of spirit. The more private letters carry some of
the evidence. In the middle of November 1912 he wrote that
writing was no longer easy for him and that he could give
only an hour daily to his pen, so that each correspondent would
get his share and no more; and in the middle of the following
March, after repeating that writing was no joke, he goes on
to say that some people seem to think paralysis is a cocktail
to be taken as a pick-up before dinner, where the truth was
that it left him consciously dependent on Aileen Tone or in her
absence (she had her periodic vacations) on someone else. He
disliked being physically alone. A year later he says that he
has stopped writing, though he took it up again within a week.
Again, in what seems to be the last extant letter to his brother
Brooks, dated February 10, 1914, he finished off: "I can't write
—also I can't read—so don't get mad about it. At least I can hold
my tongue. The other fellow must do the walking up and
down."

The other fellow must do the walking up and down: a ruse
phrase, a phrase for escape. Adams had spent a good part of his
life more or less painfully walking up and down, and all his life
trying to hold his tongue; and he was to keep on walking and
trying—and failing—to hold his tongue another four years. But
it is understandable why he put it off on the other fellow: that
wonderful creature, the perfect scapegoat of gesture. As a matter of fact, Adams' health was variable and only a graph would
have shown its steady downward trend. Writing was indeed
difficult for considerable periods; his right hand was more
affected by his paralysis than any other part; but at other
periods he wrote nearly as easily as twenty years before. The
handwriting tells the story. The copper-plate script had lost
some of its certainty before 1912 and, compared to the archetype of the 'eighties, was uneven and occasionally rough; after
1912 it varied from the merely uneven to the completely shaky
—there are words now and then, in this most legible script, that
approach the indecipherable. The principal permanent change
is in the increase in size of the individual letters, so that they
seem drawn rather than written. Otherwise the variation is

wide. In the winter of 1914 the writing is clumsy and ragged, and the letters tend to be short; but in the winter of 1915 the writing is to the contrary firm, clear, and apparently easy, and some of the letters are very long. As late as the summer of 1917 he was able to write at some length to Spring Rice. But on the other hand Miss Tone wrote a good many of his less personal letters for him.

She also read a good many of the less personal replies. For Adams' most disconcerting trouble was his vision, which had bothered him for several years but which got worse after 1912. What the trouble was and whether it could have been relieved is not known; for Adams refused on principle to see an oculist, and never could be overruled. When reading began to go hard he bought a magnifying glass, which helped a little; and when his eyesight got still worse, the only concession he made was to go to the Boston Store—a largish department store in Washington—and purchase from the open tray one pair each of all the spectacles they carried in stock. Trying them one after another, it apparently gave him a quite adequate I-told-you-so pleasure that none of them did any good. The end was that he never read by artificial light (which he disliked) and relatively little by daylight—principally the newspapers and whatever came his way on mathematics and physics. He hated to be read to, as he hated his carriage exercise; so that the reading Miss Tone did for him was limited to the duller part of his still large correspondence.

The carriage exercise was performed twice daily, by doctor's orders, behind a coachman and two black horses—which he called black rabbits. What was hateful about it was partly due to his brother Charles and partly due to the topography of Washington. Charles, who had his winter house on Massachusetts Avenue in Washington, because, like his brother Henry, he couldn't stand the combination of cold and social suffocation in Boston, was three years Henry's senior, a big, square, robust man, and rode a big horse every day for exercise and pleasure. That annoyed Henry: he had had to give up riding in his middle sixties, and here was his brother, getting on for eighty, galloping like a two-year-old. Whenever they passed each other, which was often, the small man in the carriage seeing his brother larger than life on a horse, Henry Adams could think of nothing but always the same thing: *There goes my "idjut" brother Charles!* said as brusquely—that is to say, as robustly and affectionately—as possible.

But Charles was a minor trouble, a mere matter of surface spleen, to be gotten rid of by an exclamation of dissent. For the topography of Washington there was no response possible, however you might delay it, but the same glum assent to the fact. There were only two places to go, one for the morning and one for the afternoon, and only one way of getting to each place. You came back the way you went; you doubled on your tracks—which was as hateful symbolically as it was dull actually. The great advantage of Paris over Washington was as much as anything that in Paris no matter where you went there was always another way of coming back.

The morning drive, however, was no trouble. Adams was in better spirits in the morning, and the destination was of his permanent choice. With Miss Tone for company, he was driven out to Rock Creek, and when the weather was clement walked for an hour in the woods through the last year of his life, and then returned. It was the afternoon that bothered; the spirit not only flagged but the flesh rebelled, at the one route, along the Potomac, that was always presented. Thus sometimes the afternoon drive was frittered away with calls—Miss Tone doing most of the calling, Adams waiting in the carriage for her reports. Sometimes, again, they would climb into the carriage—neither of them having an errand or a place to go—the coachman waiting for instructions. Five minutes made a gulf of silence. *No calls?* says Adams, and a little silence, followed by, *No errands?* and a good deal of silence, rather deeper than a gulf. At last Adams leaned forward and shouted at the coachman: *Along the Potomac—as usual.* And the afternoon would pass very badly indeed, for it was on such days that in half an hour they would be most likely to find brother Charles galloping by, firm and full, with no trouble at all about where he was going, or how often.

Charles' own view of his brother Henry was a little limited by his relationship, but keen. He said Henry was lonely and he sent people to see him, occasionally bringing them himself at the noon breakfast. When, in the winter of 1913 or 1914, Mr. W. C. Ford, the historian, went in one afternoon, his own impression was that Charles was right. Adams was cordial to a degree but seemed a little feeble, with a slightly thickened

voice, so that when Adams insisted on accompanying him
when he rose to go, he objected. "At least to the stairs," said
Adams—they were in the library on the second floor—and so
he did, rather slowly, escort Mr. Ford to the head of the beautiful wide stairs; which was the last Mr. Ford ever saw of him.
He left on the feeling that he had been seeing a very lonely
old man, but that may have been the quality that Mr. Ford
called out in him, for with many others Adams did not seem
outwardly lonely at all.

Charles himself did not apparently see much of Henry; there
was some obstruction in the way—not of feeling, but of social
practice—which may well have had two sources. Charles Francis Adams had a simple, direct nature, and an honesty incapable
of more than a moderate degree either of complexity or frivolity
—for he saw the value of neither. His social principles were
republican in the eighteenth-century Roman sense, and he
distrusted because he could not understand the value—except
as snobbery—of the social life of the light kind which he
thought occupied Henry overmuch. Neither on the other hand
could he make anything but insensible bewilderment and a
sense of willful frustration of the deliberately sophisticated
anarchy of Henry's mind. Both were dogmatic men; and
Charles had doubtless long since given up the attempt, begun
in his anonymous review of the *Life of Gallatin*, to correct his
sense of Henry's heresy.

Worse perhaps than either Henry's habits of mind or of
society—and it may be a consequence of both—was the obstruction that everyone came up against in Henry more or less and
sooner or later, the inner incalculable remoteness into which
he relapsed, which showed itself as periods of outer frozen
silence. There was nothing of that depth in Charles. He preferred the early Browning to St. Francis, the town meeting to
the path of economic energy, the sunlight and living air to an
imaginative identity with St. Augustine. He would not only
have disliked but also have distrusted as some form of "popery"
Henry's response to his death. Charles Adams died "in the
full tide of activity, instinct with interest in life," on the
20th of March 1915. Adams had passed his "idjut brother
Charles" only four or five days previously, when he was probably already suffering rebelliously from the pneumonia that
carried him off. The funeral was held in Washington, and

Adams sent Miss Tone, remaining himself at home, alone. When she returned she found Adams in his library, quite silent, but with the music sheets of a twelfth-century Prayer to the Virgin ready to sing.

The personal relation of Henry to his brother Brooks during these last years was closer than that to Charles. Brooks was younger, had been for years the favorite brother, and there had been a definite community of interest for twenty years in the working out of their scientific philosophy of history. The relation nevertheless gradually thinned away until, without ever disappearing, it was like a shadow in a winter noon. It could be seen only on infrequent clear days. It was again a matter of contrasted characters. Brooks himself, in his "Heritage of Henry Adams," felt the difference between the "amusing" and the "serious" sides of his brother during the later years.

Indeed, to speak the truth, I rather tried to avoid his lighter social circle, a disposition which I think he noticed and allowed for. And I have even conjectured that, because of this tendency of mine, he chose a moment when he was in Washington and I in Quincy to send me . . . the essay on "Phase," for my opinion, instead of keeping it for one of my visits to his house, and talking it over with me there.

Another way of determining the contrast is the fact that nowhere in the hundred and forty-odd extant letters to Brooks is Henry driven to more than a paragraph or so of such imaginative eloquence as is found in certain of the letters to the nieces—such as that on Michelangelo. It was not that Brooks would have failed in understanding; it was rather the lack of a subjective sense of rapport, which Adams felt mostly in children, women, and nieces, and which alone allowed him thoroughly to let go. There was, moreover, a special quality of irritation about Brooks, for Henry, that in old age made small doses of him enough. Perhaps Brooks had not the quality of silence, or the tact that belongs in speech, that together keep intimacy from turning ferret or inquisitor. Brooks was exciting and excitable, brilliant, erratic, and sometimes inconsequential, highly nervous, emphatic, and dogmatic, in manner and personality as well as mind; he often lost his intellectual temper. Henry was unable to manage, to control, all that Brooks gave; and there was no help for it, to avoid the dismay of temper, but also sometimes to avoid Brooks himself. It remained a matter of dosage entirely. When the personal point of excess was not touched, there was a special kind of unanimity in Brooks' companionship that Adams got nowhere else. They shared, among other adventures, and expressed together—and Charles as well— a common sense of the family mind so strong that it amounted almost to a myth. "The family mind"—Henry had written to Brooks in 1905, but the feeling endured—"the family mind approaches unity more nearly than is given to most of the works of God. You and I think so nearly on the same lines that, even when not directly interacting, the two minds run parallel, and you can hardly tell whether they are one or several."

It was not only with his brothers that Adams' relationships were intermittently difficult. The whole social experience was a matter of dosage; stimulus was its own surfeit unpredictably— and this most social of all men was found suddenly to have retired to his tower. In dealing with him the only safe calculation was based on weather, for on damp days he was likely to be at his worst. Gloom reigned within, and all that was visible was the gulf of bottomless reserve, until momently, or on another day, the sun poured—like Danae's golden shower—and all his tender-brusque genius for human friendship flourished again. The worst was the silence of literally not speaking, and Miss Tone remembers that once he did not speak for, she thinks, three days. These silences were usually shorter, and mostly the mood did not go to silence at all. Then, rather, he would complain of boredom, of what he called cold on the liver, and would order Miss Tone back to her bogs. Sometimes the mood was relieved by his osteopathic treatments, which he took for their obvious benefit the last five years of his life; but more often relief came without warning from nothing specific, or from the return of bright weather. All this was only the deeper version of an ordinary and predominant trait in Adams' character: that he could not open freely, but only at times, to anyone. He hated direct questions—especially from strangers but even from friends; and in response he froze on them. The ice protected him or, as we say, controlled the inner instinctive protection of anger. It was a matter of the gambit; and we have an example of variable success in two sentences from a letter William Roscoe Thayer wrote to his wife in January 1915. "Today I called on Mr. Charles Adams, who took me down to lunch with his brother Henry. That arch-egoist was interesting, and very expansive compared with last year." But no one ever knew surely what the right gambit was.

There we have the varieties at one extreme of mood. At the other extreme, Mrs. Winthrop Chanler provides us with an incident, in her *Roman Spring*, which must have occurred sometime in the winter of 1914 or 1915. One evening after dinner and talk, Adams was left alone in his library with Mrs. Chanler's youngest daughter, Gabrielle, who was, with Mrs. Chanler's other daughters, one of the junior nieces.

There was a pause; Uncle Henry leaned back with his eyes half closed and his two hands joined at the upturned fingers. Then he began to talk, softly at first as if to himself, then, gathering momentum from his surging thoughts, he went on to speak of all that lay on his mind, the mysteries of time and eternity, man and destiny, his aspiration and helplessness. It was all way over her head, but she listened breathless, feeling that something great and wonderful was happening, though she could not understand it. At last he paused and came back to earth, looked at her, and said: "Do you know why I have told you all this?" Of course she had no answer. "It is because you would not understand a word of it and you will never quote me."

The image is worth preserving because endlessly suggestive. Like an idea of Rembrandt put down to show an extreme of human possibility in terms of pure character, we know what it is visually: complete and quivering, a luminosity which increases as we absorb the details but which we lose as we try to say what it is that shines in any other language than that of the picture itself. Here the picture is simple but with details as infinite as you care to pick out. The small old man, nearing eighty, in dark clothes, with white beard and shirt, and the young girl of sixteen, sitting opposite each other in the low, deep maroon leather chairs, under the honeycomb-beamed ceiling; flowers on the big table and Chinese bronzes; the bookcases along the walls, some of them overflowing, and with watercolors and drawings on top; the little tables with lamps; the golden carpet; the Turner over the fireplace of carved onyx, and the fire burning, giving most of the light in the large room so that it falls mostly on the two human figures, and also darkness gathering from the ends and from above.

Light, at least to human eyes, fastens always upon the human face. Here our imaginary light falls on the faces of Henry

Adams and Gabrielle Chanler, the younger face incipient with character and the older explicit. The girl we cannot see very well, and do not need to; for we know what freshness is, what beginning is, partly by memory and partly by living instinct, quite well enough; we could hardly see more if we had the face in front of us. The old man's face is quite another matter, and there we need everything possible to see; for the fine faces of the old, when they have not fallen awry or grown dismayed, represent everything in life that can be finished and also every-thing that endures or can be endured: the character that is fate. Fortunately we may borrow where our eyes fail us from John Briggs Potter's drawing of Adams, which was delivered to him in January 1914. You may think what you will of the drawing, of the great domed head with its impression of magnitude; the rising, frownless dark eyebrows over the steady buried eyes; the strong, large, family nose; the beard which seems to cover a firm but not a tight mouth—and, so thinking, find what tokens please you. It is a face at once naked and reserved, shy and deliberately declaratory; it suggests restlessness controlled, motion arrested but not stopped, and shows a kind of con-templative intensity on the verge of expression—but momently held back by those conflicting motives toward repose and to-ward action which once felt are seldom resolved—a face, that is, on the verge of sufficing form.

Having seen so much, dismiss it; it is only a possibility; here it is the scene that counts: the room, the girl, the old man— the silence and the ensuing speech, the after-silence and the return into the shell of urbane and daily life. Our concern is in the interval burst of speech, the poetry of character expressing itself through a channel miraculously open to it. Commonly we respond to the young face, the young body, the young life suddenly seen, only with a hidden gesture; it is all we can dare in manners and all we can manage expressively of the deep access of imagination that enlivens us. There are the barriers of circumstance and convention and timidity, and, as a rule— were even these barriers put down—there remains a cramping shortage of speech. Here, for the interval, and by a miracle of justice, not only was every confederated circumstance right, but the imagination was ready too. The gesture was released from hiding, and the man let go. No doubt he *heard* himself speak, for on these occasions words seem to be called out willy-nilly, and life itself, at the very height of intimacy, seems spontaneous, full, and remote. No wonder the girl Gabrielle remembered nothing but time and eternity, and her own exhilaration; but who would wish to remember more of what was a gesture at heart? No wonder the old man Adams, coming back, as we put it, to himself—to the loneliness which we feel as echo—should have found safety in the conviction that what was shared was not understood—it was beyond that—and have found comfort in the assurance that his words could no more be quoted than the look on his face. Who would wish, really, experience to be otherwise than fleeting? It is enough ever afterward to be haunted.

It was indeed because he had a sensibility haunted by experiences such as this that Adams provided to the end his unfailing gift of friendship that should be, as he had told Spring Rice, "all give and no take." Perhaps it was for that reason also that his curiosity about men and women never flagged or fell into dulled habit. If anything, his curiosity increased in certain respects. For many years he had gone little into society, much preferring to entertain his friends—and those whom his friends brought him—at his own house. Formal society bored him—and the farther from home the more formal and the more boring—because it lacked both a center of interest and general conversation, and even more because it lacked genuine frivolity. But even in his last years he well knew that it might be fun in the thinking and the telling. Miss Tone was often delegated the duty he had hardly himself borne for twenty years; she was "sent," she says, to every party or function she could find time for, and was expected the morning after to turn it to lively account. If there was something vicarious in this, and appropriate to old age, no matter; there is nothing so refreshing as a sense of popular folly; and it was that aspect of Miss Tone's accounts which Adams found amusing. He had not been his father's private secretary half a century before without learning a game far better worth following than playing—except lightly—oneself. It was one more instance where the values society gave were more important than the principles it abandoned—or never had.

In his own house the twelve o'clock breakfast remained perennial; the table was still permanently set for four and still always ready to be set for six if William, being asked, was able to smile upon the prospective guest. In the evenings there were often dinners, running to as many as eight, which though less casual than the breakfasts, since the guests were invited, were hardly less informal. The barriers Adams put up against society were chiefly against formality and dullness; the rest being his private taste in people. What were called exclusiveness and snobbery and coldness and eccentricity were for Adams the necessary defenses of a strongly developed taste and an attempt to guarantee amusement after his own kind. Your snob may well be only a man whose principles of selection irritate you. But social life was less than ever Adams' occupation, more than ever a help to living; but most it was something that must be made good enough to be enjoyed for its own sake. His peculiar social ambition, upon which he sometimes pretended to hang the picture of success in life, never faltered; it gave him unremitting value for the work he put into it. When William Roscoe Thayer wrote him in December 1913 to ask him for help upon his projected life of John Hay, Adams answered him at once.

My dear Sir
Your letter of the 23rd has just arrived.

Such ambition as I retain has of late years been directed to creating round my group of friends a certain atmosphere of art and social charm. They were not numerous, but all were superior. John La Farge, Alex Agassiz, Clarence King, St. Gaudens, Hay, and their more-or-less close associates like Bret Harte, John Sargent, Henry James, etc., etc., were distinguished men in any time or country. John Hay alone was a public character, and needs separate treatment. I am glad you have undertaken him.

The only comment that seems to be required is that only in America would the labor of holding such a group together be thought of as an exercise in snobbery or the vain subterfuge of a dilettante.

But now, in 1913, the group was mostly dead, and with those not dead the connections had fallen away; the investment was wasting, like copper stocks, the Supreme Court, and Adams himself. It needed a stoic with a gift for nieces to put up with the change, which was just what it had needed, since 1885, all along; it needed humor and a sense of history; brightness and youth; the Virgin of Chartres and a philosophy of history. The rest was memory and the old songs, persisting habits and the sense of coming the full round. So far as his social group was concerned, although its calibre was different, Adams got all he needed, because he still had more than enough to give. With age, his personality was only plainer to feel, his vitality more concentrated.

On the physical side it was the same. His hands were warm to the touch—he preferred open fires to central heating. His appetite was voracious; at dinner, even the late dinners, he finished always ahead of everybody else out of robustious delight in his food; and his champagne, which was all he permitted himself to drink and all he cared for after his illness, he took by the pint in a single gulp—for the full mouth was the only way, as he said, of getting all the taste of it all at once. Yet he could not help, any more than could his ancestors —and no matter what the scope in which he felt he moved— either asserting human warmth so that it showed to strangers as cold, forbidding, and barren, or exemplifying the normal without showing as individual to the point of egoism and eccentricity. Providential character, the accident of a lifetime, and the habit of imagination—almost the habit of an artist—produced a combination of stresses which one either reacted against violently or which one discovered to be an example of singular human unity.

IV

Paris in the spring of 1913 was a draught of champagne unusually copious and with an effect unusually stimulating, both for reaction and discovery, however worked for and anticipated it had been for a long four months. Adams had sailed toward the end of March or the first of April, taking with him Elsie Adams, Louisa Hooper, Florence Keep, and Aileen Tone. He had also taken a masseur, who had to be dismissed on account of bad behavior. Mistaken instinct had led him to instruct his brother Charles, in almost his first intelligible words after his shock, to break up his own Paris apartment, which Charles had done, and the plan was now to take over Mrs. Cameron's apartment—she being then far away, in Egypt or Abyssinia or wherever. But on their arrival, her apartment was not quite ready, and for the time Adams, Elsie Adams, and Aileen Tone moved into Mrs. Keep's apartment, while Louisa Hooper occupied her own.

The whole group went at once and furiously to work. Ward Thoron had seen about an automobile and chauffeur, and Bessie Lodge (George Cabot Lodge's widow) had provided a piano, which was all the equipment they needed. Days were passed at the Conservatoire asking questions. The services of a M. Expert were engaged to teach the young ladies the twelve modes of the ancient music, and a M. Gastuet helped on the theory of rendition. They attended concerts and gave concerts of their own—but precisely for themselves. As Adams had written Ward Thoron at the end of many requisitions: *We want lots of things, but thank the Holy Virgin we don't want audiences*. Altogether they were so busy and delighted that it was not till they had been six weeks in Paris that Adams reports his first appearance *en monde*—as it happened, with Edith Wharton, who had just turned up. As Adams said, he employed everybody, and the task seemed ready to stretch to the twenty-second century. Meanwhile he kicked himself with astonishment every day when he woke up.

The transcription, study, and singing of hundreds of songs, with four young ladies to help, was a long and arduous business; but even the joy of its provision and the depth of its obsessive reach could only dominate and never extinguish Adams' other interests. The world was always there—the grasses and colored flowers of St. Francis, and also the social world—which were together the medium through which every interest flowed; and it was one's natural pride to keep track, through every pretense of indifference and every feeling of difference, of what the world was doing.

The auto and the chauffeur were more for the countryside than anything else; there were constant drives out of Paris, and always, when possible—which was often, as in Washington it was not—by different routes. In Paris itself, besides the auto, there were the cabs, the buses, and the feet. Adams walked almost every day. But the cab was the usual vehicle, the bus being a resort on principle. When Adams felt that a cabby had cheated him (which was common enough in Paris), he paid the full amount without complaint but did not use a cab again until he both felt charitable and felt that he had used up on bus fares the amount he had been cheated. This alternation was in some years pretty regular, and gave satisfaction both ways. The end was that Adams had a familiarity with the streets of Paris which must have equaled Henry James' with those of London; and it was that cultivated experience of its flora, I think, that made Adams in his last years more at home and alive in Paris than anywhere in the world. It is Bostonians who by their characteristic inconsequence, rather than Americans in general, go to Paris when they die.

Certainly Paris was full of Bostonians, and fuller of Americans of all sorts than Adams cared to contemplate or wanted to see. There were a few old friends—especially the younger Mrs. Lodge and her children—whom he saw little or much. They called on Elsie DeWolfe, Anne Morgan, and Miss Marbury at the Trianon. On another occasion Adams climbed six flights of stairs to pay a call and prove himself alive. As for the young ladies, they must, on his own pedagogical principle, see as much of the world as they could, just as they must dress as well as possible: to be brighter, more complete, in color and light. One of the present batch of nieces was not naturally given to making the most of her possibilities in clothes; and now in Paris, Adams had his chance. It was as if he remembered what he told his wife in 1879 when she was bored with the idea of getting any new gowns: "People who study Greek must take pains with their dress," and now made the application to those who studied twelfth-century music. At any rate he packed her off to Worth's, in charge of two other and delighted nieces. She stormed and cried and said *I won't! I won't!* But she did. At length she was fitted, and finally gowned; and to her own surprise was much pleased with herself sitting at Adams' table, and Adams was as much pleased with her pleasure as he was with his own. He never tired of smart women.

As the weather got hot and the city filled and the store of music got stout enough to last their lives out, they looked around for a country place which should be both secluded and easily available to Paris. Toward the end of June they took the Château Marivault, in St. Crépin in the Oise, hardly twenty miles from Paris in the ducal country, and remained there until the middle of September. The Château Marivault was eighteenth century and quite large enough to require six servants to run it. There were five bedrooms and two old-style bathrooms: of which the most modern feature was a metal bathtub on legs, that could be heated from underneath. The first floor had been done over—walls and furniture—in various colors and designs of French mattress ticking. Most successful was the dining room in blue and white four-inch checks. Outside there was a large garden with a pool and a view of the Paris road.

Characteristically, Adams' first act after he got there was to drive to the Post Office, leaving a heavy tip, and then to all the railroad stations, of which there were several within easy reach, having trains for Paris. Adams never felt safe in a new place until his lines of communication had been laid down with fussy accuracy. But once the lines were settled the fuss was gone and free movement became not only natural but orderly. The young ladies played and Adams looked on. Miss Tone sang and Adams listened. M. Gastuet was brought down to instruct; new methods of reading the scores were devised, the greatest advance being when the music was felt in units of natural phrasing instead of in arbitrary units of three-four measure. Adams began to feel at home in what had seemed a labyrinth. Thibaut of Navarre was the great mine of wealth, for himself and for what he stole from the Vidame of Chartres. By the end of the summer the collection was first-rate; the elements of taste were formed; the general enthusiastic acceptance of the winter and spring gave way to discrimination and rejection—a few songs even being found poor or dull or empty, so that what was good seemed even better than before.

The summer was no more all music than the spring had been: there was correspondence at the rate of a letter a day; the newspapers; politics at home and abroad. Europe swarmed with relatives and friends, and a few came to Marivault. Brooks and his wife came in August to stimulate and irritate along the old tracks, and to emphasize still further the almost welcome idea of universal collapse in its most logical and terrifyingly attractive form, as it was just about to appear in his *Theory of Social Revolutions*. At about the time of Brooks' visit, Adams wrote to Ward Thoron that the end of the world would not be till July 1938, so that he had twenty-five years to spare; and he finished the letter by saying that he was stuck in the mud trying to pretend to look on. A little later, from Paris, he wrote that at Washington only L. P. Morton and himself were left, and both had lost their minds, but that to lose one's mind was a favor of God. Morton was then eighty-nine

to Adams' seventy-five, but by Adams' principle it came to
the same thing. After the 'eighties Adams almost habitually
added something to his age when speaking of it in a letter,
although he always kept good track, as we see above and in the
last paragraph of the *Education,* of his centennial. Real relief
from both social collapse and old age was, as always in France,
in looking at the two extremes of nature, the land and the
churches. Every side road was tried and every church looked at
within driving range.

By the 15th of December he was back in Washington. He
was worse. Everybody was worse. The stock market was worst
of all. The lame ducks crawled all about. And "the Architects"
had stolen his Virgin—by which he meant that the American
Institute of Architects had brought out the first published
edition of the *Chartres.* So he wrote to Ward Thoron. But the
moods were variable, for two days previously he had written
his brother Brooks: "Certainly I am better than the rest of you!
I've only one hand, one foot, one eye, and half a brain, but
I see no one else who has more than half that."

Perhaps he was right. On the whole, the winter of 1913–1914
seems to have been low in tone—a continuation, an interlude,
a waiting—a winter of omens at home and abroad, and of failing spirits generally. But it had to be dealt with; as Adams
once said he could not think of feet without thinking of kicking,
neither could he grow old and prepare to die without resolute
vigor. Miss Tone walked him in the woods every morning and
sang him to sleep every evening. When Miss Tone suggested
that he was not well enough to have John Briggs Potter come
to do his drawing, and that he had better wait till he looked
better, he insisted that on the contrary he should come. Let
him come! Or he may never! Never put anything off.

One thing he had put off now attended to itself by making
its own crisis. Since the death of Maggie Gray, the cook, in
1909, William the butler had grown more and more mindful
of the wine cellar, of which he had the keys. Maggie had, with
her prestige as a *grande dame* in her own world, always been
able to keep William in order. With Maggie gone it was only
a matter of time; Adams would not or could not interfere—
William had been with him too long and had done too well
by him. The time came, one evening, at an English dinner—
with the guests entirely from the English Embassy, where

Spring Rice was now the head. William served the soup fairly enough, but when the plates had been taken away he brought in, without a flicker, the ice cream. Adams inquired quietly for the meat; William answered politely that there could be no meat that night—it was too expensive. Descending to the kitchen, two of the young Englishmen found the meat all cooked and the cook dismayed. With an aplomb equal to William's own, the young Englishmen served the rest of the dinner themselves. The end was that William had to be sent away, and was eventually replaced by another colored butler named Charles, who never provided much satisfaction except as a living sign of an old connection broken off.

Continuing connections were intellectual or imaginative and showed as attitudes or as style—or both. When "the Architects" stole Adams' Virgin, it was part of his amusement to pretend that the book was no longer his. Henry Osborn Taylor wrote Adams about the new edition, and for answer Adams told him a little story. The Mr. Cram referred to is of course Boston's medievalist architect Ralph Adams Cram, who had been responsible for the publication and who had in his Editor's preface relieved Adams, by his own stipulation, of all responsibility for publication. "Many thanks!" Adams wrote. "You should meet Mr. Cram and give him your views about his book. As for me, I only recall some old story of fifty years ago about Ruskin that his landlady in London objected strenuously to his sacrificing a bull in her front parlor. I am reminded of it because I sympathised strongly with him—and with the landlady."

"And then what a glorious thing it is to have a landlady and a bull!" This was written the last day of March 1914. The reader may think what he likes as to who the bull was, who the landlady, and who took the part of Ruskin.

About three weeks later Adams and Elsie Adams and Aileen Tone and Louisa Hooper climbed down a ladder into a tender at quarter before midnight and landed at Cherbourg, where they sat up till half-past-three drinking chocolate until their beds were ready. The next day they were met in Paris by Mrs. Cameron, her daughter Martha, and Ward Thoron. They also got the news that one more contact with the past was gone: Mrs. John Hay had died while they traveled.

A little later, in a letter to Ward Thoron, who had gone to

Switzerland, Adams shows his spirits as still low. He thought of himself, he wrote, as more than ever a waif tossed upon this rotten atmosphere. He watched the show with "amused superiority," and he detected a singular odor of rotten apples. Finally, his thirty-thousand-year-old-baby was his only joy. The "amused superiority" and the bull in the front parlor were on about the same level of dramatic projection; his book and its fate were as dear to him as his interest was terrible in the world, social and political, then visibly breaking up around him. When he says together, in a letter of July, that only the Châtelain de Coucy keeps him alive and that the whole show—the show of Europe—is a what-do-you-call-it?—a movie, the reader has only to remember the mechanical, abrupt violence and the glaring unreality of the movies of that time, and he will have a sound clue to the expressive value of the baby and the poet and of Adams himself.

The war struck Adams with all the greater shock because he had so long and so surely seen it coming. His first impulse was to get away. They were that summer at the Château Coubertin, a few miles south of Paris, all but Louisa Hooper, who had gone to visit her sister Mabel La Farge in Switzerland. Before even the war actually came, the picture was clear. One day Adams, needing a haircut, drove up to Paris with Aileen Tone and Elsie Adams, got the haircut, had lunch at Henri's, and started back. The tension had been so much in the air that Adams, who sat between the two women, put a hand on the knee of each and said, "It has come, I want to go home." Brooks Adams and his wife, and possibly Mrs. Cameron, were visiting him when the end came. The *affiches* were posted, the tocsin rung, all their men servants were called up except one, and their car was requisitioned. They stayed a few days to make plans. A single skittish horse was gotten in the village and their remaining servant volunteered to drive them about in a victoria. On one occasion the horse ran away with them, the servant holding hard, Adams and his two young women giggling in terror.

Then Martha Cameron Lindsay telegraphed them, offering her place in England for as long as they wanted; and they fled to Paris—the end of their world yelping at their heels in the form of the unknown.

Mrs. Cameron had gone to Switzerland to be with Martha,

and Adams never saw either of them again, though he corresponded with Mrs. Cameron till he died. Brooks and his wife went home. Adams and his young ladies drove to Dieppe, equipped with special permissions but stopped every few miles, and found the hospitals already filled with wounded. They were just in time, for they caught the last boat for fleeing passengers across the Channel, and after a week in a London hotel with the Lodges, went down to Stepleton House in Dorset.

The war was then expected to be short in the sense that few could imagine it long, and those who did were greedy to think themselves wrong. There would either be a decisive battle, or money, or men, or both, would run out; embattled *nations* was a mere figure of speech, as when we say the heavens rain, meaning a few clouds. At any rate Adams waited, taking what proved to be only the first mild lesson in four years of exhausting strain. No situation could have made the lesson more tolerable than the Dorset countryside in late summer and early autumn. Their music they had brought with them; the landscape was there; and old friends could be imported.

Among these last was Henry James, who came over twice from Rye and talked with Adams late into the night. This was the final and perhaps an unusually full meeting of the two extreme—and therefore deeply related—types of American imagination. Report must be regrettably conjectural, but with an element of firm predictability on two counts—their past lives and the war.

There had been an exchange of letters the previous spring over James' *Notes of a Son and Brother* in which James had attempted to re-imagine—or, as he would have himself said —to revise, his own version of post-bellum America. Both men were concerned with experience as education, and to both the judgment of education called for a specialized form of autobiography in which the individual was suppressed in the act, only to be caught in the style. James imagined human reality always through dramatizing the bristling sensual record of the instance—almost any instance that had a story in it— and let the pattern, the type, the *vis a tergo*, take care of itself, which under the stress of the imaginative process it commonly did. Adams, on the other hand, tended in a given case to depend on his feeling for human type and pattern—for history and lines of force—as the source of drama, and hence saw the in-

dividual as generalized *first:* so that whatever happened would
fall into the pattern, if you only had the wit to see how—which
Adams by the strength of his conceptual imagination did commonly see. To put it another way, Adams' set of intellectual
instruments more or less *predicted* what he would discover;
James resorted to instruments only to ascertain what his sensibility had *already* discovered.

If we may quote T. S. Eliot's remark that Henry James had
a mind—a sensibility—so fine that no mere idea could ever violate it, then we should say that Henry Adams had an intellect
so fine—so energized—that no mere item of sensibility could
ever violate that. To be inviolate in one respect fairly calls for
penalties in another. Adams paid in a want of freshness, James
in a want of restraint. Adams might run dry, James frequently
ran off the track. The thinness in James comes from excess of
feeling; in Adams thinness comes, not from want of feeling,
but from excess of consideration. To make a maxim of it: excess
of sensibility sterilizes the significance of form; excess of intellect reduces form, and sometimes imagination itself, to formula;
the tendency of excess in either direction is toward the disappearance of subject matter. There is a kind of shrinkage of value
that occurs under the stress of the general excess we call
sophistication, which is one trait common to James and Adams.

It was the signs of that shrinkage that James and Adams felt
in each other as the penalty for the extraordinary riches provided. In the following letter from James to Adams I think we
may feel a struck balance of the weakness and strength of both
men: of James directly, of Adams by implication—for both men
were obstinately artists at bottom.

March 21, 1914

My dear Henry,

I have your melancholy outpouring of the 7th, and I know not how
better to acknowledge it than by the full recognition of its unmiti-
gated blackness. *Of course* we are the lone survivors, of course the
past that was our lives is at the bottom of an abyss—if the abyss *has*
any bottom; of course, too, there's no use talking unless one particularly *wants* to. But the purpose, almost, of my printed divagations
was to show you that one *can*, strange to say, still want to—or at least
can behave as if one did. Behold me therefore so behaving—and
apparently capable of continuing to do so. I still find my consciousness interesting—under *cultivation* of the interest. Cultivate it *with*

me, dear Henry—that's what I hoped to make you do—to cultivate yours for all that it has in common with mine. *Why* mine yields an interest I don't know that I can tell you, but I don't challenge or quarrel with it—I encourage it with a ghastly grin. You see I still, in presence of life (or of what you deny to be such) have reactions —as many as possible—and the book I sent you is a proof of them. It's, I suppose, because I am that queer monster, the artist, an obstinate finality, an inexhaustible sensibility. Hence the reactions— appearances, memories, many things, go on playing upon it with consequences that I note and "enjoy" (grim word!) noting. It all takes doing and I *do*. I believe I shall do yet again—it is still an act of life. But you perform them still yourself—and I don't know what keeps me from calling your letter a charming one! There we are, and it's a blessing that you understand—I admit indeed alone—your all-faithful

Henry James.

Neither man thought of the other in terms of his full work. Their relationship was personal; their knowledge of each other on the social rather than the imaginative plane; and their community of purpose only instinctively recognized. Yet they made naturally the most valuable criticism of each other: in their work and in their personalities as seen side by side. They had both enough in common and enough in radical opposition to be complementary figures. Perhaps they talked their late hours out only in London in the 'seventies and Washington in the 'eighties; they had been members of a vanishing society and each had kept a sharp eye—astigmatic, selective, but preternaturally sharp—upon what vanished, including each other. It would be more artistically probable—more just—to think of the two men, at last, in their seventies, baldheaded, and precisely at the moment that their world did blow up, finding a common ground, each strengthening the other, in a common vision of all that had happened—of all that they had, exactly, by the power of imagination, actually survived.

However that may be, it is certain that they talked of the war; and there the listener would have gotten a contrast in response sharper than any other blow could have provided. The war assaulted each man with equal violence. For each it was a long, never-subsiding panic of emotion, felt physically as stress and queasiness. Under that stress James broke down, and Adams did not. James had nothing but his sensibility, which withstood nothing but sucked up the horror like a vacuum; he thought it criminal to think of anything but the war, and in the end resorted to hatred and fury and utter surrender of his sensibility to every idea and device of the Allied cause. In James' letters of the war years we see the unsteady stages of the violation of a great sensibility.

Adams, on the contrary, had a formed and provisional intellect which guided and controlled his sensibility without excess. He was partisan—even as partisan as James—but he kept what he had previously most to depend on, he kept his head. He knew the war was coming: it was the outward toppling of a collapse that had already occurred. Another world, or else a dead world, was coming, in which he would take no part. He was the morning star fading unnoticed in a thunderstorm at dawn. He wanted greatly to live the war through to see what would happen. Meanwhile he could bear the stress because it was only the critical accentuation of normal stress, and because he knew it would be criminal *not* to think of something else. He could write to W. R. Thayer on December 17, 1915, that he was sorry for the Germans, and proceed to compare, jocularly, his own plight with theirs. He had an imaginative refuge, characteristically his own, ready for everything. He wrote to Professor Luquiens on the 29th of December 1914, from Washington, that they had sung all the best of the *chansons* and that the "charm of the pursuit has almost obliterated that of the other studies."—"Throughout all the terrors and roars of German howitzers," he wrote at the end, "we have lived on 'Seigneurs Sachez' and 'A vous amants,' in France and England as here, and they alone have given us repose. Reims fell, but Thibaut rose."

It should be said that both these songs are songs of the Crusades. Professor Luquiens thought Adams' words wonderfully beautiful because they referred to the songs "of the men unafraid to die." Perhaps another perspective would be more illuminating. Certainly it is a perspective more appropriate to our own day, when we have again the sense of waiting a third time our own turn to share in a new catastrophe that is but an extension, or a contagion, of the old. Before the explosive spectacle of human failure in the form of "energy without direction" —which is how Adams characterized the war—what is better, what possible other refuge could there be for the assaulted imagination than an art that still lived, and still intimately witnessed perhaps the surest and straightest direction human energy ever took.

V

No refuge was complete, or was meant to be. In Washington, with his old friend Spring Rice, now the British Ambassador, at one elbow and the war itself (in the form of newspapers) at the other, Adams wrote to Ward Thoron in the middle of December that the war kept him awake nights. The world had ended; then let Thoron come home and help make a new one. Adams had always expected the worst and it had always been worse than he expected. Here was Christmas—Peace and Good Will—and he, Adams, reminded himself of St. Augustine correcting syntax before the Germans came. This letter was signed "Marmot"—a kind of rodent that curls up in its fur for the winter's sleep. Just after the New Year he wrote succinctly to Louisa Hooper, who remained in Lausanne, but there was in Washington a curious odor of W. J. Bryan, Wilson, sixty-odd Senators, Roger Warner, and Beacon Street, and that he had said ten years ago all he had to say about war. To both he wrote also about the music: there was much still to explore; and the songs to the Virgin were best.

Here we may find ourselves striking once again the major theme of Adams' life. He was, in an imaginative, wholly poetic sense, increasingly the Virgin's man, as he remained historically an eighteenth-century republican, as he had become intellectually a twentieth-century speculative skeptic, and as he was also, all along and always committedly, a man of the world. In his poem called "Buddha and Brahma," written in 1891 but not printed until October 1915 in the *Yale Review*, Adams had expressed the central aspect of the predicament in which so complex an allegiance might find itself.

> But we, who cannot fly the world, must seek
> To live two separate lives; one, in the world
> Which we must ever seem to treat as real;
> The other in ourselves, behind a veil
> Not to be raised without disturbing both.

The right solution, or one right solution, might consist—since one could actively deny the world like Buddha—in imaginatively giving one's inner allegiance to the Virgin. In *Chartres*, Adams emphasizes the possibility by comparing Milton's "They also serve, who only stand and wait" to the lines spoken by a thirteenth-century chevalier when reprehended by his squire for lingering at a Mass to the Virgin when the tournament was about to begin.

> "Amis!" ce dist li chevalier,
> "Cil tournoie moult noblement
> Qui le servise dieu entent."

> "Friend!" said to him the chevalier,
> "He tourneys very nobly too,
> Who only hears God's service through!"

It remained, however, only a possibility, and as a practical formula never reached the condition of temptation. Neither the Virgin nor Gautama Buddha could any longer be brought into the world without destruction except as poetry, and even as poetry, if the symbol was made too explicit, the risk was imminent—both to one's sense of the world and to one's sense of oneself. Yet the religious necessity was at times paramount; the veil had to be raised: by a mere fatality of insight or shock or understanding, frequent enough to seem habitual, one again and again saw it tremble to the thinnest transparency; and both lives were profoundly disturbed. Recovery—repose—was either in silence or in a kind of symbolic dramatization where one both participated and looked on, hardly knowing which; or it might be, rarely, that recovery was found in expression, which might be serious or poetic as in the talk with Gabrielle Chanler, or might be mocking and cryptically diffident, or might be, too, a combination, a blending of both. We are concerned with the disturbance seen as recovery, and we fasten, for our signs, both on the strokes of character and the strokes of imagination, strokes where the pattern of a life shows like a luminous embroidery.

For the Catholic Church itself, Adams had in his last years as always the respect due to a great historical institution and the interest due to a philosophy which, admirable in itself, he could not share. With Catholics as individuals he felt, as he often told Miss Tone, more and more *en rapport*. They had by virtue of their faith a security and fullness of spiritual tenure—or seemed to have—which non-Catholics only got if at all, precariously, and by the constant uncertain stress of the individual imagination. It was a matter for envy as well as admiration. The Catholic instincts were right; Catholic practice, for him, impossible. Rapport was not unanimity; rapport was dramatic understanding, provisional and poetic, at arm's length, altogether in parallel. One was oneself always something else again; something tough, resonant within and not easily played upon from without: always, at bottom, a little willfully independent. One might give up by final default, and confess failure; but one could not give in—however near one came to doing so—precisely because such a surrender, to a scrupulous and provisioned soul, would amount to the surrender of integrity, would seem indeed a plain giving out. This sentiment, if correctly drawn, is characteristic of the Puritan Protestant tradition, which Adams consciously inherited, as qualified by the *riches* of that skepticism which sets every movement of the mind upon a provisional and frankly questionable basis.

For the Protestant, who lacked the intercessory human grace and imagination of the Virgin, there was always agony in the approach to God. As skepticism increased, it either impaired the sensibility as in Huxley and Sam Butler or, with a certain sophistication and a brand-new excruciating agony, it added to and richened the texture of the imagination as in Emily Dickinson, Henry James, and Henry Adams. If Adams had known Emily Dickinson's line, "Faith is the Experiment of our Lord," he would not only have approved it but would also have borrowed it and transformed it to his own purpose. For twenty years he had saturated himself in the great imaginative experiment of the Virgin which had brought the diverse energies of the twelfth century to unified purpose, and now in his last years he was lost in her music, the ultimate, ethereal form that the imagination took. But he knew, unrelentingly, that the faith was experimental, however necessary, and that the experiment was imaginative, however vital its sources. Once it had enlivened and humanized a church; now the church was a simulacrum, a set shell, a spent experiment, a formula of imagination that no longer applied—though individuals might and did occasionally rehearse the old imagination by instinct rather than formula: when one sympathized, deeply—as with an anachronism which one might not reach and which could not be efficacious—with the charm, the humanity, the frailty, and the personal aspiration that now alone replaced, almost fortuitously, what was once a faith past reason.

To the individual Catholics whom he knew he was sympathetic to the point where some thought he was at heart one of them. His niece Mabel La Farge seems to have thought so and gave her views at the end of her introduction to her *Letters to a Niece*. Certainly there were many Catholics at Adams' house in the late years. Mrs. La Farge and Aileen Tone were both Catholic. Father John La Farge, the youngest son of the artist, a Jesuit, was stationed at a missionary parish in Maryland from about 1912 to 1914. Pale, intellectual, of what some call an Oriental—a Buddhistic—demeanor, Father La Farge, by birth a family friend, often visited Adams' house at this time, both out of friendship and to help with the music. Father Fay, of the Catholic University of America, was a constant visitor from 1912 to the end. Round, jolly, worldly to a degree that only an ordained priest can attain without loss of spirituality, he was quite the opposite type to Father La Farge and quite as useful. He, too, helped with the music. Besides the clergy, there were of course such Catholics as the Winthrop Chanlers, who came in whenever they were in Washington. It would be as true to say that Catholics were attracted to Adams as that Adams was attracted to Catholics. In either case there was a barrier when what seemed to either the proper scope of the imagination was overpassed. For example, in offering indirectly to send to Justine Ward—who in the zeal of conversion had become a sort of lay nun—copies of such *chansons* as she wanted, Adams differentiated himself from her as being emphatically "of the world." And to the contrary, he reports in the spring of 1914 that he had been accused of being too "intimate with Our Lady."

On the worldly plane the whole matter is best shown in a report Mrs. Winthrop Chanler gives in her *Roman Spring*.

I asked him once [she writes] how it was that he did not become a Catholic, seeing he assented so warmly to what we believed.

"Do you think, my child, that Rhadamanthus would be less severe?" He said this half solemnly with a defiant twinkle in his eye.

That was all; it makes an ellipsis lucid precisely because it is tantalizing. Rhadamanthus, the son of Zeus by Europa, was, it will be remembered, translated to Elysium because of the ideal justice of his life and opinions. Rhadamanthus, for any Church, would be better outside, and probably better off for himself, too. One would not wish to see one's sense of justice forced to operate as a sense of mockery.

On the plane of the rational, but driven, imagination, which was for Adams always behind the worldly plane and disturbing it, the predicament of the modern sensibility confronted with the religious problem is expressed in the following extraordinary letter, dated February 15, 1915, to Henry Osborn Taylor. Taylor had sent Adams his *Medieval Mind* and this was Adams' answer.

My dear Scholar and Master

As you know, I am a poor and ignorant besides being a senile, reptile, and in one respect also am morally bad, for I never loved or taught facts, if I could help it, having that antipathy to facts which only idiots and philosophers attain; but with these drawbacks perhaps you will allow me to thank you for your last volume. I have read it with grateful attention.

I cannot criticise. The field is not mine. I am concerned with it only as a spectator, and now a very blind one. I cannot correct or suggest, but I can do what may be equally useful.—I can tell you what effect your treatment has on me, and as I am probably an extreme case, you may infer its effect on opposite natures.

Perhaps I ought to say first, that once, at the most trying crisis of my life—and of his—our old teacher in wisdom, Gurney, said to me that of all moral supports in trial only one was nearly sufficient. That was the Stoic. I cannot say that I have found it so, except in theory, but I am talking theory. Putting myself in that position I read your book.

You see at once what must follow,—what did in fact follow. Of course all that goes before is futile except as failure; all that follows after is escape—flying the ring,—by assuming an unprovable other world. Logically, the religious solution is inadmissible,—pure hypothesis. It discards reason. I do not object to it on that account: as a working energy I prefer instinct to reason; but as you put it, the Augustinian adjustment seems to be only the Stoic, with a supernatural or hypothetical supplement nailed to it by violence. The religionists preached it, and called it Faith.

Therefore to me the effect is of ending there. The moral adjustment, as a story, ended with Marcus Aurelius. There you lead us with kind and sympathetic hands; but there, over the door to the religious labyrinth, you, like Lord Kelvin, write the word Failure. Faith, not Reason, goes beyond.

What you intend, either as reason or faith, is another matter. I am giving only the effect on one mind. At the present moment, perhaps, the moral is somewhat pointed,—to me decidedly peaked. If you are writing Failure over one door and Lord Kelvin over another, and the Germans over the third and last—that of energy without direction,— I think I had better quit. I said so ten years ago, but I put it down to my personal equation then, and I cannot believe that you mean it now. Are we, then, to go back to Faith? If so, is it to be early Christian or Stoic?

The early Christian I take to have been abandoned long ago by the failure of Christ to reappear and judge the world. Whatever faith is to save us, it cannot be that. Is it, then, the Stoic?

I do not ask these questions for answers,—only to show you what questions are roused by your book, in order that, if you like, you may in any case, insert some provision against misapprehension. Of course, had I been the author, I should perhaps have been drawn into giving different values to the solutions, and should very likely have laboured damnably over the Buddhists and the Stoics. Marcus Aurelius would have been my type of highest human attainment. Even as it is, I would give a new cent to have a really good book on the Stoics. If there is one, lend it me. I need badly to find one man in history to admire. I am in near peril of turning Christian, and rolling in the mud in an agony of human mortification. All these other fellows did it,—why not I?

> Ever yrs
> Henry Adams

Characteristically, Adams' answer set up an attitude different from Taylor's and raised questions that neither mind could answer except provisionally, speculatively, imaginatively. In the mind's conversations as in those of manners the great thing was, as Adams never tired of saying, to keep the ball rolling, to furnish the cue, to *donner la replique*. Other comment would be superfluous, except this, that while the letter may seem to represent the whole of Adams' intelligence at the age of 77, it actually does nothing of the sort. Rhadamanthus is still there. Adams' unity was a product, not a multiplier, and the product varied from time to time. The unity of such a mind is what happens when you experience all you can manage of its aspects together. Here we may go on, with two pertinent illustrations of aspects not touched on in the long letter above. One is from a letter to Taylor written a year later (April 17, 1916), which began by sympathizing with Taylor's cold, and proceeds with the following fable.

Yesterday I walked in the spring woods, and met a fly. To that fly I said:—"Fly! do you want me to tell you the truth about yourself?" And that fly looked at me—carefully—and said:—"You be damned."

They have told me that now, just seventy-eight times. They are not tired, but I am. If you happen on a copy of my Education, kindly burn it. I have no longer a wish to educate. I think that, as an insect, I know! that is, I don't care to know any more. So, I'll join the beetles. They were, I think, the first, the greatest, and most successful experiment of nature. Read Fabre! Talk to Aileen!

So much for the fable and its gloss. Then he continues: "We go to Lenox! Seek us there! You can be as futile there as in New York:—almost as futile as here. No! I hate extreme and violent expressions! No! not as futile as here!" And, serious again, he ends off: "Stick to Montaigne. Never mind the rest. I can't find the book on the stoics."

The fable is a seminal form; because it can never be applied exactly it can always be applied anywhere with unfailing freshness; which is why Adams indulged in the form—it caught meaning from the air as it flew. The beetles are another matter, an obsessional image for energy as instinct, but used by Adams to refresh the powers of imagination: if you *imagine* life as instinctive, then your experience of it will once again be equivalent to, or will declare, its own meaning.

But the transition to our second illustration is in neither the fly nor the beetle but in the admonition *Stick to Montaigne.* Montaigne is the great master of ironic wisdom, of wisdom which by the poetry of its manners suggests another version of itself in the very act of finishing or polishing off its present expression. That is its irony, the riches of its skepticism, that in reconciling two points of view into one it manages to imply the possibility of a third and quite unadjusted point of view. It was this aspect of Montaigne that I think Adams would have meant Taylor and himself to stick to; certainly there is something of the ironic *and* poetic quality of Montaigne in the following anecdote—both in itself and as it illuminates by contrast the letter, the fable, and the Rhadamanthine reserve.

One evening toward the end of his life the conversation turned on John Singer Sargent. It may have been in the fall of 1917, when Sargent was in Washington painting President Wilson. Someone asked Adams why Sargent had not done him, and Adams answered immediately and with force: "I never

would let Sargent paint my portrait. I knew too well what he
would do to me, and I was too much of a coward." He paused,
then added in a different tone, "But there *is* a portrait of me,
and I have it here"—he rose and went to a drawer—"a twelfth
century portrait";—he came back—"I have it here."

What he had was a postcard photograph of a sculptured panel
of the Nativity from the rood loft or choir of Chartres Cathedral.
He had sometimes sent copies to friends, calling it his favorite
poem; but it had not hitherto been called a portrait. It has been
said that Adams himself discovered the panel lost in a cellar
and had caused it to be restored. The scene is traditional but
executed with more familiar and intimate grace than is usual.
The Virgin is reclining, weary and delicate, her right hand
holding her head, her left arm a long curve running down to
two fingers tenderly at the throat of the baby's swaddling clothes
as he lies in the manger. Joseph, unfortunately decapitated,
leans over the Virgin looking down at the baby and holding
back a fold of the drapery of the Virgin's bed in his hands.
At one end of the manger is a sheep and at the other a donkey,
his nose in the manger. The unknown artists had been faithful
to the point of imagination. Adams handed the card. "That is
my portrait," he said patiently. "It is the donkey sniffing the
straw."

The story is all there: Marcus Aurelius, Fly, Rhadamanthus,
and all. This was as near as Adams ever came to the Virgin or
her Son. It happened some seven or eight centuries ago; very
near in the direction of faith but not very near in the direction
of a Church—exactly how near, the reader will have to figure,
as his own imagination bids him. It was a poem as well as a
portrait; in neither art should a meaning be too closely nailed
down, for in time another is sure to spring the nails.

Here, through the focus of Adams' relation to religion, all we
have been saying comes to this: Increasingly as he grew older,
Adams was able to feel his own complexity as unity only in
the form of a fable or a riddle. He could no longer—if indeed
he ever had—feel the complexity as resolvable into a single
energy. Even wisdom had to become poetry to be efficacious,
and the poetry, as like as not, was not one's own but just what
was available or came to hand. But let us protect ourselves
from a false emphasis on religion, or wisdom, or poetry. We
have been dealing with a relation as if it were sudden, and a

relation of old age, which was actually the relation and the damage of a lifetime, and only transpired in old age. We could as well, for truth, turn imagination backward, even as far back as the ganoid fish *Pteraspis* or the Civil War, and find in the seed, pressed and perfect but a little cramped for expression, the final flower. Our ends resort to their means; constantly the pattern, like character (of which it is the inert form), reasserts itself, until in the end nothing but pattern is left—and character only its last sophistication.

As old age waxed, reserve waned: pattern *and* character began to show clearer and clearer. Perhaps the War telescoped time as well as human purpose. If speed were vertiginous, experience might well be vertigo—from which release must either be paralysis or spontaneous expression. When the *Lusitania* went down, May 7, 1915, off the coast of Ireland, the news found Adams in Dublin, New Hampshire, where he had taken a house for the summer. He responded with a temporary paralysis of the tongue; he actually could not speak a word for some hours, and for several days his speech was thickened. No wonder he played with Florence Keep's children—the Keeps had a summer place near at hand—and drove them about the countryside either in his own car or Mrs. Keep's. No wonder, too, that when his niece Ellen Potter asked him if men of affairs like himself and Harry White (who was also in New Hampshire that summer) were not bored in the country, Adams answered her that he was never bored in the country if there was grass to sit on and no trolley cars. Children and grass and the absence of noise were a convenient and far from imaginary substitute for paralysis.

When Adams returned to Washington in the fall, Thayer's *Life of John Hay* had appeared and was already a best seller. Adams read it, and the effect was so direct and startling that he wrote the author a letter of unusual candor—a candor hitherto impossible to him even to his intimate friends, let alone to a man so much a stranger that he addressed him as "My dear Sir." "I have long delayed writing, though it has been much on my mind," he begins, "and I have felt some self-reproach at the omission. The truth is, I felt a little as though you had written a life of me as well as Hay, and I ought to take time to think it over, and to learn what people said about it." The letter goes on for two pages on biography as fact and as art, the necessity of

interest and partisanship, and the difficulty of making a "satisfactory life of what the French call an homme d'esprit or an
homme du monde." In Washington, he writes,

no reader knows what it is; they know only politicians. For that
reason I have watched to see their attitude before your picture of
Hay. Curious it is,—much like that of a Danubian Hun before a
statue of Alcibiades. The figure is much too complex for them. Yet I
have seen thus far no active hostility, though I do not doubt it will
come. I shall be artistically disappointed if it does not, but meanwhile
I am sure it interests, which is the essential. Most wits and talkers
bore one in biography. Yours is interesting.

Then he goes on directly—the break here is made only for emphasis:

This is a considerable triumph, for which I was hardly prepared, but
you have actually made a greater, for which I was wholly unprepared.
You have positively created a new city here at Washington,—a centre
of art and taste. Of course, I was trying hard, with Hay's help, to do
what you say we did, but your insight into it amounts to genius. It is
a creation, almost as striking and original as Bret Harte. No one else
has seen it, or approached it, and when I think of your feeling that
group of women,—my wife, Mrs. Lodge and Mrs. Cameron, under
the shadow of St. Gaudens' figure at Rock Creek, I am astounded. It
is true insight of a most unusual kind.

This was the first time, so far as is known, that Adams had
ever mentioned his wife as a direct and continuous influence
upon him, and it was the first time in all his years of conspicuous
contemplation of it, that he had ever lighted the anonymity of
Saint-Gaudens' statue with a name. Of the monument he had
always spoken with studied objectivity; of his wife, even to her
nieces, he had never spoken directly at all, though he had a
few times, upon necessity, referred to her as "your aunt." Her
memory had been his, and hidden, husbanded as his sole store
against adversity—the blackness of her loss, the very violence
of it—at the bottom of every effort he had made. It should all
the more convince us of the strength of his feeling that his
response altogether outran any incentive that Thayer's book
might have raised. Thayer was matter-of-fact, and spoke at
most in remote admiration of something almost as alien to him
in practice as the statue of Alcibiades to the Hun, although natural enough in theory. In return Adams laid himself bare—as

bare as an Adams could—and it almost seems, from what he said, that the whole charm and meaning of his social life were to be found in the memory of his wife, just as the leap of his imagination from competence to mastery had its impetus in the shock of her suicide. As with Villon and Dante in their measure, we should be grateful for Adams' evil luck in his measure.

Perhaps it was easier for him to re-enter the past freely, now everyone concerned in it was far away or dead. Mrs. Lodge had died in the fall of 1915. Mrs. Cameron, the lone survivor, was in France fighting the Germans. As Adams wrote farther on in the letter above to Thayer, "I am sorry for the Germans; I am sorry for myself to be still here, alone, without allies, and blind as well as idiotic." Death, absence, the War, and his backward mood had cut him off.

It was a combination of these elements that led to another and explosive release as remarkable as the breaking down of his reserve about his wife. The story is simple, but needs a little preface to make its point. The relation between Adams and Henry Cabot Lodge had begun as that of master and pupil; later they had something in common in the reform politics of the early 'eighties. Then Lodge had set as the extreme and fanatical party man; and so far as Adams was concerned his friendship was centered entirely in the Senator's beautiful and charming wife and their children. As for Lodge himself, as any careful reader of the *Education* will see, Adams distrusted the type, finding it less honest in every valuable sense than the frankly practical, even venal, type represented by Senator Cameron, to whom a bargain was a bargain. Adams also disliked the man. As the war lengthened, Lodge became more and more a member of the English party, more and more fanatic, and more and more scurrilous in his attacks on Wilson.

By the winter of 1917 Adams saw that American entry into the War on the Allied side was inevitable, and would have hurried it if he could. He also seems to have disliked Wilson, as uncertain in mind and temper; but he held his counsel and kept his temper, as by principle he always had, even to those he hated. But one evening when Lodge was dining at his house Adams let go with all the obliterating vigor and emotional honesty of his whole personality. Lodge had just launched into a snarling tirade against Wilson. Adams suddenly turned white, pounded his fist upon the table, and shouted: "I have never permitted treasonable conversation in my house, and I don't propose, Cabot, to allow it now."

This is as good a juncture as any to mention the posthumous glancing blow Adams had reserved for Lodge. In the package containing the copy of the *Education* delivered to Lodge as President of the Massachusetts Historical Society after Adams' death, there was a preface written by Adams but with instructions that Lodge must sign it before publication could be made. Thus Lodge sponsored a work with which he not only had no sympathy but which actually condemned him, and furthermore he sponsored it on terms not his own.

Though it was only to Lodge that he lost his temper, it was not only to Thayer that Adams was able now, in his own way, to show his allegiance to the gone time. At the first sign of spring, in early March 1917, the subject of summer encampment came up for discussion. The summer of 1916 had been spent at Ashentully, an enormous house in Tyringham in the Berkshires, a house so big that it took eight furnaces to keep it moderately warm in the fall. It had been a good summer with many guests, and so pleasant a house, indeed, that—if the owner, Mrs. Grace McClellan, was to be trusted—the ghost of Adams afterward came back to haunt it. However that may be, Adams had no intention of returning to it in life. One day Elsie Adams and Aileen Tone were discussing possibilities, when Adams astonished them by bursting in: "We will go to Beverly Farms."

This was of course his own house, which he had not used since 1885—the last summer of his wife's life—although he had kept it in repair and had lent it to his Hooper nieces and their father whenever they wanted it. He had kept away from it as he had kept away from every public reference to either his wife or her death, except in the Saint-Gaudens monument. Now he spoke firmly and naturally of going there, and looked forward to it with enjoyment, exactly as if he had been planning for thirty years to return there in 1917. Elsie Adams was sent on to get the house ready, and in Boston the Thorons (Louisa Hooper had married Ward Thoron in 1915) also went to work arranging details of servants and housekeeping. Meanwhile Adams kept the summer much in mind.

On another but associated level, another outward sign of the old life was reasserted at about this time. Adams and his wife had had three Dinmont terriers—Possum, Marquis, and Boojum —of whom they were very fond, but after the last one died, while he was in the South Seas, Adams had never got another. Now at the end of his life, when Aileen Tone suggested that it would be a good idea to accept a Scotty puppy that Brooks was willing to give away (he raised Scotties at Quincy), Adams at first put up rhetorical objections. *A dog? Have one if you like! Dogs are a nuisance. They always get run over. But go ahead.* So they "borrowed" one of Brooks' puppies called Louis. Actually the dog was Adams' and he enjoyed it greatly, though he refused to admit owning it in so many words.

It was in the midst of their preparations for Beverly Farms that President Wilson rode from the White House to the Capitol, guarded by cavalry from Fort Myers, and delivered, "as though he had put on the black cap to deliver judgment," the message calling for a declaration of war. Adams sat at home, heard the cavalry across the open square, then listened to nothing much but the rain until the newsboys cried *Extra!* outside his door. Miss Tone got a paper and read Wilson's address complete. Adams expressed, and showed, relief. "Now I can go to bed," he said, and did—and slept better than he had done for a long time. For the next week he was gay as a lark—as many were, for a month or so, and even into the summer, thinking that America's entry into the War would forthwith end it. Adams was glad, too, in a special and subsidiary sense, at the relief from pressure on his old friend Spring Rice and on La Bouillé of the French Embassy, both of whom were always in and out of the house.

But he was gladder still when the weather warmed into May and they all went up to Beverly Farms, to stay for nearly six months. The old-fashioned, rather ugly summerhouse with red roof, red bottom trim, and yellow clapboards, had changed as little as the oak and pine woods around it or the sea, which could be seen half a mile away. The furniture, the carpets, the La Farge glass in two windows, even the colors of the paint on the floors, were all much as his wife had left them. The wallpapers had of course been renewed, but that was almost all. The real change was in the addition of three rooms—a sitting room on the first floor, and a bedroom and bathroom on the second—which had been made by Edward Hooper about 1900 to accommodate his daughter's growing family.

Except that the War bothered him, and that his mind was sometimes abstracted, Adams was happy all summer. There was a constant stream of visitors: nieces and nephews of all generations, relatives and friends. Adams had a car again and drove miles around the countryside, calling on people he had not seen for thirty years. Father Fay came for a long visit, and while he was there Adams rose early enough to escort him, in the car, to early Mass. His health was as good as his spirits; he still walked a great deal in the woods and clambered over the rocks, but still had no need of a cane. He had recently to give up his champagne and cigars, as he had earlier given up most of his reading—and said firmly that he never missed them—but he never gave up exercise.

Beverly Farms was all he could possibly have expected; it perfected his rejuvenescence and brought out, in a final form, the bare elements of his pattern—a form marked by a certain enigmatic ambiguity appropriate to the pattern itself. On July 10, 1917, he wrote the following letter to Spring Rice.

My dear Springy,

I enclose to you a copy of the two sonnets, prepared for the press. I wish you would look over them and see if they suit you. I have not yet taken any further steps about them or read them to anyone else, but I wish that in case it comports with your high dignity you would return them to me at your earliest convenience; and further that, if Your Excellency pleases, there might be added a few lines of Your Excellency's own, giving the legend you recited to me, and which I apprehend, entered into your conceptions of the sonnets, which, if you do not object, I will insert between the two sonnets, in such a manner as to connect the two, but without heading. Do you think it would comport with Your Excellency's high dignity to return me the document this time, with your high approval?

Ever yours,
Henry Adams.

When the sonnets were printed in the *Atlantic Monthly* that fall there were prefixed to them the "lines of His Excellency's own" and also a text from Ezekiel, presumably supplied by Adams.

It is told of the founder of one of the Sufi sects in Western Asia, that, hearing of the great beauty of a certain lady, he sought her in marriage and promised her parents to build a beautiful house for her. The request was granted and the house built. The bride was brought into it veiled, according to custom. When the veil was removed, the bridegroom saw before him, not a bride, but the angel Azrael. He fell at the angel's feet, crying, "Have mercy!" And the angel answered, "I am Mercy."

Son of man, behold, I take from thee the desire of thine eyes at a stroke—yet shall thou neither mourn nor weep—neither shall thy tears run down. So spake I unto the people in the morning; and in the evening my wife died.—Ezekiel xxiv.16

I

I built my love a temple and a shrine,
And every stone of it a loving thought:
And far and wide and high and low, I sought
For sweetest fancies on the walls to twine,
And deeds of gold and words of purest shine
And strength of marble faithfulness, enwrought
With love's enchantments.—Lady, dearly bought
Nor lightly fashioned was that house of thine.
Who came to dwell within it? Not the face
I dreamed of—not the dear familiar eyes,
The kind, the soft, the intimately sweet.
Dread presence—great and merciful and wise—
All humbly I draw near thy dwelling place
And lay the vacant crown before thy feet.

II

O steadfast, deep, inexorable eyes,
Set look inscrutable, nor smile nor frown!
O tranquil eyes that look so calmly down
Upon a world of passion and of lies!
For not with our poor wisdom are you wise,
Nor are you moved with passion such as ours,
Who, face to face with those immortal powers
That move and reign above the stainless skies,
As friend with friend, have held communion—
Yet have you known the stress of human years,
O calm, unchanging eyes! And once have shone
With these our fitful fires, that burn and cease,
With light of human passion, human tears,
And know that, after all, the end is peace.

Azrael was, in the Mohammedan belief, the angel of death. "It is he who separates the soul from the body, doing this gently or harshly, as the case may be. When a man has been God-fearing, the soul leaves as gently as water from a bag; but the

soul of an infidel is drawn out as a hot spit out of wet wool." So
much for Azrael. The choice of the text from Ezekiel was
far from being accidental or surprising. When Adams and his
wife went to England on their honeymoon in 1872, almost the
first wedding present they received there was from Frank Palgrave: Blake's picture of Ezekiel mourning his dead wife.
Adams had had the picture hanging in his study at Washington,
in full view from his desk chair, ever since. These are the facts
that heighten the significance of Adams' letter to Spring Rice.

As for the sonnets themselves, they are intended to represent
Spring Rice's interpretation of the Saint-Gaudens monument,
of which he had long been, in Stephen Gwynn's word, a votary;
and they were published as his, both that fall and in a posthumous edition of his poems. It is not meant to suggest that Spring
Rice did not write the sonnets but only to suggest that the evidence points toward an integral collaboration on Adams' part.
Of external evidence there is the high, frivolous formality of
tone which Adams takes on a matter near to his heart—a tone
not at all surprising if Adams had a share in the sonnets but
quite surprising if he had no share in them—if, that is, they
were entirely Spring Rice's offering to Adams. There is also
the initial statement that Adams has "prepared" them for the
press, and his final hope that Spring Rice may return "the document *this time*, with your high approval." These statements may
have only the meaning of manners, or again they may carry a
positive, if ambiguous, conclusion.

Of internal evidence—versification, turn of speech, vocabulary
—the data are more difficult to handle. Neither man ever accomplished a poetic style, and both had always depended on
the stock properties of English verse. We have to look, then,
more for traits than means of expression, more for verbal bias
than poetic skill. There is, I think, a striking difference between
both the intellectual bent and the vocabularies of the two sonnets, and also, as a consequence, between the attitudes that
would seem to have inspired them. The first sonnet is in every
way lighter than the second, more tender in the romantic sense,
and more commonplace in terms of the general poetic vocabulary. The second is simpler and more compact than the first.
The first reaches for an emotion, the second generalizes an
emotion, and not the same emotion. There is nothing in the
first, except the twelfth line, which we would think of as Adams;

on the contrary, in the second, for turn of speech, for philosophical despair—a quality Spring Rice did not show—and the choice of the words themselves, there is little that could not have been Adams. Barring some of the rhyme phrases and the fillers, which might have been written by either, the second sonnet sounds and feels like Adams. It is therefore ventured that, while Adams had little to do with the first sonnet, he had a great deal to do with the second. It seems almost certain that he at least rewrote the second. If the reader can accept an approximation to this view, then the letter and the poems and the mottoes reach a clear and imaginative unity, through which we may, once again, and in a principal aspect, feel the unity of Adams himself.

At any rate, even if he only "prepared" the poems for publication, it made the last act of expression, the last assertion of deep pattern, which his luck afforded him. Washington in the late fall of 1917 was the crowded, frantic, confused, capital of a nation at war. It was with something like panic that Adams, Aileen Tone, and the dog started back. Actually they traveled well, arriving in a storm, and were met by Charles the idiot butler (as Miss Tone called him) at the station. People poured in before they were unpacked. Henry White came in, full of importance; Mrs. Winthrop Chanler came with news of her husband in Italy. Elizabeth Hoyt, later the second wife of Sir Ronald Lindsay, was working for the Red Cross, and Adams gave her a bedroom, so that the house was full of Red Cross people at all hours. Spring Rice and La Bouillé came in from their respective embassies every day. Father Fay, Mrs. Chanler, and John Singer Sargent—talking of Wilson, whom he was painting, describing his face as quite marvelous, "like an ancient Japanese mask"—all came in to dinner one night. Many others came in, and went out, for an hour, an evening, a week: Shane Leslie, Dr. Dakin, Dr. Edward Dunham from New York, Dr. and Mrs. Draper. Elsie Adams was of course there, as she had been since her father's death in 1915, about two weeks a month. Altogether it was a perfect caravansery.

Adams kept his good humor, and for the most part his good spirits, despite the noise—it was war noise—which he always hated, and the confusion, which was alien to him in every form except nature's own form of chaos. He was with friends, he was admired, the value of his work was becoming generally recognized; he was seen almost to bask—to enjoy without vanity—in the winter sun of the tributes he received. The Prison Song was almost sung, and the old tragic tone had become, as in Beethoven's last quartets, heaven-sweet.

In February the outward mood was changed and the inward deepened. Spring Rice, who had been recalled by an ungrateful government, died suddenly and inexplicably on St. Valentine's Day while waiting in Canada for his ship to England. The blow was both sharp and dulling. Adams had not only seen him constantly for the last three years but also he represented for Adams the last link with his own generation. It was, as he had so often said and felt before, but now indeed, time to go. He was down to the bare point.

The Germans, too, hurried the time, for by the middle of March the world was filled to echoing with the terrifying noise of their last push. The universe had not only abandoned him but also seemed about to abandon itself. Where was the Stoic discipline for that?

On the evening of the 26th of March 1918 the time was spent as usual. There was conversation. Miss Tone sang some of the old songs. Then there was bed. The morning began, too, as usual. Adams rose, took his bath, and returned to his room. A few minutes later, as he did not come down, they found him, dressed, lying across his bed—dead on Maunday Thursday. Miss Tone laid the body out in a white silk dressing gown, which had been purchased for him in 1912 to wear in his convalescence but which in life he rarely wore, and tucked a white soft shawl under his shoulders. On Easter Saturday he was buried under the monument in Rock Creek beside his wife. By his will, "no inscription, date, letters, or other attempt at memorial, except the monument I have already constructed," was placed over their graves. None was needed. The pattern had been finally bared, which he had felt first only as a blow, in the chaos of her death; it is now part of our general imagination.

AT ROCK CREEK

Adams: Images: Eidolon

Adams at Rock Creek looked at himself, to see what he could see beyond himself: the portrait of the beyond-self: the shrouded, havened, stable self: the trembling of the self unto stone: the inner swaying of the stone in self. The rocking in the rock, rock in all rocking. Not aspiration, not an arrow of God: but the thing that aspires; hence, and so, by empathy and absorption, the object of aspiration itself. But to the live man, to the sleeper reawakened, the dreamer lost from his dream, to the man pursued and driven and drawn, to the man cut away: to him, to that Adams, the monument was the reminder of other desire: of all that cumulative waiting, the waiting arrested and rewarded in death. Adams the small man, given to sitting down, awaited his death: and the monument to his wife gave him all the beautiful pang and incentive to perfect his waiting.

Ripeness is all. We have here perhaps a mature and meditated form of that exercise of the consciousness of death that compelled Donne to shroud himself and sleep in his coffin. Death was ripeness, the moment of ripeness the verge of unity. We await, we watch, we pray; we cannot help nor harm; the plum—ripest of all fruits—colors as it will, falls as it must. But this plum is eat, if at all, in the premeditating imagination. Of this aspect of Adams—and it was a continuing, emphatic aspect; of this version of his soul—can we not say, to make it actual, "Thou hast nor youth nor age but as it were an after dinner's sleep, dreaming on both." We engage, by memory, by hope that memory makes, in the long digestion of things to come. So within. But we still breathe, still live, and act and fill out the habits of body and mind.

Adams was used to considerations of force—they made the preoccupations of history—and obsessed with the expressions of force and human reactions to the forms of expression. A cemetery could not help representing human force run out. The force of life expressed itself in death, willy-nilly. Death was the perfection of waywardness; gave it order and end and a kind of limitation that amounted to unity. The rule is to protect ourselves from the intolerable anonymity of that unity by ascribing death to individuals. We put names and dates on tablets and add sentiments which are for the most part as belittling as they are irrelevant. Such is our incapacity for the infinite and our terror of the eternal silence, we make a fiction of small identities and qualify silence with the experience of the individual. John Patric, b. 1800 d. 1900 R.I.P. The advantage is momentary and the relief specious; in time, not even the genealogists can prevent John, his century, and his peace from returning to the anonymity, for the keenest wondering eye, where actually he lay all along.

There is nothing so anonymous as the name that names nothing—like the name of a vanished god or a dead love. The Adams monument bore no name and no inscription during Henry's life, and by the direction of his will was to bear none afterward: it was the monument, the expression, and the aspiration—and deliberately so conceived by Henry—of that anonymity which, without a monument, without a face and a visible being, had indeed been intolerable. It is the anonymity of all the meaning we know and cannot grasp, of all the suffering wonder in us that is never satisfied and, too, of all the need in us that ends in peace without emptiness, and, finally, in emptiness without terror. Such an image is, if you like, the smile upon the Sphinx that is not seen but felt; better, it is the face upon chaos: the rejoicing in the abyss.

But Adams was a worldly man, too; like Hamlet with his tablets; like Dante who put all his enemies in hell; he widened his experience in terms of his pride. As he could not take his eyes off his monument, neither could he help standing aside to watch what others brought to it. What each brought would add to its meaning; and those who brought nothing, who felt nothing, would add the worst pang of all, the ironic pang that is the very anguished idiom of the wakened and attentive soul. The soul is committed to so much that it does not know; and our best snobbery, confronted with the instance, is but reminded the more, with a pang, of its own ignorance. As Adams brought himself, in different years, to the vantage of Gibbon's mount in Rome, a vantage of dedication and perspective, as he saw himself arrogant in his humility, humbled at the arrogance of his ambition, so, also, he brought himself often to Rock Creek to watch the reactions of others—of the tourists and simple souls and priests—to the dark figure that seemed, at the time, the whole object and only source of his own reaction. The passage [in the *Education*] in which he describes what he saw provides a kind of negative focus, in others, for what he felt positively in himself.

From the Egyptian Sphinx to the Kamakura Daibuts; from Prometheus to Christ; from Michael Angelo to Shelley, art had wrought on this eternal figure almost as though it had nothing else to say. The interest of the figure was not in its meaning, but in the response of the observer. As Adams sat there, numbers of people came, for the figure seemed to have become a tourist fashion, and all wanted to know its meaning. Most took it for a portrait-statue, and the remnant were vacant-minded in the absence of a personal guide. None felt what would have been a nursery-instinct to a Hindu baby or a Japanese jinricksha-runner. The only exceptions were the clergy, who taught a lesson even deeper. One after another brought companions there, and, apparently fascinated by their own reflection, broke out passionately against the expression they felt in the figure of despair, of atheism, of denial. Like the others, the priest saw only what he brought. Like all great artists Saint-Gaudens held up the mirror and no more. The American layman had lost sight of ideals; the American priest had lost sight of faith. Both were more American than the old, half-witted soldiers who denounced the wasting, on a mere grave, of money which should have been given for drink.

In the tone, half-agonized, half-contemptuous, is all the witness we need of the humiliating irony Adams must have implicitly felt in the scene before him—or in the scene, rather, that the disgust of memory reconstructed for him—the irony against oneself of the second point of view. If each saw only what he brought with him, and if the priests, who brought most, stood aghast at what they saw precisely where Adams felt most the experience of assent, then where was Adams? If Adams did not feel the irony, let us feel it for him: it is in his words, in his reaction, and only needs to be brought out to stun the awakened senses. Life as it is lived—life as one lives it oneself—becomes radically impossible and intolerable to contemplate by one's ordinary living self if the Sphinx, the Church, Michelangelo, or one's private sense of death be taken literally. No wonder the priests stood back; their judgment was right, from the point of view of life; only the point of view was irrelevant, like one's own, before the coming experience itself. The deepest insights sink in quicksand once they reveal themselves to have their final source in the extremity of personal need. If it was what one brought that counted, in the end one brought nothing, one groveled, and the money of human insight should have been given for drink, as the old, half-witted soldiers said. The expense would have been sooner made and the gain identical.

If we may speculate upon the springs of sensibility as we speculate upon the springs of matter—with a sense of rashness greater than our sense of daring, with a feeling of imaginative resource greater than our sentiment of truth—here surely in the image of Adams and his monument that he makes for us we are as near the first wellspring as we are likely to come. We see the water rise and lift and stir the particles of bright sand; then see the sand settle and the wet disappear; and as we know each instance to be eternal, we know also that the process is recurrent: and know most that these qualities of eternity and recurrence together make up the only meaning the process shows.

If there is a truth here, it is that we are on the primitive level of sensibility. What is primitive is what is nearest to chaos. And as imagination begins on the primitive level, so it ends there, making the primitive actual. But it takes great imagination, which is the greatest form of human courage, to envisage the actual in the primitive, to unite, in the single eye, the chaos which comes before with the blacker, because more actual, chaos which comes after. The very greatness of Adams' imagination, which led him to see in the artist's stone figure the supreme affirmative enactment of that unity, was also the source of the courage with which he met and accepted the full horror of denial of that unity. It was not the blind tourists, nor the revolted priests, nor even the drunken soldiery; it was Adams himself who by the strength of his imagination could feel the blindness, the revulsion, and the drunken despair, and feel them in himself, the bottom need in his affirmation. If there are great believers, almost as great are those who know the horror where belief ends; for it is only through them that we know what it is we believe, and lose, and must needs believe again. Adams was one of these.

Adams was one of these, as we have just seen, to the point of excruciation; and it is perhaps an extreme measure of the value of his personal imagination—a measure of what we can do with it as an example—that he knew himself to be excruciated, and how, and why. The truth of his picture is dramatic, and he meant it to be taken so, with all the expenses as well as all the rewards that the dramatic form provides. It was not for nothing, but deliberately to satisfy the need of his mind for objective drama, that he composed his autobiography in the dramatic mode of the third person. Only so, by detaching himself from himself, could he respond to himself with anything like unity and definition; and only so could he expect to control the response of his readers in the later day when he should expect to have readers and awake responses—when the whole story, and all its lessons, were well behind, and there was only the persuasive worth of the story—the focused point of the education— left for consideration.

The dramatic form is meant for purification; the impulse to use it, classic and universal; Hamlet had it and left its expression to Horatio, Othello tried in his death speech, being without a Horatio, to express the essence of it himself; Adams, in the peculiar exigence in which he found himself—his best friends were either dead or dying or otherwise lost, and there was no immediate or tragic death possible for him—Adams tried a combination. He wrote of himself as a friend or even a blessed enemy might write, and, granting him his chosen perspective, his necessary bias, and his almost intolerable reticence, he wrote without extenuation of the man he saw and felt himself to be: a man so objectively experienced, with such a unity of felt being, as to be altogether beyond the need for belief. You might see him or not see him, accept him or reject him. Whatever your alternative, here was the pure Adams; and he gave you the means to respond to him if you would. If you refused to respond, or denied the possibility of meaning to your response,

Adams had refused and denied before you. Just that refusal and profoundly that denial beat in the heart of the man he dramatized. You saw and felt and learned only what you brought; and it might well be that all you could bring was horror at the awful pride of human expression forcing itself to the verge of chaos in a monument of anonymity. If you saw that, you saw everything, you saw *what it was*, created out of chaos, that comes again to chaos. Beyond that there was nothing to see, because beyond that the human imagination could not go, except that by sheer multiplication you could see it again and again until your eyes tired and the vertigo in which vision ends set in. Vertigo is the feeling of chaos itself, and ends ignominy as well as consciousness; it brings peace therefore to aspiration as well as to the sensibility which aspired.

If Adams returned again and again to the monument Saint-Gaudens made for him over his wife's grave, it was the same spirit, the same drive in him, that compelled him to make an objective monument of his autobiography, and it was the same insight that led him to call the autobiography an *education*. If the monument was nothing to his wife, the education was nothing to him: yet each represented both or all or any at the limit of expression. The meaning is in the intention; the response in that unanimity of experience that awakens recognition; the education in the emphasized example. Here we have a delicious burden to assume: the burden of a dramatic image.

A Note on Blackmur's Sources

Blackmur's sources are, for the most part, identified within his text. He did not use footnotes or endnotes in his published work, and left no such apparatus among his papers. He usually quotes sequentially from his sources in the manner of a New Critic giving a "close reading." The following editions of works by Henry Adams were found in Blackmur's library at his death and are preserved in the Department of Rare Books at Firestone Library, Princeton University:

The Degradation of the Democratic Dogma. New York: The Macmillan Company, 1919.

Democracy: An American Novel. New York: Henry Holt and Company, 1880.

The Education of Henry Adams: An Autobiography. Boston and New York: Houghton Mifflin Company, 1918.

Historical Essays. New York: Charles Scribner's Sons, 1891.

History of the United States. New York: Charles Scribner's Sons, 1889, vols. 1 and 2.

Letters of Henry Adams. Ed. Worthington Chauncey Ford. Boston and New York: Houghton Mifflin Company, 1938, vols. 1 and 2.

Letters of Mrs. Henry Adams. Ed. Ward Thoron. Boston: Little, Brown, and Company, 1936.

Letters of a Niece. Ed. Mabel La Farge. Boston and New York: Houghton Mifflin Company, 1920.

Mont-Saint-Michel and Chartres. Boston and New York: Houghton Mifflin Company, 1925, 15th impression.

In two instances Blackmur's sources are less evident to the reader. In "King Richard's Prison Song" he is quoting from unpublished letters to which he was given access by Mr. and Mrs. Ward Thoron. The letters of Henry Adams to his brother Brooks quoted in "King Richard's Prison Song" were transcribed by Ward Thoron from the originals in the possession of Abigail Adams Homans, the former Hetty Adams.

For background on Henry Adams the reader may consult the three-volume life by Ernest Samuels (Harvard University Press, 1948–1964), or his thoroughly annotated edition of *The Education of Henry Adams* (Houghton Mifflin, 1973).

Blackmur's Writings on Henry Adams

I. *Published Articles*

"The Failure of Henry Adams." *Hound and Horn* 4 (1931): 440–46.

"The Expense of Greatness: Three Emphases on Henry Adams." *Virginia Quarterly Review* 12 (1936): 396–415. Also in *The Expense of Greatness* (New York: Arrow Editions, 1940), pp. 253–76, and *The Lion and the Honeycomb* (New York: Harcourt, Brace and Company, 1955), pp. 79–96.

"Letters of Marian Adams." *Virginia Quarterly Review* 12 (1937): 289–95. Also in *The Expense of Greatness*, pp. 245–52.

"Henry and Brooks Adams: Parallels to Two Generations." *Southern Review* 5 (1939): 308–34.

"Henry Adams: Three Late Moments." *Kenyon Review* 2 (1940): 7–29. Also in *A Primer of Ignorance*, ed. Joseph Frank (New York: Harcourt, Brace and World, 1967), pp. 251–73.

"Novels of Henry Adams." *Sewanee Review* 51 (1943): 281–304. Also in *A Primer of Ignorance*, pp. 201–25.

"The Pedagogue of Sensibility." *Chimera* 2 (1944): 2–16.

"The Atlantic Unites." *Hudson Review* 5, No.2 (1952): 212–32.

"The Virgin and the Dynamo." *Magazine of Art* 45 (1952): 147–53.

"The Harmony of True Liberalism: Henry Adams' *Mont-Saint-Michel and Chartres*." *Sewanee Review* 60 (1952): 1–27. Also in *A Primer of Ignorance*, pp. 226–50.

"Adams Goes to School: The Problem Laid Out." *Kenyon Review* 17 (1955): 597–623.

II. *Materials in the Department of Rare Books*, Princeton University Library, Blackmur Collection, Boxes 9–13.

Boxes 9–10: The Virgin and the Dynamo, Chapters I–IX in typescript, Chapter X and the incomplete Chapter XI in manuscript.

Boxes 10–11: Henry Adams and National Politics, 1868–1885, typescripts:
    I. The Family Go-Cart
    II. The Independents in the Canvas
    III. The Corvée
    IV. Sac and Soc

Box 11: Henry Adams and Foreign Affairs, 1895–1907, typescripts:
  I. The Burial of My Grandfather's Doctrine
  II. From Rock to Rock
  III. The Atlantic Unites

Box 12:
  Folder 1: "The Pedagogue on Michael Angelo and Athens," type-script. Became the published article "The Pedagogue of Sensibility."
  Folder 2: "Henry and Brooks Adams: Parallels to Two Generations," manuscript, notes, typescript, and clipping of published article.
  Folder 3: "The Novels of Henry Adams," typescript and clipping of published article.
  Folders 4 and 5: "Richard's Prison Song," manuscript and typescripts. Excerpts were published as "Henry Adams: Three Late Moments" in *A Primer of Ignorance.*
  Folder 6: Notebook with 2½ manuscript pages on Adams at Harvard.

Box 13: A miscellany of notes for and scraps of articles, quotations from Adams's letters and works, and photographs of Adams and related subjects. These boxes are most useful for piecing together the development of Blackmur's thoughts on Adams. Of particular interest are the various outlines for a book-length work on Adams which Blackmur never completed.

Index